Networking

with Microsoft®

Windows Vista™

Your Guide to Easy and Secure
Windows Vista Networking

Paul McFedries

800 East 96th Street,
Indianapolis, Indiana 46240

Networking with Microsoft® Windows Vista™:
Your Guide to Easy and Secure Windows Vista Networking

Copyright © 2008 by Pearson Education, Inc.

ISBN-13: 978-0-7897-3777-9
ISBN-10: 0-7897-3777-9

Library of Congress Cataloging-in-Publication Data
McFedries, Paul.
  Networking with Microsoft Windows Vista : your guide to easy and secure Windows Vista networking / Paul McFedries.
     p. cm.
  Includes index.
  ISBN-10: 0-7897-3777-9
  ISBN-13: 978-0-7897-3777-9
  1. Computer networks--Management--Computer programs. 2. Microsoft Windows (Computer file) 3. Operating systems (Computers) I. Title.
  TK5105.5.M33945 2008
  005.4'46--dc22
                                2007045275

Printed in the United States of America

First Printing: December 2007

Trademarks

Warning and Disclaimer

Bulk Sales

Que Publishing offers excellent discounts on this book when ordered in quantity for bulk purchases or special sales. For more information, please contact

> **U.S. Corporate and Government Sales**
> **1-800-382-3419**
> **corpsales@pearsontechgroup.com**

For sales outside of the U.S., please contact

> **International Sales**
> **international@pearsoned.com**

This Book Is Safari Enabled

The Safari® Enabled icon on the cover of your favorite technology book means the book is available through Safari Bookshelf. When you buy this book, you get free access to the online edition for 45 days.

Safari Bookshelf is an electronic reference library that lets you easily search thousands of technical books, find code samples, download chapters, and access technical information whenever and wherever you need it.

To gain 45-day Safari Enabled access to this book:

- Go to http://www.quepublishing.com/safarienabled.
- Complete the brief registration form.
- Enter the coupon code Y2J9-P52K-IH31-PCKM-MBRZ.

If you have difficulty registering on Safari Bookshelf or accessing the online edition, please email customer-service@safaribooksonline.com.

Associate Publisher
Greg Wiegand

Acquisitions Editor
Rick Kughen

Development Editor
Rick Kughen

Managing Editor
Patrick Kanouse

Project Editor
Mandie Frank

Copy Editor
Keith Cline

Indexer
Ken Johnson

Proofreader
Leslie Joseph

Technical Editor
Terri Stratton

Publishing Coordinator
Cindy Teeters

Designer
Ann Jones

Composition
Bronkella Publishing

Contents at a Glance

Introduction

Part I: **Networking Hardware for Windows Vista**

1   Understanding Ethernet Networking

2   Understanding Wireless Networking

3   Configuring Your Router

4   Putting Your Network Together

Part II: **Managing and Using Your Network**

5   Working with Vista's Basic Network Tools and Tasks

6   Managing Network Connections

7   Managing Wireless Network Connections

8   Accessing and Sharing Network Resources

9   Setting up Vista as a Digital Media Hub

10   Taking Advantage of Your Network

11   Work with Network Files Offline

12   Collaborating with Windows Meeting Space

Part III: **Securing Your Network**

13   Securing Windows Vista

14   Implementing Network Security

15   Implementing Wireless Security

Part IV: **Advanced Networking with Windows Vista**

16   Making Remote Network Connections

17   Monitoring Your Network

18   Troubleshooting Network Problems

19   Setting up a Website

20   Setting up an FTP Site

Glossary of Network Terms

Index

Table of Contents

Introducion 1

How This Book Is Organized 3
    Part I: Networking Hardware for Windows Vista 3
    Part II: Managing and Using Your Network 3
    Part III: Securing Your Network 4
    Part IV: Advanced Networking with Windows Vista 4

Conventions Used in This Book 4

Part I: Networking Hardware for Windows Vista 7

    1   Understanding Ethernet Networking 9

        What Is Ethernet? 10
            10BASE-T 12
            100BASE-T (Fast Ethernet) 12
            1000BASE-T (Gigabit Ethernet) 13
            Beyond Gigabit Ethernet 13

        Understanding Network Interface Cards 13

        Understanding Network Cables 18
            Twisted-Pair Cable 18
            Crossover Cable 20

        Understanding Switches 22

        Understanding Routers 24
            Understanding IP Addresses 25
            The Router and Dynamic IP Addressing 26
            The Router as Firewall 27
            The Router as Switch 28

        Understanding Other Ethernet Devices 30
            Network Attached Storage 30
            Print Server 31
            Digital Media Receiver 32
            Powerline Adapter 32

        A Buyer's Guide to Ethernet Hardware 32
            Purchasing a NIC 33
            Purchasing Cables 34
            Purchasing a Switch 35
            Purchasing a Router 36

        From Here 37

2   Understanding Wireless Networking 39

What Is Wireless Networking? 40
   Understanding Wi-Fi 41
   Understanding Wireless Hot Spots 43

Understanding Wireless NICs 44

Understanding Wireless Access Points 47

Understanding Other Wireless Network Devices 50
   Wireless Range Extender 50
   Wireless Network Finder 51
   Wireless Print Server 52
   Wireless Digital Media Receiver 53

A Buyer's Guide to Wireless Networking Hardware 53
   Purchasing a Wireless NIC 54
   Purchasing a Wireless AP 55

From Here 57

3   Configuring Your Router 59

Connecting the Router for Configuration 60

Displaying the Router's Setup Pages 60
   Entering the Router's IP Address 61
   Using the Network Window 62

Changing the Router's IP Address 63
   Belkin 64
   D-Link 64
   Linksys 64
   Netgear 66

Updating the Firmware 66
   Belkin 67
   D-Link 68
   Linksys 69
   Netgear 70

Setting Up Your Broadband Connection 71
   Belkin 73
   D-Link 74
   Linksys 75
   Netgear 75

Enabling UPnP 77
   Belkin 78
   D-Link 78

Linksys 79
Netgear 79

Enabling the DHCP Server 81
Belkin 82
D-Link 83
Linksys 83
Netgear 84

Modifying Wireless Settings 85
Belkin 86
D-Link 87
Linksys 88
Netgear 89

Checking the Router Status 90
Belkin 90
D-Link 91
Linksys 91
Netgear 92

Testing Your Router's Capabilities 93

From Here 96

4   Putting Your Network Together 97

Inserting an Internal NIC 98
Installing the NIC's Device Driver 98
Installing the NIC 100
Making Sure the NIC Installed Properly 104

Connecting the Broadband Modem 105
Attaching the Internet Connection Cable .105
Registering the Modem 107

Connecting the Router 108

Connecting the Switch 110

Laying the Network Cable 111

Changing the Computer and Workgroup Name 112

Making Wireless Network Connections 113
Connecting to a Wireless Network 114
Disconnecting from a Wireless Network 117

From Here 118

Part II: Managing and Using Your Network   119

   5   Working with Vista's Basic Network Tools and Tasks 121
       Understanding Vista's Network Icon 122
           Accessing Common Networking Commands 122
           Viewing the Current Network Status 123
           Turning Off the Network Icon 124
       Accessing the Network and Sharing Center 125
       Turning On Network Discovery 128
       Viewing Network Computers and Devices 130
       Displaying a Network Map 131
       Viewing Network Status Details 133
       Customizing Your Network 135
       From Here 137

   6   Managing Network Connections 139
       Opening the Network Connections Window 140
       Renaming a Network Connection 141
       Enabling Automatic IP Addressing 142
           Confirming That Windows Vista Is Configured for Dynamic IP
             Addressing 142
           Displaying the Computer's Current IP Address 143
       Setting Up a Static IP Address 145
           Displaying the Current DNS Addresses 146
           Specifying the Static IP Address 147
       Finding a Connection's MAC Address 149
       Using a Network Connection to Wake Up a Sleeping Computer 151
       Disabling a Network Connection 154
       From Here 155

   7   Managing Wireless Network Connections 157
       Opening the Manage Wireless Networks Window 158
       Making Other Wireless Connections 158
           Connecting to a Hidden Network 159
           Creating an Ad Hoc Wireless Network 161
       Working with Wireless Connection Properties 163
           Modifying Connection Properties 164
           Modifying Security Properties 165

Renaming Wireless Connections 166

Reordering Wireless Connections 167

Creating User-Specific Wireless Connections 168

Removing Wireless Connections 170

From Here 170

8   Accessing and Sharing Network Resources 171

Accessing Shared Network Resources 172
    Viewing a Computer's Shared Resources 172
    Working with Network Addresses 174

Mapping a Network Folder to a Local Drive Letter 177
    Creating the Mapped Network Folder 177
    Mapping Folders at the Command Line 179
    Disconnecting a Mapped Network Folder 180

Creating a Network Location for a Remote Folder 180

Accessing a Shared Printer 182

Sharing Resources with the Network 184
    Activating File and Printer Sharing 185
    Sharing the Public Folder 186
    Activating Printer Folder Sharing 187
    Using Password Protected Sharing 187
    Using Public Folder Sharing 188
    Creating User Accounts for Sharing 189
    Sharing a Resource with the File Sharing Wizard 190
    Viewing Your Shared Resources 192

From Here 192

9   Setting Up Vista as a Digital Media Hub 195

Understanding Digital Media Hardware 196
    Digital Media Computer 196
    Television 201
    Television Connectors 202
    Audio Receiver Connectors 203
    Digital Media Receivers 204

Connecting Your Digital Media Hub 205
    Adding an Xbox 360 to the Network 205
    Connecting an Xbox 360 to Windows Vista 206

Sharing Your Media Player Library 207

From Here 209

10 Taking Advantage of Your Network 211

Backing Up to the Network 212

Publishing a Windows Vista Calendar on the Network 216
Publishing Your Calendar 217
Subscribing to a Calendar I: Using the Subscribe Message 219
Subscribing to a Calendar II: Using Windows Calendar 220
Working with Shared Calendars 221

Importing Pictures to a Network Share 221

Ripping Audio CDs to a Network Share 223

Recording TV Shows to a Network Share 225

Setting Up a Network-Based Slideshow 228
Running a Screensaver Slideshow from the Network 228
Running a Slideshow from the Network 230
Display Network Images in the Slide Show Gadget 234

From Here 236

11 Working with Network Files Offline....................................237

Activating the Offline Files Feature 238

Making a File or Folder Available for Offline Use 239

Changing the Amount of Disk Space Used by Offline Files 240

Prohibiting a Network Folder from Being Made Available Offline ...242

Encrypting Offline Files 244

Working with Network Files While You're Offline 245
Working with Offline Files via the Sync Center 245
Working with Offline Files via the Remote Computer 247

Synchronizing Your Offline Files 248
Scheduling a Synchronization by Time 248
Scheduling a Synchronization by Event 250

Dealing with Synchronization Conflicts 252

From Here 253

12 Collaborating with Windows Meeting Space 255

Working with the People Near Me Service 257
Signing In to People Near Me 257
Working with Trusted Contacts 258
Setting People Near Me Options 261
Signing Out of People Near Me 264

Configuring Windows Meeting Space 264

Launching Windows Meeting Space 265

Joining an Existing Meeting 266

Starting Your Own Meeting 267

Sending a Meeting Invitation 269
 Sending a Meeting Invitation Using People Near Me 269
 Sending a Meeting Invitation via Email 270
 Creating an Invitation File 271

Handling a Meeting Invitation 272
 Handling a People Near Me Invitation 272
 Opening an Invitation File 274

Sharing a Handout 275

Starting a Shared Session 276

Controlling the Shared Session 277

Ending the Shared Session 278

From Here 278

Part III: Securing Your Network   279

13   Securing Windows Vista 281

Understanding Vista's Security Groups 282

Understanding User Account Control 283
 Understanding the Least-Privileged User 283
 Elevating Privileges 284

Implementing Parental Controls 286
 Setting Up User Accounts for the Kids 287
 Turning On Parental Controls and Activity Reporting 288
 Securing the Web 290
 Allowing Only Specific Programs 291

Building a Strong Password 292

Checking Your Computer's Security Settings 294
 Making Sure Windows Firewall Is Turned On 294
 Making Sure Windows Defender Is Turned On 295
 Controlling Automatic Updates 298
 Making Sure User Account Control Is Turned On 301
 Making Sure the Administrator Account Is Disabled 302

Thwarting Spyware with Windows Defender 303

Protecting Yourself Against Email Viruses 304

Protecting Yourself Against Phishing Scams 307
   Making Sure Internet Explorer's Phishing Filter Is Turned On 308
   Making Sure Windows Mail Phishing Protection Is Turned On 310
From Here 311

14   Implementing Network Security 313
Deactivating the Sharing Wizard 314
Setting Sharing Permissions on Shared Folders 315
Setting Security Permissions on Shared Folders 318
Hiding Your Shared Folders 320
Disabling the Hidden Administrative Shares .322
Removing Stored Remote Desktop Credentials 323
Preventing Users from Logging On at Certain Times 325
   Setting a User's Logon Hours 326
   Automatically Logging Off a User When the Logon Hours Expire 327
Hiding the Usernames in the Logon Screen 328
Running the Baseline Security Analyzer on Your Network 330
From Here 333

15   Implementing Wireless Security 335
Specifying a New Administrative Password 336
   Belkin 336
   D-Link 337
   Linksys 338
   Netgear 339
Positioning the Access Point for Maximum Security 340
Encrypting Wireless Signals with WPA 341
   Belkin 342
   D-Link 343
   Linksys 344
   Netgear 345
   Changing the Wireless Connection Security Properties 345
Disabling Network SSID Broadcasting 347
   Belkin 348
   D-Link 349
   Linksys 349
   Netgear 351
Changing the Default SSID 352
   Belkin 352
   D-Link 353

Linksys 353
Netgear 355

Enabling MAC Address Filtering 356
Getting the MAC Address of Your Wireless NIC 356
Belkin 358
D-Link 359
Linksys 360
Netgear 361

From Here 362

Part IV: Advanced Networking with Windows Vista   363

16   Making Remote Network Connections 365

Setting Up the Remote Computer as a Host .366
Windows Versions That Can Act as Hosts 366
Setting Up User Accounts on the Host 367
Configuring Vista to Act as a Remote Desktop Host 367
Configuring XP to Act as a Remote Desktop Host 371

Installing Remote Desktop on an XP Client Computer 372

Connecting to the Remote Desktop 373
Making a Basic Connection 373
Making an Advanced Connection 374
Working with the Connection Bar 379

Disconnecting from the Remote Desktop 380

Connecting to a Remote Desktop via the Internet 380
Changing the Listening Port 381
Configuring Windows Firewall 382
Determining the Host IP Address 383
Setting Up Port Forwarding 384
Connecting Using the IP Address and New Port 388

Using Dynamic DNS to Access Your Network 389
D-Link 390
Linksys 391
Netgear 392

From Here 393

17   Monitoring Your Network 395

Monitoring Network Performance 396
Monitoring Network Performance with Task Manager 397
Monitoring Network Performance with Performance Monitor 400

Monitoring Shared Folders 405
Launching the Shared Folders Snap-In 405
Viewing the Current Connections 406
Viewing Connections to Shared Folders 407
Viewing Open Files 407
Closing a User's Session or File 408
From Here 409

18   Troubleshooting Network Problems 411
Repairing a Network Connection 412
Checking the Connection Status 413
General Solutions to Network Problems 413
Checking for Solutions to Problems 415
Troubleshooting Using Online Resources 417
Checking Connectivity with the PING Command 419
Troubleshooting Cables 421
Troubleshooting the NIC 422
Viewing the NIC in Device Manager 423
Updating the NIC Device Driver 425
Troubleshooting Wireless Network Problems 426
Reverting to an Earlier Configuration 427
From Here 429

19   Setting Up a Website 431
Understanding Internet Information Services 432
Installing Internet Information Services 433
Accessing Your Website 434
Creating a Windows Firewall Exception for the Web Server 434
Accessing Your Website Over the Network 436
Accessing Your Website Over the Internet 436
Understanding the Default Website 437
Viewing the Default Website Folder 437
Viewing the Default Website with IIS Manager 438
Adding Folders and Files to the Default Website 440
Setting Permissions on the Default Website Folder 440
Adding a File to the Default Website 441
Changing the Default Website Home Page 443
Adding a Folder to the Default Website 443

Controlling and Customizing Your Website 447
  Stopping Your Website 447
  Restarting Your Website 448
  Renaming the Default Website 448
  Changing the Website Location 448
  Setting the Website's Default Document 449
  Working Without a Default Document 451
  Disabling Anonymous Access 454
  Viewing the Server Logs 456

From Here 459

20 Setting Up an FTP Site 461

Installing the FTP Publishing Service 462

Starting the FTP Publishing Service 462

Accessing Your FTP Site 464
  Creating a Windows Firewall Exception for the FTP Server 464
  Accessing Your FTP Site Over the Network 466
  Accessing Your FTP Site Over the Internet 466

Understanding the Default FTP Site 467
  Viewing the Default FTP Site Folder 467
  Viewing the Default FTP Site with IIS 6 Manager 468

Adding Folders and Files to the Default FTP Site 469
  Setting Permissions on the Default FTP Site Folder 469
  Adding a File to the Default FTP Site 470
  Adding a Folder to the Default FTP Site 471

Working with Your FTP Site 473
  Stopping Your FTP Site 473
  Restarting Your FTP Site 474
  Renaming the Default FTP Site 475
  Changing the FTP Site Location 475
  Displaying Messages to FTP Users 477
  Disabling Anonymous Access 478
  Securing an FTP Folder 480

From Here 481

Glossary of Networking Terms 483

Index 503

Introduction

Only connect!

—E. M. Forster

I f you have just a single computer in your home or small office, and if you're the only person who uses that computer, your setup is inherently efficient. You can use the machine whenever you like, and everything you need— your applications, your printer, your CD/DVD drive, your Internet connection, and so on—are readily available.

Things become noticeably less efficient if you have to share the computer with other people. For instance, you might have to wait for someone else to finish a task before you can get your own work done, you might need to have separate applications for each person's requirements, and you might need to set up separate folders to hold each person's data. User accounts and fast user switching in Vista ease these problems, but they don't eliminate them. For example, you still have to twiddle a thumb or two while waiting for another person to complete his work.

IN THIS INTRODUCTION

- How This Book Is Organized
- Conventions Used in This Book

A better solution is to increase the number of computers available. Now that machines with fast processors, ample RAM, and massive hard disk space can be had for just a few hundred dollars, a multiple-machine setup is an affordable proposition for most homes. At home, for example, the current trend is to buy a nice system for Mom and Dad to put in their office, while the kids inherit the old machine for their games and homework assignments.

Now you have several computers kicking around the house or office, but they're all islands unto themselves. If you want to print something using another computer's printer, you're forced to copy the file to a memory card or other removable media, walk that media over to the other computer, and then print from there. Similarly, if multiple computers require Internet access, you face the hassle (and expense) of configuring separate connections

So now you must take the final step on this road: Connect everything together to create your own small network. This will give you all kinds of benefits:

- A printer (or just about any peripheral) that's attached to one computer can be used by any other computer on the network.
- You can transfer files from one computer to another.
- Users can access disk drives and folders on network computers as though they were part of their own computer. In particular, you can set up a folder to store common data files, and each user will be able to access these files from the comfort of her machine. (For security, you can restrict access to certain folders and drives.)
- You can set up an Internet connection on one device and share that connection with other machines on the network.
- You can stream images, music, and videos from one computer to another computer or to a digital media receiver, such as an Xbox 360.
- You can set up a wireless portion of your network, which enables you to access other computers and the Internet from just about anywhere in your house or office.

The benefits of a network are clear; but if you've been hesitating because you think getting the right equipment and putting it all together seem like complex tasks, you've come to the right book. Here, in *Networking with Windows Vista*, you get a complete beginner's guide to creating, configuring, administering, and using a small network using Windows Vista computers. This book includes comprehensive coverage of networking hardware, including both wired and wireless devices. You get handy buyer's guides that tell you how to make smart choices when purchasing network hardware. Then, when you have your hardware in hand, this book shows you how to put everything together, including installing the devices, laying the cable, and connecting all the pieces.

With your hardware tasks complete, the book switches to the software side and examines Windows Vista networking features. These include the Network and Sharing Center, managing wired and wireless connections, accessing shared network resources, sharing local resources on the network, implementing security, and much more.

How This Book Is Organized

To help give you a sense of the overall structure of the book, the next few sections offer a brief summary of the four main parts of the book.

Part I: Networking Hardware for Windows Vista

Part I gives you a complete look at the hardware side of networking, with a focus on networking for homes and small offices. The first two chapters describe the hardware and devices you need for wired networking (Chapter 1, "Understanding Ethernet Networking") and wireless networking (Chapter 2, "Understanding Wireless Networking"). As you learn in those chapters, your network needs a device called a router to share your Internet connection with the network, and the book next tells you how to configure your router (Chapter 3, "Configuring Your Router"). Part I ends by showing you how to bring everything together and get your network connected and running (Chapter 4, "Putting Your Network Together").

Part II: Managing and Using Your Network

Part II, with eight chapters, is the biggest section of the book, and it's where you learn the real meat and potatoes of Windows Vista networking. You begin by learning about some basic Vista networking tools (Chapter 5, "Working with the Network and Sharing"), and you then move on to managing your wired and wireless network connection (Chapters 6, "Managing Network Connections," and 7, "Managing Wireless Network Connections," respectively). You next learn how to access resources on the network and how to share your computer's resource with the network (Chapter 8, "Accessing and Sharing Network Resources"), and then how to configure a Vista machine to act as your network's digital media hub (Chapter 9, "Setting Up Vista as a Digital Media Hub"). You learn a few Vista techniques for taking advantage of your network (Chapter 10, "Taking Advantage of Your Network"), how to work with network files even when you're not connected to the network (Chapter 11, "Work with Network Files Offline"), and how to collaborate with other people on the network using Vista's Meeting Space program (Chapter 12, "Collaborating with Windows Meeting Space").

Part III: Securing Your Network

Network security is a serious and important topic, so I devote three chapters to it here in Part III. You first learn how to secure each Vista computer (Chapter 13, "Securing Windows Vista"), and you then learn techniques for general network security (Chapter 14, "Implementing Network Security"), and then specific techniques to enhance wireless security (Chapter 15, "Implementing Wireless Security").

Part IV: Advanced Networking with Windows Vista

The book closes with five chapters that take your networking skills to a higher (although still practical) level. You learn how to connect to your network from remote locations (Chapter 16, "Making Remote Network Connections"), how to monitor network users and activity (Chapter 17, "Monitoring Your Network"), how to troubleshoot network woes (Chapter 18, "Troubleshooting Network Problems"), how to set up your own website on the network (Chapter 19, "Setting Up a Website"), and how to set up an FTP site (Chapter 20, "Setting up an FTP Site").

Conventions Used in This Book

To make your life easier, this book includes various features and conventions that help you get the most out of this book and Windows Vista networking:

Steps	Throughout the book, I've broken many networking tasks into easy-to-follow step-by-step procedures.
Things you type	Whenever I suggest that you type something, what you type appears in a **bold monospace** font.
Filenames, folder names, and code	These things appear in a `monospace` font.
Commands	Commands and their syntax use the `monospace` font, too. Command placeholders (which stand for what you actually type) appear in an `italic monospace` font.

Pull-down menu commands

I use the following style for all application menu commands: *Menu, Command*, where *Menu* is the name of the menu that you pull down and *Command* is the name of the command you select. Here's an example: File, Open. This means that you pull down the File menu and select the Open command.

Code continuation character

When a line of code is too long to fit on only one line of this book, it is broken at a convenient place and continued to the next line. The continuation of the line is preceded by a code continuation character (➡). You should type a line of code that has this character as one long line without breaking it.

This book also uses the following boxes to draw your attention to important (or merely interesting) information:

note The Note box presents asides that give you more information about the current topic. These tidbits provide extra insights that offer a better understanding of the task.

tip The Tip box tells you about Windows Vista methods that are easier, faster, or more efficient than the standard methods.

caution The all-important Caution box tells you about potential accidents waiting to happen. There are always ways to mess things up when you're working with computers. These boxes help you avoid those traps and pitfalls.

Networking Hardware for Windows Vista

1 Understanding Ethernet Networking

2 Understanding Wireless Networking

3 Configuring Your Router

4 Putting Your Network Together

1

Understanding Ethernet Networking

All computing topics begin, at some level, with hardware. No matter what you want to do digitally, you do it with and through hardware. From the computer itself and all of its internal components, to external devices such as the keyboard, mouse, monitor, printer, modem, and speakers, software requires hardware. But there's one computing topic that is particularly hardware intensive, and that's the subject of this book: networking. Although connecting a couple of computers together can be as simple as slinging a special cable between them, true networking requires not only a number of different devices, it also requires devices that work well together. To set up a network that not only works, but is also fast, reliable, affordable, and expandable, you need to make the right decisions at the start *before* your network is a going concern. (Although, of course, you can always modify your configuration if you've already got some kind of network on the go; it's just more expensive that way.) This chapter will help you do that by explaining the hardware and devices you need to set up the wired portion of your network. Chapter 2, "Understanding Wireless Networking," takes you through the devices you need to make wireless connections.

IN THIS CHAPTER

- What Is Ethernet?
- Understanding Network Interface Cards
- Understanding Network Cables
- Understanding Switches
- Understanding Routers
- Understanding Other Ethernet Devices
- A Buyer's Guide to Ethernet Hardware
- From Here

What Is Ethernet?

When networking geeks gather, they often talk about *network architecture*, which (to give you a definition that would be about a tenth as long as the one you'd get from a networking geek) refers to the hardware components that encompass a network, how those components connect together, and the methods those components use to send data from one part of the network to another. In other words (to give you an even shorter definition), the network architecture is the overall design of the network.

Networking geeks also seem overly fond of inventing new networking architectures, so the computing world has seen its share of designs, from *Token Ring* to *ArcNet* to *FDDI* (Fiber Distributed Data Interface, if you must know). Fortunately, you don't need to know a thing about any of these architectures. That's because, in recent years, one networking architecture has come to dominate most of computing, and is in fact universal in the small home and office networks that I talk about in this book. That architecture is called *ethernet*, and it's the subject of this chapter.

Ethernet technology exists in what network mavens call the *physical layer* and the *data link layer* of the networking model. The physical layer deals with the technical specifications of networking hardware, and the data link layer deals with the basic transfer of data from one part of the network to another.

THE OSI MODEL

The specifics of the networking model aren't important for day-to-day networking, but I'll provide you with some details here, just in case you're curious. The full networking model is called the *Open System Interconnection* (OSI) *model*, and it contains seven layers in all. Layer 1 is the physical layer; layer 2 is the data link layer; layer 3 is the *network layer*, which deals with how data is routed from one network location to another; layer 4 is the *transport layer*, which deals with ensuring that data is successfully and accurately transferred from network location to another; layer 5 is the *session layer*, which deals with initiating, managing, and terminating connections between network devices (the period between the initial connection and the termination of that connection is called a *session*); layer 6 is the *presentation layer*, which deals with formatting, converting, or encrypting data received from the session layer so that it can be used by the application layer (discussed next); and finally, layer 7 is the *application layer*, which provides the connection between the network and network-based applications such as email programs, web browsers, and FTP clients.

1

The specifics of how ethernet works are hideously complex, and you don't need to know any of it to get your own small network operating successfully. However, it doesn't hurt to have at least a high-level understanding of what's going on when your ethernet devices are hard at work.

All ethernet devices are given a unique identifier called the *Media Access Control* (MAC) *address*. When data is ready to be sent over the network, ethernet divides the data into small chunks called *frames*, which include part of the data (this is often called the *payload*) and an extra header that includes (among other things) the MAC addresses of the sending and receiving devices. The ethernet device then waits until the network isn't transferring any data (this "wait" is typically measured in milliseconds), and it then sends the first frame. This process is then repeated until all the data has been sent. If, along the way, two devices attempt to send data at the same time (resulting in a *collision*), both machines wait for a randomly chosen amount of time (again, we're talking milliseconds here), and then resend their frames.

The medium through which all this data is transferred is the network cable. (For more information, see "Understanding Network Cables," later in this chapter.) Because of this, and because of the universality of ethernet, particularly in homes and small offices, the word *ethernet* is, for all intents and purposes, synonymous with wired networking (as opposed to wireless networking, the subject of Chapter 2). In other words, if you hear someone talking about (or see someone writing about) ethernet, rest assured that all that person is really talking (or writing) about is networking that uses cables.

However, that isn't to say that there's only one kind of "networking that uses cables." There are, in fact, a number of different ethernet standards, and it's the differences between these standards (and the ways in which these standards are compatible or incompatible) that should form the bulk of your ethernet knowledge. From the point of view of your small home or office network, the only significant difference between the standards is the speed at which they transfer data.

caution This is as good a time as any to introduce the word *theoretical* into our discussion. The data transfer rate associated with any ethernet standard (indeed, any form of communications) is the rate that would be obtained if conditions were perfect. That is, if there were no noise on the line, no nearby interference, no frame collisions, and so on. So, in the discussion that follows, the speeds I mention are purely theoretical, and it's unlikely you'll ever reach such velocities in practice. However, the comparisons are still useful because the *relative* difference between two standards will still hold in practice. That is, if the theoretical rate of standard B is 10 times faster than that of standard A, standard B's real-world rate will also be 10 times faster than standard A's real-world rate.

10BASE-T

The first commercial ethernet standard (first published more than a quarter of a century ago) was called *10BASE-T*, which breaks down as follows:

> **note** When you're talking about data communications, a *megabit* (Mb) is equal to one million bits. So, the 10Mbps transmission speed of 10BASE-T means that it can (theoretically, of course) transfer 10 million bits of data per second. Just to confuse matters, if you're talking about memory or data storage, a megabit equals 1,048,576 bits.

10   This designates the maximum theoretical data transfer rate of 10 *megabits* per second (Mbps).

BASE This is short for *baseband*, which describes a communications medium (in this case, an ethernet cable) that only allows one signal at a time. Compare this with *broadband*, which describes a communications medium that allows multiple simultaneous signals.

T   This tells you that the standard uses twisted-pair cables.

100BASE-T (Fast Ethernet)

Around 1995, a new ethernet standard was introduced: *Fast Ethernet* or *100BASE-T*. As you can tell from the latter, this standard operated at a theoretical maximum transmission speed of 100Mbps, making the new devices 10 times faster than 10BASE-T. (To be accurate, the designation *100BASE-T* is an umbrella term for the various implementations of Fast Ethernet that have appeared, including 100BASE-TX, 100BASE-T2, and 100BASE-T4; of these, only 100BASE-TX survives, so that's now the actual standard underlying the Fast Ethernet moniker.)

Although (like all new technologies) Fast Ethernet was expensive at first, the prices of Fast Ethernet devices quickly fell, and by the end of the 1990s Fast Ethernet had become the most common implementation of ethernet found in offices and, increasingly, in homes. It helped, too, that most Fast Ethernet devices were *10/100* devices, which meant that they were also backward compatible with 10BASE-T devices, so you could mix and match the two types in your network. Use of Fast Ethernet remains widespread today, mostly on older networks that haven't yet upgraded to the faster Gigabit Ethernet (discussed next).

1000BASE-T (Gigabit Ethernet)

In 1995, the *Institute for Electrical and Electronics Engineers* (IEEE), which creates and maintains the ethernet standards (among many other duties), published a new standard technically labeled 802.3ab, but more commonly known as *Gigabit Ethernet* or *1000BASE-T*. This standard boasts an impressive top speed of 1,000Mbps, or 1Gbps, making it 10 times faster than Fast Ethernet.

> **note** In the context of data communications, a *gigabit* (Gb) is equal to one billion bits. As with megabits, if you're talking about memory or data storage, a gigabit equals the more exact value of 1,073,741,824 bits.

The prices of Gigabit Ethernet devices have fallen rapidly over the past few years, to the point now where a gigabit-speed network is affordable for almost any home or small office. As with Fast Ethernet, the adoption of Gigabit Ethernet is being helped by the availability of *10/100/1000* devices, which are backward compatible with both 10BASE-T devices and Fast Ethernet devices.

Beyond Gigabit Ethernet

Right now, Gigabit Ethernet is the fastest ethernet standard that's both affordable and readily available. However, it's not the fastest version of ethernet. That distinction goes to the most recent ethernet standard—*10 Gigabit Ethernet* or *10GBASE-T*—which the IEEE published in 2006. As these names imply, this implementation of ethernet comes with a theoretical transmission speed of 10Gbps, an order of magnitude faster than Gigabit Ethernet. However, as I write this in late 2007, 10GBASE-T devices are extremely rare and extremely expensive. It will likely be a few years before this standard becomes affordable and easy to find.

The need for network speed can never be satisfied, of course, so the folks at the IEEE have started work on an even faster ethernet standard: 100 Gigabit Ethernet, which will ship data at the giddy rate of 100Gbps. It will certainly be quite a few years before this standard is even published, and quite a few years after that before 100 Gigabit Ethernet devices become available.

Understanding Network Interface Cards

The starting point for your ethernet network is the *network interface card* (NIC). This is a device that serves as the connection point between some network node and the rest of the network. (A *node* is a device connected to a network. Example nodes include desktop computers, notebooks, and network devices such as routers and print servers.) As you'll see in the next section, an ethernet NIC connects a node to the network by means of a cable. The back of the NIC contains a port into which you plug the cable.

→ If you're looking for information on wireless network cards, **see** "Understanding Wireless NICs," **p. 41**.

After the physical connection is established, the NIC works with a device driver to process incoming and outgoing network data. As such, the NIC is the focal point for the computer's network connection, so it plays a big part in the overall performance of that connection. Most NICs sold today (or that come preinstalled in new computers) are either Fast Ethernet or, increasingly, Gigabit Ethernet, and the vast majority are either 10/100 or 10/100/1000 devices that you can add seamlessly to your existing network.

Ethernet NICs come in four main varieties:

Motherboard NIC   The components required by a NIC have become so small that most PC manufacturers can now easily place them directly on the computer's motherboard. (The *motherboard* is the computer's main circuit board, which includes connectors for the CPU, memory chips, hard drives, ports, expansion slots, controllers, and BIOS—the basic input/output system.) The NIC is added in such a way that the port for the network cable appears flush with the back of the computer, usually among the other built-in ports such as USB, FireWire, monitor, and so on. The motherboard NIC port is almost always labeled in some way, either with text such as LAN or Ethernet (as shown in Figure 1.1), or with some kind of network icon (as shown in Figure 1.2).

Text label marks the Ethernet port

FIGURE 1.1

On some PCs, the motherboard NIC comes with a text label.

An icon marks the Ethernet port

FIGURE 1.2

Other PCs label the motherboard NIC with a network icon.

Network adapter
If your computer doesn't have a motherboard NIC or if the built-in NIC is only Fast Ethernet and you want to upgrade to Gigabit Ethernet, you need to purchase and attach your own NIC. One common NIC type is an internal adapter card that you insert into a free slot on the computer's bus. Most computers today use a PCI bus, so you need to get a PCI network adapter. If your computer has a free *PCI Express* (PCIe) slot, there are PCIe network adapters available. Figure 1.3 shows a typical ethernet network adapter.

→ To learn how to install a network adapter, **see** "Inserting an Internal NIC," **p. 98**.

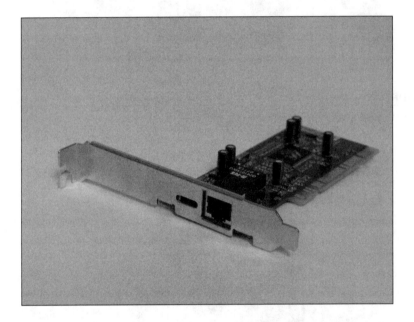

FIGURE 1.3

An ethernet network adapter goes inside the computer and attaches to a free slot on the system bus.

USB NIC
If you don't like the idea of cracking open your computer's case to insert an Internet network adapter, the alternative is to get an external NIC that you plug into

an available USB port. In this case, make sure you get a USB 2.0 NIC to ensure top performance. Figure 1.4 shows an example of a USB-based NIC.

FIGURE 1.4

For easy installation, insert a USB 2.0 NIC into a free USB slot on your computer.

PC Card NIC   Most modern notebook computers come with a built-in ethernet NIC that exposes a port. If your notebook doesn't have a built-in NIC, or if you want to upgrade your note- book to a faster version of ethernet, you have a few options. One possibility (albeit often an expensive one) is to purchase a docking station for the notebook, because almost all docking stations come with built-in NICs. Alternatively, because almost all notebooks come with one or more USB ports, you can also attach a USB NIC. Finally, all notebooks come with at least one PC Card (or PCMCIA) slot, so you can purchase and attach a PC Card (or PCM- CIA) ethernet NIC. Figure 1.5 shows an example.

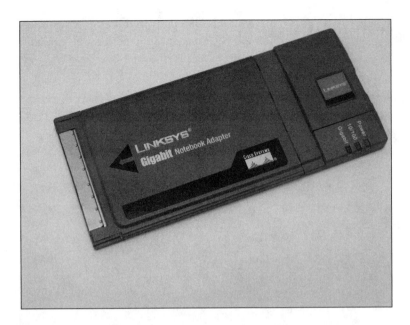

FIGURE 1.5

For a notebook computer, you can insert a PC Card (or PCMCIA) Ethernet NIC.

Understanding Network Cables

As mentioned earlier, when it comes to small networks, ethernet networking is synonymous with wired networking, where *wired* means that each computer or device is connected to the network by means of a network cable.

The "starting point" (figuratively speaking) for any cable is the network adapter. As mentioned in the preceding section, every NIC comes with a port into which you insert a network cable, which can be either a twisted-pair cable or a crossover cable.

Twisted-Pair Cable

There are several different types of network cable, such as coaxial cable and fiber-optic cable, but virtually all small ethernet networks use twisted-pair cable. It consists of four pairs of twisted copper wires that together form a circuit that can transmit data. The wires are twisted together to reduce interference. This is similar to the cable used in telephone wiring, but network cables are often shielded by a braided metal insulation to further reduce interference problems. This type of cable is called, not surprisingly, *shielded twisted-pair*, or

STP. You can use *unshielded twisted-pair* (UTP) cabling, which doesn't have the insulation layer of STP cable. UTP cable is usually cheaper than STP cable, but it does tend to be less reliable than STP.

A twisted-pair cable comes with an RJ-45 jack on each end. (Networking purists cringe if you use the term *RJ-45* to refer to a network cable plug; they insist that the correct term is *8P8C*, which is short for *8 Position 8 Contact*; the rest of us ignore this unwieldy term and stick with RJ-45 or RJ45. (The *RJ*, by the way, is short for *registered jack*.) Figure 1.6 compares a network cable's RJ-45 jack with the RJ-11 jack used by a telephone cable.

RJ-45 jack (network cable)

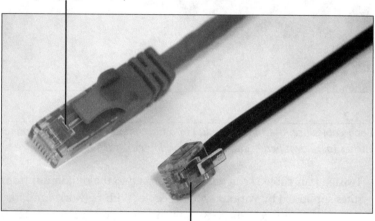

RJ-11 jack (telephone cable)

FIGURE 1.6

Network cables come with RJ-45 connectors at each end, which are similar to, but considerably larger than, the RJ-11 connectors used with telephone cables.

The RJ-45 jack on a network cable plugs into the corresponding RJ-45 port on a NIC or on some other type of network device, such as a switch or router, as shown in Figure 1.7.

FIGURE 1.7

Twisted-pair cables use RJ-45 jacks to plug into the complementary RJ-45 connectors in network switches (as shown here) and in network adapter cards.

Twisted-pair cable is categorized according to the maximum transmission rates supported by various types of cable. With network data, for example, Category 3 (also called Cat 3) cable only supports up to a 16Mbps transmission rate, so it only works with 10BASE-T networks. These days, however, few people purchase anything less than Category 5 (Cat 5) cable, which is rated at 100Mbps and so can handle the transmission rate associated with Fast Ethernet. If you think you're going to move to Gigabit Ethernet at some point, you will want Category 6 (Cat 6) cables, which support 1Gbps throughput. (Category 5e cables also support 1Gbps, but Category 6 cables are higher quality.)

Crossover Cable

Plugging one end of an RJ-45 network cable into a computer's NIC is the first step in getting the computer on the network. The second step is clear: Plug in the other end of the network cable. But, plug it in to what, exactly? Your first guess might be to plug the other end of the cable into the NIC of a second computer. Good try, but that won't work.

To understand why, you need to know that each network cable has both a transmit line and a receive line, and signals on those lines specify which direction the data is flowing. The NIC's port also has transmit and receive pins, so it can specify or detect the direction of the data flow. For example, suppose you have Computer A and Computer B connected by a network cable. When Computer A wants to send data, the transmit pin on Computer A's NIC is activated, which in turn activates the transmit line on the network cable.

That's fine, but the problem occurs when this signal reaches the NIC port on Computer B. The cable's transmit line will correspond with the transmit pin on the other NIC, so Computer B will get a signal that it should be transmitting data. This won't make sense (because Computer B isn't transmitting), so no data goes through.

The solution is to use a special kind of network cable called an ethernet *crossover cable*. This cable reverses the position of the transmit and receive lines. So when Computer A transmits data and activates the transmit pin of its NIC port, the signal goes through the crossover cable's receive line. This in turn activates the receive pin of Computer B's NIC, so the data transfer occurs successfully.

As with regular network cable, crossover cables also come in the same categories—Cat 3, Cat 5, Cat 5e, and Cat 6—so get a cable that corresponds to the ethernet standard supported by your NICs.

IDENTIFYING A CROSSOVER CABLE

From a distance (or, heck, sometimes even up close), crossover cables look identical to regular network cables. To help you identify them, many crossover cables come with a label such as "CROSS" taped to them. If you don't see such a label, I suggest you add your own so that you can keep the two types of cable separate. If you didn't do that and now you're not sure which of your cables is a crossover, there's a way to tell. Take the connectors on each end of the cable and place them side by side so that you have a good view of the colored wires inside. (A clear plastic covering helps here.) Make sure you hold the connectors with the same orientation (it's usually best to have the plastic tabs facing down). If the layout of the wires is identical on both connectors, then you've got a regular network cable. If you see, instead, that two of the wires—specifically, the red and the green— have switched positions, then you've got a crossover cable.

Understanding Switches

In the preceding section, you learned that you can use an ethernet crossover cable to connect two computers directly via their NIC ports. That's fine if you only want to network two computers, but what if your network consists of three or more computers, or if it also includes other network devices such as a printer or an Xbox gaming console? In these more complex—and decidedly more common—scenarios, direct connections with crossover cables won't work.

To work around the limitations of direct connections, you need some other way to combine multiple computers and devices into a network. Specifically, you need a central connection point that each device can use. On simple networks, that connection point is often a *switch*, which is a device with multiple RJ-45 ports. Figure 1.8 shows two switches: a basic 5-port switch and a larger 16-port switch.

FIGURE 1.8

Switches contain multiple RJ-45 ports for connections to computers and other network devices.

The idea here is that each ethernet device on the network connects to a port on the switch using a network cable, as shown in Figure 1.9. The result is a *network segment,* a collection of network devices connected to a single switch. (If this network segment comprises your entire network, you can call it a *switched network.*)

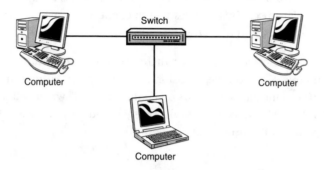

Switch

Computer   Computer

Computer

FIGURE 1.9

You can use a switch as the central connection point for your network.

The switch then forwards data from one network node to another. On basic switches such as the type used in homes or small offices, the switch usually reads the MAC address of the destination node in each ethernet frame and sends the frame directly to that device. Most switches maintain a *switching table,* a record of the MAC addresses and network port numbers used by each device on the network. As you use your network, the switch makes note of each new MAC address and adds it to the switching table, which improves overall switch performance.

You can also use a switch to send data across multiple network segments. For example, you might have a network segment in one room or office and a second segment in the room or office next door. Similarly, if your network outgrows your original switch, you might add a second switch to the network instead of upgrading to a switch with more ports. To join the two segments, you have three choices:

■ Many older switches come with a special *uplink* port that's designed to connect two switches by running a network cable from the uplink port of one switch to the uplink port of the other switch. On some of these switches, a button controls whether the port is used as a regular RJ-45 port or an uplink port.

note The network configuration shown in Figure 1.9—that is, multiple network nodes joined to a central connection point—is called the *star topology.*

- Use an ethernet crossover cable to link two switches by running the cable from any port in the first switch to any port in the second switch.

- Get switches where the ports support *Auto Crossover* (also called *Auto MDI/MDI-X* crossover detection; MDI stands for *Medium-Dependent Interface*). This enables you to connect two switches without using an uplink port or a crossover cable.

As with NICs and cables, all switches support one or more of the ethernet standards. For example, a Fast Ethernet switch will almost always support 10/100 connections, whereas a Gigabit Ethernet switch will usually support 10/100/1000 connections. Make sure you match your switch to the ethernet standard you're using on your network.

Understanding Routers

You saw in the previous section that a switch forwards ethernet packets according to the device MAC address in the frame header. This works extremely well, and most modern switches are high-performance devices. However, the inherent limitation of a switch becomes obvious when you want to add an Internet connection to your network:

- When you want to request data from a web server, it's impossible to know the MAC address of the remote server computer, so the switch has no way to forward the data request.

- When a web server wants to send data to your computer, it's impossible for the remote machine to know your computer's MAC address, so the switch cannot get the data to your computer.

In other words, the MAC address-based forwarding performed by a switch is limited to LAN traffic and cannot be used to handle WAN (*wide area network*) data.

To solve this problem, you need to add a *router* to your network (see Figure 1.10). A router is a device that makes decisions about where to send the network packets it receives. So far, this sounds suspiciously similar to a switch. The major difference is that while a switch uses a MAC address-based switching table to forward data, a router uses a *routing table* that tracks *IP addresses*, unique addresses assigned to every Internet host and to

note A *wide area network* is network that covers a wide geographical area. Some corporations use wide area networks, but the Internet is *the* wide area network.

every computer on your network. For example, this is useful when the computers share a high-speed Internet connection, because the router ensures that the Internet data goes to the computer that requested it. To make this work, you plug your high-speed modem directly into the special WAN port in the back of the router.

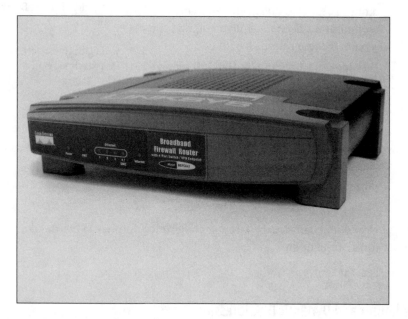

FIGURE 1.10

You add a router to your network when you want to add Internet access.

Understanding IP Addresses

An IP address is a 32-bit value assigned to a computer by a network administrator or, if you've signed up for an Internet account, by your *Internet service provider* (ISP). As you'll see in a minute, these addresses are designed so that every host and router on the Internet or within a network has a unique address. That way, when an application needs to send data to a particular locale, it knows that the destination address it plops into the packet header will make sure that everything ends up where it's supposed to.

The problem with IP addresses is their "32-bitness." Here's an example:

```
11001101110100001110000100000010
```

Not very inviting, is it? To make these numbers easier to work with, you use *dotted-decimal notation* (also known in the trade as *dotted-quad notation*). This notation divides the 32 bits of an IP address into four groups of 8 bits each (each of these groups is called a *quad*), converts each group into its decimal equivalent, and then separates these numbers with dots.

Let's look at an example. Here's the previous IP address grouped into four 8-bit quads:

```
11001101 11010000 01110001 00000010
```

Now you convert each quad into its decimal equivalent. When you do, you end up with this:

```
11001101 11010000 01110001 00000010
   205      208      113        2
```

Now you insert dots between each decimal number to get the dotted-decimal form of the address:

```
205.208.113.2
```

> **tip** You can convert a value from binary to decimal using Windows Vista's Calculator. Select Start, All Programs, Accessories, Calculator, and then, in the Calculator window, select View, Scientific. Click the Bin (binary) option, use the text box to type the 1s and 0s of the binary value you want to convert, and click the Dec (decimal) option.

The Router and Dynamic IP Addressing

The MAC addresses of network devices are assigned in advance by the device manufacturer. How, then, are IP addresses assigned? For the servers and other remote machines you deal with on the Internet, each network that wants on the Internet must sign up with a domain registrar (such as VeriSign.com or Register.com). In turn, the registrar assigns that network a block of IP addresses that the administrator can then dole out to each computer (or, in the case of an ISP, to each customer).

For your own network, however, the IP addresses are assigned as follows:

■ Your router is given its own IP address—called the *public IP address*—from the pool of addresses controlled by your ISP. Internet data sent to any computer on your network is first sent to the router's external IP address.

■ The computers on your network are assigned IP addresses. In other words, when a computer logs on to the network, it is assigned an IP address from a pool of available addresses. When the computer logs off, the address it was using is returned to the pool. The system that manages this dynamic alloca- tion of addresses is called the *Dynamic Host Configuration Protocol* (DHCP), and the computers or devices that implement DHCP are called *DHCP servers*. In most home networks, the router acts as a DHCP server.

> **note** When a device such as a router is set up as the sole connection point between a network and the Internet, that device is called a *gateway*.

In most cases, the range of addresses is from 192.168.1.1 to 192.168.1.254. (On some routers, the range is from 192.168.0.1 to 192.168.0.254.) The router itself usually takes the 192.168.1.1 address (this is called its *private IP address*), and the pool of possible addresses is usually some subset of the total range, such as between 192.168.1.100 and 192.168.1.150.

The big advantage of this setup is that your network is never exposed to the Internet. All communication goes through the router's public IP address; so as far as, say, a web or email server is concerned, it's communicating with a device at that address. The router is able to get the correct data to your com- puter because when you initially request data, it adds your computer's private IP address and the number of the communications port your computer is using and stores this data in a *routing table*. When data comes back from the Internet, the router converts the public destination IP address of the data to the private address of your computer, a process known as *network address translation* (NAT).

The Router as Firewall

On a small network, the main function of a router is to be used as a gateway between your network and the Internet. Through the magic of NAT, your net- work cannot be seen from any device attached to the Internet; as far as the Internet is concerned, your network is nothing but a router. (For this reason, an Internet-connected router that performs NAT duties is sometimes called an *edge router*.) NAT, therefore, acts as a kind of simple *firewall*, a technology that prevents unwanted data from reaching a network.

However, most modern routers go one step further and come with separate firewall software. This gives you an interface for controlling and managing the firewall, which mostly means opening and closing specific software ports used by applications. For example, you'll see in Chapter 19, "Setting Up a Website," that to successfully use a web server on your network you need to configure the router's firewall to allow incoming connections on port 80.

The Router as Switch

You've seen that a router can act as a gateway device and a firewall device, but there's a third hat that's worn by most modern routers: a switch device. A typical router has a few RJ-45 ports (usually four; see Figure 1.11); so, as with a dedicated switch, you can create ethernet connections for computers and other devices by running ethernet cable from each device to a router port.

WAN port (for broadband modem)   RJ-45 ports

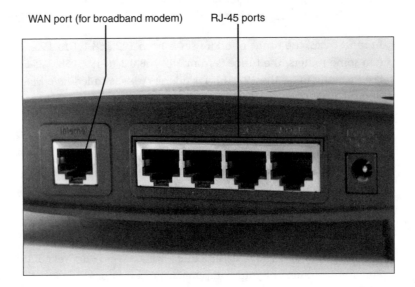

FIGURE 1.11

Most routers have built-in switches, meaning you can use the router's ports to connect devices to your network.

This means that if you have a small ethernet network, you might be able to get away with using just a router as your network's connection point. Figure 1.12 shows this network configuration.

On the other hand, if your network is larger or if you have a number of other devices you need to connect, your router might not have enough ports. Similarly, you may be upgrading your network to Gigabit Ethernet and your router only comes with Fast Ethernet (or 10/100) ports. In both cases, the easiest solution is to leave your existing router in place and add to the network a dedicated switch that meets your needs. In this scenario, you connect the broadband modem to the router's WAN port, you run a network cable from one of the router's RJ-45 ports to an RJ-45 port on the switch, and you connect your network devices to the switch. Figure 1.13 shows this network configuration.

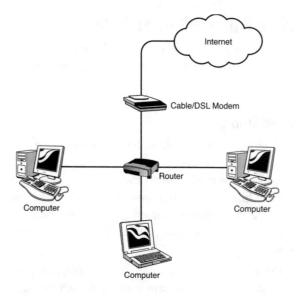

FIGURE 1.12

A small ethernet network can use a single router as both the gateway and the switch.

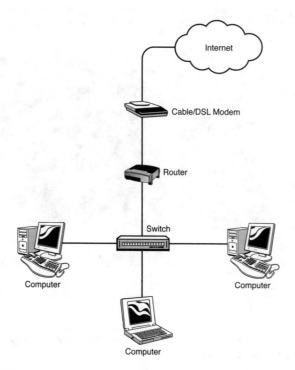

FIGURE 1.13

Larger ethernet networks may require a dedicated switch as the central network connection point.

Understanding Other Ethernet Devices

To round out your look at ethernet hardware, the next few sections give you a quick overview of a few other devices you can connect to your ethernet network.

Network Attached Storage

A *network attached storage* (NAS) device contains one or more hard drives and plugs into a switch or router. This enables the client computers on the network to store files on the device rather than on a network share. If you have one or two internal hard drives lying around, you can purchase just the NAS enclosure and attach the drives yourself. In this case, make sure that the NAS enclosure's interface supports your hard drive type (for example, ATA versus SATA).

Many NAS devices also come with one or more USB ports, which means you can expand the device's storage space by attaching one or more external USB hard drives. Figure 1.14 shows a typical NAS enclosure.

FIGURE 1.14

With a NAS enclosure, you attach one or more internal and external hard drives that a network computer can then access directly.

Print Server

To print over the network, you normally share a printer that's attached to one of the network computers. However, this requires that the computer with the printer share that printer, it requires each person who wants to use the printer to connect to it, and it requires that the network computer always be on. These aren't onerous demands, but they sometimes create enough of a hassle to make network administrators turn to dedicated *print servers*, devices that connect printers directly to the network.

In some cases, a printer comes with a built-in RJ-45 port, so you need only run ethernet cable from the printer to an RJ-45 port in the switch or router. However, most consumer-grade printers don't have a built-in NIC. In that case, you can get a print server that's a separate box with either a parallel port or a USB port (or both), as well as an RJ-45 port (see Figure 1.15). You connect the printer to the print server's parallel or USB port, and then connect the print server's RJ-45 port to the switch or router.

FIGURE 1.15

A print server device enables you to connect a printer directly to the network without having to share it through a network computer.

Digital Media Receiver

Windows Vista programs such as Windows Media Player and Windows Media Center can broadcast digital media over an ethernet connection. This is called *streaming* the media, and the data itself is called a *stream*. Other Windows Vista computers on your network can pick up and play that stream. However, you can also use a device called a *digital media receiver* (DMR) to access a media stream being sent over an ethernet connection and then play that stream through connected equipment such as speakers, audio receivers, or a TV. Examples of DMRs include the Xbox 360, the Roku SoundBridge, and the D-Link MediaLounge. Other DMR types include certain digital media players (such as MP3 players) and digital picture frames, which display images streamed over a network connection.

Powerline Adapter

You use a powerline adapter to connect a computer to your network using the AC power lines in your home or office. This device isn't a NIC per se. Instead, it acts as a kind of bridge that connects a regular ethernet NIC to your network without having to connect that NIC directly to a switch or router. You actually need at least two powerline adapters. One adapter plugs into an AC outlet near your switch or router, and you then run ethernet cable from the switch/router to the powerline adapter, which effectively connects your home or office power lines to the network. You then plug a second powerline adapter into an AC outlet near the device you want to network, and you run an ethernet cable from the device's NIC to the powerline adapter. You can repeat this for any number of devices.

A Buyer's Guide to Ethernet Hardware

If you're looking to purchase new ethernet hardware, whether you're starting from scratch or looking to upgrade your existing equipment, the buying process is not always easy because you often face a thicket of jargon terms and a list of product specifications that seems to require an advanced degree in electrical engineering to figure out. To make it easier to choose the right ethernet hardware, the next few sections give you a few pointers on what to look for and what to avoid when purchasing the four main hardware types: NICs, cables, switches, and routers.

Before getting to those specific tips, I should mention that when it comes to ethernet hardware, quality counts. That is, whenever possible, you should purchase only devices manufactured by reputable companies because that's the closest you can come to a guarantee that the products will be reliable, will conform to ethernet standards, will have device drivers that work with Windows Vista, and will provide good support, either on the Web or via phone. Yes, you can save a dollar or three on devices made by obscure manufacturers, but my experience has been that it's simply not worth the grief of buying an inferior product. Here's a list of networking companies that manufacture quality ethernet devices suitable for the home, home office, or small office:

Belkin (belkin.com)

Cables To Go (cablestogo.com)

Cables Unlimited (cablesunlimited.com)

D-Link (dlink.com)

Hewlett-Packard (hp.com)

Intel (intel.com)

Linksys (linksys.com)

NETGEAR (netgear.com)

TRENDnet (trendnet.com)

Zonet (zonetusa.com)

Purchasing a NIC

Here are a few pointers to bear in mind when shopping for a new NIC:

Internal or external? If you're looking for a NIC to go with a desktop computer, your first decision is whether to go for an internal adapter card or an external USB device. The USB NIC is obviously much easier to install; so, if your network uses Fast Ethernet (USB NICs are too slow to support Gigabit Ethernet) and your computer has lots of free USB ports, USB is definitely the way to go.

Get USB 2.0. If you do go the USB route, check the NIC's specifications carefully to make sure you're getting a USB 2.0 NIC. USB 1.1 has a maximum data transfer rate of only 12Mbps, so it's only useful for 10BASE-T connections; if your network uses Fast Ethernet, you need USB 2.0, which supports data transfer rates of up to 480Mbps.

Fast Ethernet or Gigabit Ethernet? Your next major decision is which Ethernet standard to use: Fast Ethernet or Gigabit Ethernet (don't even consider 10BASE-T). Fast Ethernet NICs are cheaper than their Gigabit Ethernet cousins; so, if your budget is tight, go with the former. On the other hand, you're really only looking at spending a few more dollars for a Gigabit Ethernet NIC, and those few measly dollars buy you 10 times the performance. The downside with Gigabit Ethernet is that you must purchase an internal adapter card, which is harder to install.

Check your available bus slots. Internal NICs insert into a slot on the computer's bus. The most common type of bus is PCI, but some older systems have one or more ISA slots and some newer systems have one or more PCIe slots. Make sure the internal NIC you buy matches your computer's bus, and make sure that your computer has at least one slot available to hold the NIC.

Make sure it's Vista-ready. You should only purchase a NIC that displays the Certified for Windows Vista logo on the box. This guarantees that the NIC's drivers work with Vista, so the device will install automatically and should work properly right out of the box.

Purchasing Cables

Network cables might seem like the simplest of all networking hardware to purchase, but you do need to consider a few things. Here are a few pointers:

Get the right cable category. Make sure the cable you buy matches your ethernet standard. If you're setting up a Fast Ethernet network, you need Cat 5 cable; if you're going with Gigabit Ethernet, load up on Cat 6 cable (or Cat 5e if you can't find Cat 6).

Shielded or unshielded? For a small network, *shielded twisted-pair* (STP) cable is probably overkill, so in most cases you'll be fine with *unshielded twisted-pair* (UTP) cable. The exception to this is when you know that the cable will be running near a source of electromagnetic radiation such as an electronic device, a power line, an air conditioner, fluorescent lights, or a motor.

Get the right length. You can reduce cable clutter in your home or office by not purchasing cables that are excessively too long. For example, if you know that a computer is 8 feet from the switch or router, don't purchase a 25-foot cable for that computer. Instead, examine the available cable lengths and buy one that's a bit longer than what you need. (A bit of slack on the cable is a good idea because it reduces the pressure on the RJ-45 connectors.) The most typical cable lengths are as follows, in feet: 1, 3, 5, 7, 10, 14, 25, and 50.

Mix your colors. Color might not seem like an important consideration when purchasing cable, but it can actually be extremely handy. The basic idea is that you buy your cables using the widest variety of colors possible: ideally, a different color for each device that you'll be connecting to the switch or router.

> **note** If you're a dedicated do-it-yourselfer, you can create your own custom cable lengths. Most computer retailers sell bulk cable rolls and cable kits that include a stripping tool for removing a section of the cable's plastic covering, a collection of RJ-45 connectors, a crimp tool for attaching a connector the cable, and even a cable tester that tells you whether the new cable works properly.

That way, later on when you need to, say, swap out a computer's network cable for a new one, you know immediately which cable to disconnect from the switch or router.

Go snagless. All RJ-45 connectors come with a plastic tab that snaps into place when you insert the connector into an RJ-45 port. This prevents the cable from falling out of the port, because you need to hold down the plastic tab to remove the connector. Unfortunately, that plastic tab has a nasty habit of snagging on whatever's under your desk when you try to pull out a loose cable. Tugging on the cable usually breaks the plastic tab, which renders the cable useless. To avoid this problem, get cables that have *snagless* connectors, which include a rounded bit of rubber just behind or on either side of the plastic tab. The rubber helps the connector slide over any obstacles, thus preventing the plastic tab from snagging. This extra bit of rubber is called, variously, the *cable boot*, the *connector boot*, the *mold boot*, or just the *boot*.

Purchasing a Switch

The technical specifications for most switches are a maze of impenetrable jargon, acronyms, and abbreviations. People who build massive networks need to know all that minutiae; but for your small network, you need to concern yourself with only four things:

The number of ports. Purchasing a switch is usually a trade-off between price and the number of ports. That is, the more ports a switch has, the more expensive it usually is. The minimum number of ports you need is, obviously, the same as the number of ethernet devices you'll be connecting to the switch. However, networks do have a habit of growing over time, so it's almost always a good idea to get a switch that has at least a few extra ports. On the other hand, if you think it's extremely unlikely that you'll ever need more than about a half dozen ports or so, don't waste your money buying a 16-port switch.

The port speed. As the central connection point for your network, the ethernet standard supported by the switch is crucial. For example, even if you have nothing but Gigabit Ethernet cards and Cat 6 cable, it won't matter a bit if your switch's ports only operate at Fast Ethernet speeds. If you want gigabit performance, get a gigabit switch. If you're slowly making your way from Fast Ethernet to Gigabit Ethernet, you can ease the transition by getting a switch that supports 10/100/1000.

Does the switch support Auto Crossover? If you think you might expand your network down the road by adding a second switch, make sure the first switch supports Auto Crossover (Auto MDI/MDI-X). This enables you to add a second switch to the network just by running a regular network cable between the two switches.

Do you even need a dedicated switch? As mentioned earlier, most routers nowadays come with a built-in switch, so you might be able to get away with using the router as your network's central connection point. This is usually only the case with small networks, because most routers come with 4-port switches (although 8- and 16-port routers are available).

Purchasing a Router

Most home and small offices now have Internet access via a broadband modem, and to share that access among the network computers and devices requires a router. Here are a few ideas to keep in mind when you need to purchase a router for your network:

Do you need a separate router? Some broadband modems come with a built-in router; so, if you need only basic connectivity, you can forego a separate router. The downside to the modem-as-router is that they only rarely include some kind of interface for configuring the router, usually because these are barebones routers without much to configure. Getting the most out of a router almost always means accessing the router's setup program, so I recommend a dedicated router for most small networks.

Do you want to use the router as a switch? If your network is small, you can save a few bucks by using the router as the network switch. Most modern routers have the capability, but double-check the product specifications to make sure. Check the ethernet standards supported by the router, and get the largest number of ports that you can afford.

Do you need wireless access? If you want to access your network with a wireless connection, then your router will also need to include a wireless access point. I discuss this in more detail in Chapter 2.

→   **See** "Understanding Wireless Access Points," **p. 47**.

Make sure it has a firewall. All routers support NAT for security, but for maximum safety make sure the router comes with a dedicated firewall that you can configure. This will help keep out Internet intruders.

Do you need VPN? If you think you'll need to make secure *virtual private network* (VPN) connections to your network, get a router that supports VPN.

From Here

- To learn how to configure various router settings, **see** Chapter 3, "Configuring Your Router," **p. 59**.

- To learn how to install a NIC adapter, **see** "Installing an Internal NIC," **p. 98**.

- For tips and pointers on running network cable, **see** "Laying the Network Cable," **p. 111**.

- For more information on using digital media over your network, **see** Chapter 9, "Setting Up Vista as a Digital Media Hub," **p. 195**.

- To learn how to configure Windows Vista as a simple web server, **see** Chapter 19, "Setting Up a Website."

Understanding Wireless Networking

IN THIS CHAPTER

- What Is Wireless Networking?
- Understanding Wireless NICs
- Understanding Wireless Access Points
- Understanding Other Wireless Network Devices
- A Buyer's Guide to Wireless Networking Hardware
- From Here

C hapter 1, "Understanding Ethernet Networking," was all about wired networking, where each computer and device connects to the network via a cable that runs from the device's *network interface card* (NIC) to a port on a switch or router. If you want maximum network speed, then ethernet, particularly Gigabit Ethernet, is the only way to connect.

However, sometimes a wired connection just isn't practical or even possible. For example, if your switch is in the den, how do you set up a wired connection for the computer in the bedroom next door? One solution is to drill holes in the adjoining walls and then snake a long ethernet cable through the hole. That will work, but holes in the wall are rarely attractive. Even more daunting, how do you connect a computer that's downstairs in the kitchen or even two floors down in the basement? Diehard ethernet types might consider getting special outdoor ethernet cables and poking more holes in the appropriate walls, but at some point the hole-making madness must stop. Finally, consider the simple scenario where you're tired of working in the den and you'd prefer to take your notebook PC outside to enjoy the sunshine. Do you purchase a 500-foot cable for the privilege of occasionally working away from your desk?

A much more convenient solution in all these scenarios is to forego the cables and go wireless. It's not as fast as either Fast Ethernet or Gigabit Ethernet, but if you get the right hardware, it's fast enough, and it means that you can easily and quickly connect almost any computer or wireless device to your network. And wireless signals extend out of doors, so you can go ahead and enjoy the day.

Modern wireless networking can be both fast and reliable, but achieving such a state requires a bit of planning and the know-how to purchase the right hardware for your needs. This chapter tells you everything you need to know.

What Is Wireless Networking?

Wireless devices transmit data and communicate with other devices using *radio frequency* (RF) signals that are beamed from one device to another. Although these radio signals are similar to those used in commercial radio broadcasts, they operate on a different frequency. For example, if you use a wireless keyboard and mouse, you have an RF receiver device plugged into, usually, a USB port on your computer. The keyboard and mouse have built-in RF transmitters. When you press a key or move or click the mouse, the transmitter sends the appropriate RF signal, that signal is picked up by the receiver, and the corresponding keystroke or mouse action is passed along to Windows, just as though the original device had been connected to the computer directly.

A *radio transceiver* is a device that can act as both a transmitter and a receiver of radio signals. All wireless devices that require two-way communications use a transceiver. In wireless networking (also called *wireless local area network* [WLAN]), you still use a NIC, but in this case the NIC comes with a built-in transceiver that enables the NIC to send and receive RF signals. (For more information, see "Understanding Wireless NICs," later in this chapter.) The resulting beam takes the place of the network cable. The wireless NIC communicates with a nearby *wireless access point*, a device that contains a transceiver that enables the device to pass along network signals. (For more details, see "Understanding Wireless Access Points," later in this chapter.) A WLAN that uses an access point is called an *infrastructure* wireless network; as you see later in the book, it's also possible to set up a quick-and-dirty WLAN by having two or more wireless devices communicate directly with each other. This type of configuration is called an *ad hoc* wireless network.

→   To learn how to use Windows Vista to set up an ad hoc WLAN, **see** "Creating an Ad Hoc Wireless Network," **p. 161**.

Understanding Wi-Fi

The most common wireless networking technology is *wireless fidelity*, which is almost always shortened to *Wi-Fi* (which rhymes with *hi-fi*), and the generic *Institute of Electrical and Electronics Engineers* (IEEE) designation for this wireless networking standard is *802.11*. There are four main

caution As with the ethernet standards discussed in Chapter 1, all wireless speeds are theoretical because interference and bandwidth limitations almost always mean that real-world speeds are slower than the optimum speeds.

types—802.11a, 802.11b, 802.11g, and 802.11n—each of which has its own range and speed limits, as you see in the next few sections.

802.11b

The original 802.11 standard was published by the IEEE in 1997, but few people took it seriously because it was hobbled by a maximum transmission rate of just 2Mbps. By 1999, the IEEE had worked out not one but *two* new standards: 802.11a and 802.11b. The 802.11b standard became the more popular of the two, so I discuss it first.

802.11b upped the Wi-Fi data transmission rate to 11Mbps, which is just a bit faster than 10BASE-T, the original ethernet standard, which has a maximum rate of 10Mbps. The indoor range of 802.11b is about 115 feet.

802.11b operates on the 2.4GHz radio frequency, which is an unregulated frequency often used by other consumer products such as microwave ovens, cordless telephones, and baby monitors. This keeps the price of 802.11b hardware down, but it can also cause interference problems when you attempt to access the network near another device that's using the 2.4GHz frequency.

802.11a

The 802.11a standard was released at around the same time as the 802.11b standard. There are two key differences between these standards: 802.11a has a maximum transmission rate of 54Mbps, and it operates using the regulated 5.0GHz radio frequency band. This higher frequency band means that 802.11a devices don't have the same interference problems as 802.11b devices, but it also means that 802.11a hardware is more expensive, offers a shorter range (about 75 feet), and has trouble penetrating solid surfaces such as walls. So, despite its impressive transmission speed, 802.11a just had too many negative factors against it, and 802.11b won the hearts of consumers and became the first true wireless networking standard.

802.11g

During the battle between 802.11a and 802.11b, it became clear that consumers and small businesses really wanted the best of both worlds. That is, they wanted a WLAN technology that was as fast and as interference free as 802.11a, but had the longer range and cheaper cost of 802.11b. Alas, "the best of both worlds" is a state rarely achieved in the real world. However, the IEEE came close when it introduced the next version of the wireless networking standard in 2003: 802.11g. Like its 802.11a predecessor, 802.11g has a theoretical maximum transmission rate of 54Mbps, and like 802.11b, 802.11g boasted an indoor range of about 115 feet and was cheap to manufacture. That cheapness came from its use of the 2.4GHz RF band, which means that 802.11g devices can suffer from interference from other nearby consumer devices that use the same frequency.

note In the same way that many ethernet devices support multiple standards by offering 10/100 or 10/100/1000 support, so too do many WLAN devices support multiple Wi-Fi standards. Older devices often offer *a/b* support, meaning you can use the device with both other 802.11a and 802.11b devices. Newer WLAN devices now often offer *b/g* support, meaning you can use the device with both 802.11b and 802.11g devices. A few devices even offer *a/b/g* support for all three Wi-Fi standards.

Despite the possibility of interference, 802.11g quickly became the most popular of the Wi-Fi standards, and almost all WLAN devices sold today support 802.11g.

802.11n

The IEEE is working on a new wireless standard called 802.11n as this book goes to press, and this amendment is expected to be finalized sometime in 2009. 802.11n implements a technology called *multiple-input multiple-output* (MIMO) that uses multiple transmitters and receivers in each device. This enables multiple data streams on a single device, which will greatly improve WLAN performance. For example, using three transmitters and two receivers (the standard configuration), 802.11n promises a theoretical transmission speed of up to 248Mbps. It's still not Gigabit Ethernet, but 802.11n devices could finally enable us to stream high-quality video over a wireless connection. 802.11n also promises to double the wireless range to about 230 feet.

These are all impressive numbers, to be sure, and even if the real-world results are considerably less, it appears as though 802.11n devices will be about five times faster than 802.11g devices, and will offer about twice the range. That's why some manufacturers have jumped the gun and started offering 802.11n Draft 2.0 devices. "Draft 2.0" refers to the second draft of the amendment, which was approved by the IEEE in March 2007. The word on the street is that there are unlikely to be substantive changes to the amendment between the Draft 2.0 version and the final version.

Does this mean that it's safe to purchase Draft 2.0 devices now? The answer is a resounding *maybe*. Most WLAN manufacturers are saying that their current Draft 2.0 products will be upgradeable; so, if there are changes between now and the final draft, you'll be able to apply a patch to the device to make it conform to the new standard. Trusting that this will be so means taking a bit of a chance on your part, so *caveat emptor*.

Understanding Wireless Hot Spots

With Wi-Fi RF signals extending about 115 feet (and weaker signals extend even farther), you won't be surprised to learn that wireless communication is possible over a reasonably long distance. In your home or small office, this means that your wireless network is probably available *outside* the building, which is why you need to pay extra attention to wireless security.

> **note** What does it mean to say that a device is "upgradeable"? Most devices are controlled by *firmware*, programming code embedded in the device, often stored in a special memory chip called an *EPROM*, which is short for erasable programmable read-only memory. The "erasable" part means that the firmware can be replaced by a newer version, and hence the device's firmware is upgradeable.

> **tip** You can eliminate a bit of the risk associated with 802.11n Draft 2.0 products by purchasing only those that have been certified by the Wi-Fi Alliance, a consortium of Wi-Fi manufacturers. After the Draft 2.0 amendment was approved, the Wi-Fi Alliance began testing Draft 2.0 devices to ensure not only that they conform to the draft specifications, but also that they work well with older 802.11a/b/g devices. See http://www.wi-fi.org for more information.

→   Wireless security is such an important topic that I devote an entire chapter to it later in the book; **see** "Implementing Wireless Security," **p. 335**.

However, there are circumstances where the relatively long range of a wireless network—or even *extending* the network's range with special equipment—see "Understanding Other Wireless Network Devices," later in this chapter—is an advantage. I'm talking here about the wireless networks that are popping up in cities all across the world: in coffee shops, cafés, restaurants, fast-food outlets, hotels, airports, trains, even dental offices. Some cities have even started offering universal Wi-Fi access in the downtown area.

These wireless networks share an Internet connection, so you can connect to the network and then use it to surf the Web, check your email, catch up on your RSS feeds, log on to the office network, and more. A public wireless network that shares an Internet connection is called a *wireless hot spot* (or just a hot spot). In some cases, the establishment offers Internet access free of charge as a perk for doing business with them. However, most hot spots charge a fee to access the network.

> **note** Another popular wireless technology is *Bluetooth*, a wireless networking standard that uses RFs to set up a communications link between devices. This is another example of an ad hoc wireless network. The Bluetooth name comes from Harald Bluetooth, a tenth-century Danish king who united the provinces of Denmark under a single crown, the same way that, theoretically, Bluetooth will unite the world of portable wireless devices under a single standard. Why name a modern technology after an obscure Danish king? Here's a clue: two of the most important companies backing the Bluetooth standard—Ericsson and Nokia—are Scandinavian.

Understanding Wireless NICs

Whether you're setting up a simple ad hoc wireless network with another computer, or a full-fledged infrastructure wireless network with an access point, your computer requires a wireless NIC.

A wireless NIC is a transceiver that can both transmit data to the network and receive signals from the network. The rate at which the NIC processes this data and the distance from the network that you can roam depend on the 802.11 standard implemented by the NIC. Almost all wireless NICs sold today (or that come preinstalled in new computers) are 802.11g compliant, and most implement b/g support, meaning that the NIC will also work seamlessly with 802.11b NICs and devices.

There are four main types of wireless NIC:

Internal card   One common wireless NIC type is an internal adapter card that you insert into a free slot on the computer's bus. Most computers today use a PCI bus, so you need to get a PCI network adapter. The NIC's backplate usually includes a small post onto which you screw the antenna, either directly or via a longish wire that enables you to position the antenna to avoid interference. Figure 2.1 shows both types.

→   To learn how to install an adapter card, **see** "Inserting an Internal NIC," **p. 98**.

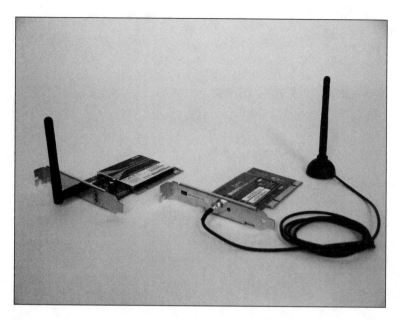

FIGURE 2.1

You insert an internal wireless NIC into a free slot on the system bus inside your computer.

USB   If you don't feel comfortable installing an internal circuit board
             (and there's no one hardware savvy nearby to do it for you), you
             can still go wireless by attaching an external wireless NIC to an
             open USB port. As with all USB devices, get a USB 2.0 wireless
             NIC for optimum performance. USB wireless NICs either attach
             directly to the USB port or they come with a USB cable, as shown
             in Figure 2.2.

PC Card   Almost all notebooks nowadays come with Wi-Fi built in. In some
             cases, you can enable or disable the built-in wireless NIC by tog-
             gling a button (usually labeled Wi-Fi or WLAN). If you want to
             upgrade your notebook to a faster version of Wi-Fi, you can attach
             a USB wireless NIC, if you have a free USB port. Alternatively, every
             notebook comes with at least one PC Card (or PCMCIA) slot, so you
             can purchase and attach a PC Card (or PCMCIA) wireless NIC.
             Figure 2.3 shows an example.

FIGURE 2.2

A USB wireless NIC attaches to a free USB slot on your computer.

FIGURE 2.3

You can upgrade you notebook's Wi-Fi capabilities by inserting a PC Card (or PCMCIA) wireless NIC.

Motherboard NIC   A few manufacturers are now offering a wireless NIC built directly into the computer's motherboard. The NIC is added in such a way that the post onto which you screw the antenna appears flush with the back of the computer, usually among the other built-in ports, such as USB, FireWire, monitor, and so on, as shown in Figure 2.4.

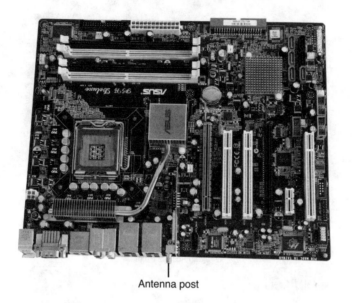

Antenna post

FIGURE 2.4

A wireless NIC built in to a motherboard.

Understanding Wireless Access Points

If you just want to exchange a bit of data with one or more nearby computers, Windows Vista enables you to set up and connect to an ad hoc wireless network where the computers themselves manage the connection. A longer-term solution is to set up and connect to an infrastructure wireless network, which requires an extra device called a *wireless access point* (AP). A wireless AP (Figure 2.5 shows a couple of examples) is a device that receives and transmits signals from wireless computers to form a wireless network, as shown in Figure 2.6.

FIGURE 2.5

Examples of wireless APs.

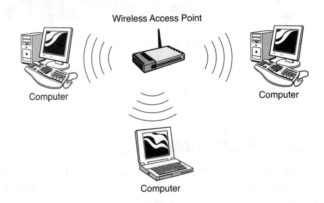

FIGURE 2.6

Add a wireless AP to create an infrastructure wireless network.

For a wireless AP to work properly, it must support an 802.11 standard that's compatible with all of your wireless NICs. For example, if all your wireless NICs use 802.11g, your wireless AP must also support 802.11g. Similarly, if your wireless NICs are a mixture of 802.11b and 802.11g, your wireless AP must implement 802.11b/g. Most wireless APs support both 802.11b and 802.11g, and the AP's setup pages usually enable you to choose between support for 802.11b/g or just 802.11g.

→   For more information about configuring 802.11 support, **see** "Modifying Wireless Settings," **p. 85**.

These days, standalone wireless AP devices are rare. Instead, most wireless APs are multifunction devices and usually come with some or all of the following features built in:

Switch   Almost all wireless APs also implement an ethernet switch and offer several (usually four) RJ-45 ports. This enables you to mix both wired and wireless connections on your network. As with a standalone ethernet switch, make sure the wireless AP's switch supports an ethernet standard that's compatible with the ethernet NICs you want to use for your wired connections (such as Fast Ethernet, Gigabit Ethernet, or 10/100).

Router   Most wireless APs also come with a built-in router. (Actually, to be accurate, in the vast majority of cases it's the router that's the main device, and it's the wireless AP that's the built-in feature.) This enables you to give your wireless network users access to the Internet (see Figure 2.7) by connecting a broadband modem to the WAN port in the back of the wireless AP.

FIGURE 2.7

With a combination wireless AP and router, you can give wireless network users access to the Internet.

> Firewall   Most wireless APs come with a built-in firewall, which hides your wireless network from the Internet and prevents unwanted packets from reaching your wireless devices.

Understanding Other Wireless Network Devices

To complete your tour of wireless hardware, the next few sections give you a quick overview of a few other devices you can connect to your wireless network.

Wireless Range Extender

If you find that your wireless AP is not reaching certain areas of your home or office, you can use a *wireless range extender* to boost the signal. Depending on the device and wireless AP, the extender can more than double the normal wireless range. Bear in mind, however, that range extenders are notoriously difficult to incorporate into an existing network. For best results, use an extender from the same company that makes your wireless AP, and make sure the extender is compatible with the AP. (For example, they implement compatible 802.11 standards and support the same wireless security protocols.) Figure 2.8 shows a wireless AP and wireless range extender from Linksys.

FIGURE 2.8

You can use a wireless range extender to boost your wireless signal and extend the range of your network.

Wireless Network Finder

If you're traveling with your notebook PC and you stop for a while at a business establishment or other public location, it would be nice to know whether a wireless hot spot is nearby that you can use. Unless you see a sign telling you that a hot spot is available, the only way to tell is to start up your notebook, log on to Windows Vista, and then display Vista's list of available networks.

→   To learn how to display Vista's list of available wireless networks, **see** "Making Wireless Network Connections," **p. 113**.

caution The advent of wireless network finders as mainstream consumer devices has a darker side: It means that a wider range of people can look for unsecured wireless networks and use them to get free Internet access or to play havoc with the network. Therefore, even if you never own a wireless network finder, their very existence should be the catalyst you need to secure your network, as I describe in Chapter 15.

That's a lot of work, particularly if the result is that there's no network in sight. To avoid this kind of hassle, you can purchase a *wireless network finder* (also called a *Wi-Fi detector* or a *hot spot finder*), a device that detects signals that are unique to a wireless network. Most models beep or flash an LED when a Wi-Fi network is within range, and some units also show you the strength of the wireless signal. Figure 2.9 shows a typical example.

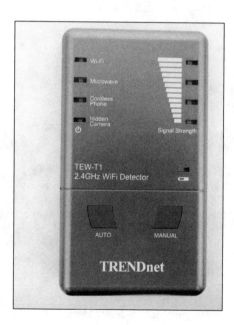

FIGURE 2.9

You can use a wireless network finder to detect nearby Wi-Fi signal without booting up your notebook.

Wireless Print Server

One of the major reasons people set up a network is to share equipment among multiple PCs. A printer is a good example, because it's overkill (not to mention expensive) to supply every PC in the house or office with its own printer. Instead, you can share a single printer on the network and then any computer can use it. Most networks install the printer on one computer, and then that computer shares the printer with the network. However, a simpler way to accomplish the same thing is to add the printer directly to the network.

The most straightforward way to do this is to purchase a printer that has a wireless NIC built in, which is becoming increasingly common. After you connect the printer to your wireless network, every other network PC can see the printer and connect to it directly.

If you don't have a printer with built-in wireless, you can get a wireless print server that's a separate box with either a parallel port or a USB port (or both), as well as a built-in wireless NIC (see Figure 2.10). You connect the printer to the print server's parallel or USB port, and then connect the print server to your wireless network.

FIGURE 2.10

Attach a printer to a wireless print server device to make the printer available directly to the computers on your wireless network.

Wireless Digital Media Receiver

If you've set up a Windows Vista computer to stream media through Windows Media Player or Windows Media Center, other Windows Vista computers on your network can pick up and play that stream. However, you can also use a device called a *wireless digital media receiver* (DMR) to access the media stream over a wireless connection. This doesn't work so well for streaming video, because even 802.11g is too slow, but it's fine for music and still images.

In some cases, you need to convert a DMR into a wireless receiver by purchasing an add-on accessory. A good example is the Xbox 360 console, which doesn't support wireless connection out of the box, so you need to purchase a Wi-Fi adapter. Many other DMRs have wireless capabilities built in, including the Roku SoundBridge and the D-Link MediaLounge and most digital picture frames.

A Buyer's Guide to Wireless Networking Hardware

Purchasing wireless hardware is, unfortunately, no easier than buying other types of networking hardware because the acronyms and jargon are just as prevalent. If there's an advantage to outfitting a wireless network, it's that to get started you really only need two types of equipment: wireless NICs for each computer that needs one, and a wireless AP to manage the network. The next two sections offer you a few tips and suggestions on what to look for and what to avoid when purchasing devices in these two wireless hardware categories.

Before getting to those tips, I want to reiterate the point I made in Chapter 1 about quality versus price when it comes to wireless networking devices. There is an inherent finicky quality to Wi-Fi networking because of interference from other devices, humidity, and even the phase of the moon (or so it seems on occasion). Quality wireless devices minimize this flakiness, so on that point alone they're worth the extra few dollars. Of course, wireless devices manufactured by reputable companies are also reliable, conform to the 802.11 standard, come with Vista device drivers, and offer decent support. The following list of companies that manufacture quality wireless networking devices is similar to, but not quite the same as, the list you saw for ethernet devices in Chapter 1:

Belkin (belkin.com)

Buffalo (buffalo.com)

D-Link (dlink.com)

Linksys (linksys.com)

NETGEAR (netgear.com)

TRENDnet (trendnet.com)

USRobotics (usr.com)

Zonet (zonetusa.com)

Purchasing a Wireless NIC

When you need to purchase a wireless NIC or two, here are some things to think about in advance:

Internal or external? You saw in Chapter 1 that ethernet users face a stark choice: If you want the speed of Gigabit Ethernet, you can get it only in the form of an internal adapter card. You face no such choice in the wireless world because the fastest NICs—those that support 802.11g or even 802.11n Draft 2.0 if you want to take the plunge (more on this below)—are available both as internal cards and as external USB devices. The choice really comes down to whether you have a free USB port. Most computers come with a decent collection of USB ports these days, but more and more devices are coming out in USB form, so it's not unusual for USB ports to fill up.

Only get USB 2.0 NICs. If you want to purchase a USB wireless NIC, make sure it uses the faster USB 2.0 technology, and not USB 1.1. Wireless USB 1.1 NICs are actually hard to find nowadays, but it pays to read the fine print in the specifications, just to make sure.

Wireless security. As you see in Chapter 15, "Implementing Wireless Security," wireless security is a crucial topic, and it's important that all your wireless devices use the same type of security. You get all the details in Chapter 15, but for now you should only consider purchasing a wireless NIC that offers the strongest possible security. Right now, that means the NIC must support the *Wi-Fi Protected Access* (WPA) security standard, ideally the latest iteration, which is WPA2. At all costs, avoid any wireless NIC that only supports *Wired Equivalent Privacy* (WEP), an older security scheme that is easily compromised.

802.11b or 802.11g? This one's a no-brainer: Go with 802.11g, no matter what. If you can even find 802.11b

> **note** If your computer's USB ports are full, consider purchasing a *USB hub*, a device that offers multiple USB ports (usually three, four, or seven).

devices (perhaps at a geek's garage sale), they'll be temptingly cheap. However, remember that you get five times the speed with 802.11g, and that extra speed is worth it, believe me.

To 802.11n or not to 802.11n? As I write this, 80211.n Draft 2.0 devices are still relatively rare, but they should be thick on the ground by the time you read this. Should you take a chance on these products, even though they'll be more expensive than their 802.11g counterparts? My own feeling is that if you have a real need for more wireless speed—for example, if you're itching to stream video over a wireless connection—you should probably jump in. As mentioned earlier, you should ideally stick to devices that have been certified by the Wi-Fi Alliance. Another strategy to consider is purchasing all your 802.11n devices from the same manufacturer, the theory being that devices from the same company should work well together. So, for example, if you want to purchase 802.11n NICs from, say, Linksys, you should also purchase your 802.11n wireless AP from Linksys. The important thing is to make sure you're getting a Draft 2.0 device. Previous 802.11n products used the "Draft N" moniker, and you want to stay away from those.

Check the claims. Lots of wireless NICs claim that they use fancy new technology to, say, double the data transmission rate or triple the range of standard 802.11g. In some cases, these claims are true. For example, I mentioned earlier that 802.11n uses MIMO technology to improve speed and range, but some companies are incorporating MIMO into 802.11g NICs, too, and those NICs show genuine improvements in speed and range. Other claims may or may not be true. It's best in these cases to do some homework by reading reviews of the NICs to see whether the claims hold up under real-world conditions. Most online retailers solicit reviews from purchasers, online networking sites review the latest NICs, and you can use sites such as Epinions (epinions.com) and ConsumerReview (consumerreview.com) to search for reviews of devices you're considering.

Purchasing a Wireless AP

The wireless AP is the most complicated of the wireless products, so not surprisingly the ads and specifications for these devices are riddled with ten-dollar technical terms, acronyms and abbreviations, and a fair dose of marketing hype. Fortunately, you can ignore most of what you read and just concentrate on the following points:

Wireless security. I mentioned in the previous section that you should only get wireless NICs that support WPA security, ideally WPA2. It's important that your wireless AP supports the same security standard. To see why, understand that most new wireless NICs support multiple security standards, usually WEP, WPA, and WPA2. If you purchase an older wireless AP that supports only, say, WEP, *all* your wireless activity will use WEP because the NICs will lower their security to work with the AP. So, again, you should ideally only purchase a wireless AP that supports the WPA2 standard.

Get a router. It's a rare wireless network that doesn't also need to share an Internet connection. If you want your wireless users to be able to access the Internet from anywhere in the house or office, make sure the wireless AP comes with a router (or purchase a router that comes with a built-in wireless AP).

Do you need a separate switch? As mentioned earlier, almost all new wireless APs come with a built-in switch, so you might be able to get away with using the wireless AP as your network's central connection point. This is usually only the case with networks that require only a few wired connections, because most wireless APs come with four-port switches (although eight-port APs are available). If your network comes with quite a few devices that require ethernet connectivity, you should consider adding a dedicated switch to the network. Check the ethernet standards supported by the AP ports to ensure that they match the standards used by your ethernet devices, and get the largest number of ports that you can afford.

Check the 802.11 support. Because it's the AP's job to manage your network's wireless connections, you must make sure that the AP supports the same 802.11 standards as your wireless devices. For example, if all your wireless devices use 802.11g, you can get a wireless AP that only supports 802.11g. However, if your wireless devices use a mixture of 802.11b and 802.11g, your AP must support both standards. If you go with an 802.11n Draft 2.0 wireless AP, make sure it also supports 802.11b and 802.11g, because you'll certainly have other devices on your network that use those standards. Look for certification from the Wi-Fi Alliance to ensure that the 802.11n AP correctly implements 802.11b/g.

Make sure it has a firewall. All wireless APs that have built-in routers support *network address translation* (NAT) for security, but for maximum safety make sure the AP comes with a dedicated firewall that you can configure.

From Here

- To learn how to configure various router settings, **see** Chapter 3, "Configuring Your Router," **p. 59.**

- For more information on configuring 802.11 support, **see** "Modifying Wireless Settings," **p. 85.**

- To learn how to install a NIC adapter, **see** "Installing an Internal NIC," **p. 98.**

- To learn how to display Vista's list of available wireless networks, **see** "Making Wireless Network Connections," **p. 113.**

- To learn how to use Windows Vista to set up an ad hoc WLAN, **see** "Creating an Ad Hoc Wireless Network," **p. 161.**

- Wireless security is such an important topic that I devote an entire chapter to it later in the book; **see Chapter 15**, "Implementing Wireless Security," **p. 335.**

2

Configuring Your Router

You learned in Chapter 1, "Understanding Ethernet Networking," that you need to add a router to your network if you want to share a broadband Internet connection with the users on your network. This saves you money in the long run because it means you do not need multiple broadband modems or multiple Internet connections. It's also more convenient because you don't have to set up a particular computer to share its Internet connection with the network. After you have the router configured, you almost never have to think about it again.

Of course, getting to that state requires taking a few minutes now to configure various aspects of the router, including the broadband connection to your *Internet service provider* (ISP), the feature that supplies IP addresses to each network computer, and more. Also, if your router doubles as a wireless *access point* (AP), you need to configure the wireless network settings. This chapter takes you through these configuration and other chores. I demonstrate each configuration task using routers from four major manufacturers: Belkin, D-Link, Linksys, and Netgear.

→ If you need a bit of router background before you start, **see** "Understanding Routers," **p. 24**.

IN THIS CHAPTER

- Connecting the Router for Configuration
- Displaying the Router's Setup Pages
- Changing the Router's IP Address
- Updating the Firmware
- Setting Up Your Broadband Connection
- Enabling UPnP
- Enabling the DHCP Server
- Modifying Wireless Settings
- Checking the Router Status
- Testing Your Router's Capabilities
- From Here

Connecting the Router for Configuration

I take you through the steps for configuring and connecting your networking hardware in Chapter 4, "Putting Your Network Together," and that includes connecting the router to the network. For now, you need to connect your router to one of your network computers so that you can configure the router.

Here are the general steps to follow:

1. Attach the router's AC cord and plug it in.
2. Turn off the router and your broadband modem.
3. Run a network cable from the broadband modem's LAN port to the WAN port on the back of the router.
4. Run another network cable from one of your computers to any RJ-45 port on the back of the router.
5. Turn on the router and modem.

note Most routers include a card or sticker that tells you to insert and run the router's CD before connecting it. This is good advice for many devices that require a driver to be installed in advance, but that's not the case with a router. Therefore, you're free to ignore the note (no matter how dire the manufacturer makes the consequences sound) and go ahead and connect the router.

note You must connect the router to a computer even if you're going to use your router solely as a wireless AP. The initial configuration requires a wired connection. After you have your wireless network set up (see "Modifying Wireless Settings," later in this chapter), you can remove the wired connection and access the router's setup pages wirelessly when you need them.

Displaying the Router's Setup Pages

All routers come with a built-in configuration program. This program is a series of web pages that you access via a web browser on one of your network computers. (This is why you connected the router directly to a computer in step 4 of the previous section.) These pages enable you to configure many different aspects of the router, including its IP address, its password, the connection settings for your broadband ISP, and much more. You learn about these and other configuration tasks later in this chapter. For now, the next two sections show you two methods you can use to access the router's setup pages.

note Here are the default IP addresses used by the router manufacturers that I discuss in this section:

Belkin   192.168.2.1

D-Link   192.168.0.1

Linksys   192.168.1.1

Netgear   192.168.1.1

Entering the Router's IP Address

Follow these steps to access the router's setup pages using the device's IP address:

1. On the computer connected to the router, start Internet Explorer.

2. In the Address bar, type the router address, and then press Enter. See your device documentation for the correct address, but in most cases the address is either http://192.168.1.1 or http://192.168.0.1. You usually see a Connect dialog box like the one shown in Figure 3.1.

> **note** On Belkin routers, you see the Setup Utility right away. To make changes, you must click Login and then enter the router password. (The default password is blank.)

FIGURE 3.1

You must log on to the router to access its setup pages.

3. Type the default username and password. Note that in most cases you only need to enter the password; again, see the device documentation for the logon details.

4. If you're the only person who uses your computer and your user account is protected by a password, activate the Remember My Password check box so that you don't have to enter the logon information again in the future.

5. Click OK. The router's setup page appears. Figure 3.2 shows a sample setup page.

> **tip** If you're not sure which username and password to use, try **admin** for both. If that doesn't work, leave the username blank and try either **admin** or **password** for the password. If you still can't get in, see whether your device is listed in the Default Password List maintained at http://www.phenoelit.us.org/dpl/dpl.html.

FIGURE 3.2

A typical router setup page.

Using the Network Window

For routers that support *Universal Plug and Play* (UPnP), follow these steps to access the setup pages:

1. On the computer connected to the router, select Start, Network. Vista displays the Network window, which contains a list of devices on your network. If your router supports UPnP, you should see an icon for the router. The name of the icon usually is the same as the router's model number. In Figure 3.3, for example, the router is the icon named WRT54GS.

2. Right-click the router icon.

3. Click View Device Webpage (see Figure 3.3). The Connect dialog box appears.

caution The only problem with telling Windows Vista to remember a password is that you open up a small security hole when you leave your desk for any length of time after you've logged on to your user account. Another person could sit down at your computer and easily access the protected feature. To plug this hole, be sure to lock your computer before you leave your desk unattended. To lock the computer, either press Windows Logo+L, or click Start and then click the Lock icon. This displays the Vista logon screen. To unlock the PC, you type your password and press Enter.

FIGURE 3.3

If your router supports UPnP, you should see an icon for it in the Network window.

4. Type the default username and password. (See the device documentation for the logon details.)

5. If you don't want to enter the logon information again in the future, activate the Remember My Password check box.

6. Click OK. The router's setup page appears.

Changing the Router's IP Address

In the previous section, you might find that you can't access the router's setup page. First, check that the router is turned on and that the computer you are using has a wired connection that runs from the computer's *network interface card* (NIC) to an RJ-45 port on the router.

If you still can't access the router, your broadband modem might be the culprit. Some broadband providers are using "smart" modems that include routing features. That's fine, but these modems almost always have a static IP address, and that address is usually either http://192.168.1.1 or http://192.168.0.1, which may conflict with your router's IP address.

If you have connection problems after adding the router, the likely culprit is an IP address conflict. Disconnect or turn off the broadband modem and access the router's

caution After you change the IP address, the router's setup program might not change the IP address in Internet Explorer's Address bar, so Internet Explorer may display an error message. In that case, modify the IP address by hand and press Enter to access the router's new location.

setup pages as described in the previous section. (This should work now.) Use the techniques shown in the following sections to change the router's IP address (to, say, http://192.168.1.2 or http://192.168.0.2) .

Belkin

For most Belkin routers, follow these steps to modify the IP address:

1. Under LAN Setup, click the LAN Settings link to display the LAN Settings page, shown in Figure 3.4.

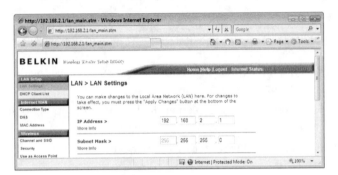

FIGURE 3.4

On your Belkin router, use the LAN Settings page to change the IP address.

2. Use the IP Address text boxes to modify the default IP address.

3. At the bottom of the page, click Apply Changes.

D-Link

Follow these steps to modify the IP address on most D-Link routers:

1. Click the Setup tab (or, on some D-Link routers, the Basic tab).

2. Click Network Settings to display the Network Settings page, shown in Figure 3.5.

3. Use the Router IP Address text box to modify the IP address.

4. Click Save Settings. The router restarts to put the new setting into effect.

Linksys

For most Linksys routers, follow these steps to modify the IP address:

1. Click the Setup tab.

2. Click the Basic Setup subtab.

3. In the Router IP section, modify the Local IP Address text boxes, as shown in Figure 3.6.

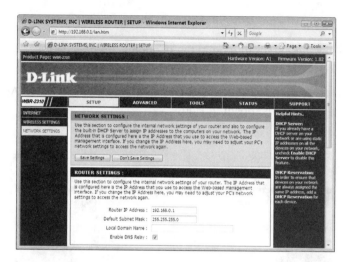

FIGURE 3.5

On your D-Link router, use the Network Settings page to change the IP address.

FIGURE 3.6

On your Linksys router, use the Setup tab to change the IP address.

4. At the bottom of the page, click Save Settings. The router reports that the `Settings are successful`.

5. Click Continue.

Netgear

Follow these steps to modify the IP address on most Netgear routers:

1. In the Advanced section, click the LAN IP Setup link.

2. In the LAN TCP/IP Setup section, modify the Local IP Address text boxes, as shown in Figure 3.7.

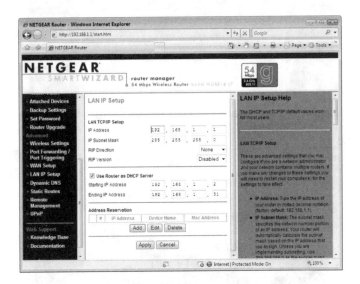

FIGURE 3.7
On your Netgear router, use the LAN TCP/IP Setup section to change the IP address.

3. At the bottom of the page, click Apply.

→ One of your first tasks with your new router should be to change the default administrative password; **see** "Specifying a New Administrative Password," **p. 336.**

Updating the Firmware

The *router firmware* is the internal program that the router uses to perform its routing chores and to display the setup pages and process any configuration changes you make. Router manufacturers frequently update their firmware to fix bugs, to improve performance, and to add new features. For all these reasons, it's a good idea to update the router's firmware to get the latest version, as shown in the next few sections. In case you're wondering, updating the firmware doesn't cause you to lose any of your settings.

Before getting to the specifics, however, here's the general procedure for finding out and downloading the latest firmware version:

1. Use Internet Explorer to navigate to the router manufacturer's website.

2. Navigate to the Support pages.

3. Navigate to the Downloads pages.

4. Use the interface to navigate to the download page for your router.

5. You should now see a list of firmware downloads. Examine the version numbers and compare them to your router's current firmware version.

6. If the latest version is later than the current version on your router, click the download link and save the firmware upgrade file on your computer.

Belkin

Here are the steps to follow to determine the current firmware version and, if necessary, upgrade the firmware on most Belkin routers:

1. Under Utilities, click the Firmware Update link to display the Firmware Upgrade page, shown in Figure 3.8.

tip As described later when I discuss updating the firmware for different router manufacturers, the router's setup pages usually show you the current firmware version. However, if your router supports UPnP, you can usually get the router's firmware version through Windows Vista. Select Start, Network to open the Network window, right-click the router's icon, and then click Properties. In the property sheet that appears, click the Network Device tab. The current firmware version usually appears as the Model Number value in the Device Details group.

tip Most product support pages require the name and model number of the router. You can usually find this information on the underside of the router.

tip A good place to save the firmware upgrade file is the Downloads folder, which is a subfolder of your main Windows Vista user account folder.

caution Most router manufacturers require that you upgrade the firmware using a wired link to the router. Using a wireless link can damage the router.

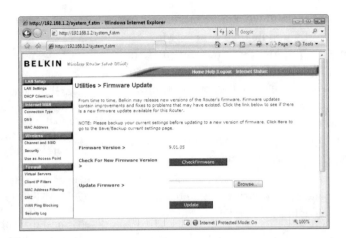

FIGURE 3.8

On most Belkin routers, use the Firmware Update page to check the current firmware version and upgrade to a newer version, if necessary.

2. The Firmware Version setting tells you the current version of the router's firmware. If you're not sure whether a newer version exists, click Check Firmware.

3. To upgrade the firmware using a downloaded upgrade file, click Browse to open the Choose File dialog box.

4. Navigate to the folder that contains the firmware upgrade file, click the file, and then click Open.

5. Click Update. The router asks you to confirm.

6. Click OK. The router warns you not to interrupt the firmware update.

7. Click OK.

D-Link

Most D-Link routers give you two ways to determine the current firmware version:

- The firmware version appears in the upper-right corner of most setup pages.

- Click the Tools tab, click Firmware, and then read the Current Firmware Version text.

note Some Belkin routers come with a feature that automatically checks for a newer firmware version, but that feature is usually disabled by default. To enable this feature, first click System Settings (under Utilities) to display the System Settings page, and then scroll down until you see the Auto Update Firmware Enabling group. Click Enable, and then click Apply Changes.

For most D-Link routers, follow these steps to update the firmware:

1. Click the Tools tab.

2. Click Firmware to display the Firmware Upgrade page, shown in Figure 3.9.

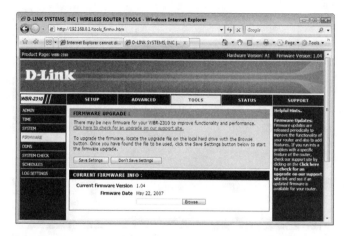

FIGURE 3.9

On your D-Link router, use the Firmware Upgrade page to update the router's firmware.

3. Click Browse to open the Choose File dialog box.

4. Navigate to the folder that contains the firmware upgrade file, click the file, and then click Open.

5. Click Save Settings. The router installs the firmware and then restarts.

Linksys

Most Linksys routers give you two ways to determine the current firmware version:

- The firmware version appears in the upper-right corner of most setup pages.

- Click the Status tab, click the Router subtab, and then read the Firmware Version text.

If the current version is earlier than the latest version, follow these steps to upgrade the firmware on most Linksys routers:

1. Click the Administration tab.

2. Click the Firmware Upgrade subtab, shown in Figure 3.10.

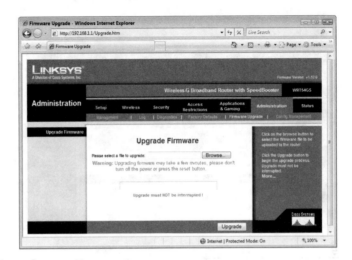

FIGURE 3.10

On most Linksys routers, use the Administration tab's Firmware Upgrade subtab to upgrade the router's firmware.

3. Click Browse to open the Choose File dialog box.

4. Navigate to the folder that contains the firmware upgrade file, click the file, and then click Open.

5. Click Upgrade.

6. When you see the `Upgrade is Successful. Rebooting...` message, click Continue.

Netgear

To check the current firmware version on most Netgear routers, click the Router Status link under the Maintenance section. Note, too, that many Netgear routers also offer to check to see whether a newer firmware version is available when you log on to the router.

Follow these steps to check for and, if necessary, upgrade to a new firmware version on most Netgear routers:

1. In the Maintenance section, click the Router Upgrade link. The Router Upgrade page appears, as shown in Figure 3.11.

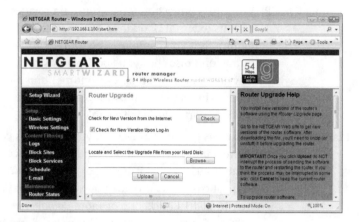

FIGURE 3.11
On most Netgear routers, use the Router Upgrade page to check for a new version of the router firmware.

2. If you're not sure whether a newer firmware version exists, click Check.
3. To perform the upgrade, click Browse to open the Choose File dialog box.
4. Navigate to the folder that contains the firmware upgrade file, click the file, and then click Open.
5. Click Upload. The router asks you to confirm.
6. Click OK.

Setting Up Your Broadband Connection

The main point of adding a router to your network is to share a broadband Internet connection with the network computers, which means users don't have to worry about either setting up a connection or logging on to the Internet. With the broadband modem connected to the router's WAN port, the router takes over the duties of initiating and managing the Internet connection. Before it can do that, however, you need to configure the router with the Internet connection settings provided to you by your broadband provider.

Your broadband connection will almost certainly fall under one of the following types:

Dynamic (DHCP)	With this connection type, your ISP provides the router with its external IP address automatically. Some ISPs require that you configure the router with a specific name, and also that you specify a hostname (also called a system name or an account name) and a domain name. This is the most common type of broadband connection, particularly with cable providers.
Static	With this type of connection, your ISP gives you an IP address that never changes, and you must configure the router to use this as its external IP address. Your ISP will in most cases also provide you with a subnet mask, gateway IP address, and one or more *domain name server* (DNS) addresses. This type of broadband connection is rare these days.
PPPoE	With this connection type, your ISP provides you with a username and password that you use to log on. Some ISPs also require that you configure the router with a specific name, and also that you specify a hostname and a domain name. This type of broadband connection is most commonly used with *Digital Subscriber Line* (DSL) providers.
PPTP	With this type of connection, your ISP usually provides you with a static IP address, a subnet mask, a gateway IP address, a username, and a password. This broadband connection type is mostly used by DSL providers in European countries.
Telstra BigPond	With this connection type, your ISP provides you with a user name and password. This broadband connection type is used by Australian DSL providers.

The next few sections show you how to configure your broadband Internet connection on some different routers.

Belkin

Follow these steps to set up your Internet connection on most Belkin routers:

1. Under the Internet WAN section, click Connection Type. The Connection Type page appears, as shown in Figure 3.12.

FIGURE 3.12

On most Belkin routers, use the Connection Type page to set up the broadband Internet connection.

2. Click the connection type used by your ISP.

3. Click Next.

4. Fill in the connection settings provided by your ISP.

5. Click Apply Changes.

6. Under the Internet WAN section, click DNS. The DNS page appears.

7. If your ISP didn't give you one or more DNS addresses, click to activate the Automatic from ISP check box. Otherwise, make sure that the Automatic from ISP check box is deactivated, and then use the DNS Address and Secondary DNS Address text boxes to type the DNS addresses provided by your ISP.

8. Click Apply Changes. The router saves the new settings and connects to your ISP.

D-Link

On most D-Link routers, here are the steps to follow to set up your Internet connection:

1. Click the Setup tab (or, on some D-Link routers, the Basic tab).

2. Click Internet.

3. Click Manual Configure to display the Internet Connection page.

4. Use the My Internet Connection Is list to select the connection type your ISP uses. Figure 3.13 shows the settings that appear when you select PPPoE.

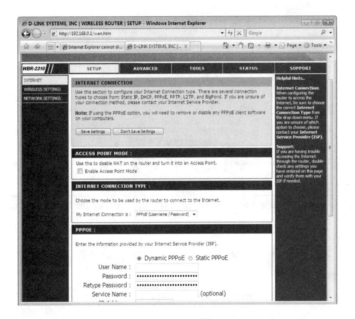

FIGURE 3.13

On your D-Link router, use the Internet Connection page to set up the broadband connection.

5. Fill in the connection settings provided by your ISP.

6. Click Save Settings. The router restarts to put the new settings into effect.

> **note** You can connect to the Internet on most D-Link routers by clicking the Status tab, clicking Device Info, and then clicking Connect. Click Disconnect on the same page to close the connection.

Linksys

Follow these steps to set up your Internet connection on most Linksys routers:

1. Click the Setup tab.

2. Click the Basic Setup subtab.

3. Use the Internet Connection Type list to select the connection type your ISP uses. Figure 3.14 shows the settings that appear when you select PPPoE.

FIGURE 3.14

On most Linksys routers, use the Setup tab's Basic Setup subtab to set up the broadband Internet connection.

4. Fill in the connection settings provided by your ISP.

5. At the bottom of the page, click Save Settings. The router reports that the Settings are successful.

6. Click Continue.

Netgear

On most Netgear routers, here are the steps to follow to set up your Internet connection:

note On most Linksys routers, you connect to the Internet by clicking the Status tab, clicking the Router subtab, and then clicking Connect. When you're connected, you can click Disconnect on the same page whenever you need to shut down the connection.

1. Under Setup, click the Basic Settings link. The Basic Settings page appears.

2. Choose one of the following options to specify whether your ISP requires you to log on:

   Yes   After you click this option, select an item in the Internet Service Provider list, and then fill in the connection settings for your ISP (see Figure 3.15).

   No   After you select this option, fill in the connection settings required by your ISP.

FIGURE 3.15
On most Netgear routers, use the Basic Settings page to set up the broadband Internet connection.

3. Fill in the other ISP connection settings, as required.

4. Click Apply. The router applies the new settings and then connects to the ISP.

<aside>
note   On most Netgear routers, you connect to the Internet by clicking Router Status, clicking Connection Status to open the Connection Status window, and then clicking Connect. When you're connected, you can open the Connection Status window and click Disconnect whenever you need to close the connection.
</aside>

Enabling UPnP

Most newer routers support *Universal Plug and Play* (UPnP), a technology designed to make networking devices easier to manage and configure. Traditionally, devices are controlled by a *device driver*, a small software program that serves as an intermediary between hardware devices and the operating system. Device drivers encode software instructions into signals that the device understands, and conversely, the drivers interpret device signals and report them to the operating system. However, device drivers are difficult to code and need to be upgraded as operating systems and hardware architectures change.

UPnP is designed to overcome the limitations of device drivers by eliminating them altogether. In their place, UPnP devices are controlled by software protocols, particularly TCP/IP (*Transmission Control Protocol/Internet Protocol*; the protocols used to transmit and receive information over the Internet, including email and *File Transfer Protocol* [FTP]), UDP (*User Datagram Protocol*; a protocol used for sending short bits of data called *datagrams*, a form of packet), and HTTP (*Hypertext Transfer Protocol*; the protocol used to transmit and receive information on the World Wide Web). This allows any UPnP-enabled device to run in any network environment and under any operating system.

For small networks, the main advantage of UPnP is that it allows software programs to automatically read and configure a router's settings. For example, you saw earlier that Windows Vista can recognize the presence of a router and display an icon for that router in the Network window, but it can also glean the router's IP address and use that address to open the router's setup page (via the View Device Webpage command). All of this is made possible by UPnP.

Similarly, software sometimes needs to configure the router. For example, a program may need to modify the router's firewall to allow data through a particular port and have that data go directly to a particular computer on the network. For example, Windows Home Server has a remote-access feature that enables you to access computers on your network via the Internet, which requires forwarding data from two different ports to the Windows Home Server computer. So that you don't have to set this up yourself, Windows Home Server comes with a feature that configures the router automatically. Again, all of this is accomplished via UPnP.

So, UPnP is a valuable and useful technology, particularly on small networks. Most routers that support UPnP come with the technology enabled, but some have UPnP disabled by default. The next few sections show you how to enable UPnP on a few different routers.

3

Belkin

Follow these steps to enable UPnP on most Belkin routers:

1. Under the Utilities section, click System Settings. The System Settings page appears.

2. Scroll down until you see the UPNP Enabling group, shown in Figure 3.16.

FIGURE 3.16

On most Belkin routers, use the UPNP Enabling group on the System Settings page to enable UPnP.

3. Click Enable.

4. Click Apply Changes.

D-Link

On most D-Link routers, here are the steps to follow to enable UPnP:

1. Click the Advanced tab.

2. Click Advanced Network to display the Network Settings page, shown in Figure 3.17.

3. Click to activate the Enable UPnP check box.

4. Click Save Settings. The router restarts to put the new setting into effect.

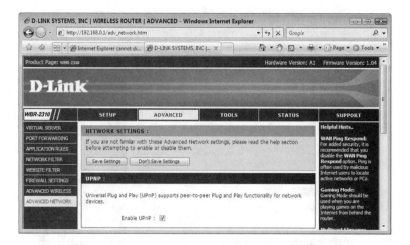

FIGURE 3.17

On your D-Link router, use the Network Settings page to enable UPnP.

Linksys

Follow these steps to enable UPnP on most Linksys routers:

1. Click the Administration tab.
2. Click the Management subtab.
3. In the UPnP section (see Figure 3.18), click Enable.
4. At the bottom of the page, click Save Settings. The router reports that the Settings are successful.
5. Click Continue.

Netgear

On most Netgear routers, here are the steps to follow to enable UPnP:

1. Under Advanced, click the UPnP link. The UPnP page appears, as shown in Figure 3.19.

FIGURE 3.18

On most Linksys routers, use the Administration tab's Management subtab to enable UPnP.

FIGURE 3.19

On most Netgear routers, use the UPnP page to enable UPnP.

2. Click to activate the Turn UPnP On check box.

3. Click Apply.

Enabling the DHCP Server

You learned in Chapter 1 that most small networks allocate IP addresses to computers and devices dynamically. That is, instead of going to the trouble of configuring each network node with a static IP address, you can use a *Dynamic Host Configuration Protocol* (DHCP) server to automatically assign an IP address from a range of addresses each time a device starts up.

→   For more about DHCP, **see** "The Router and Dynamic IP Addressing," **p. 26**.

→   If you only have a few computers, setting and managing static IP addresses isn't difficult in Windows Vista; **see** "Setting Up a Static IP Address," **p. 145**.

In your small network, the best choice for dynamic IP addressing is the router, because almost all routers come with a built-in DHCP server. When configuring your router, you need to enable the DHCP server, specify the range of addresses from which the server will allocate the IP addresses, and optionally specify the length of the *DHCP lease*, the amount of time each client can use an IP address. The next few sections show you how this is done with various router types.

→   After you enable the router's DHCP server, make sure each client computer is set up to use DHCP; **see** "Enabling Automatic IP Addressing," **p. 142**.

note The Netgear UPnP page also includes an Advertisement Period setting. You can use this setting to control how often the router broadcasts its UPnP data to the network. The default value is 30 minutes, which should be fine in most small networks. However, if you change, say, your router's IP address, there will be a period before the next broadcast when Vista thinks the router is using a different address. If you want to make sure that Windows Vista and your software programs always have the most current data, you can change this to a shorter interval. Also, the Advertisement Time to Live property controls the number of hops each broadcast is allowed to make, where a *hop* is a step from one network device to another. For example, the path from the router to a network switch is one hop, and the path from the switch to a network computer is another hop. It shouldn't take more than four hops (the default value) for a UPnP broadcast to reach any computer on your home network. However, if you find that some devices aren't receiving UPnP data from the router, try increasing the Advertisement Time to Live value.

caution When you configure the range of IP addresses that the DHCP server can assign, be sure not to include the router's static IP address in that range. For example, if your router's IP address is 192.168.1.1, the DHCP server's range of IP addresses should begin at 192.168.1.2 or higher.

Belkin

Follow these steps to enable the DHCP server on most Belkin routers:

1. Under LAN Setup, click the LAN Settings link to display the LAN Settings page.

2. In the DHCP Server group, click On, as shown in Figure 3.20.

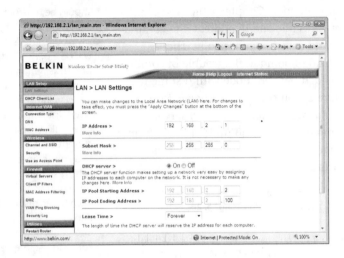

FIGURE 3.20
On most Belkin routers, use the DHCP Server group on the LAN Settings page to enable the router's DHCP Server.

3. Use the IP Pool Starting Address text box to specify the first address in the range of IP addresses that the server can assign.

4. Use the IP Pool Ending Address text box to specify the last address in the range of IP addresses that the server can assign.

5. Use the Lease Time list to specify the length of the DHCP lease. The default is Forever, which means each computer always keeps the same IP address. If you prefer to recycle addresses, use the list to specify a time interval (such as One Day, which is a typical lease time).

6. Click Apply Changes.

> **note** After you have the DHCP server enabled, the router will maintain a list of DHCP clients and the IP addresses they're using. You can see this list on most Belkin routers by clicking the DHCP Client List link under LAN Setup.

D-Link

On most D-Link routers, here are the steps to follow to enable the DHCP server:

1. Click the Setup tab (or, on some D-Link routers, the Basic tab).

2. Click Network Settings to display the Network Settings page.

3. In the DHCP Server Settings section (see Figure 3.21), click to activate the Enable DHCP Server check box.

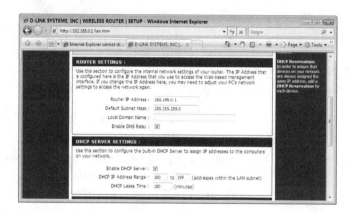

FIGURE 3.21

On your D-Link router, use the Network Settings page to enable and configure the DHCP server.

4. Use the DHCP IP Address Range text boxes to specify the first and last addresses in the range of IP addresses that the server can assign.

5. Use the DHCP Lease Time text box to specify the time, in minutes, that each client can keep its IP address.

6. Click Save Settings. The router restarts to put the new setting into effect.

Linksys

Follow these steps to enable the DHCP server on most Linksys routers:

1. Click the Setup tab.

2. Click the Basic Setup subtab.

> **note** To see the list of DHCP clients on most D-Link routers, click the Setup tab, click Network Settings, and then scroll down to the Dynamic DHCP Client List section.

3. In the Network Address Server Settings (DHCP) section (see Figure 3.22), click Enable.

FIGURE 3.22

On most Linksys routers, use the Setup tab's Basic Setup subtab to enable the DHCP server.

4. Use the Starting IP Address text box to specify the first address in the range of IP addresses that the server can assign.

5. Use the Maximum Number of DHCP Users text box to limit the number of DHCP leases that the server can assign. This isn't important on a small network, and the default value of 50 is more than enough.

6. Use the Client Lease Time text box to specify the time, in minutes, that each client can keep its IP address. The default value of 0—which corresponds to one day—is fine for most small networks.

7. At the bottom of the page, click Save Settings. The router reports that the Settings are successful.

8. Click Continue.

Netgear

On most Netgear routers, here are the steps to follow to enable the DHCP server:

1. Under Advanced, click the LAN IP Setup link. The LAN IP Setup page appears, as shown in Figure 3.23.

2. Click to activate the Use Router as DHCP Server check box.

3. Use the Starting IP Address text box to specify the first address in the range of IP addresses that the server can assign.

note You can see a list of DHCP clients on most Linksys routers by clicking the Status tab, clicking the Local Network subtab, and then clicking DHCP Clients Table.

4. Use the Ending IP Address text box
to specify the last address in the
range of IP addresses that the
server can assign.

5. Click Apply.

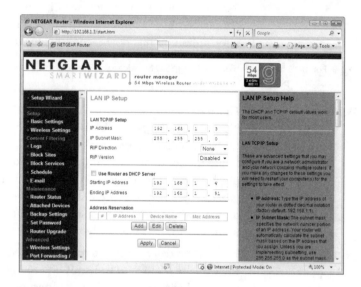

note You can see the list
of DHCP clients on
most Netgear routers by clicking
the LAN IP Setup link under
Advanced and then scrolling to
the Address Reservation section.

FIGURE 3.23

On most Netgear routers, use the LAN IP Setup page to enable the DHCP server.

Modifying Wireless Settings

If your router includes a wireless *access point* (AP), you need to configure a few
settings before making wireless connections to the AP. On most routers, you
can configure the following settings:

Network name   This is the name of your wireless network, which is often
called the *service set identifier*, or SSID. All routers come
with a default SSID, usually some variation on the manufacturer's name, such as linksys or belkin54g.
Changing the SSID to something memorable will help
you to identify your network in Vista's list of available
wireless networks, and it will avoid confusion with other
nearby wireless networks that still use the default name.

SSID broadcasting   This setting determines whether your router broadcasts the SSID, which makes the wireless network visible in Windows Vista's list of available networks. It's best to enable SSID broadcasting when you first make your connections to the wireless network. However, Windows Vista can remember the networks you've connected to in the past, so you can later disable SSID broadcasting as a security measure. (Although see Chapter 15, "Implementing Wireless Security," for some important information on just how secure this tactic really is.)

→   For more information on disabling SSID broadcasting, **see** "Disabling Network SSID Broadcasting," **p. 347**.

Wireless mode   This tells the router which Wi-Fi standard—802.11a, 802.11b, 802.11g, or 802.11b—to implement. If your router supports more than one standard, you can configure the router to use multiple standards (for example, both 802.11b and 802.11g; this is often called *mixed mode*) or just a single standard. For example, if all your wireless devices use 802.11g, you should configure the router to use only that standard.

Wireless channel   This setting determines the *radio frequency* (RF) band that the wireless AP uses to transmit and receive signals. For successful wireless networking connections, all your networking devices must use the same channel.

The next few sections show you how to configure these wireless settings in various routers.

Belkin

Follow these steps to configure wireless settings on most Belkin routers:

1. Under Wireless, click the Channel and SSID link to display the Channel and SSID page, shown in Figure 3.24.
2. Use the SSID text box to specify the network name you want to use.
3. Use the ESSID Broadcast group to click either Enable or Disable.
4. Use the Wireless Mode list to select a wireless mode.
5. Use the Wireless Channel list to select a frequency (or click Auto to let the router select the correct frequency automatically).
6. Click Apply Changes.

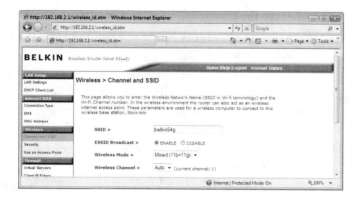

FIGURE 3.24

On most Belkin routers, use the Channel and SSID page to configure the wireless settings.

D-Link

On most D-Link routers, here are the steps to follow to configure wireless settings:

1. Click the Setup tab (or, on some D-Link routers, the Basic tab).

2. Click Wireless Settings to display the Wireless Network page, shown in Figure 3.25.

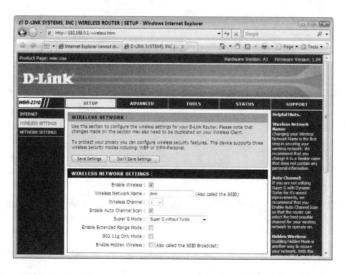

FIGURE 3.25

On your D-Link router, use the Wireless Network page to change the wireless settings.

3. Make sure the Enable Wireless check box is activated.

4. Use the Wireless Network Name text box to specify the network name you want to use.

5. If you want the router to automatically select the correct channel for your network, leave the Enable Auto Channel Scan check box activated; otherwise, deactivate Enable Auto Channel Scan, and then use the Wireless Channel list to select a frequency.

6. If you want the router to only use 802.11g, click to activate the 802.11g Only Mode check box.

7. To prevent the router from broadcasting the network name, click to activate the Enable Hidden Wireless check box.

8. Click Save Settings. The router restarts to put the new settings into effect.

Linksys

Follow these steps to configure wireless settings on most Linksys routers:

1. Click the Wireless tab.

2. Click the Basic Wireless Settings subtab, shown in Figure 3.26.

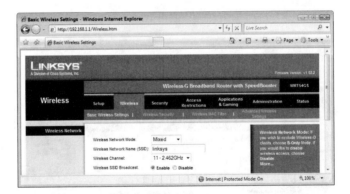

FIGURE 3.26

On most Linksys routers, use the Wireless tab's Basic Wireless Settings subtab to configure the wireless AP.

3. Use the Wireless Network Mode list to select a wireless mode.

4. Use the Wireless Network Name (SSID) text box to specify the network name you want to use.

5. Use the Wireless Channel list to select a frequency.

6. Use the Wireless SSID Broadcast group to click either Enable or Disable.

7. At the bottom of the page, click Save Settings. The router reports that the Settings are successful.

8. Click Continue.

Netgear

On most Netgear routers, here are the steps to follow to configure the wireless AP settings:

1. Under Setup, click the Wireless Settings link. The Wireless Settings page appears, as shown in Figure 3.27.

FIGURE 3.27
On most Netgear routers, use the Wireless Settings page to configure the wireless AP.

3. Use the Name (SSID) text box to specify the network name you want to use.

4. Use the Channel list to select a frequency.

5. Use the Mode list to select a wireless mode.

6. Click Apply.

7. Under Advanced, click the Wireless Settings link to display the Advanced Wireless Settings page.

8. Use the Enable SSID Broadcast check box to toggle SSID broadcasting on and off.

9. Click Apply.

Checking the Router Status

All routers come with a status page that provides you with the router's current settings in various categories, including the following:

■ The router's current firmware version and serial number.

■ The router's *Media Access Control* (MAC) address and internal IP address.

■ Whether features such as the DHCP server, *network address translation* (NAT), and the firewall are enabled or disabled.

■ The wireless network settings (SSID, mode, channel, and so on).

■ Internet connection settings such as the external MAC address, the external IP address, and the addresses for your ISP's gateway and DNS servers.

The next few sections show you how to display the status page for various routers.

Belkin

To view the status page in most Belkin routers, click the Home link in the top navigation bar. Figure 3.28 shows an example of the Status page that appears.

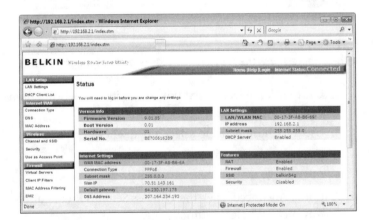

FIGURE 3.28

On most Belkin routers, click the Home link in the top navigation bar to display the Status page.

D-Link

On most D-Link routers, here are the steps to follow to view the status page:

1. Click the Status tab, (or, on some D-Link routers, the Basic tab).
2. Click Device Info to display the Device Information page, shown in Figure 3.29.

FIGURE 3.29

On your D-Link router, use the Device Information page to view the router's status.

Linksys

Follow these steps to display the status pages on most Linksys routers:

1. Click the Status tab.
2. Click the Router subtab, shown in Figure 3.30.
3. Click the Local Network subtab to see the router's internal MAC and IP addresses, as well as the current DHCP server settings.
4. Click the Wireless subtab to see the router's wireless mode, SSID, and channel.

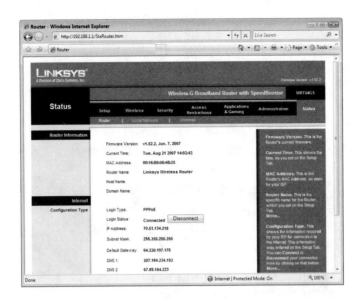

FIGURE 3.30

On most Linksys routers, use the Status tab's Router subtab to view the current router settings.

Netgear

On most Netgear routers, here are the steps to follow to view the router status:

1. Under Maintenance, click the Router Status link. The Router Status page appears, as shown in Figure 3.31.

2. To view statistics related to the router's WAN, LAN, and WLAN connections, click the Show Statistics button.

3. To view the WAN connection status, click the Connection Status button.

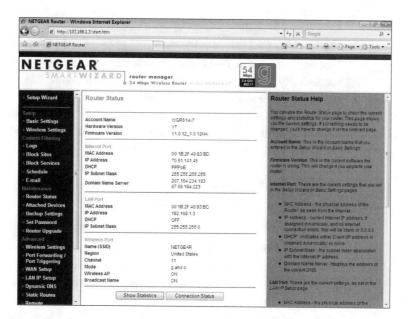

FIGURE 3.31

On most Netgear routers, use the Router Status page to see the router's current settings.

Testing Your Router's Capabilities

Microsoft offers a useful Internet Explorer add-on called the *Internet Connectivity Evaluation Tool* that examines your router and determines whether it supports several advanced features that Windows Vista can take advantage of to maximize Internet and network performance. The tests performed by the Internet Connectivity Evaluation Tool include the following:

■ **Network Address Translation Type.** This test determines the NAT support provided by your router. Specifically, the tool checks to see whether your router supports cone NAT or symmetric NAT. *Cone NAT* means that when a client with a specific internal address uses a port, all external hosts can communicate with the client by sending data through that port to the external address. *Symmetric NAT* means that when a client with a specific internal address uses a port to communicate with an external host, NAT creates a unique mapping for the internal address and port, and only that external host can use the mapping. If the client uses the same port to communicate with a different external host, an entirely new address/port mapping is created. This is less efficient than cone NAT, and fewer protocols support this type of NAT.

- **Traffic Congestion Test.** This test determines whether your router can successfully handle a technology called *Explicit Congestion Notification* (ECN), which enables your router to alert hosts that they are sending data too fast and that they should throttle back the transmission. If the test shows that your router can handle ECP, you can enable ECP in Windows Vista by selecting Start, All Programs, Accessories, right-clicking Command Prompt, clicking Run As Administrator, and then entering your *User Account Control* (UAC) credentials. At the command prompt, enter the following command:

```
netsh interface tcp set global ecncapability=enabled
```

- **TCP High Performance Test.** This test determines whether your router can handle *window scaling*, a technology that modifies the size of the *TCP window*, which is the amount of data that can be transmitted before the sending host must stop and wait for the receiving host to acknowledge that the data has been received. The bigger the TCP window, the better the performance of the connection. The TCP High Performance Test uses a series of data transfers to scale up the size of the TCP window until either a data transfer fails or the maximum window size is reached. If your router supports window scaling, it means Windows Vista can negotiate the best TCP window size with the router and so improve transmission speeds.

- **UPnP Support Test.** This test determines whether your router supports UPnP and whether UPnP is enabled on the router. (See "Enabling UPnP," earlier in this chapter.)

- **Multiple Simultaneous Connection States Test.** This test determines whether your router can handle multiple computers, devices, and programs accessing Internet sites at the same time. The text sets up 80 simultaneous connections to websites and attempts to keep them activate for 2 minutes.

Here are the steps to follow to download, install, and run the Internet Connectivity Evaluation Tool:

1. Run Internet Explorer and navigate to the following URL:

   http://www.microsoft.com/windows/using/tools/igd/default.mspx

2. Accept the license agreement and click Continue.

3. Click Internet Explorer's Information bar, and then click Install ActiveX Control. The User Account Control dialog box appears.

4. Enter your UAC credentials. The Security Warning dialog box appears.

5. Click Install. Internet Explorer installs the add-on.

6. Click Start Test. The User Account Control dialog box appears.

7. Enter your UAC credentials. The Internet Connectivity Evaluation Tool begins testing your router.

8. When the test is complete, the results page show whether your router passed or failed each test, as shown in Figure 3.32. To see more information about the test results, scroll to the bottom of the page and click View Detailed Report.

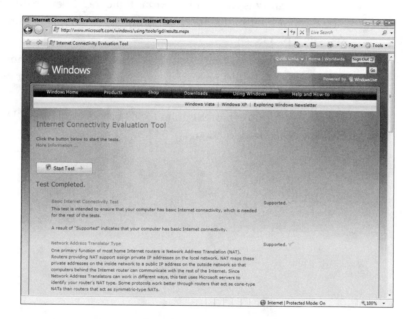

FIGURE 3.32

Use the Internet Connectivity Evaluation Tool to test various advanced features of your router.

3

From Here

- If you need a bit of router background, **see** "Understanding Routers," **p. 24**.

- For more about DHCP, **see** "The Router and Dynamic IP Addressing," **p. 26**.

- After you enable the router's DHCP server, make sure each client computer is set up to use DHCP; **see** "Enabling Automatic IP Addressing," **p. 142**.

- If you only have a few computers, setting and managing static IP addresses isn't difficult in Windows Vista; **see** "Setting Up a Static IP Address," **p. 145**.

- Wireless security is such an important topic that I devote an entire chapter to it later in the book; **see Chapter 15**, "Implementing Wireless Security," **p. 335**.

- One of your first tasks with your new router should be to change the default administrative password; **see** "Specifying a New Administrative Password," **p. 336**.

- For more information on disabling SSID broadcasting, **see** "Disabling Network SSID Broadcasting," **p. 347**.

4

Putting Your Network Together

B
y now, you've assembled your ethernet devices (see Chapter 1, "Understanding Ethernet Networking") and your wireless networking devices (see Chapter 2, "Understanding Wireless Networking"), and you've set up your router for networking and Internet access (see Chapter 3, "Configuring Your Router"). All that's left now is to put everything together to create your network, and that's the subject of this chapter. Here I take you step by step through the entire process of taking those scattered networking bits and pieces and molding them into a solid, reliable network. You learn how to insert an internal *network interface card* (NIC); how to connect your broadband modem, router, and switch; and how to run cables to connect the ethernet portion of your network. You also learn some basic Windows Vista networking chores, such as configuring the workgroup and computer names. Finally, you learn how to connect to your new network.

IN THIS CHAPTER

■ Inserting an Internal NIC

■ Connecting the Broadband Modem

■ Connecting the Router

■ Connecting the Switch

■ Laying the Network Cable

■ Changing the Computer and Workgroup Name

■ Making Wireless Network Connections

■ From Here

Inserting an Internal NIC

If you have an internal NIC that you need to install, and you don't have
someone who is hardware savvy that you can dragoon into doing the job for
you, not to worry: Installing an internal circuit board isn't that hard as long
as you follow a few simple instructions, which is what this section is all about.

Installing the NIC's Device Driver

Before you get to the hardware part, it's likely you have to take care of a bit of
software, first. Most internal NICs require you to install the NIC's device driver
before you attach the card to the computer. This is always a good idea
because it ensures that Windows Vista will immediately recognize the NIC
after you install it, and you'll be able to start networking right away.

First, you need to determine whether the NIC comes with a driver that works
with Windows Vista. Check out the box to see whether it displays the
Windows Vista logo. You have two ways to proceed:

■ If you see the Windows Vista logo on the box, it means the CD that
comes with the NIC contains the Vista driver. Insert the CD, launch the
setup program when the AutoPlay window appears, and then run
through the steps in the setup program. In particular, look for a setup
option that installs the device driver (see Figure 4.1 for an example).
Note that you'll need to enter your User Account Control (UAC) credentials at some point during the install.

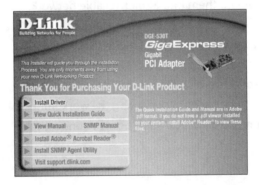

FIGURE 4.1
In the NIC's install program, look for an option that installs the device driver.

■ If you don't see any Windows logo or you see a logo for an earlier version of Windows, you need to download and install the device driver yourself (assuming the NIC is compatible with Vista). Go to the manufacturer's website and locate the Windows Vista driver for your device. In most cases, you need to go to the Support section of the site, and then look for a Downloads section. Along the way you'll be asked to specify the make and model number of the NIC, so keep the box handy.

note If you're not sure whether the NIC is Vista-compatible, and you don't have any drivers for it, don't give up just yet. Go ahead and install the NIC as described in the next section. If you're lucky, Vista will recognize the NIC anyway and install the drivers for it.

note If the downloaded driver comes in a compressed (ZIP) file, be sure to extract the driver files from the download file. Right-click the ZIP file, click Extract All, specify the folder in which you want to store the file, and then click Extract.

If you downloaded the Windows Vista device driver for the NIC, first check to see whether the downloaded files include an installation program (usually setup.exe, but it could also be autorun.exe). If so, run that program to install the driver. Otherwise, you need to follow these steps to install the driver:

1. On the computer in which you'll be installing the NIC, select Start, right-click Computer, and then click Properties. (You can also press Windows Logo+Pause/Break.) Vista displays the System window.

2. Click Device Manager in the taskbar. The User Account Control dialog box appears.

3. Enter your UAC credentials to continue. The Device Manager window appears.

4. Right-click the computer name at the top of the tree, and then click Add Legacy Hardware. Device Manager launches the Add Hardware Wizard.

5. Click Next. The wizard asks how you want to install the hardware.

6. Select Install the Hardware That I Manually Select from a List, and then click Next. The wizard displays the Select Network Adapter dialog box.

7. Select Network Adapters and then click Next. The wizard displays lists of network adapter manufacturers and models.

8. Click Have Disk to display the Install from Disk dialog box.

9. Click Browse to open the Locate File dialog box.

10. Navigate to the folder containing the NIC's downloaded driver files, click the INF file that appears in the folder (see Figure 4.2), and then click Open. Vista returns you to the Install From Disk dialog box.

FIGURE 4.2
The folder containing the NIC's downloaded device driver files will contain an INF file that you need to select.

11. Click OK.

12. If you see a list of network adapters, click the one you'll be installing, and then click Next. Vista installs the driver.

13. Click Finish.

Installing the NIC

With the drivers installed, you're now ready to physically install the NIC. The only tool you need is a Phillips screwdriver. Here are the steps to follow:

1. If the computer is running, select Start, click the arrow beside the Lock button, and then click Shut Down.

2. Vista's Shut Down command should turn off your computer. If it doesn't, press the power button to turn off the machine.

3. Remove all cables that are attached to ports on the back of the computer, including (I should say *especially*) the power cable.

4. If the computer is under your desk or in some other inconvenient or dark location, move the unit so that you can more easily work with it and so that you have lots of light to allow you to see what you're doing.

5. Remove the computer's access panel. If the computer has a tower case, this is usually the left side of the case (that is, the left as you face the front of the computer); if the computer has a desktop case, the access panel is usually the top of the case. Loosen or remove any screws that attach the access panel to the chassis, and then slide or lift the access panel away from the chassis. (Some cases require you to hold down a lever as you do this.)

6. If the computer is a tower case, either raise the case so that you can easily see and reach inside or gently lay the case on its side so that the exposed area faces up.

7. You now have two ways to proceed:

   ■ If your computer has an empty PCI or PCIe slot (depending on which type of NIC you have), remove the screw that holds the slot cover (the long, thin piece of metal attached to the chassis; see Figure 4.3). Place the screw in a handy place.

tip Before removing the cables, make a mental note of where they're currently attached so that you'll know where to reattach them when you're putting your system back together.

caution At this point, it's very important to ground yourself by touching the chassis, the power supply unit, or some other metal object. This discharges your static electricity and ensures that you won't damage any of the computer's sensitive electronic components. Ideally, you shouldn't walk around the room until you've finished the installation. If you need to walk away from the computer for a bit, be sure to ground yourself again when you're ready to resume the installation.

tip When the screw is out, the slot cover should come out easily; it might even fall out on its own, so it's a good idea to hold on to the slot cover with your free hand to ensure that it doesn't fall onto the motherboard and damage a component. If the slot cover won't budge, it's probably being held in place by the slot cover above it (or, less often, the slot cover below it). Loosen (but don't remove) the screw on the other slot cover. This should give you enough slack to remove the cover for the empty slot. When that slot cover is out, you can tighten the screw on the other slot cover.

4

Slot cover   PCI slot

FIGURE 4.1

An empty PCI slot with slot cover.

- If you're removing an existing PCI or PCIe card to make room for the NIC, remove the screw that attaches the card's metal bracket to the chassis and place the screw nearby. Using the thumb and forefinger of both hands, grasp empty sections of the card (usually near the edges) and pull the card away from the slot; you might need to jiggle the card back and forth a bit to loosen it. Pull the card out of the chassis, being careful not to hit any other components.

8. Place the NIC so that its bracket is flush with the open slot cover, and slowly slide the NIC toward the slot. When the NIC's connectors are touching the slot and are perfectly aligned with the slot opening, place your thumbs on the edge of the card and press the card firmly into the slot (see Figure 4.4).

tip How do you know whether the card is completely inserted into the slot? The easiest way to tell is to look at the portion of the bracket that screws onto the chassis. If that portion isn't flush with the chassis, the card isn't fully inserted.

FIGURE 4.4
Press the NIC firmly into the slot.

9. Screw the bracket to the chassis, as shown in Figure 4.5.

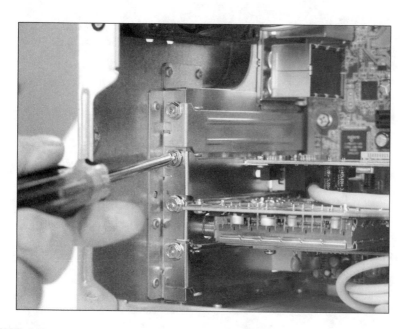

FIGURE 4.5
Screw the NIC's bracket to the computer chassis.

10. Replace the access panel and move the computer back to its original location.

11. Reattach the cables using the same ports. (If the computer has an existing motherboard NIC and you had an Ethernet cable attached to that NIC, be sure to attach the cable to the new NIC, instead.)

12. Power up the computer.

Making Sure the NIC Installed Properly

With the device driver preinstalled, Vista shouldn't have any problem recognizing the NIC and configuring it for use. Just to be sure, here are the steps to follow to check that the NIC installed correctly:

1. On the computer where you installed the NIC, select Start, right-click Computer, and then click Properties. Vista displays the System window.

2. Click Device Manager in the taskbar. The User Account Control dialog box appears.

3. Enter your UAC credentials to continue. The Device Manager window appears.

4. Open the Network Adapters branch. You should see your device listed, as shown in Figure 4.6.

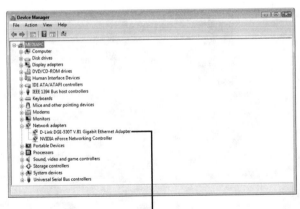

The new NIC should appear in the Network Adapters branch.

FIGURE 4.6

Use Device Manager to ensure the NIC installed properly.

If you see a yellow or red icon over the device icon, the device has a problem. Similarly, if the device isn't listed in the Network Adapters branch, open the Other Devices branch (if one exists) and look for Ethernet Controller (or possibly Unknown Device). In both cases, the solution is to either reinstall the existing driver or install a different driver (perhaps an older Vista driver, if one exists, an XP driver, or whatever driver came with the NIC; see Chapter 18, "Troubleshooting Network Problems").

→ For the details on installing a different a NIC driver, **see** "Updating the NIC Device Driver," **p. 425**.

Connecting the Broadband Modem

A *broadband modem* is a high-speed modem used for ADSL (*Asymmetric Digital Subscriber Line*), cable, or satellite Internet access. In almost all cases, the *Internet service provider* (ISP) provides you with a broadband modem that's compatible with their service. Getting the broadband modem connected is the first step in putting your network together.

Begin by connecting and plugging in the modem's power adapter. Make sure the modem is turned off. If the modem doesn't come with a power switch, unplug the power adapter for now.

Attaching the Internet Connection Cable

Next, attach the cable that provides the ISP's Internet connection. For example, if you have an ADSL broadband modem, run a phone line from the nearest wall jack to the appropriate port on the back of the modem, which is usually labeled ADSL or DSL, as shown in Figure 4.7.

Similarly, if you have a cable broadband modem, connect a TV cable to the cable connector on the back of the modem, which is usually labeled Cable, as shown in Figure 4.8.

note Many ADSL providers require that you install a phone filter device to protect your telephones. Each phone filter comes with two RJ-11 (phone) jacks, usually labeled Line and Phone. Run a phone cable from the wall jack to the Line port on the phone filter, and run a second phone cable from the Phone port on the filter to your telephone. You need to do this for each telephone in your home or office.

FIGURE 4.7

For an ADSL broadband modem, plug a phone cable into the DSL (or ADSL) port on the back of the modem.

FIGURE 4.8

For a cable broadband modem, plug a TV cable into the Cable connector on the back of the modem.

Registering the Modem

How you proceed from here depends on the ISP. Nowadays, many ISPs insist that you register the broadband modem by accessing a page on the ISP's website and sometimes entering a code or the serial number of the modem. Read the instructions that come with your ISP's Internet kit to determine whether you must first register your broadband modem online.

caution Use either the ethernet port or the USB port, but not both. Connecting both ports to your computer can damage the modem.

If you don't need to register, skip to the next section. If you do need to register, you must first connect the modem directly to a computer (instead of to your router, as described in the next section). Most broadband modems give you two ways to do this (see Figure 4.9):

Ethernet All broadband modems have an RJ-45 port on the back that is labeled Ethernet, LAN, or 10BASE-T. Run an ethernet cable from this port to the RJ-45 port on your computer's NIC.

USB Most newer broadband modems also come with a USB port on the back. If you're working with a computer that doesn't yet have a NIC, or if the NIC already has a cable attached, you can use USB instead. Run a USB cable from the USB port on the modem to a free USB port on your computer. You also need to install the broadband modem's USB device driver, which should be on a CD that your ISP provided.

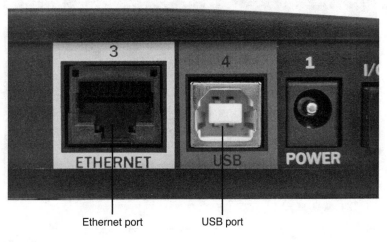

Ethernet port   USB port

FIGURE 4.9

Almost all newer broadband modems come with both an ethernet (RJ-45) and a USB port.

Turn on the broadband modem and wait until it makes a connection with the line. All broadband modems have an LED on the front that lights up to indicate a good connection. Look for an LED labeled Online, DSL, or something similar, and wait until you see a solid (that is, not blinking) light on that LED. You can now use a web browser to access the ISP's site (depending on the ISP, you may need to log on first) and register your modem.

Connecting the Router

You're now ready to set up your broadband modem so that its Internet connection can be shared with each computer and device on your network. You do that by connecting the broadband modem to your router.

If you had to register your broadband modem as described in the previous section, turn off the modem and disconnect the ethernet or USB cable from your computer.

Examine the back of your router and locate the port that it uses for the Internet connection. Some routers label this port WAN (see Figure 4.10), whereas others use Internet (see Figure 4.11). Some routers don't label the Internet port at all, but instead place the port off to the side so that it's clearly separate from the router's RJ-45 ports.

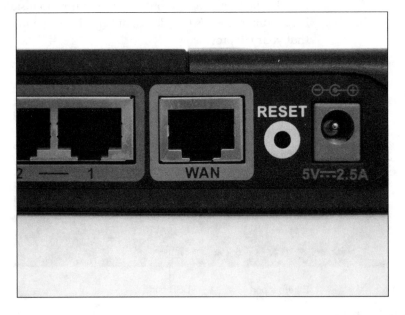

FIGURE 4.10

Some routers use the label WAN to indicate the port used for the Internet connection.

FIGURE 4.11

On other routers the Internet connection port is labeled Internet.

4

With the broadband modem and the router turned off, run an ethernet cable from the broadband modem's ethernet port to the WAN port on the router. Figure 4.12 shows an example setup (using ADSL).

You're now ready to turn on your devices. Begin by turning on the broadband modem and waiting until it has a solid connection with the line. Then turn on your router. Because you already configured your ISP's Internet settings in Chapter 3, "Configuring Your Router," the router will automatically connect to the ISP. The front of the router should have an LED labeled WAN or Internet that will go solid when the Internet connection has been made.

> **tip** On my network, I keep the broadband modem and the router side by side on a desk so that I can easily see the LEDs on the front of both devices (particularly the LED on the broadband modem that indicates a good Internet connection). If you do this, purchase a 1-foot Ethernet cable to connect to the two devices.

→   For the details on configuring your router to connect to your ISP, **see** "Setting Up Your Broadband Connection," **p. 71**.

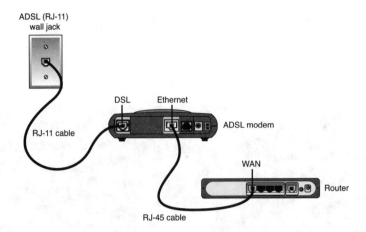

FIGURE 4.12

Connect the broadband modem's ethernet port to the router's WAN or Internet port.

Connecting the Switch

If your network setup includes a switch, the next step in your network configuration involves adding the switch. After plugging in the switch's power adapter, all that's required is to run an ethernet cable from any RJ-45 port on the router to any RJ-45 port on the switch, as shown in Figure 4.13.

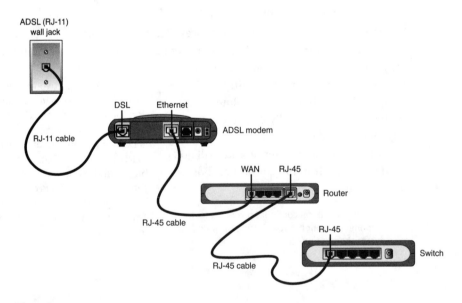

FIGURE 4.13

If your network includes a switch, run an ethernet cable from an RJ-45 port on the router to an RJ-45 port on the switch.

Laying the Network Cable

Your final hardware-related network configuration chore is to lay the ethernet cable for those computers and devices that will use a wired connection to the network. To do this, for each wired computer or device you run an ethernet cable of the appropriate length from any RJ-45 port on your network's router or switch, to the RJ-45 port on the computer's or device's NIC.

You can prevent some cable problems and simplify your troubleshooting down the road by taking a few precautions and "ounce of prevention" measures in advance:

■ First and foremost, always buy the highest-quality cable you can find. With network cabling, you get what you pay for.

■ Make sure the cable you use is appropriate for the ethernet standard your network uses. If you're running Fast Ethernet, you need Cat 5 cable; if you're running Gigabit Ethernet, you need Cat 5e or, even better, Cat 6 cable.

■ Try to use a different-color cable for each computer or device. This makes it easy to know which computer or device is plugged into which port on the router or switch, and it simplifies the task of tracing a cable's path (for example, to see if the cable is lying close to a source of electromagnetic radiation). If all your cables are the same color, consider adding your own labels for things such as the source and destination of the cable.

■ To avoid electromagnetic interference, don't run cable near electronic devices, power lines, air conditioners, fluorescent lights, motors, and other electromagnetic sources.

■ Try to avoid running cable in parallel with phone lines because the ringer signal can disrupt network data.

■ To avoid the cable being stepped on accidentally, don't run it under carpet.

■ To avoid people tripping over a cable (and possible damaging the cable connector, the NIC port, or the person doing the tripping!), avoid high-traffic areas when laying the cable.

■ If you plan to run cable outdoors, either get special outdoor ethernet cable or use conduit or another casing material to prevent moisture damage.

■ Don't use excessive force to pull or push a cable into place. Rough handling can cause pinching or even breakage.

Changing the Computer and Workgroup Name

At this point, you've pretty much got yourself a working network: The data line is connected to the broadband modem, the modem is connected to the router, the router is connected to the switch (if you have one), and all of your wired devices are connected to the switch (or router). What's left? Just a couple of things:

> **note** The default workgroup name in Windows Vista is Workgroup. If your network uses exclusively Vista machines, you probably won't have to change any workgroup names. However, it's a good idea to check the workgroup name for each computer.

- For both wired and wireless clients, the machines will be able to access the network and your network chores will be easier if each computer has a unique name and every computer uses the same workgroup name. This section shows you how to modify the computer and workgroup names in Windows Vista.

- For your wireless clients, you need to know how to connect them to your wireless network. That's the topic of the next section.

Here are the steps to follow to change the computer name and workgroup name in Vista:

1. Click Start, right-click Computer, and then click Properties. (You can also press Windows Logo+Pause/Break.) The System window appears.

2. In the Computer Name, Domain, and Workgroup Settings section, click the Change Settings link. The User Account Control dialog box appears.

3. Enter your UAC credentials to continue. The System Properties dialog box appears with the Computer Name tab displayed.

4. Click Change. The Computer Name/Domain Changes dialog box appears, as shown in Figure 4.14.

5. Use the Computer Name text box to modify the name of the computer, if necessary.

> **tip** Another way to open the System Properties dialog box with the Computer Name tab displayed is to press Windows Logo+R (or select Start, All Programs, Accessories, Run), type `systempropertiescomputername` (you can also type `control sysdm.cpl,,1`), click OK, and then enter your UAC credentials.

> **note** Computer names can be a maximum of 64 characters and should include only letters, numbers, or hyphens (-).

FIGURE 4.14

Use the Computer Name/Domain Changes dialog box to change your computer and workgroup names.

6. Select the Workgroup option.

7. Use the Workgroup text box to type the common workgroup name; you can enter a maximum of 15 characters.

8. Click OK. A dialog box welcoming you to the new workgroup appears.

9. Click OK. Windows Vista tells you that you must restart the computer to put the changes into effect.

> **note** You only need to change the computer name if the current name conflicts with another computer on the network or if you want to use a more descriptive name. (The computer names appear in Vista's Network window, so descriptive names help you differentiate your computers.)

10. Click OK to return to the System Properties dialog box.

11. Click Close. Vista prompts you to restart your computer.

12. Click Restart Now. Vista restarts your computer.

Making Wireless Network Connections

You learned in Chapter 3 how to configure the wireless settings on your router's wireless *access point* (AP). With that chore complete and with a wireless NIC installed, you're ready to access your wireless network. Note, however, that although connections to wired networks are automatic, Vista doesn't establish the initial connection to a wireless network automatically. This is mostly a security concern because a password or security key protects most wireless networks. This might not be the case just yet in your wireless network, because we haven't yet talked about wireless security; we get to that in Chapter 15, "Implementing Wireless Security."

> **note** It's perfectly okay for one computer to have both a wired and a wireless connection for your network. In fact, as long as your computer has both an ethernet and a wireless NIC, having both connections running simultaneously is a good idea because it gives you connection redundancy: if one connection goes down, you still have the other connection to perform your network chores.

→   To learn how to configure the wireless option of your router's AP, **see** "Modifying Wireless Settings," **p. 85**.

→   To learn how to set up a security key for your wireless network, **see** "Encrypting Wireless Signals with WPA," **p. 341**.

However, it's also usually the case (particularly in dense, urban neighborhoods) that Vista might detect multiple wireless networks within range, so it's up to you to specify which of those networks is your own. Fortunately, you can configure Vista to remember a wireless network's settings and automatically connect to your network the next time you log on to Vista. So, in most cases, you need to run through the connection procedure only once.

Connecting to a Wireless Network

Here are the steps to follow to connect to your wireless network:

1. Select Start, Connect To. Vista opens the Connect to a Network dialog box, which displays a list of the available wireless networks, as shown in Figure 4.15. Each network displays three pieces of information:

   ■ The left column displays the network name (the SSID).

   ■ The middle column tells you whether the network requires a password or security key (Security-enabled network) or not (Unsecured network). After you connect to a wireless network, this column displays Connected for that network.

   ■ The signal strength, as indicated by the five bars to the right; the more green bars you see, the stronger the signal. Note that the networks are in descending order of signal strength.

FIGURE 4.15
The Connect to a Network window displays a list of the wireless networks that are in range.

2. Select your network.

3. Click Connect. If the network that you want to use is unsecured—as your network may be, and as are most public hot spots—Vista connects to the network immediately (so skip to step 6). However, most private wireless networks are (or should be) secured against unauthorized access. In this case, Windows Vista prompts you to enter the required security key or password.

4. Type the security key or password. Note that Vista displays dots in place of each character, as shown in Figure 4.16. This is a security feature just in case someone is looking over your shoulder.

5. Click Connect. Vista attempts to connect to the wireless network. If the connection went through, you see a dialog box named Successfully Connected to *Network*, where *Network* is the name of the network.

> **note** If your network's security key is long or complex, you might not be sure whether you entered the security key correctly. Because the prospect of something peeking over your shoulder isn't much of an issue in most home or small office networks, it's okay to activate the Display Characters check box to tell Vista to display the actual security key characters rather than dots.

4

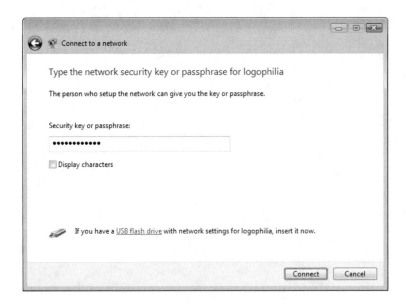

FIGURE 4.16

To access a secured wireless network, you must enter a security key or password.

6. This dialog box gives you two options (both activated by default; see Figure 4.17):

Save This Network   When activated, this check box tells Vista to save the network in the Manage Wireless Networks window (described in Chapter 7, "Managing Wireless Network Connections"). You must leave this check box activated if you want to connect to the network in the future without having to reenter the security key.

→   To learn more about the Manage Wireless Networks window, **see** "Opening the Manage Wireless Networks Window," **p. 158**.

Start This   When activated, this check box tells Vista to
Connection   connect to the network automatically the next
Automatically   time you log on to Vista. If you always want to connect to the network manually, deactivate this option. Note that if you deactivate the Save This Network check box, Vista deactivates and disables the Start This Connection Automatically check box.

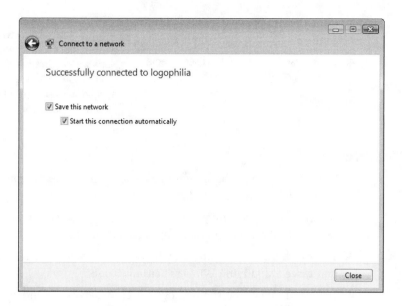

FIGURE 4.17

After a successful connection, Vista prompts you to save the wireless network.

→   If you can't connect successfully, **see** "Troubleshooting Wireless Network Problems," **p. 426**.

7. Click Close. Vista prompts you to choose the location of your network.

8. Click Home or click Work (as the case may be; they both set up your network as a private network). The User Account Control dialog box appears.

9. Enter your UAC credentials to continue.

10. Click Close.

Disconnecting from a Wireless Network

If you no longer need to use your current wireless connection, follow these steps to disconnect it:

1. Select Start, Connect To. Vista displays the Connect to a Network dialog box.

2. Select your current connection. (This is the network that displays Connected in the middle column.)

3. Click Disconnect. Vista asks you to confirm.

4. Click Disconnect. Vista disconnects from the network.

5. Click Close.

> **tip** A faster way to disconnect is to right-click the Network icon in the taskbar's notification area, select Disconnect From, and then select your current connection.

From Here

■ To learn how to configure various router settings, **see** Chapter 3, "Configuring Your Router," **p. 59**.

■ For the details on configuring your router to connect to your ISP, **see** "Setting Up Your Broadband Connection," **p. 71**.

■ To learn how to configure the wireless option of your router's access point, **see** "Modifying Wireless Settings," **p. 85**.

■ To learn more about the Manage Wireless Networks window, **see** "Opening the Manage Wireless Networks Window," **p. 158**.

■ To learn how to set up a security key for your wireless network, **see** "Encrypting Wireless Signals with WPA," **p. 341**.

■ For more information on what to do when you see either the Disconnected icon or the Error icon, **see** "Checking the Connection Status," **p. 413**.

■ For more information about the Diagnose and Repair command, **see** "Repairing a Network Connection," **p. 412**.

■ For the details on installing a different NIC driver, **see** "Updating the NIC Device Driver," **p. 425**

■ If you can't connect to your wireless network successfully, **see** "Troubleshooting Wireless Network Problems," **p. 426**.

4

Managing and Using Your Network

5 Working with Vista's Basic Network Tools and Tasks

6 Managing Network Connections

7 Managing Wireless Network Connections

8 Accessing and Sharing Network Resources

9 Setting Up Vista as a Digital Media Hub

10 Taking Advantage of Your Network

11 Work with Network Files Offline

12 Collaborating with Windows Meeting Space

Working with Vista's Basic Network Tools and Tasks

With your network hardware purchased, unpacked, plugged in, and connected, your network should be up and running. (If not, you might want to pay a visit to Chapter 18, "Troubleshooting Network Problems.") For the most part, you'll be using your network for useful tasks such as sharing files, streaming media, making backups, and accessing the Internet. However, it's inevitable that some of your network chores will be network related, because even the smallest networks demand a certain amount of administration and configuration. These network tasks range from simply viewing the current status of the network to viewing the computers and devices attached to the network to customizing settings such as the network name.

These are all basic network chores, and if you're the person who's wearing the Network Administrator nametag in your home or office, you need to know how to perform these chores. Fortunately, none of this is at all complex, so it won't take much time away from your more useful or interesting pursuits. This chapter tells you everything you need to know.

IN THIS CHAPTER

- Understanding Vista's Network Icon
- Accessing the Network and Sharing Center
- Turning On Network Discovery
- Viewing Network Computers and Devices
- Displaying a Network Map
- Viewing Network Status Details
- Customizing Your Network
- From Here

Understanding Vista's Network Icon

If you have any type of network card attached to your computer, Windows Vista always displays a Network icon in the taskbar's notification area. The Network icon serves two purposes (as described in more detail in the next two sections):

- To give you quick access to several common networking commands
- To give you a quick and visual method of seeing the current network status

Accessing Common Networking Commands

If you right-click the Network icon, you see a shortcut menu of commands, as shown in Figure 5.1. Here's a summary of what you can do with these commands:

- **Disconnect From.** Select this command to see a list of wireless networks to which your computer is currently connected. (In practice, this list will almost always contain just your local wireless network. However, I should mention that Vista also uses this list to display dial-up and direct broadband connections to the Internet.) Click a wireless network to disconnect from it.

- **Connect to a Network.** Select this command to open the Select a Network dialog box.

- **Turn On Activity Animation.** Select this command to configure the Network icon to indicate when network activity occurs on this computer. That is, whenever the computer is either sending data to or receiving data from the network, the Network icon signals this activity by blinking the screens of the two small monitors that make up the Network icon. Select Turn Off Activity Animation to disable this feature.

- **Turn Off Notification of New Networks.** Windows Vista normally alerts you when a new wireless network comes within range of your computer. This is useful if you're running Vista on a laptop computer that you take to different places. However, it's not much use on a desktop machine, so you might want to select this command to turn this feature off.

5

■ **Diagnose and Repair.** Select this command to have Vista try to solve a network problem, as described in Chapter 18.

→   For more information about the Diagnose and Repair command, **see** "Repairing a Network Connection," **p. 412.**

■ **Network and Sharing Center.** Select this command to open the Network and Sharing Center, which is Vista's hub for networking information and tasks. See "Accessing the Network and Sharing Center," later in this chapter.

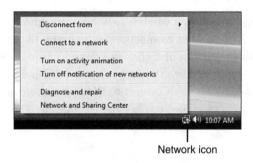

Network icon

FIGURE 5.1

Right-click Vista's Network icon to see this list of commands.

Viewing the Current Network Status

The Network icon consists of two small monitors, but the look of those monitors, and the extra icon superimposed on the monitors, gives you a visual indication of the general network status. There are four different status indicators:

Connected with Internet access

Vista indicates this status by showing the monitors with blue screens and superimposing a globe in the lower-right corner of the icon.

Connected without Internet access

Vista indicates this status by showing the monitors with blue screens, but without superimposing a globe in the lower-right corner of the icon.

Disconnected

![Disconnected icon showing 10:35 AM]

Vista indicates this status by showing the monitors with gray screens and superimposing a red *X* in the lower-right corner of the icon.

Error

![Error icon showing 10:34 AM]

Vista indicates this status by showing the monitors with blue screens and superimposing a yellow triangle with an exclamation mark (!) in the lower-right corner of the icon.

➜   For more information about what to do when you see either the Disconnected icon or the Error icon, **see** "Checking the Connection Status," **p. 413**.

If your computer uses a wireless network connection, you can see the current signal strength for that connection by hovering the mouse pointer over the Network icon. You can also click the Network icon, in which case Vista displays the fly-out window shown in Figure 5.2. Note, too, that you can also use this window to click the Connect or Disconnect command to open the Connect to a Network dialog box, or click the Network and Sharing Center command, to open the Network and Sharing Center.

FIGURE 5.2

Click the Network icon to see the signal strength of your wireless network connection.

Turning Off the Network Icon

The Network icon is a useful tool when you first set up your network because it shows you the status of the connection and gives you easy access to the Network and Sharing Center, which you'll probably use quite often at first. However, if after a while you find that you rarely use the Network icon and you'd like to reduce the clutter in the notification area, you can follow these steps to turn off the Network icon:

1. Right-click an empty section of the taskbar, and then click Properties. Vista displays the Taskbar and Start Menu Properties dialog box.

2. Click the Notification Area tab.

3. Deactivate the Network check box, as shown in Figure 5.3.

4. Click OK.

FIGURE 5.3

If you no longer use the Network icon, turn it off by deactivating the Network check box.

Accessing the Network and Sharing Center

One of the things people often griped about with previous versions of Windows was that the networking features were often scattered about the interface and it was hard to find what you needed. Windows XP's My Network Places folder helped a bit because it offered the Network Tasks section in the tasks pane, but it only had a few useful commands.

Microsoft realized that more work needed to be done to make network administration easier, particularly for nonprofessionals. The result in Windows Vista is the Network and Sharing Center, which acts as a kind of home base for networking. Proof that Microsoft is heading in the right direction here is the long list of network-related tasks that you can either perform or launch using the Network and Sharing Center:

- See a list of your current network connections.

- Visualize your network with a network map (see "Displaying a Network Map," later in this chapter).

■ Customize the network name, type, and icon (see "Customizing Your Network," later in this chapter).

■ Change your computer discovery and sharing options (see "Turning On Network Discovery," later in this chapter, and Chapter 8, "Accessing and Sharing Network Resources").

→ **See** "Activating File and Printer Sharing," **p. 185**.

■ View the status of each network connection (see "Viewing Network Status Details," later in this chapter).

■ View the computers and devices on the network (see "Viewing Network Computers and Devices," later in this chapter).

■ Connect to another network.

■ Manage your network connections (see Chapter 6, "Managing Network Connections").

→ **See** "Opening the Network Connections Window," **p. 140**.

■ Manage your wireless networks (see Chapter 7, "Managing Wireless Network Connections").

→ **See** "Opening the Manage Wireless Networks Window," **p. 158**.

■ Diagnose and repair a network connection (see Chapter 18).

→ **See** "Repairing a Network Connection," **p. 412**.

The Network and Sharing Center is a handy networking tool that you'll probably use a great deal, particularly when you're first getting your new network configured the way you want. That might be why Microsoft offers so many ways to open it. Here's a summary of the various methods you can use:

■ Select Start, Control Panel, and then, under the Network and Internet icon, click the View Network Status and Tasks link. (You can also click Network and Internet and then Network and Sharing Center.)

■ Click (or right-click) the Network icon in the notification area, and then click Network and Sharing Center.

■ Select Start, Network, and then click Network and Sharing Center in the taskbar.

■ Select Start, Connect To, Open Network and Sharing Center.

- Select Start, type **net** in the Search box, and then select Network and Sharing Center in the search results.

- In the Manage Wireless Networks window (see Chapter 7), click Network and Sharing Center in the taskbar.

Whichever method you use, the Network and Sharing Center window appears, and it will look similar to the window shown in Figure 5.4.

FIGURE 5.4

The Network and Sharing Center is Vista's networking hub.

The Network and Sharing Center window comprises four main areas:

- **Map.** This section gives you a miniature version of the network map: a visual display of the current connection. See the "Displaying a Network Map" section, later in this chapter.

- **Network.** This section tells you the name of the network to which you're connected, the network category (private or public), whether you have Internet access via that connection, and which of your computer connections is in use. (This will usually be either Local Area Connection for a wired connection or Wireless Network Connection). If you're connected to multiple networks or have multiple connections to a single network (wired and wireless, for example), all the connections appear here.

■ **Sharing and Discovery.** This area shows the current network detection and sharing settings. See "Turning On Network Discovery," next, to learn about the Network Discovery setting; see Chapter 8 to learn about the other settings in this area.

■ **Tasks.** This pane on the left side of the Network Center window gives you one-click access to some useful network tasks.

The rest of this chapter takes you through a few of the most common network administration chores, all of which you initiate using the Network and Sharing Center. (Although if there are other methods you can use to start a task, I'll let you know.)

Turning On Network Discovery

Networking your computers is all about access. You may want to access another computer to view one of its files or use its printer, and you may want other computers to access your machine to play your digital media. In Windows Vista, however, this access is not always automatic. Vista comes with a feature called *network discovery* that, when turned on, means you can see (discover) the other computers on your network and that the other computers can see (discover) yours. In networking, it's generally true that if you can see something, you can access it. (I say that this is *generally* true because there may be security issues that prevent or restrict access to a computer.)

Whether you have discovery turned on for a network depends on the type of network you're connected to:

■ In a private network such as the one in your home or office, you want to see other computers and have them see you, so network discovery should be turned on.

■ In a public network, such as a wireless hot spot, network discovery should be turned off because you probably don't want other users in the coffee shop (or wherever) to see your computer.

These aren't hard-and-fast rules, however, and there might be times when you need to flaunt these rules. For example, there might be one computer on your home or office network that you don't want others to see because, for instance, it contains sensitive information; in this case, it makes sense to turn off network discovery for that computer. Similarly, you and a friend might want to see each other's computers in a public setting so that you can perform a quick file exchange; in such a scenario, you can turn on network discovery, if only temporarily.

Here are the steps to follow to change the current network discovery setting:

1. Open the Network and Sharing Center, as described earlier (see "Accessing the Network and Sharing Center").

2. In the Sharing and Discovery section, find Network Discovery (the first item in the list) and click the current setting. (That is, click either On or Off; you can also click the downward-pointing arrow to the right of the Network Discovery setting.) Vista expands the Network Discovery item, as shown in Figure 5.5.

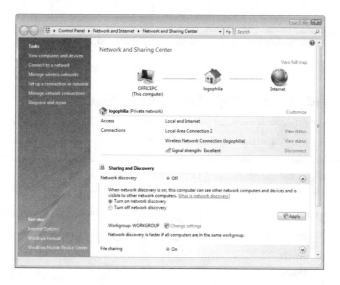

FIGURE 5.5

In the Network and Sharing Center's Sharing and Discovery section, expand the Network Discovery item to change its current setting.

3. Click either Turn On Network Discovery (which works only while you're connected to a network) or Turn Off Network Discovery.

4. Click Apply. Vista displays the User Account Control dialog box.

5. Enter your UAC credentials to put the new setting into effect.

If you have Network Discovery turned off and you open the Network window (select Start, Network), Vista displays an Information bar message warning you that network discovery is turned off (see Figure 5.6), which is why you don't see any icons in the window. If you want to turn network discovery on, click the Information bar, click Turn On Network Discovery and File Sharing, and then enter your UAC credentials.

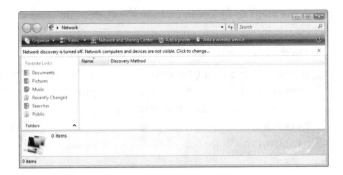

FIGURE 5.6
The Network window displays an Information bar warning if network discovery is turned off.

Viewing Network Computers and Devices

If the Network icon is showing that you have a good connection to the network (see "Viewing the Current Network Status," earlier in this chapter), you can go right ahead and see what's out there. One way to do this is to view Vista's network map (see "Displaying a Network Map," later in this chapter). However, Vista offers a more straightforward method: the Network window.

To open the Network window, you can use any of the following methods:

- Select Start, Network.
- In the Network and Sharing Center, click View Network Computers and Devices.
- Select Start, Control Panel, Network and Internet, and then click the View Network Computers and Devices link.

Figure 5.7 shows the Network window for a typical small network, where you see the network's main resources, such as the computers and media devices. As you can see in Figure 5.8, Details view (select Views, Details) shows you the resource name, category, workgroup name, and the name of the network profile.

You probably noticed in Figures 5.7 and 5.8 that some of the network resource names appear multiple times (for example, once in the Computer category and again in the Media Devices category). Multiple network icons mean that the computer or device has other networking features, and these appear as "devices" in the Network window. The most common secondary icon is the Windows Media Connect device,

> **note** To change the columns shown in Details view, right-click any column header, and then click a column name to toggle that column on and off.

which appears when the computer has configured Windows Media Player (in the case of a Windows Vista computer) to stream media to the network.

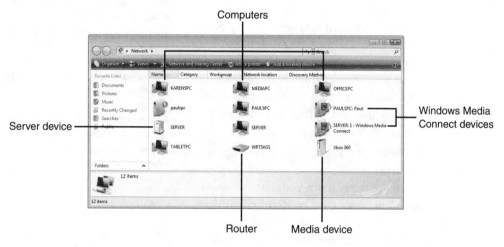

FIGURE 5.7

The Network window shows you the main resources on your network.

FIGURE 5.8

The Network window in Details view.

Displaying a Network Map

The Network window gives you a list of the network computers and devices, but it tells you nothing about how these devices connect to your network. This bird's-eye view of your network is available via Vista's Network Map feature, which gives you a visual display of everything your computer is connected to: network connections (wired and wireless), ad hoc (computer-to-computer) connections, Internet connections, and the devices associated with these connections. Network Map also gives you a visual display of the connection status so that you can easily spot problems.

The Network and Sharing Center displays your local portion of the network map, and the layout depends on your current connections. You always see an icon for your computer on the left. If your computer is connected to a network (as shown earlier in Figure 5.4), a green line joins the computer icon and the network icon. If the network is connected to the Internet, another green line joins the network icon and the Internet icon on the right. If there is no connection, you see a red X through the connection line.

> **note** The three Server icons you see in Figures 5.7 and 5.8 come from a Windows Home Server computer, which always shows icons for the server itself, its shared folders, and Windows Media Connect if the server has been configured to share media. See my book *Microsoft Windows Home Server Unleashed* (Sams, 2007) for a complete look at what Windows Home Server can do for your home or small office network.

> **note** In the full network map, a double solid line indicates a wired connection, and double dashed line indicates a wireless connection.

The Network and Sharing Center also comes with a more detailed version of Network Map. To view it, click the View Full Map link. Figure 5.9 shows an example of the full network map. If you have multiple network connections, use the Network Map Of list to select a different connection and see its map.

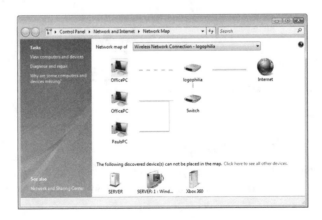

FIGURE 5.9
The full version of a network map.

Viewing Network Status Details

You saw earlier that you can use the Network icon in Vista's notification area to get a quick visual read on the current network status (see "Viewing the Current Network Status," earlier in this chapter). If the Network icon shows that your computer is connected to the network, you might find yourself wondering about some related status data: How long has the connection been running? How fast is the connection; that is, what is the connection's data transfer rate?

> **note** In this case, the data transfer rate is the theoretical maximum rate supported by the networking hardware. For example, if Vista detects that at least one component of a wired connection (the NIC, the cable, or the switch/router) supports only Fast Ethernet, Vista will report a connection speed of 100Mbps.

Windows Vista can supply you with these and other details about your network connection. Follow these steps to see them:

1. Open the Network and Sharing Center, as described earlier (see "Accessing the Network and Sharing Center").

2. In the Connections section, click the View Status link beside the connection you want to work with. Figure 5.10 shows the Status dialog box that appears for a wired connection. Figure 5.11 shows the Status dialog box for a wireless connection, which also shows the network's *service set identifier* (SSID) and then the connection's current signal strength.

FIGURE 5.10

The Status dialog box for a wired network connection.

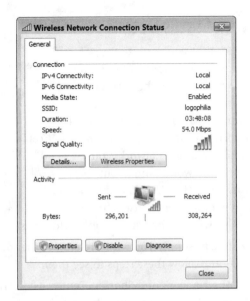

FIGURE 5.11

The Status dialog box for a wireless network connection.

→   For information about the Wireless Properties button in the Status dialog box for a wireless connection, **see** "Working with Wireless Connection Properties," **p. 163**.

3. Click Details. Vista displays the Network Connection Details dialog box, shown in Figure 5.12. This dialog box tells you, among other things, your NIC's MAC address (the Physical Address value), your computer's IP address, and the addresses of your ISP's DNS servers.

4. Click Close to return to the Status dialog box.

5. Click Close.

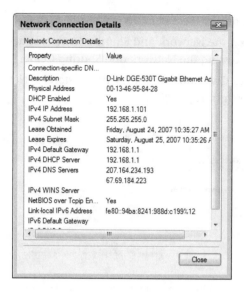

FIGURE 5.12

The Network Connection Details dialog box displays your computer's IP address, among other values.

Customizing Your Network

When you first open the Network Center, in most cases, you won't have a profile set up for the network, so Vista configures the network with three default settings:

- A default name, usually either *Network* or the SSID of the wireless network.

- The network type, which depends on the network location you chose when you first connected to the network.

- A default network icon, which depends on the network location you chose when you first connected to the network. (In the miniature network map shown in Figure 5.4, the default Home icon is the one shown above logophilia.)

note Windows Vista supports three types of network categories: private, public, and domain. Private networks are usually home or small office networks where you need to work with a few nearby computers. To that end, Windows Vista turns on network discovery and file and printer sharing. Public networks are usually wireless hot spot connections in airports, coffee shops, hotels, and other public places. When you designate a network as public, Vista turns off network discovery and file and printer sharing. The domain category applies to networks that are part of a corporate domain.

5

To change any of these defaults, follow these steps:

1. Open the Network and Sharing Center, as described earlier (see "Accessing the Network and Sharing Center").

2. Click Customize to display the Customize Network Settings dialog box shown in Figure 5.13.

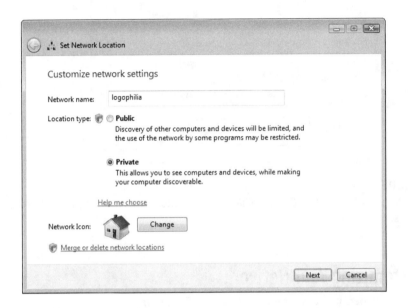

FIGURE 5.13
In the Network and Sharing Center, click Customize to display this dialog box so that you can change the network name, type, and icon.

3. Type a name in the Network Name text box.

4. Select either Public or Private. (You see the Domain option only if you are connected to a network with a domain.)

5. To change the icon, click Change to open the Change Network Icon dialog box, select an icon, and then click OK.

6. Click Next. Vista displays the User Account Control dialog box.

> **tip** The Change Network Icon dialog box initially shows you a small collection of icons from the `%SystemRoot%\system32\pnidui.dll` file. To get a larger choice of icons, type any of the following pathnames into the Look for Icons in This File text box (and press Enter after you enter the pathname):
> `%SystemRoot%\system32\shell32.dll`
> `%SystemRoot%\system32\pifmgr.dll`
> `%SystemRoot%\explorer.exe`

7. Enter your UAC credentials. Vista applies the new network settings.

8. Click Close. Vista updates the Network and Sharing Center window with the new settings.

From Here

- To find out more information about the Network Connections window, **see** "Opening the Network Connections Window," **p. 140**.

- For information on the Wireless Properties button in the Status dialog box for a wireless connection, **see** "Working with Wireless Connection Properties," **p. 163**.

- To learn more about the Manage Wireless Networks window, **see** "Opening the Manage Wireless Networks Window," **p. 158**.

- To learn how to enable sharing, **see** "Activating File and Printer Sharing," **p. 185**.

- If you can't connect to your wireless network successfully, **see** "Troubleshooting Wireless Network Problems," **p. 426**.

5

6

Managing Network Connections

I n Windows Vista, you can link to many different types of remote resources, including dial-up and broadband Internet services, dial-up and Internet-based *virtual private networking* (VPN), and the ethernet and wireless networking that are the subject of this book. In Vista, all of these remote links are called *network connections*, and Vista maintains a Network Connections window that lists all your network connections. Each *network interface card* (NIC) attached to your computer gets its own connection icon in the list, and you can use those icons to work with your network connections.

For example, you can rename a connection, disable an unused connection, switch a connection between using a dynamic and a static IP address, and find out a connection's *Internet Protocol* (IP) and *Media Access Control* (MAC) addresses. You learn about these and other tasks in this chapter. For more information about wireless connections, see Chapter 7, "Managing Wireless Network Connections."

IN THIS CHAPTER

■ Opening the Network Connections Window

■ Renaming a Network Connection

■ Enabling Automatic IP Addressing

■ Setting Up a Static IP Address

■ Finding a Connection's MAC Address

■ Using a Network Connection to Wake Up a Sleeping Computer

■ Disabling a Network Connection

■ From Here

Opening the Network Connections Window

You do most of your work in this chapter in Vista's Network Connections window, and Vista gives you two main ways to access this window:

- In the Network and Sharing Center, click the Manage Network Connections link in the Tasks list.

- Press Windows Logo+R (or select Start, All Programs, Accessories, Run) to open the Run dialog box, type `control ncpa.cpl`, and then click OK.

Figure 6.1 shows an example of the Network Connections window.

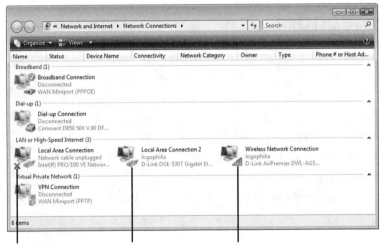

Connection has a problem   Wired connection   Wireless connection

FIGURE 6.1

Windows Vista's Network Connections window.

By default, Vista groups the Network Connections window via the Type field. If you've previously created a direct broadband Internet connection, a dial-up Internet connection, or a connection to a VPN, you see groups named Broadband, Dial-up, and Virtual Private Network, respectively (as shown in Figure 6.1). However, you always see the LAN or High-Speed Internet group, which usually includes two types of icons:

Wired   These ethernet connections take the default name Local Area Connection, and you can recognize them by the RJ-45 jack shown with the icon. If you have more than one ethernet NIC installed in your computer, you see a wired connection icon for each one (with subsequent connections named Local Area Connection 2, and so on).

Wireless   These connections take the default name Wireless Network Connection, and you can recognize them by the green signal bars shown with the icon.

When you're in the default Tiles view, both wired and wireless icons show the name of the network to which they're connected (or the icon shows `Disconnected` if no current connection is present) and the name of the NIC through which each connection is made. (Details view shows you more data such as the current connectivity setting—such as `Access to Local Only` or `Access to Local and Internet`—and the network category—Private, Public, or Domain.) If the network connection currently has a problem, you see a red X added to the icon (see Figure 6.1), and the connection's Status field may display an error message (such as `Network cable unplugged`).

Renaming a Network Connection

The default network connection names—Local Area Connection and Wireless Network Connection—don't tell you much other than whether the connection is wired or wireless. Similarly, if your computer has two ethernet NICs, having connections named Local Area Connection and Local Area Connection 2 doesn't give you much to go on if you need to differentiate between them.

For these reasons, you might consider renaming your connections. For example, if you have Linksys and D-Link routers on your network, you could rename your connections as Linksys Connection and D-Link Connection. Here are the steps to follow:

1. Open the Network Connections window, as described earlier.

2. Click the icon of the network connection you want to rename.

3. Click Rename This Connection in the taskbar, or press F2. Vista adds a text box around the connection name.

4. Type the new name and press Enter. The Use Account Control dialog box appears.

5. Enter your *User Account Control* (UAC) credentials to continue.

note You use the same rules for naming network connections as you use for naming files. That is, the maximum name length is about 255 characters, and you can include any letter, number, or symbol except the following: * | \ : " < > / and ?.

Enabling Automatic IP Addressing

note The instructions in this section work for both wired and wireless connections.

Every computer on your network requires a unique designation so that packets can be routed to the correct location when information is transferred across the network. In a default Microsoft peer-to-peer network, the network protocol that handles these transfers is *Transfer Control Protocol / Internet Protocol* (TCP/IP), and the unique designation assigned to each computer is the IP address.

By default, Windows Vista computers obtain their IP addresses via the *Dynamic Host Configuration Protocol* (DHCP). In Chapter 3, "Configuring Your Router," you learned how to turn on your router's DHCP server, which the router uses to provide each network computer at logon with an IP address from a range of addresses.

→ **See** "Enabling the DHCP Server," **p. 81.**

However, activating the router's DHCP server is only the first step toward automating the assignment of IP addresses on your network. The second step is to make sure that each of your Vista machines is configured to accept automatic IP addressing. This feature is turned on by default in most Windows Vista installations, but it's worth checking, just to be sure.

Confirming That Windows Vista Is Configured for Dynamic IP Addressing

Here are the steps to follow to check (and, if necessary, change) Vista's automatic IP addressing setting:

1. Open the Network Connections window, as described earlier.

2. Select the connection you want to work with.

3. In the taskbar, click Change Settings of This Connection. The User Account Control dialog box appears.

4. Enter your UAC credentials to continue. Vista display's the connection's Properties dialog box.

5. In the Networking tab's list of items, select Internet Protocol Version 4 (TCP/IPv4).

tip If you don't see the Change Settings of This Connection command, either maximize the window or click the double arrow (>>) that appears on the right side of the task bar to display the commands that won't fit. Note, too, that you can also right-click the connection and then click Properties.

6

6. Click Properties to display the Properties dialog box for Internet Protocol Version 4.

7. Select the Obtain an IP Address Automatically option, as shown in Figure 6.2.

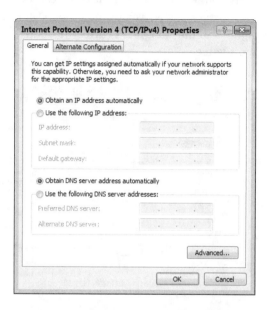

FIGURE 6.2

Select the Obtain an IP Address Automatically option to configure Vista to accept the dynamic IP addresses assigned by your network's router.

8. Select the Obtain DNS Server Address Automatically option.

9. Click OK to return to the connection's Properties dialog box.

10. Click Close.

11. Repeat steps 2 through 10 for your other network connections.

Displaying the Computer's Current IP Address

There may be times when you need to know the current IP address assigned to your Vista machine. For example, one networking troubleshooting process is to see whether you can contact a computer over the connection, a process known as *pinging* the computer (because you use Vista's PING command). In some cases, you need to know the computer's IP address for this method to work.

→   For the details on using PING as a troubleshooting tool, **see** "Checking Connectivity with the PING Command," **p. 419**.

To find out the current IP address of the Windows Vista machine, use any of the following methods:

- In the Network Connections window, click the network icon, click the taskbar's View Status of This Connection command (or double-click the network connection) to open the connection's Status dialog box. Click Details to open the Network Connection Details dialog box. As shown in Figure 6.3, the computer's current IP address appears as the IPv4 IP Address value.

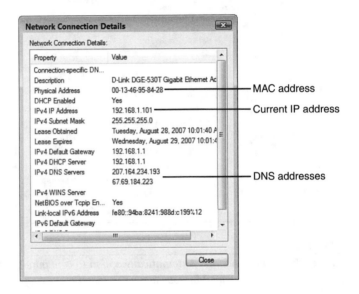

FIGURE 6.3

In the network connection's Status dialog box, the IPv4 IP Address value displays the Vista computer's current IP address.

- Select Start, All Programs, Accessories, Command Prompt to open a command-line window. At the prompt, type **ipconfig ¦ more** and press Enter. Vista displays information about each network connection, including the IP address associated with each connection, as shown in the following (partial) example output:

note I've added the MORE command here to control the output of the IPCONFIG results. Vista displays a screenful of data, then displays — More — at the bottom of the screen. Press Enter to scroll through the rest of the results one line at a time, or press Space-bar to see the results one screen at a time.

```
Windows IP Configuration


Ethernet adapter Local Area Connection 2:

   Connection-specific DNS Suffix  . :
   Link-local IPv6 Address . . . . . : fe80::94ba:8241:988d:c199%12
   IPv4 Address. . . . . . . . . . . : 192.168.1.101
   Subnet Mask . . . . . . . . . . . : 255.255.255.0
   Default Gateway . . . . . . . . . : 192.168.1.1

Wireless LAN adapter Wireless Network Connection:

   Connection-specific DNS Suffix  . :
   Link-local IPv6 Address . . . . . : fe80::130:2a68:fde5:d668%8
   IPv4 Address. . . . . . . . . . . : 192.168.1.105
   Subnet Mask . . . . . . . . . . . : 255.255.255.0
   Default Gateway . . . . . . . . . : 192.168.1.1
```

Setting Up a Static IP Address

Your router's DHCP server offers each client a lease on the IP address, and in most cases that lease expires after 24 hours. When the expiration time approaches, the client asks for a new IP address. In small networks, the DHCP server often assigns each client the same IP address each time, but that's not guaranteed. Because when you're working with Vista you rarely need to know a connection's IP address, however, a changing IP address is no big deal the vast majority of the time.

However, there are times when a constantly changing IP address can be a big problem. For example, when you learn how to turn a Windows Vista machine into a lightweight web server in Chapter 19, "Setting Up a Website," you see that a dynamic IP address makes it much harder for people to find and use the website. You can fix this problem by assigning a static IP address to a network connection.

tip Instead of assigning a static IP address to the Vista computer, you might be able to get your router to handle this for you. Log on to your router's configuration pages and look for an option that enables you to map a static IP address to the computer MAC (see "Finding a Connection's MAC Address," later in this chapter) address. This means that whenever the computer requests a new DHCP lease, the router supplies the computer the same IP address each time. Note that not all routers offer this option.

note The instructions in this section work for both wired and wireless connections.

Displaying the Current DNS Addresses

When you use a dynamic IP address, in most cases you also use dynamic DNS (*domain name system*) addresses, which are supplied by your *Internet service provider* (ISP). (The DNS enables computers and servers connected to the Internet to find resources using domain names rather than IP addresses.) When you switch your Vista computer to a static IP address (as shown in the next section), Vista also disables the feature that allows Vista to obtain DNS addresses automatically. In other words, when you specify a static IP address, you must also specify static DNS addresses.

note Remember that when using MORE, you control the output of the results by either pressing Enter (to scroll through the results one line at a time) or press Spacebar (to see the results one screen at a time).

Therefore, before performing the procedure for converting Vista to a static IP address, you need to determine your ISP's current DNS addresses. To find out the current DNS addresses for a network connection, use either of the following methods:

- In the Network Connections window, click the icon of the connection you want to work with, click the taskbar's View Status of This Connection command (or double-click the network connection) to open the connection's Status dialog box. Click Details to open the Network Connection Details dialog box. As shown earlier in Figure 6.3, the current DNS addresses appear as the IPv4 DNS Servers values.

- Select Start, All Programs, Accessories, Command Prompt to open a command-line window. At the prompt, type `ipconfig /all ¦ more` and press Enter. Vista displays information about each network connection, including the IP addresses of your ISP's DNS servers, as shown in the following (partial) example output:

```
Windows IP Configuration

    Host Name . . . . . . . . . . . . : OfficePC
    Primary Dns Suffix  . . . . . . . :
    Node Type . . . . . . . . . . . . : Hybrid
    IP Routing Enabled. . . . . . . . : No
    WINS Proxy Enabled. . . . . . . . : No
```

6

```
Ethernet adapter Local Area Connection 2:

    Connection-specific DNS Suffix  . :
    Description . . . . . . . . . . . : D-Link DGE-530T Gigabit Ethernet Adapter
    Physical Address. . . . . . . . . : 00-13-46-95-84-28
    DHCP Enabled. . . . . . . . . . . : Yes
    Autoconfiguration Enabled . . . . : Yes
    Link-local IPv6 Address . . . . . : fe80::94ba:8241:988d:c199%12(Preferred)
    IPv4 Address. . . . . . . . . . . : 192.168.1.101(Preferred)
    Subnet Mask . . . . . . . . . . . : 255.255.255.0
    Lease Obtained. . . . . . . . . . : Tuesday, August 28, 2007 10:01:41 AM
    Lease Expires . . . . . . . . . . : Wednesday, August 29, 2007 10:01:40 AM
    Default Gateway . . . . . . . . . : 192.168.1.1
    DHCP Server . . . . . . . . . . . : 192.168.1.1
    DHCPv6 IAID . . . . . . . . . . . : 301994822
    DNS Servers . . . . . . . . . . . : 207.164.234.193
                                        67.69.184.223
    NetBIOS over Tcpip. . . . . . . . : Enabled
```

Specifying the Static IP Address

You're now just about ready to assign a static IP address to your Vista computer. The last bit of information you need to know is the IP address to use. This is important because you don't want to use an address that your router has already assigned to another computer. The easiest way to do this is to choose an address outside of the DHCP server's range. For example, if you configured the DHCP server to assign addresses from the range 192.168.1.100 to 192.168.1.150, an address such as 192.168.1.50 or 192.168.1.200 will work. (Remember, too, not to use the address assigned to your router.)

With an IP address in hand, follow these steps to assign it to a network connection in Windows Vista:

1. Open the Network Connections window, as described earlier.
2. Select the connection you want to work with.
3. In the taskbar, click Change Settings of This Connection. (You can also

> **tip** It's probably a good idea to check your router's DHCP table to see which addresses it has assigned. I showed you how to do this in Chapter 3.

right-click the connection and then click Properties.) The User Account Control dialog box appears.

4. Enter your UAC credentials to continue. Vista display's the connection's Properties dialog box.

5. In the Networking tab's list of items, select Internet Protocol Version 4 (TCP/IPv4).

6. Click Properties to display the Properties dialog box for Internet Protocol Version 4.

7. Click to activate the Use the Following IP Address option.

8. Use the IP Address box to type the IP address you want to use.

9. Use the Subnet Mask box to type the IP addresses for the subnet mask. (Windows Vista should fill this in for you automatically; the most common value is 255.255.255.0.)

10. Use the Default Gateway box to type the IP address of your network's router.

11. Use the Preferred DNS Server and Alternate DNS Server boxes to type the IP addresses of your ISP's DNS servers. Figure 6.4 shows a completed version of the dialog box.

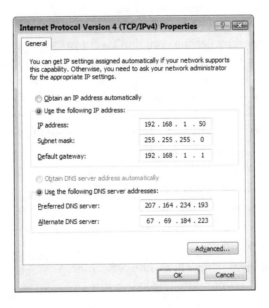

FIGURE 6.4

You can assign a static IP address to a network connection on a Windows Vista computer.

12. Click OK to return to the connection's Properties dialog box.

13. Click Close.

Finding a Connection's MAC Address

A NIC's MAC address seems like a pretty obscure value, but you'd be surprised how often it comes up. Here are two instances in this book:

> **note** The instructions in this section work for both wired and wireless connections.

- Later in this chapter, I show you how to wake up a remote computer that's in Vista's Sleep mode, and the utility I mention requires the MAC address of a NIC on the remote computer.

- In Chapter 15, "Implementing Wireless Security," you learn that you can use wireless NIC MAC addresses to beef up the security of your wireless network.

→ **See** "Enabling MAC Address Filtering," **p. 356**.

To find out the MAC address of the NIC associated with a network connection, use either of the following methods:

- In the Network Connections window, click the icon of the connection you want to work with, click the taskbar's View Status of This Connection command (or double-click the network connection) to open the connection's Status dialog box. Click Details to open the Network Connection Details dialog box. As shown earlier in Figure 6.3, the connection's MAC address appears as the Physical Address value.

- Select Start, All Programs, Accessories, Command Prompt to open a command-line window. At the prompt, type `ipconfig /all ¦ more` and press Enter. Vista displays information about each network connection, including the MAC addresses, as shown in the following (partial) example output (see the Physical Address value):

```
Windows IP Configuration

   Host Name . . . . . . . . . . . . : OfficePC
   Primary Dns Suffix  . . . . . . . :
   Node Type . . . . . . . . . . . . : Hybrid
```

6

```
   IP Routing Enabled. . . . . . . . : No
   WINS Proxy Enabled. . . . . . . . : No

Ethernet adapter Local Area Connection 2:

   Connection-specific DNS Suffix  . :
   Description . . . . . . . . . . . : D-Link DGE-530T Gigabit Ethernet Adapter
   Physical Address. . . . . . . . . : 00-13-46-95-84-28
   DHCP Enabled. . . . . . . . . . . : Yes
   Autoconfiguration Enabled . . . . : Yes
   Link-local IPv6 Address . . . . . : fe80::94ba:8241:988d:c199%12(Preferred)
   IPv4 Address. . . . . . . . . . . : 192.168.1.101(Preferred)
   Subnet Mask . . . . . . . . . . . : 255.255.255.0
   Lease Obtained. . . . . . . . . . : Tuesday, August 28, 2007 10:01:41 AM
   Lease Expires . . . . . . . . . . : Wednesday, August 29, 2007 10:01:40 AM
   Default Gateway . . . . . . . . . : 192.168.1.1
   DHCP Server . . . . . . . . . . . : 192.168.1.1
   DHCPv6 IAID . . . . . . . . . . . : 301994822
   DNS Servers . . . . . . . . . . . : 207.164.234.193
                                       67.69.184.223
   NetBIOS over Tcpip. . . . . . . . : Enabled

Wireless LAN adapter Wireless Network Connection:

   Connection-specific DNS Suffix  . :
   Description . . . . . . . . . . . : D-Link AirPremier DWL-AG530 Wireless PCI
Adapter
   Physical Address. . . . . . . . . : 00-11-95-F5-BC-96
   DHCP Enabled. . . . . . . . . . . : Yes
   Autoconfiguration Enabled . . . . : Yes
   Link-local IPv6 Address . . . . . : fe80::130:2a68:fde5:d668%8(Preferred)
   IPv4 Address. . . . . . . . . . . : 192.168.1.105(Preferred)
   Subnet Mask . . . . . . . . . . . : 255.255.255.0
   Lease Obtained. . . . . . . . . . : Tuesday, August 28, 2007 10:02:08 AM
   Lease Expires . . . . . . . . . . : Wednesday, August 29, 2007 10:02:06 AM
   Default Gateway . . . . . . . . . : 192.168.1.1
   DHCP Server . . . . . . . . . . . : 192.168.1.1
```

6

```
DHCPv6 IAID . . . . . . . . . . . : 134222229
DNS Servers . . . . . . . . . . . : 207.164.234.193
                                    67.69.184.223
NetBIOS over Tcpip. . . . . . . . : Enabled
```

Using a Network Connection to Wake Up a Sleeping Computer

Most Windows Vista computers are configured to go into Sleep mode after a certain amount of idle time. Sleep mode is the new low-power state that Vista uses to replace the confusing Standby and Hibernate modes from earlier versions of Windows. (Standby mode preserved your work and enabled you to restart quickly, but didn't entirely shut off the machine's power; Hibernate mode preserved your work and completely shut off the machine, but also took a relatively long time to restart—faster than shutting down your computer entirely, but slower than Standby.)

Vista's Sleep state combines the best of the old Standby and Hibernate modes:

- As in Standby, you enter Sleep mode within just a few seconds.

- As in both Standby and Hibernate, Sleep mode preserves all your open documents, windows, and programs.

- As in Hibernate, Sleep mode shuts down your computer, except it maintains power to the memory chips so that it can preserve the contents of RAM for when you restart.

- As in Standby, you resume from Sleep mode within just a few seconds.

To use Sleep mode, you have two choices:

- To launch Sleep mode by hand, open the Start menu and click the Sleep button, shown in Figure 6.5. (You can also click the arrow beside the Lock button and then click Sleep.) Vista saves the current state and shuts off the computer in a few seconds.

- To configure Vista to go into Sleep mode automatically, select Start, Control Panel, System and Maintenance, Power Options. In the Power Options window, click the Change Plan Settings link under the currently selected power plan. Use the Put the Computer to Sleep list to select the number of minutes or hours of idle time after which Vista automatically puts the computer to sleep (see Figure 6.6). Click Save Changes.

Sleep button   Lock button

FIGURE 6.5

Click the Sleep button to quickly shut down your computer and save your work.

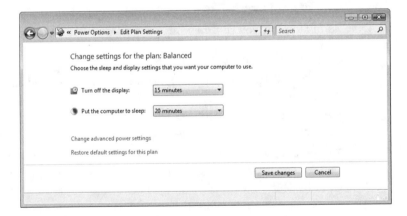

FIGURE 6.6

You can configure Vista to put the computer to sleep after a certain number of minutes or hours of idle time.

Having a computer go to sleep when you're not using it is a good idea because it conserves power. However, it can be a pain if you need to access the computer remotely over your network because you have no way to wake up the sleeping computer (which normally requires a physical action such as jiggling the mouse or pressing the computer's power button).

Fortunately, most new NICs support a feature called *wake-on-LAN*, which enables the NIC to wake up the computer when the NIC receives a special ethernet packet called a *magic packet* (usually the hexadecimal constant FF FF FF FF FF FF followed by several repetitions of the computer's MAC address) .

note If the Allow This Device to Wake the Computer check box is disabled, it probably means your NIC doesn't support wake-on-LAN. However, it may also mean that this support has been disabled. In the NIC's Properties dialog box, display the Advanced tab and look for a property named Wake Up Capabilities. Click this property, and then choose On in the Value list. Click OK to put the new setting into effect, and then retry the steps in this section.

For this to work, you must first configure the NIC to handle wake-on-LAN. Here are the steps to follow:

1. In the Network Connections window, right-click the connection that uses the NIC you want to configure, and then click Properties. The User Account Control dialog box appears.

2. Enter your UAC credentials to continue. The connection's Properties dialog box appears.

3. In the Networking tab, click Configure to open the NIC's Properties dialog box.

4. Display the Power Management tab.

5. Click to activate the Allow This Device to Wake the Computer check box (see Figure 6.7).

6. Click OK.

tip When you use the wake-on-LAN feature, you probably don't want the remote computer to wake to the Vista Welcome screen. Instead, it's almost always better to have the computer wake directly to the desktop. To disable the password requirement on wakeup, select Start, Control Panel, System and Maintenance, Power Options. In the Power Options window, click the Require a Password on Wakeup link to open the System Settings window. Click Change Settings That Are Currently Unavailable, and then enter your UAC credentials. Activate the Don't Require a Password option, and then click Save Changes.

With the computer's NIC configured, you need to download a utility that can send a magic packet to the remote computer whenever you need to wake up the

6

machine. I use MatCode Software's free Wake-on-LAN utility, available at www.matcode.com/wol.htm. (This utility requires the NIC's MAC address; see "Finding a Connection's MAC Address," earlier in this chapter.) You can also try Googling "wake-on-lan utility".

FIGURE 6.7
To turn on a NIC's wake-on-LAN support, activate the Allow This Device to Wake the Computer check box.

Disabling a Network Connection

It's possible that your Vista computer has a network connection that it doesn't use. For example, if you upgraded to a Gigabit Ethernet NIC, you may no longer use your machine's old Fast Ethernet motherboard NIC. You can't detach a motherboard NIC from your computer (not easily, anyway), so the network connection icon remains, cluttering the Network Connections window and using up a few Windows Vista resources. If you don't plan on using such a connection, you're better off disabling it by following these steps:

1. In the Network Connections window, click the connection you want to work with, and then click the taskbar's Disable This Network Device command. (You can also right-click the connection and then click Disable.) The User Account Control dialog box appears.

2. Enter your UAC credentials to continue.

As shown in Figure 6.8, Vista changes the connection's status to Disabled. If you want to use the connection again later on, click it, and then click the taskbar's Enable This Network Device command.

Disabled connection ———

FIGURE 6.8
You can disable a network connection that you no longer use.

From Here

- For information about how to turn on the DHCP server for various routers, **see** "Enabling the DHCP Server," **p. 81**.

- To learn more about wireless connections, **see** Chapter 7, "Managing Wireless Network Connections," **p. 157**.

- To learn how to enable sharing, **see** "Sharing Resources with the Network," **p. 184**.

- To learn how to use wireless NIC MAC addresses to beef up the security of your wireless network, **see** "Enabling MAC Address Filtering," **p. 356**.

- For the details on using PING as a troubleshooting tool, **see** "Checking Connectivity with the PING Command," **p. 419**.

6

Managing Wireless Network Connections

Most small networks use just a single wireless connection—the connection to your network's wireless access point. However, it's no longer unusual to have multiple wireless networks configured on your computer. For example, you might have two or more wireless gateways in your home or office; you might have a wireless hot spot nearby; and as you see in this chapter, Windows Vista also enables you to set up computer-to-computer wireless connections to share files or an Internet connection without going through a wireless access point.

Vista comes with a Manage Wireless Networks feature that lists your saved wireless networks and enables you to add new wireless connections, reorder the connections, and remove existing connections. This chapter shows you how to perform these and other wireless networking tasks.

IN THIS CHAPTER

- Opening the Manage Wireless Networks Window

- Making Other Wireless Connections

- Working with Wireless Connection Properties

- Renaming Wireless Connections

- Reordering Wireless Connections

- Creating User-Specific Wireless Connections

- Removing Wireless Connections

- From Here

Opening the Manage Wireless Networks Window

Most of the chores in this chapter take place in Vista's Manage Wireless Networks window. To get this window onscreen, open the Network and Sharing Center, and then click the Manage Wireless Networks link in the Tasks list. Figure 7.1 shows the Manage Wireless Networks window with a couple of networks displayed.

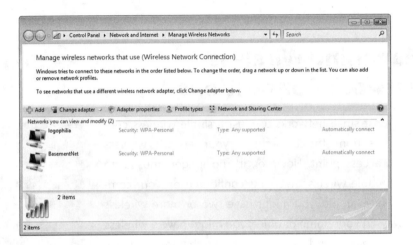

FIGURE 7.1
Windows Vista's Manage Wireless Networks window.

By default, Vista groups the wireless networks using the Extended Tiles view, and you can't change this view. The networks are listed in the order that Vista uses to attempt connections (more on this later; see "Reordering Wireless Connections"). If your computer comes with multiple wireless *network interface cards* (NICs) and you use those NICs to create separate connections, you can switch from one NIC to another by pulling down the Change Adapter list and selecting the NIC you want to work with.

Making Other Wireless Connections

In Chapter 4, "Putting Your Network Together," you learned how to make a standard connection to a wireless network. However, Windows Vista also enables you to make two other wireless connections: to a hidden

7

(nonbroadcasting) wireless network and to an ad hoc (computer-to-computer) wireless network. The next two sections provide the details.

→   For the steps required to connect to a standard wireless network, **see** "Making Wireless Network Connections," **p. 113**.

Connecting to a Hidden Network

Each wireless network has a network name: the *service set identifier*, or SSID. The SSID identifies the network to wireless devices and computers with wireless network cards. By default, most wireless networks broadcast the network name so that you can see the network and connect to it. However, some wireless networks disable network name broadcasting as a security precaution. The idea is that if unauthorized users can't see the network, they can't attempt to connect to it.

→   For more information about turning off network name broadcasting, **see** "Disabling Network SSID Broadcasting," **p. 347**.

However, you can still connect to a hidden wireless network by entering the connection settings by hand. You need to know the network name, the network's security type and encryption type, and the network's security key or passphrase. Here are the steps to follow:

1. Open the Manage Wireless Networks window, as described earlier.

2. Click Add. Vista displays the How Do You Want to Add a Network? dialog box.

3. Click Add a Network That Is in Range of This Computer. Vista displays the Select a Network to Connect To dialog box.

4. Click the Set Up a Connection or Network link. The Choose a Connection Option dialog box appears.

5. Select Manually Connect to a Wireless Network, and then click Next. Vista prompts you for the network connection data, as shown in Figure 7.2 (which shows a completed version of the dialog box).

> **tip** You can combine steps 1 through 3 into a single step by selecting Start, Connect To.

7

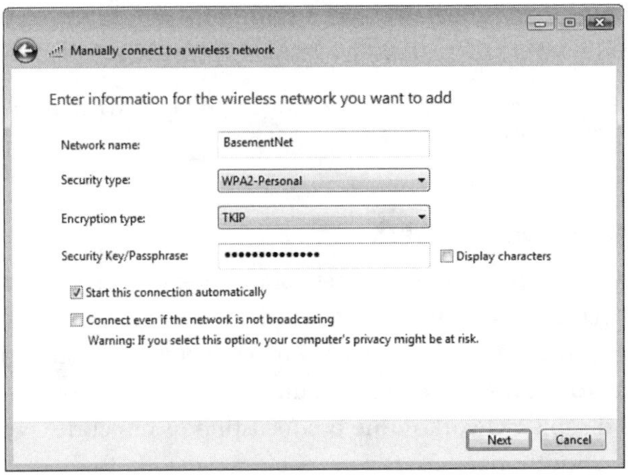

FIGURE 7.2
Use this dialog box to specify the connection settings for the hidden wireless network.

6. Provide the following connection data:

   Network Name. The SSID of the hidden wireless network.

   Security Type. The security protocol used by the wireless network. Select No Authentication (Open) if the network is unsecured.

   Encryption Type. The method of encryption used by the wireless network's security protocol.

   Security Key/Passphrase. The key or password required for authorized access to the network.

   Start This Connection Automatically. Leave this check box activated to have Vista connect to the network now (that is, when you click Next in step 7) and automatically the next time the network comes within range. If you always want to connect to the network manually, deactivate this option.

   Connect Even If the Network Is Not Broadcasting. If you activate this check box, Vista will send probe requests to see whether the network is in range even if the network isn't broadcasting its SSID. Note, however, that this lessens security (because the SSID is sent in plain text in the probe request; see Chapter 15 for more information), so you should leave this check box deactivated.

7. Click Next. Vista connects to the network and adds it to the list of wireless networks.

8. Click Close.

Creating an Ad Hoc Wireless Network

If you don't have a wireless access point, Vista enables you to set up a temporary network between two or more computers. This is an *ad hoc connection*, and it's useful if you need to share folders, devices, or an Internet connection temporarily. Note that the computers must be within 30 feet of each other for this type of connection to work.

note Another way to begin the process of creating an ad hoc wireless network is to select Start, Connect To, click the Set Up a Connection or Network link to open the Choose a Connection Option dialog box, select Set Up a Wireless Ad Hoc (Computer-to-Computer) Network, and then click Next.

Here are the steps to follow to create an ad hoc wireless network:

1. Open the Manage Wireless Networks window, as described earlier.

2. Click Add. Vista displays the How Do You Want to Add a Network? dialog box.

3. Click Create an Ad Hoc Network. Vista displays the Set Up a Wireless Ad Hoc Network dialog box.

4. Click Next.

5. Provide the following data to set up the network (see Figure 7.3):

   Network Name. The name of the ad hoc network.

   Security Type. The security protocol used by the ad hoc wireless network. Select No Authentication (Open) if you want the network to be unsecured.

   Security Key/Passphrase. Type the key or password required for authorized access to the ad hoc network.

   Save This Network. Activate this check box to save the network in the Manage Wireless Networks list.

6. Click Next. Vista sets up the ad hoc network.

7. If you want to share your computer's Internet connection, click Turn on Internet Connection Sharing.

8. Click Close. Windows Vista adds the ad hoc network to your list of networks in the Manage Wireless Networks window, as shown in Figure 7.4.

7

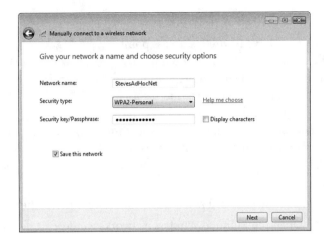

FIGURE 7.3

Use this dialog box to configure your ad hoc network's name and security type.

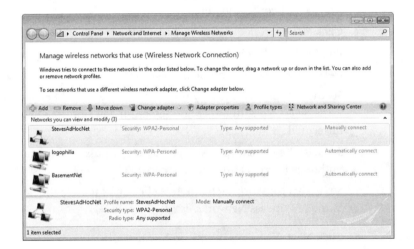

FIGURE 7.4

The new ad hoc network appears in the Manage Wireless Networks window.

Now, other people within 30 feet of your computer will see your ad hoc network in their list of available wireless networks, as shown in Figure 7.5. Note that the network remains available as long as at least one computer is connected to it, including the computer that created the network. The network is discarded when all computers (including the machine that created the network) have disconnected from it.

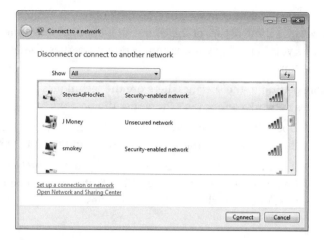

FIGURE 7.5
The ad hoc network is available to computers that are within 30 feet of the original computer.

Working with Wireless Connection Properties

When you connect to a wireless network, Windows Vista eases network management by doing two things:

■ If you tell Windows Vista to remember the network (by activating the Save This Network check box after the connection has been made), Vista stores the network in the Manage Wireless Networks window.

■ If you tell Vista to save the connection data (by activating the Start This Connection Automatically check box after the connection has been made), Vista initiates the connection as soon as it detects the network when you log on. (In the Manage Wireless Networks window, Vista displays the network's Mode value as Automatically Connect.)

These two features mean that, after running through the initial wireless network

> **tip** Connecting to a wireless network automatically is useful for those networks you use regularly. This applies to your home or office network, of course, but it may also be true of places you frequent, such as your local coffee shop or a hotel. However, if the network charges you for connection time, then it's usually a good idea to connect manually.

7

connection, you may never have to think about the connection again. However, if some aspect of the connection changes down the road, Vista enables you to modify various connection properties, as described in the next two sections.

Before getting to the specifics, here are the techniques you can use to open a wireless network connection's Properties dialog box:

- Open the Manage Wireless Networks window, as described earlier, and then double-click the wireless network you want to work with.

- If the wireless network connection appears in the Network and Sharing Center, click the connection's View Status link to open the Status dialog box, and then click Wireless Properties.

Modifying Connection Properties

In the wireless network connection's Properties dialog box, the Connection tab (see Figure 7.6) displays some basic information about the connection—the connection's local name, its SSID, the network type (Access Point or Ad Hoc Network), and the network availability (that is, which users can use the connection). You also get the following three check boxes:

- **Connect Automatically When This Network Is In Range.** Leave this check box activated to have Vista connect to the network automatically whenever the network comes within range. If you prefer to connect to the network manually, deactivate this check box.

- **Connect to a More Preferred Network If Available.** Leave this check box activated to have Vista automatically disconnect from this network if a network that is listed higher in the Manage Wireless Networks list comes within range. (See "Reordering Wireless Connections" for more information about preferred networks.)

- **Connect Even If the Network Is Not Broadcasting.** If you activate this check box, Vista checks to see whether the network is within range even if the network isn't broadcasting its SSID. Leave this check box deactivated to improve security (see Chapter 15 for the details).

7

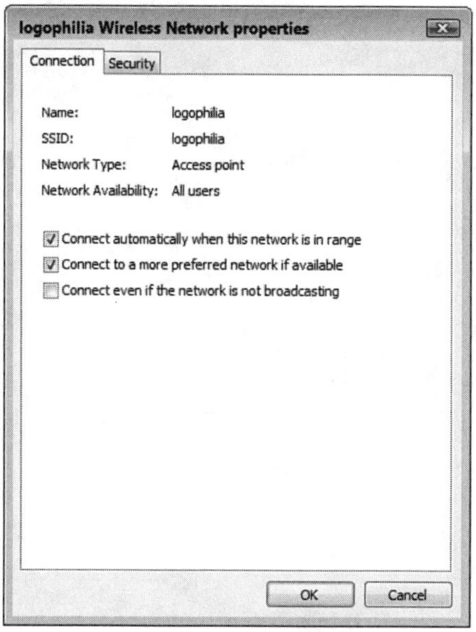

FIGURE 7.6

In the wireless network connection's Properties dialog box, the Connection tab enables you to configure a few connection-related properties.

Modifying Security Properties

After you make the initial connection to a wireless network, you may find that later on the network's security settings have changed. For example, an open network might decide to add encryption to improve security. Similarly, the person administering the network might upgrade to a more robust encryption setting or change the security key or password. You can adjust the security settings for an existing network using the settings in the Security tab of the wireless network connection's Properties dialog box. As shown in Figure 7.7, the Security tab offers the following controls:

Security Type   The security protocol used by the wireless network. Select No Authentication (Open) if the network is unsecured.

Encryption Type   The specific type of encryption used by the network's security protocol.

Network Security Key   The key or password required for authorized access to the network.

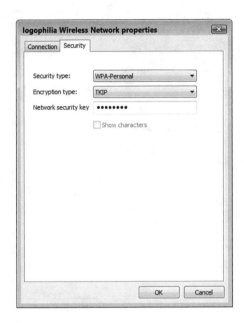

FIGURE 7.7

In the wireless network connection's Properties dialog box, the Security tab enables you to con-figure a few security-related properties.

→   For more information about securing wireless networks with encryption, **see** "Encrypting Wireless Signals with WPA," **p. 341**

Renaming Wireless Connections

By default, the local name that Windows Vista gives to a saved wireless network connection is the same as the network's SSID. Because SSIDs can sometimes be generic (for example, default is a common SSID on out-of-the-box access points) or obscure, you might want to change a network connection's local name to make it easier to work with. Here are the steps to follow to rename a connection:

1. Open the Manage Wireless Networks window, as described earlier.

2. Select the wireless network you want to rename.

> **note** Note that renaming the wireless network connection means that you're only changing the local connection name used by Windows Vista. The network's SSID is not affected.

3. Press F2. (You can also right-click the wireless network and then click Rename).

4. Type the new name for the wireless network connection.

5. Press Enter.

Reordering Wireless Connections

Windows Vista configures a wireless network with an automatic connection so that you can get on the network as soon as Vista detects it. (This is assuming that you activated the Start This Connection Automatically check box when you made the initial connection.) If you have multiple wireless networks, Windows Vista maintains a priority list, and a network higher in that list connects before a network lower in that list. (A network higher in the list is said to be a *more preferred* network.) If you are not connecting to the wireless network you want, it might be that the network is lower on the network priority list. To work around this problem, you can move the network higher in the list.

Vista's wireless network priority list is none other than the list of networks in the Manage Wireless Networks window. Here are the steps to follow to use the Manage Wireless Networks window to reorder your wireless networks:

1. Open the Manage Wireless Networks window, as described earlier.

2. Select the network you want to move.

3. As you can see in Figure 7.8, the taskbar offers either the Move Up or Move Down command, and you use these commands to prioritize the networks:

Move Up   Click this command to move the selected network to a higher priority. (You can also right-click the network and then click Move Up.)

Move Down   Click this command to move the selected network to a lower priority. (You can also right-click the network and then click Move Down.)

note You don't see both Move Up and Move Down for every network. For example, if you select the network with the highest priority (that is, the network at the top of the list), you only see the Move Down command. Similarly, if you select the network with the lowest priority (that is, the network at the bottom of the list), you only see the Move Up command.

7

Use these commands to reorder your networks

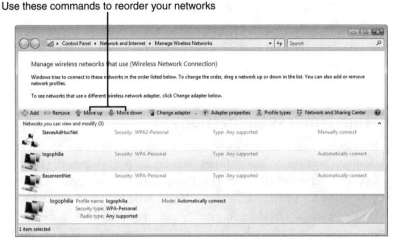

FIGURE 7.8

In the Manage Wireless Networks window, use the Move Up and Move Down commands to reorder your wireless networks.

Creating User-Specific Wireless Connections

By default, when you connect to a wireless network and then elect to save the network (by activating the Save This Network check box after the connection has been made), Windows Vista makes the wireless connection available to all users of the computer. (That is, Vista stores the wireless network connection in the computer's All Users profile, which is the profile that Vista uses to make objects available to every user account on the computer.) This is usually the best way to go because it means you only have to make the connection to the wireless network once, and then the connection is set up for every user account.

Sometimes, however, you might not want other users to have access to a particular wireless network connection. For example, your neighbor might allow you to use his wireless network, but only on the condition that your kids not use the network.

For these kinds of situations, Vista enables you to create user-specific wireless connections. This means that when a user connects to a wireless network, Vista enables that user to save the wireless network connection in the user's profile. The other users on the computer will not see the connection.

Here are the steps to follow to activate Vista's user-specific profiles (or *per-user profiles*, as Vista calls them) for wireless networks:

1. Open the Manage Wireless Networks window, as described earlier.

2. Select Profile Types in the taskbar. Vista displays the Wireless Network Profile Type dialog box.

3. Select the Use All-User and Per-User Profiles option, as shown in Figure 7.9.

FIGURE 7.9
Use this dialog box to activate per-user wireless network profiles.

4. Click Save. The User Account Control dialog box appears.

5. Enter your UAC credentials to put the new setting into effect.

Now, when a user creates a wireless network connection, Vista displays the dialog box shown in Figure 7.10, which gives the user three options:

- **Save This Network for All Users of This Computer.** The user selects this option to save the wireless network connection in the All Users profile, which means that every user account will have access to the wireless network.

- **Save This Network for Me Only.** The user selects this option to save the wireless network connection in the user's profile only. Other user accounts will not have access to the wireless network.

- **Don't Save This Network.** The user selects this option to bypass saving the network connection.

7

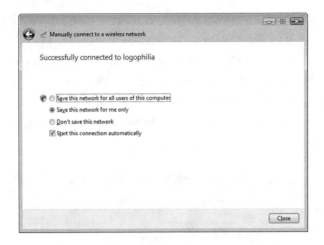

FIGURE 7.10
With per-user profiles activated, users can save wireless network connections in their own user profiles.

Removing Wireless Connections

If you no longer use a wireless network, or if an existing wireless network has changed and you'd like to create a fresh connection for it, you can remove the wireless network from the Manage Wireless Networks window. Here are the steps to follow:

1. Open the Manage Wireless Networks window, as described earlier.

2. Select the wireless network you want to remove.

3. Click Remove or press Delete. Vista warns you that you'll no longer be able to connect to the network automatically.

4. Click OK. Vista removes the wireless network.

From Here

- For the steps required to connect to a standard wireless network, **see** "Making Wireless Network Connections," **p. 113**.

- To learn more about wired connections, **see** Chapter 6, "Managing Network Connections," **p. 139**.

- For more information about securing wireless networks with encryption, **see** "Encrypting Wireless Signals with WPA," **p. 341**.

- For more information about turning off network name broadcasting, **see** "Disabling Network SSID Broadcasting," **p. 347**.

7

Accessing and Sharing Network Resources

IN THIS CHAPTER

■ Accessing Shared Network Resources

■ Mapping a Network Folder to a Local Drive Letter

■ Creating a Network Location for a Remote Folder

■ Accessing a Shared Printer

■ Sharing Resources with the Network

Many home and small office networks exist for no other reason than to share a broadband Internet connection. The administrators of those networks attach a broadband modem to a router, configure the router, run some ethernet cable (or set up wireless connections), and then they never think about the network again.

There's nothing wrong with this scenario, of course, but there's something that just feels, well, *incomplete* about such a network. Sharing an Internet connection is a must for any modern network, but networking should be about sharing so much more: disk drives, folders, documents, music, photos, videos, recorded TV shows, printers, scanners, CD and DVD burners, projectors, and more.

This expanded view of networking is about working, playing, and connecting with your fellow network users. It is, in short, about *sharing*, and sharing is the subject of this chapter. You learn how to access those network resources that others have shared, and you learn how to share your own resources with the network.

Accessing Shared Network Resources

After you connect to the network, the first thing you'll likely want to do is see what's on the network and access the available resources. Vista gives you two ways to get started:

- Select Start, Network.
- In the Network and Sharing Center, click View Network Computers and Devices.

Either way, you see the Network window, which lists the main network resources, such as the computers and media devices in your workgroup. As you can see in Figure 8.1, Details view shows you the resource name, category, workgroup or domain name, and the name of the network profile.

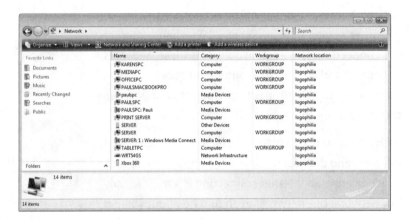

FIGURE 8.1

Vista's Network window displays the main resources on your network.

→ For a more detailed look at the types of items you see in the Network window, **see** "Viewing Network Computers and Devices," **p. 130.**

Viewing a Computer's Shared Resources

Your Network window will likely show mostly computers, and those are the network items you'll work with most often. (The computers display an icon that shows a monitor and mini tower computer; if you're not sure, select View, Details and look for the objects that have Computer in the Category column.) If you don't see a particular computer, it likely means that the machine is either turned off or is currently in Sleep mode. You need to either turn on or wake up the computer.

→ You may be able to remotely wake up a computer that's in Sleep mode; **see** "Using a Network Connection to Wake Up a Sleeping Computer," **p. 151**.

If you see the computer you want to work with, double-click the computer's icon. One of two things will happen:

■ If your user account is also a user account on the remote computer, Windows Vista displays the computer's shared resources.

■ If your user account is not a user account on the remote computer, and the remote computer has activated password protected sharing (see "Using Password Protected Sharing," later in this chapter), Windows Vista displays the Connect to *Computer* dialog box (where *Computer* is the name of the remote computer). You need to type the username and password of an account on the remote computer, as shown in Figure 8.2.

FIGURE 8.2

You may need to log on to the remote computer to see its shared resources.

Figure 8.3 shows a typical collection of shared resources for a computer.

The computer shown in Figure 8.3 is sharing a folder named Data, two hard drives (Drive D and Drive G), a DVD drive, and a printer. The computer is also sharing two folders that that many Vista computers automatically share:

Public   This folder is open to everyone on the network and usually provides users with full read/write access. However, it's also possible to protect this folder by giving users read-only access, or by not displaying the Public folder at all. See "Sharing the Public Folder," later in this chapter.

FIGURE 8.3

Double-click a network computer to see its shared resources.

Printers   This folder contains the computer's installed printers. Vista usually places an icon for each shared printer in the computer's main folder, too. You can control whether Vista displays the Printers folder; see "Activating Printer Folder Sharing," later in this chapter.

Double-click a shared folder to see its contents. For example, Figure 8.4 displays the partial contents of the Data folder shown earlier in Figure 8.3. What you can do with the shared folder's contents depends on the permissions the computer owner has applied to the folder. See "Sharing a Resource with the File Sharing Wizard" and "Sharing a Resource with Advanced Permissions," later in this chapter.

Working with Network Addresses

In Figure 8.4, the Address bar shows the breadcrumb path to the shared folder:

Network > PAULSPC > Data

caution Double-clicking a network computer to see its shared resources works because the default action (which you initiate by double-clicking) for a network computer is to run the Open command, which opens the computer's shared resources in a folder window. However, not all the devices you see in the Network window have Open as the default action. For example, with media devices, the default action is either Open Media Player or Open Media Sharing. Other devices have more dangerous default actions. On some routers, for example, the default action is Disable, which disconnects the router's Internet connection! So, instead of just double-clicking any device to see what happens, it's better to right-click the device and examine the list of commands. In particular, make note of the command shown in bold type, which is the default action.

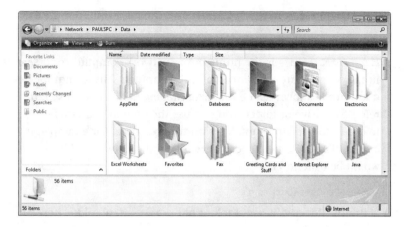

FIGURE 8.4

Double-click a shared folder to see its contents.

Clicking an empty section of the Address bar (or the icon that appears on the left side of the Address bar) changes the breadcrumb path to the following network address, as shown in Figure 8.5:

\\PAULSPC\Data

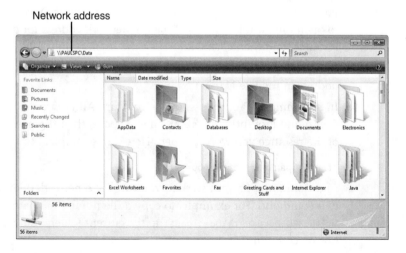

FIGURE 8.5

Click an empty section of the Address bar to see the network address.

8

As you can see, a network address uses the following format:

`\\ComputerName\ShareName`

Here, `ComputerName` is the name of the network computer, and `ShareName` is the name of the shared resource on that computer. This format for network addresses is known as the *Universal Naming Convention* (UNC). If the UNC refers to a drive or folder, you can use the regular Windows path conventions to access folders and subfolders on that resource. For example, if the resource `Data` on PAULSPC has a `Documents` folder, the network address of that folder would be as follows:

`\\PAULSPC\Data\Documents`

Similarly, if that `Documents` folder has a `Writing` subfolder, here's the network address of that subfolder:

`\\PAULSPC\Data\Documents\Writing`

So, although you'll most often use icons in folder windows to navigate through a computer's shared resources, network addresses give you an alternative way to specify the resource you want to work with. Here are some examples:

- In the Network Explorer, click an empty section of the Address bar, type the network address for a shared resource, and then press Enter.
- Press Windows Logo+R (or select Start, All Programs, Accessories, Run) to open the Run dialog box. Type the network address for a shared resource, and then click OK to open the resource in a folder window.
- In a program's Open or Save As dialog box, you can type a network address in the File Name text box.
- In a Command Prompt session (select Start, All Programs, Accessories, Command Prompt), type **start**, then a space, then the network address of the resource you want to open. Here's an example:

  `start \\paulspc\data\documents`

- In a Command Prompt session, you can use a network address as part of a command. For example, to copy a file named `memo.doc` from `\\PAULSPC\Documents\Downloads\` to the current folder, you'd use the following command:

  `copy "\\paulspc\data\documents\memo.doc"`

Mapping a Network Folder to a Local Drive Letter

Navigating a computer's shared folders is straightforward, and is no different from navigating the folders on your own computer. However, you might find that you need to access a particular folder on a shared resource quite often. That's not a problem if the folder is shared directly—see, for example, the shared Data folder in Figure 8.3. However, the folder you want might be buried several layers down. For example, you may need to open the Data folder, then the Documents folder, then Writing, then Articles, and so on. That's a lot of double-clicking. You could use the network address, instead, but even that could get quite long and unwieldy. (And, with Murphy's law still in force, the longer the address, the greater the chance of a typo slipping in.)

note You might also find that mapping a network folder to a local drive letter helps with some older programs that aren't meant to operate over a network connection. For example, I have a screen-capture program that I need to use from time to time. If I capture a screen on another computer and then try to save the image over the network to my own computer, the program throws up an error message telling me that the destination drive is out of disk space (despite having, in fact, 100GB or so of free space on the drive). I solve this problem by mapping the folder on my computer to a drive letter on the other computer, which fools the program into thinking it's dealing with a local drive instead of a network folder.

You can avoid the hassle of navigating innumerable network folders and typing lengthy network addresses by *mapping* the network folder to your own computer. Mapping means that Windows assigns a drive letter to the network folder, such as G: or Z:. The advantage here is that now the network folder shows up as just another disk drive on your machine, enabling you to access the resource quickly by selecting Start, Computer.

Creating the Mapped Network Folder

To map a network folder to a local drive letter, follow these steps:

1. Select Start, right-click Network, and then click Map Network Drive. (In any folder window, you can also press Alt to display the menu bar, and then select Tools, Map Network Drive.) Windows Vista displays the Map Network Drive dialog box.

caution If you use a removable drive, such as a memory card or flash drive, Windows Vista assigns the first available drive letter to that drive. This can cause problems if you have a mapped network drive that uses a lower drive letter. Therefore, it's good practice to use higher drive letters (such as *X*, *Y*, and *Z*) for your mapped resources.

2. The Drive drop-down list displays the last available drive letter on your system, but you can pull down the list and select any available letter.

3. Use the Folder text box to type the network address of the folder, as shown in Figure 8.6. (Alternatively, click Browse, select the shared folder in the Browse for Folder dialog box, and then click OK.)

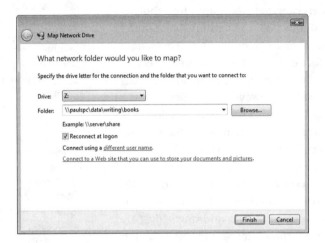

FIGURE 8.6
Use the Map Network Drive dialog box to assign a drive letter to a network resource.

4. If you want Windows Vista to map the network folder to this drive letter each time you log on to the system, leave the Reconnect at Logon check box activated.

5. Click Finish. Windows Vista adds the new drive letter to your system and opens the new drive in a folder window.

To open the mapped network folder later, select Start, Computer, and then double-click the drive in the Network Location group (see Figure 8.7).

> **tip** By default, Vista connects you to the network folder using your current username and password. If the network folder requires a different username and password, click the Different User Name link to open the Connect As dialog box. Type the account data in the User Name and Password text boxes, and then click OK.

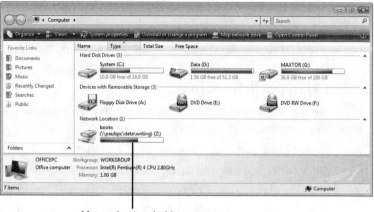

Mapped network drive

FIGURE 8.7

After you map a network folder to a local drive letter, the mapped drive appears in the Computer window for easier access.

Mapping Folders at the Command Line

You can also map a network folder to a local drive letter by using a command prompt session and the NET USE command. Although you probably won't use this method very often, it's handy to know how it works, just in case. Here's the basic syntax:

```
NET USE [drive] [share] [password] [/USER:user]
➥[/PERSISTENT:[YES ¦ NO]] ¦ /DELETE]
```

drive	The drive letter (followed by a colon) of the local drive to which you want the network folder mapped.
share	The network address of the folder.
password	The password required to connect to the shared folder (that is, the password associated with the username, specified next).
/USER:*user*	The username you want to use to connect to the shared folder.
/PERSISTENT:	Add YES to reconnect the mapped network drive the next time you log on.
/DELETE	Deletes the existing mapping that's associated with *drive*.

For example, the following command maps the shared folder \\PAULSPC\Data\Writing\Books to the Z: drive:

```
net use z: \\paulspc\data\writing\books \persistent:yes
```

Disconnecting a Mapped Network Folder

If you no longer need to map a network resource, you should disconnect it by following these steps:

1. Select Start, Computer to open the Computer window.

2. Right-click the mapped drive, and then click Disconnect.

3. If there are files open from the resource, Windows Vista displays a warning to let you know that it's unsafe to disconnect the resource. You have two choices:

   ▪ Click No, close all open files from the mapped resource, and then repeat steps 1 and 2.

   ▪ If you're sure there are no open files, click Yes to disconnect the resource.

Creating a Network Location for a Remote Folder

When you map a network folder to a drive on your computer, Vista creates an icon for the mapped drive in the Computer folder's Network Locations group. However, you may find that the supply of available drive letters is getting low if your computer has multiple hard drives, multiple CD or DVD drives, a memory card reader, a flash drive or two, and so on.

To work around this problem, you can add your own icons to the Computer folder's Network Locations group. These icons are called, appropriately enough, *network locations*, and each one is associated with a particular network folder. (They're similar to the network places you could create in Windows XP.) That is, after you create a network location, you can access the network folder associated with that location by double-clicking the icon. This is usually a lot faster than drilling down through several layers of folders on the network computer, so create network locations for those network folders you access most often.

Follow these steps to create a network location:

1. Select Start, Computer to open the Computer folder.

2. Right-click an empty section of the Computer folder, and then click Add a Network Location. Vista launches the Add Network Location Wizard.

3. Click Next in the initial wizard dialog box.

4. Select Choose a Custom Network Location, and then click Next.

5. Type the network address of the folder you want to work with. Notice that as you enter the address, the Add Network Location Wizard displays a list of objects that match what you've typed; so, you can save some typing by selecting items from the lists as they appear (see Figure 8.8). You can also click Browse to use the Browse for Folder dialog box to select the network folder.

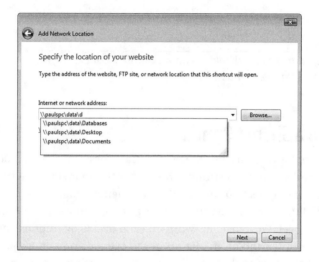

FIGURE 8.8

As you enter the network address, the Add Network Location Wizard displays a list of objects that match what you've typed.

6. Click Next.

7. Type a name for the network location and click Next.

8. Click Finish. The Add Network Location Wizard adds an icon for the network folder to the Computer window, as shown in Figure 8.9.

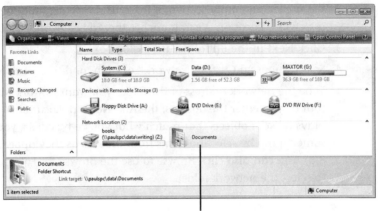

Network location

FIGURE 8.9

After you associate a network folder with a network location, an icon for the new location appears in the Computer window.

Accessing a Shared Printer

Except for perhaps disk drives, the most commonly shared device on small networks is almost certainly the printer. This makes sense because almost everyone needs to print something sometime, and those print jobs vary: One day it's a letter to send to the laser printer, and the next it's a photo to send to the ink-jet. Of course, it's wasteful (and decidedly impractical) to attach both a laser printer and an ink-jet printer to every computer. It's just so much easier (and cheaper) to share one of each type of printer on the network so that everyone can use them.

To access a shared printer, you must connect to it. Here are the steps to follow:

1. Open the network computer or print server that has the printer you want to use.

2. Right-click the shared printer.

3. Click Connect. If a Vista driver for the shared printer isn't already installed on your computer, Vista warns you that it must install the driver to use the shared printer.

4. Click Install Driver. The User Account Control dialog box appears.

5. Enter your UAC credentials to continue. Vista installs the printer driver.

You can also add a shared network printer using Vista's Add Printer Wizard. Follow these steps:

1. Select Start, Control Panel to open the Control Panel window.

2. Click the Printer link under the Hardware and Sound icon. Vista opens the Printers window.

3. Click Add a Printer in the task pane to open the Add Printer Wizard.

4. Click Add a Network, Wireless or Bluetooth Printer. Vista searches for shared printers on the network and then displays a list of the printer it found, as shown in Figure 8.10.

FIGURE 8.10

The Add Printer Wizard displays a list of the shared printers that it found on your network.

5. Select the network printer you want to use.

6. Click Next. If a Vista driver for the shared printer isn't already installed on your computer, Vista warns you that it must install the driver to use the shared printer.

7. Click Install Driver. The User Account Control dialog box appears.

8. Enter your UAC credentials to continue. Vista installs the printer driver.

> **note** The default printer is the printer that is selected automatically whenever you open the Print dialog box. Also, it's the printer that Vista uses when you click the Print toolbar button in most applications, which sends the current document directly to the printer without going through the Print dialog box.

9. If you want to use the shared printer as your default printer, leave the Set as Default Printer check box activated and click Next.

10. Click Finish.

After you connect to a shared printer, Vista adds it to the Printers window. The name of the icon you see takes the following general form:

PrinterName on *ComputerName*

Here, *PrinterName* is the name of the printer as given by its device driver, and *ComputerName* is the name of the computer or print server to which the printer is attached. For example, Figure 8.11 shows a connected shared printer that uses the following name:

HP LaserJet 5P/5MP PostScript on Paulspc

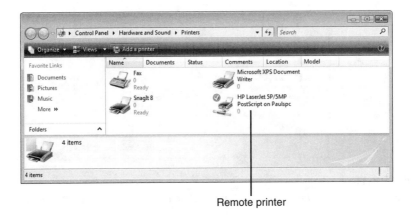

Remote printer

FIGURE 8.11

When you connect to a remote shared printer, Vista adds an icon for the printer to your Printers window.

Sharing Resources with the Network

Small networks are normally egalitarian affairs because no computer is in any significant sense more important than the others. One of the ways that this digital equality manifests itself is via the universal sharing of at least some resources on each computer. People rarely make their entire computer available to their fellow network users, but it's a rare machine that doesn't have at least a drive or folder to share.

Fortunately, when it comes to sharing resources on the network, Windows Vista come with quite a few options that enable you to share what resources you want and to control how others can access those resources. Network sharing in Vista begins by configuring the basic sharing options, of which there are five in all: general file sharing, Public folder sharing, printer sharing, password-protected sharing, and media sharing.

The next four sections cover the first four of these options; I'll leave media sharing to Chapter 9, "Setting Up Vista as a Digital Media Hub." To view and work with these options, you need to open the Network and Sharing Center (as described in Chapter 5, "Working with Vista's Basic Network Tools and Tasks," in the section "Working with Vista's Basic Network Tools and Tasks").

→   For the details about media sharing, **see** "Sharing Your Media Player Library," **p. 207**.

→   To learn how to open the Network and Sharing Center, **see** "Accessing the Network and Sharing Center," **p. 125**.

Activating File and Printer Sharing

In the Network and Sharing Center's Sharing and Discovery section, the File Sharing setting covers general file and printer sharing. If the current setting is Off, follow these steps to activate file and printer sharing:

1. Click the downward-pointing arrow to the right of the File Sharing setting to expand the setting.

2. Select the Turn On File Sharing option, as shown in Figure 8.12. This will allow other people on the network to access your shared files and printers.

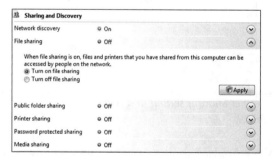

FIGURE 8.12

Expand the File Sharing setting, and then activate the Turn On File Sharing option.

3. Click Apply. The User Account Control dialog box appears.

4. Enter your UAC credentials to put the new setting into effect.

Sharing the Public Folder

The Public Folder Sharing setting covers sharing the Public folder. If the current setting is Off, here are the steps to follow to activate sharing the Public folder:

1. Click the downward-pointing arrow to the right of the Public Folder Sharing setting to expand the setting.

2. Select one of the following options (see Figure 8.13):

   ■ **Turn On Sharing So Anyone with Network Access Can Open Files.** Select this option to share the Public folder, but allow network users only to read files in that folder. (That is, users can't create new files or change existing files.)

   ■ **Turn On Sharing So Anyone with Network Access Can Open, Change, and Create Files.** Select this option to share the Public folder, and allow network users to read, edit, and create new files in that folder.

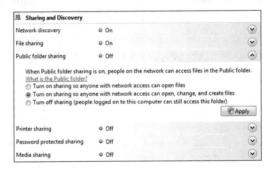

FIGURE 8.13
Expand the Public Folder Sharing setting and then activate one of the options to turn on sharing of the Public *folder.*

3. Click Apply. The User Account Control dialog box appears.

4. Enter your UAC credentials to put the new setting into effect.

Activating Printer Folder Sharing

The Printer Sharing setting covers sharing the `Printers` folder. If the current setting is Off, follow these steps to activate sharing for the `Printers` folder:

1. Click the downward-pointing arrow to the right of the Printer Sharing setting to expand the setting.

2. Select the Turn On Printer Sharing option, as shown in Figure 8.14. This will allow other people on the network to access your `Printers` folder.

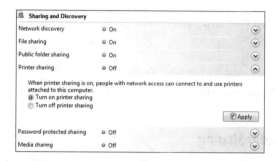

FIGURE 8.14

Expand the Printer Sharing setting and then activate the Turn On Printer Sharing option.

3. Click Apply. The User Account Control dialog box appears.

4. Enter your UAC credentials to put the new setting into effect.

Using Password Protected Sharing

The Password Protected Sharing setting covers sharing with password protection. That is, when you turn on password protected sharing, only people who know the username and password of an account on your computer can access your shared resources. If the current setting is Off, follow these steps to activate password protected sharing:

1. Click the downward-pointing arrow to the right of the Password Protected Sharing setting to expand the setting.

2. Select the Turn On Password Protected Sharing option, as shown in Figure 8.15.

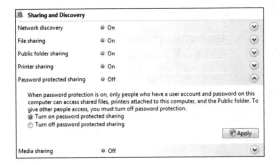

FIGURE 8.15

Expand the Password Protected Sharing setting, and then activate the Turn On Password Protected Sharing option.

3. Click Apply. The User Account Control dialog box appears.

4. Enter your UAC credentials to put the new setting into effect.

Using Public Folder Sharing

If you have the Public Folder Sharing setting turned on (see "Sharing the Public Folder," earlier in this chapter), you can use the Public folder to share files or other folders with the network. This is often the easiest way to share resources with the network because you only have to worry about one shared location, which keeps your life simple and makes it easier for other people to find what you're sharing.

To get to the Public folder, follow these steps:

1. Open any folder window.

2. Click Folders to display the Folders list.

3. At the top of the list, click Desktop.

4. Double-click the Public icon.

Figure 8.16 shows the default Public folder, which includes a half dozen subfolders: Public Documents, Public Downloads, Public Music, Public Pictures, Public Videos, and Recorded TV.

FIGURE 8.16

The Public *folder and its subfolders offer a simple way to share files and folders with the net-work.*

Creating User Accounts for Sharing

If you activated the Password Protected Sharing option (see "Using Password Protected Sharing," earlier in this chapter), you have to do one of the following:

■ **Set up separate accounts for each user that you want to access a shared resource.** Do this if you want to assign each user a different set of permissions, or if you want the usernames and passwords to match each user's local username and password.

■ **Set up a single account for all remote users to use.** Do this if you want to assign the same set of permissions for all users.

Here are some notes to bear in mind for creating users who will access your computer over a network:

■ Windows Vista does *not* allow users without passwords to access network resources. Therefore, you must set up your network user accounts with passwords.

■ The usernames you create do not have to correspond with the names that users have on their local machines. You're free to set up your own usernames, if you like.

■ If you create a user account that has the same name and password as an account of a user on his or her local machine, that user will be able to access your shared resources directly. Otherwise, as you saw earlier (see Figure 8.2), a Connect To dialog box appears so that the user can enter the username and password that you established when setting up the account on your computer.

8

You create a new user account in Windows Vista by following these steps:

1. Select Start, Control Panel to open the Control Panel window.

2. Under the User Accounts and Family Safety icon, click the Add or Remove User Accounts link. The User Account Control dialog box appears.

3. Enter your UAC credentials to continue. Vista displays the Manage Accounts window.

4. Click Create a New Account. The Create New Account window appears.

5. Type the name for the account. The name can be up to 20 characters and must be unique on the system.

6. Activate either Administrator (to add the user to the Administrators group) or Standard User (to add the user to the Users group).

7. Click Create Account. Vista creates the new account and returns you to the Manage Accounts window.

8. Click the account you just created. The Change An Account window appears.

9. Click the Create a Password link. Vista displays the Create Password window.

10. Type the user's password in the New Password and Confirm New Password text boxes.

11. Use the Type a Password Hint text box to type a reminder for the user in case he forgets the password.

12. Click Create Password.

Sharing a Resource with the File Sharing Wizard

By default, Windows Vista comes with the File Sharing Wizard activated. This is a simplified sharing feature that removes some of the complexity from sharing folders and files. However, it also removes much of the power and flexibility of sharing, so Vista also enables you to turn off the File Sharing Wizard. I show you how to do that in the next section. So that you can compare the two methods, here are the steps to follow to use the File Sharing Wizard to share a folder or file:

1. Select Start, and then click your username to open your user profile folder.

2. Click the folder you want to share. If you want to share a subfolder or file, instead, open its folder, and then click the subfolder or file.

3. Click the Share button in the task pane. Vista launches the File Sharing Wizard, which asks you to choose the user accounts you want to share the item with.

4. Type the username and click Add.

5. Repeat step 4 as necessary to share the folder or file with other users.

6. For each user you added, assign a permission level by clicking the downward-pointing arrow and selecting one of the following (see Figure 8.17):

Reader	This is the default level, and it means the user can only view the shared file or folder and open its contents. The user can't create, change, or delete anything.
Contributor	This level means that the user can add new files to the shared folder, and that the user can make changes to or delete any file that the user has added to the folder.
Co-owner	This level means that the user can create new items, and that the user can make changes to or delete any item.

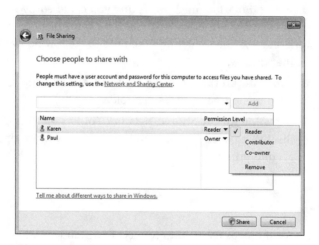

FIGURE 8.17
The Sharing Wizard asks you to choose the permission level for each user.

7. Click Share. The User Account Control dialog box appears.

8. Enter your UAC credentials to continue. The File Sharing Wizard sets up sharing for the file or folder.

8

9. If you want to send an email to the users to let them know the folder or file is shared, click the E-mail link; otherwise, click Done.

If you no longer want to share a folder or file, you can change the sharing using either of the following methods:

- **To remove a user from the sharing.** Follow steps 1 through 3 in this section, and then click Change Sharing Permissions to display the list of shared users. Click the permission level for the user you want to work with, and then click Remove.

- **To stop sharing the folder or file entirely.** Follow steps 1 through 3 in this section, and then click Stop Sharing.

→   To learn how to share a folder using advanced permissions, **see** "Setting Sharing Permissions on Shared Folders," **p. 315.**

Viewing Your Shared Resources

After a while, you might lose track of which folders you've shared. You could look through all your folders to look for those that have the Shared icon attached, but that's too much work, and you could easily miss some shared folder. Fortunately, Windows Vista offers a couple of easier methods. Open the Network and Sharing Center and then use the following two links at the bottom of the window:

- **Show Me All the Files and Folders I Am Sharing.** Click this link to open the Shared By Me search folder.

- **Show Me All the Shared Network Folders on This Computer.** Click this link to open a folder window showing your computer's shared folders and printers.

From Here

- For the steps required to connect to a standard wireless network, **see** "Making Wireless Network Connections," **p. 113.**

- To learn how to open the Network and Sharing Center, **see** "Accessing the Network and Sharing Center," **p. 125.**

- For a more detailed look at the types of items you see in the Network window, **see** "Viewing Network Computers and Devices," **p. 130.**

■ To learn more about wired connections, **see** Chapter 6, "Managing Network Connections," **p. 139**.

■ For information about how to remotely wake up a computer that's in Sleep mode, **see** "Using a Network Connection to Wake Up a Sleeping Computer," **p. 151**.

■ To learn more about wireless connections, **see** Chapter 7, "Managing Wireless Network Connections," **p. 157**.

■ For the details about media sharing, **see** "Sharing Your Media Player Library," **p. 207**.

■ To learn how to share a folder using advanced permissions, **see** "Setting Sharing Permissions on Shared Folders," **p. 315**.

8

Setting Up Vista as a Digital Media Hub

One of the main benefits of setting up a small network is that it frees at least some content from the shackles of whichever computer stores that content. For example, without a network, if you have a digital photo stored on a computer, the only way for another person to see that photo is to either pull up a chair beside the computer or to get a copy of the photo on a CD or memory card or via email. With a network, however, you have lots of ways to get others to see the photo:

IN THIS CHAPTER

■ Understanding Digital Media Hardware

■ Connecting Your Digital Media Hub

■ Sharing Your Media Player Library

■ From Here

■ You can share the folder that stores the photo.

■ You can move or copy the photo to a central network location that is shared with the network.

■ You can use Vista's Media Player to stream the photo over the network, which enables other Vista machines to access and view the photo.

Of course, you can do all of this not just with digital photos, but also with other images, digital music, digital video, and recorded TV. My focus on media here is deliberate. After all, a typical home network has no need to collaborate on a Word memo, an Excel budget, or a PowerPoint presentation. But most homes are teeming with media and media devices. That's why modern-day small networks, particularly home networks, are increasingly becoming *digital media* networks.

Sharing media over the network is fine, but it soon becomes apparent that for the best network-based media experience, you need a computer that sits at the center of it all. You need a machine to store and stream the media, record the TV shows, rip the music CDs, and view the media in whatever playback format you prefer (whether it's a slideshow, a live feed, a music shuffle, or a seat-of-the-pants playlist). A computer that performs all these tasks is called a *digital media hub*, and Windows Vista with its strong media applications—notably Media Center, Media Player, and Photo Gallery—can be the ideal device for the job, as you see in this chapter.

Understanding Digital Media Hardware

Earlier I said that Windows Vista "can be" an ideal digital media hub. Why did I hedge my bets? For the simple reason that these things are never straightforward. Digital media is a hardware-intensive subject, and to get the most out of using Vista as your home's digital media hub, you need to configure the Vista box with the right components, and you need to surround the Vista box with devices and other hardware that work well together and that accomplish your goals. The sections that follow give you the details on these and other hardware considerations.

Digital Media Computer

The main component of your digital media setup is the hub itself: the Vista computer. Yes, if your budget's tight, you can dragoon just about any old Vista box to serve as the hub. However, to get the most out of your networked digital media now, and to allow for future needs, it's better to have a machine designed to handle the media workload. You can either get a new machine that does the job or, to save some money, you can upgrade an older machine so that it passes the media muster. Here are some points to bear in mind:

Windows Vista If you only want to use your hub to view slideshows and play music and videos through Windows Media Player, any version of Vista will do. However, most digital media hubs also use Windows Media Center to play media, stream media to a digital media receiver such as an Xbox 360, and perhaps most important, record TV shows.

> **note** Lots of companies are now coming out with *home theater PCs* (HTPCs) that are designed to look more like a typical audio/video component than a computer. For example, see VoodooPC (Voodoopc.com) and Shuttle (Shuttle.com).

If you want to include these and other Media Center features as part of your hub's capabilities, the computer must run either Vista Home Premium or Vista Ultimate.

Form factor

Most PCs reside under or beside desks, so the size and look of the case isn't too important. A computer that you use as a digital media hub is a different story, however. The hub will sit in your family room or den along with your TV and other media equipment, so you don't want some beige eyesore with a full-tower case that dominates the room. Instead, look for a *small form factor* (SFF) PC, particularly one designed for home theater setups. The most common SFF PCs come as small cubes or flat (pizza box) cases. Here are three things to consider when looking at the specs of an SFF PC:

> **caution** Many SFF PCs come with low-profile bus slots that are packed closer together. The upside of this is that it enables the computer to offer multiple slots for hardware upgrades; the downside is that most regular PCI cards won't fit into these slots, so you need to purchase a low-profile version of the card. (Note that some cards come with two brackets—one regular and one low-profile—so that you can use the card in either type of system.) Even then, the compressed positioning of the slots means that only the thinnest cards can fit next to each other, so it's possible that even some low-profile cards might not fit.

- If you plan on storing the computer inside a cabinet or other entertainment unit, examine the dimensions of the case to make sure it will fit into whatever space you're going to use.

- Most SFF PCs come with only a limited number of internal expansion slots. If you plan on replacing integrated components such as the video adapter, network adapter, and audio adapter, the computer must have the requisite number of bus slots available.

- Most SFF PCs come with only a limited number of internal drive bays. If you want to add more internal hard drive storage to the computer, make sure the computer has at least one available drive bay.

Fan noise

Whether you care how much noise your digital media hub makes depends on what other activities occur in the same room. If the room is used solely for relatively noisy activities such as watching TV and movies, and playing music and games, the noise level on a typical modern PC won't be a problem. However, if you also use

caution Low-noise components are almost always more expensive than their louder cousins, and then have a tendency to run hot. The latter means that it might not be a good idea to use low-noise components if you'll be sticking the PC inside a cabinet where there is less ventilation and so a greater chance of heat buildup. Fortunately, in this case, whatever noise the PC makes will be less noticeable if the computer sits inside a cabinet.

the room for reading, playing board games, or napping, you'll want to tone down the noise caused by a PC's multiple whirring fans and other spinning components. Many HTPCs are designed as low-noise machines, so that's a good place to start. It's also possible to find low-noise versions of hard drives, video cards, and computer power supplies.

Storage

In a digital media hub, storage space is paramount for one very obvious reason: Digital media files take up a *lot* of space. Most digital media repositories contain thousands of multimegabyte music files, hundreds of multimegabyte digital images, and perhaps dozens of multigigabyte video files (mostly in the form of recorded TV shows). A hard drive with just a few hundred gigabytes of storage is going to fill up fast. Fortunately, hard drive prices are incredibly cheap now, so adding a couple of 500GB or 750GB drives to your hub won't put you in the poorhouse. Make sure these are either internal Serial ATA drives or external eSATA, USB 2.0, or FireWire drives for best performance. Look for drives with spin rates of at least 7,200rpm, and with a large memory buffer of at least 16MB (but 32MB is better).

Processor

Digital media hubs often have to perform multiple tasks at once. For example, the machine may have to stream an audio file while also recording a TV show. Therefore, your hub should have a dual-core processor, either from Intel or AMD, running at 2.4GHz or better. (You'll want at least 3.6GHz to play high-definition video in the H.264 format used by HD-DVD and Blu-ray.)

Memory

Your digital media hub will be required to process massive video streams, manipulate huge images, play back multiple music streams simultaneously, and perform other heavy-duty chores. All of this requires prodigious amounts of memory to happen smoothly and without delays or dropped frames. System memory of 2GB should be considered the minimum for such a system; although if money's tight, you can probably get away with 1GB for most operations. If you can afford the extra couple of hundred dollars, go with 3GB of RAM; you won't regret it.

Video card

Most modern video cards come with enough processing power and onboard memory to handle not only whatever day-to-day computing you'll perform on the digital media hub, but also most media tasks. The exception is video playback of high-definition video, which requires a card that supports H.264 acceleration and HDCP (*High-Bandwidth Digital Content Protection*). Even more important, you need to make sure that the card comes with connectors that are compatible with the rest of your system. In particular, the connectors on the video card must match the connectors on the back of your TV. See "Television Connectors," later in this chapter.

TV tuner

If you want to watch and capture TV via the digital media hub, you need a TV tuner device. Some video cards have TV tuners built in, but you can also purchase standalone TV tuners, either as internal adapter cards or external boxes. (In general, standalone TV tuners give you a better signal and are less flaky overall than all-in-one cards that try to do both graphics and TV.) Match the TV tuner device to the type of signal you receive. For example, if your signal arrives via a digital or analog TV cable, you need a digital or analog cable connector; similarly, *over-the-air* (OTA) broadcast signals require the appropriate type of antenna to capture the signal.

CableCard

If you have an HDTV signal that you want to record using Windows Media Center, out of the box you'll only be able to watch and record over-the-air signals. If you want to view and record specialty channels that are broadcast in HD, then you need to add a CableCard to your home theater PC. This device enables your PC to recognize cable-based HD signals, which means you can view and record HD channels on your PC.

Network card

In most home theater setups, the digital media hub is the only computer in the room, so an ethernet card is only necessary if you're also connecting the computer directly to a broadband modem for Internet access. However, one of the primary roles of a hub is to stream media to other computers, digital media receivers, and other devices in the house. It's unlikely your house is completely wired with Cat 6 (or whatever) cable, so that means you must stream your media over a wireless network signal. For music and images, you'll be fine with 802.11g. However, if you want to stream video, too, you'll need to take a chance on 802.11n. Alternatively, look into powerline networking adapters, which offer theoretical data transfer rates of up to 200Mbps, more than enough for streaming even high-definition video.

→   For the details about wireless networking standards, **see** "Understanding Wi-Fi," **p. 41**.

Audio card

As with the video card, the key feature of your digital media hub's audio card is having a set of connectors that match your audio equipment. If you'll be connecting audio output directly to your TV or, more likely, to an audio receiver, you need connectors that match.

Keyboard

You'll be operating your digital media hub from a nearby chair or sofa (the so-called 10-foot interface), so a wireless keyboard is a must. Look for a Wi-Fi or Bluetooth keyboard, ideally one designed to work with Media Player or Media Center.

Television

It used to be that purchasing a TV was a happily simple affair. You just decided what size you could afford, plunked down the plastic, and you were watching *The Brady Bunch* before you knew it. These days, however, buying a TV has become almost as complex as buying a computer. The problem, as is usually the case when things get complex, is the terminology. Whereas before the only crazy abbreviations and words you had to deal with were TV manufacturer names (RCA, Zenith, and so on), now they're TV feature names: HDTV, aspect ratio, horizontal resolution, and many more.

For starters, your new digital set may support HDTV (*High-Definition TV*), a relatively new broadcast format that supports better picture and sound quality. HDTV replaces the old NTSC (*National Television System Committee*) sets that we've used up until now.

One of the reasons HDTV is better involves the *aspect ratio*, the width of the screen in relation to its height. NTSC has a 4:3 aspect ratio, which means that if the screen is four units wide, it's also three units tall (say, 40 inches wide and 30 inches tall). HDTV uses a 16:9 aspect ratio, which is called *widescreen*. This is the same aspect ratio that's used in the movies, so that's why you often see the following disclaimer when watching a movie on TV: "This film has been modified from its original version. It has been formatted to fit your screen."

What they mean is that the movie has been altered so that it fits a screen with a 4:3 aspect ratio. If they didn't do this, the picture would be shrunk to fit the width of the screen, leaving black areas on the top and bottom, a format called *letterbox*. Because HDTV uses 16:9, movies are displayed in their original format, meaning they don't get chopped off on the sides to fit a 4:3 screen or squished into the letterbox display.

The other thing that HDTV improves upon is the *resolution*, which determines how sharp the picture will appear. The keys here are the *pixels* (short for "picture elements"), which are the thousands of teeny pinpoints of light that make up the picture display. Each pixel shines with a combination of red, green, and blue, which is how they produce all the colors you see.

The important figures when buying a TV are the *horizontal resolution* and the number of *scan lines*. The horizontal resolution is the number of pixels there are across the screen. The scan lines are the horizontal lines created by these pixels. The number of scan lines is also called the *vertical resolution*. Basically, the higher these numbers are, the better the picture will be.

9

NTSC sets have a horizontal resolution of 720 pixels, and they have 486 scan lines. This is often written as 720×486, and multiplying these numbers together, it means the set has 349,920 total pixels to display each frame. The highest quality HDTV broadcast is 1920×1080, which multiplies out to 2,073,600 pixels, or about six times the NTSC value. That, in a nutshell, is why HDTV looks so much better than NTSC. A second HDTV format is 1280×720, which is still much better than NTSC.

Other terms related to resolution that TV sales types bandy about are *interlaced scanning* (or just *interlacing*) and *progressive scanning*. Both refer to how the set "draws" each video frame on the screen. Inside the set is an electron gun that shoots a beam that runs along each scan line and lights up the pixels with the appropriate colors. With interlaced scanning, the beam first paints only the odd-numbered scan lines and then starts again from the top and does the even-numbered lines. With progressive scanning, the beam paints all the lines at once. In general, progressive scanning is better because it produces a more stable picture.

A set that supports interlaced scanning over 1,080 scan lines is called *1080i capable*, and a set that supports progressive scanning over 720 scan lines is called *720p capable*. If you see a set advertised as *HDTV capable*, it means it supports both formats.

Television Connectors

How you connect your digital media hub PC to your TV depends on the connectors you have on the PC side (that is, on your video card / TV tuner) and on the TV side. There are five possibilities:

Composite   This is a yellow RCA-style connector, and it's available on most standard-definition TVs and on some PC video cards. This is old technology, however, so you won't get great video quality from such a connection.

S-Video   This connector is fairly common on newer TVs and on recent video cards. S-Video offers decent video quality, so it's a good choice.

Component   This is the set of red, green, and blue connectors that is available on

> **note** If you don't have connectors that match, you're not out of luck. You can purchase adapters that will convert the output of one type of connector to the input of a different type. For example, if your video card has a DVI connector and your HDTV has an HDMI connector, you can buy a DVI-to-HDMI converter.

most newer TVs, although they're still relatively rare on video cards. You get good video quality here, but it's unlikely your video card has component outputs.

DVI   *Digital Visual Interface* (DVI) is a high-definition video connector available on most older digital TVs and on many modern video cards.

HDMI   *High-Definition Multimedia Interface* (HDMI) is currently the gold standard for displaying digital video signals. However, although it's now relatively common to find an HDMI connector on a digital TV, it's still rare to have an HDMI connector on a video card.

caution When you're working with DVI, note that there are three types: DVI-A, DVI-D, and DVI-I. DVI-A works with only analog signals; DVI-D works with only digital signals; and DVI-I works with both analog and digital. Unfortunately, each type of DVI uses a slightly different pin arrangement, so when you're purchasing a DVI cable, you need to make sure that it matches the DVI connectors on your video card and TV. Just to confuse matters, DVI-D and DVI-I connectors also come in *single-link* and *dual-link* configurations. In this case, make sure you get dual-link; it will also work with single-link.

9

In each case, your job is to match the connector on your video card with the equivalent connector on your TV. Ideally, you want to use the highest-quality common connection, and then buy good quality cables to make the connection.

Audio Receiver Connectors

Connecting the sound component of your computer to your home theater means running cables from the PC's sound card to the audio input connectors on your audio receiver (or on your TV, if you want to play PC audio directly through the TV's speakers). You have three basic choices:

Single-channel analog   This sound system usually consists of a stereo mini jack connector (usually labeled something like Line Out) on the sound card and red and white RCA-style connectors on the receiver. You occasionally see sound cards with the red and white RCA output jacks.

9

| Multichannel analog | If your sound card supports Dolby 5.1 sound, the card will have three stereo mini connectors, usually labeled something like Front Left/Right, Center/Subwoofer, and Surround Left/Right. These connect to red and white RCA connectors on the receiver (assuming it also supports Dolby 5.1), which will have similar labels. If the card and receiver support Dolby 7.1, the card will have an extra stereo mini connector labeled something like Surround Back Left/Right, and the receiver will have the equivalent red and white RCA connectors. |
| Digital | Many modern sound cards and audio receivers support digital audio connections. This connection usually uses the *Sony/Philips Digital Interface Format* (S/PDIF), and the sound card connector will be labeled S/PDIF or Digital Out. The connectors will either by coaxial on the sound card and RCA style on the receiver, or TOSLink (also called optical) on both. |

> **note** As with video cables, you can also purchase adapters that convert one type of audio output to another type of audio input. For example, you can get an adapter that enables you to connect a single-channel stereo mini jack on the sound card with a digital (coaxial or TOSLink) input on the receiver.

Digital Media Receivers

Windows Vista comes with support for Windows Media Connect 2.0, which is software that streams digital media from (in this case) the Vista machine to programs and devices that support Windows Media Connect. Supported programs include digital media players such as Windows Media Player 11 and devices such as the Xbox 360 and Roku SoundBridge. The latter two are examples of *digital media receivers* (DMRs), devices that can access a media stream being sent over a wired or wireless network connection and then play that stream through connected equipment such as speakers, audio receivers, or a TV. Note, too, that Windows Media Connect uses standard protocols—specifically *Hypertext Transfer Protocol* (HTTP) and *Universal Plug and Play* (UPnP)—so, theoretically, any device that supports these protocols should also be able to receive Windows Vista media streams.

> **note** Most UPnP devices have options to disable and enable UPnP, or "network control" as it's sometimes called. Access the device settings and make sure that UPnP is enabled.

Connecting Your Digital Media Hub

With your computer and other hardware at hand, you're ready to connect everything together to add a digital media hub to your home theater setup. Power everything off, and then run through the following general steps:

1. If you want your Vista machine to connect directly to the Internet via a broadband connection, run an ethernet cable from the broadband modem's LAN port to the computer's NIC. (On most broadband modems you can instead run a USB cable from the modem's USB port to a free USB port on the PC.)

2. If you have a set-top box for your TV signal, run the appropriate cable from the set-top box output connector to the input connector on your computer's TV tuner card.

3. Run video cable from the computer's video card to the TV's video input connectors.

4. If your TV tuner or video card has a connector for a digital TV antenna (to pick up OTA digital broadcast signals), attach the antenna.

5. Run audio cable from the computer's sound card to the audio receiver's input connectors (or to the TV's audio input connectors) .

Adding an Xbox 360 to the Network

The Xbox 360 and Windows Vista go together well because the Xbox can access and play media streamed from Vista. First you need to get the Xbox 360 connected to your network. Follow these steps:

1. Connect your Xbox 360 to the network. If you have physical access to the network, you can plug a network cable into the Xbox 360's network port. Otherwise, you need to attach a wireless networking adapter (sold separately) to the Xbox 360.

2. Turn on the Xbox 360.

3. When the Dashboard appears, display the System blade.

4. Highlight Network Settings and press Select.

5. Highlight Edit Settings and press Select.

6. In the Basic Settings tab, if the IP Settings field isn't set to Automatic, highlight the IP Settings section, press Select, highlight the Automatic setting, and then press Select.

7. If the DNS Settings field isn't set to Automatic, highlight the DNS Settings section, press Select, highlight the Automatic setting, and then press Select.

8. Highlight the section that includes the Network Name (SSID) field and press Select. The Xbox 360 displays a list of available wireless networks.

9. Highlight your network and press Select. (Tip: If you don't see your network listed, press X to rerun the network search.)

10. If your network uses Wired Equivalent Privacy (WEP) or Wi-Fi Protected Access (WPA) security, use the onscreen keyboard to enter the security key. When you have finished, select Done. The Xbox 360 updates the network settings.

11. Highlight Test Media and press Select. You should see Connected in the Wireless Network field and Confirmed in the IP Address field. (If not, highlight Edit Settings, press Select, and repeat steps 6 through 10.)

Connecting an Xbox 360 to Windows Vista

Just follow these steps to connect the Xbox 360 to Windows Vista:

1. Turn on the Xbox 360 without a game disc in the console.

2. When the Dashboard appears, display the Media blade.

3. Highlight Music or Photos and press Select.

4. Highlight Computer and press Select. The Xbox 360 asks whether you have installed *Windows Media Connect* (WMC) on the computer.

5. WMC is already part of Windows Vista, so highlight Yes, Continue, and press Select. The Xbox 360 displays a list of WMC computers.

6. Highlight your Windows Vista computer and press Select. The Xbox 360 connects to the computer and displays a list of media.

7. Use the Xbox 360 interface to play the music or run a slideshow.

Sharing Your Media Player Library

With your digital media hub up and running, you'll mostly use Vista to run slideshows, play digital music, and record TV shows via Media Center. However, if you're using the Windows Vista computer as the central storage location for your network's media files, you'll want to share that media with the rest of the users on your network. One way to do that is to share the media folders directly. However, Windows Media Player 11 gives you a second option: *media sharing*.

The idea behind media sharing is simple. As you might know, it can take quite a while to set up and customize a Media Player Library just the way you like it with playlists, album art, views, and other features. If you want other people to see and use the same setup, it's way too much work to configure each computer's Media Player separately. Fortunately, you don't have to bother with all that because the media sharing feature enables you to share your Media Player library with other network users or devices, just as you'd share a folder or a printer.

To activate media sharing, follow these steps:

1. On the Windows Vista computer that you're using as a digital media hub, launch Windows Media Player by selecting Start, All Programs, Windows Media Player.

2. Pull down the Library tab's menu and select Media Sharing. The Media Sharing dialog box appears.

3. Click to activate the Share My Media check box, as shown in Figure 9.1.

4. Click OK. Media Player expands to show the devices connected to Media Player (see Figure 9.4, later in this section).

When computers or devices connect to your network, Media Player recognizes them and displays an icon in the notification area. Place your cursor over the icon to see the message Windows Media Player found: *computer*, where *computer* is the name of the new computer or device (see Figure 9.2). Double-click the message to open the Windows Media Player Library Sharing dialog box shown in Figure 9.3. Then, click either Allow (if you want the computer or device to share your media) or Deny (if you don't).

tip After you run Media Player for the first time, Vista adds an icon for Media Player to the Quick Launch toolbar on the left side of the taskbar. For subsequent Media Player sessions, you can launch the program quickly by clicking that icon.

note Another route to the Media Sharing dialog box is to pull down the menu for any other tab, select More Options to open the Options dialog box, display the Library tab, and then click Configure Sharing.

9

FIGURE 9.1

Activate the Share My Media check box to turn on Media Player's media sharing feature.

FIGURE 9.2

Media Player displays this message when it detects a new computer or device connected to your network.

FIGURE 9.3

You can allow or deny other computers and devices access to your media library.

To control media sharing, display the Media Sharing dialog box again. This time, you see the configuration shown in Figure 9.4. The large box in the middle lists the network computers and devices that Media Player has detected. In each case, click an icon and then click either Allow or Deny. If you allow an item, you

note To control the default sharing settings, click the Settings button in the Media Sharing dialog box.

can also click Customize to specify exactly what you want to share based on three criteria: media types, star ratings, and parental ratings. Deactivate the Use Default Settings check box, and then use the controls to customize what you want to share.

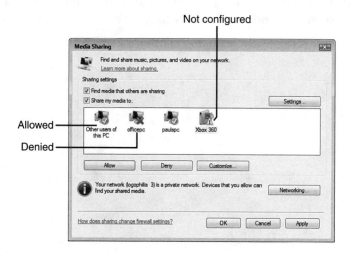

FIGURE 9.4

Use the Media Sharing dialog box to allow or deny other network devices access to your Media Player library.

From Here

- For the details about wireless networking standards, **see** "Understanding Wi-Fi," **p. 41**.

- For the steps required to connect to a standard wireless network, **see** "Making Wireless Network Connections," **p. 113**.

- To learn more about wired connections, **see** Chapter 6, "Managing Network Connections," **p. 139**.

- To learn more about wireless connections, **see** Chapter 7, "Managing Wireless Network Connections," **p. 157**.

- For information about importing images directly to a shared network folder, **see** "Importing Pictures to a Network Share," **p. 221**.

■ To learn how to rip music CDs directly to a shared network folder, **see** "Ripping Audio CDs to a Network Share," **p. 223**.

■ For information about recording a TV show directly to a shared network folder, **see** "Recording TV Shows to a Network Share," **p. 225**.

■ To learn how to run a slideshow based on the images stored in a shared network folder, **see** "Setting Up a Network-Based Slideshow," **p. 228**.

9

Taking Advantage of Your Network

N ow that you've gone to the trouble of purchasing network hardware, connecting that hardware, and getting your Vista machines on the network, a natural question arises: Now what? That is, your computers are connected, so what should you do to take advantage of this connectedness? You've seen some early answers to these questions in the previous two chapters. In Chapter 8, "Accessing and Sharing Network Resources," you learned how to view and use the shared resources of other computers on the network and how to share your own computer's resources; in Chapter 9, "Setting Up Vista as a Digital Media Hub," you learned how to configure a Vista machine to act as a digital media warehouse for the network and to stream that media over the network.

This idea of taking advantage of network connectedness also comes up quite often later in this book. For example, you learn how to collaborate with other network users in Chapter 12, "Collaborating with Windows Meeting Space"; how to connect to the desktops of other computers in Chapter 16, "Making Remote Network Connections"; how to use Vista as a web server in Chapter 19, "Setting Up a Website"; and how to use Vista's FTP server features in Chapter 20, "Setting Up an FTP Site."

IN THIS CHAPTER

- Backing Up to the Network

- Publishing a Windows Vista Calendar on the Network

- Importing Pictures to a Network Share

- Ripping Audio CDs to a Network Share

- Recording TV Shows to a Network Share

- Setting Up a Network-Based Slideshow

- From Here

However, there's a large range of other Vista features you can use to take advantage of your network. For example, you can use the network as a backup location; you can publish a calendar on the network; you can save imported images, ripped audio CD tracks, and recorded TV shows to the network; and you can run slideshows based on the images in a network folder. This chapter shows you how to perform these and other tasks.

Backing Up to the Network

The idea of backing up your computer has been hampered in recent years by a strange and increasingly vexatious paradox:

- We all have more data than ever on our computers, so backing up that precious data is more important than ever.

- The more data we have, the harder it is to perform the backup because tens or hundreds of gigabytes of data require multiple media (writable optical discs, USB flash drives, or whatever). Even a separate hard drive might not have enough free space to hold a full computer backup.

The most obvious solution is to add a hard drive with enough storage capacity to handle a full backup. With 500GB external hard drives available for about 25 cents a gigabyte, and 750GB hard drives only slightly more expensive (and with affordable terabyte drives just around the corner), you can add an easy-to-use backup medium to your computer.

Backing up to an attached hard drive is a useful solution, but it's by no means a perfect one. For example, if your computer is stolen, the second hard drive might get stolen along with it, and then you're in big trouble. Similarly, a fire in your office or den could torch both the computer and the second hard drive.

A solution that avoids both of these problems is to use the network as your backup location:

- You can back up to a folder on a network share that has lots of free space.

- You can add a large hard drive to a network computer, share that drive, and then back up to the drive.

- You can add a *network-attached storage* (NAS) device to the network and back up to that device.

note Yes, it's still possible that a thief could make off with *all* your computer equipment, or a large house fire could destroy everything. If you're still worried, buy two network hard drives and swap them once a week or so. When you're using one, keep the other in an offsite location, such as a safety deposit box or storage locker.

Even better, the backup feature in Windows Vista supports backing up to a network share and, after you set up the program, backing up is completely automated, particularly if you back up to a resource that has plenty of room to hold your files (such as a roomy network share).

note The backup feature is not available in Windows Vista Home Basic.

Windows Vista gives you two ways to get the initial backup configuration started:

■ Select Start, All Programs, Maintenance, Backup and Restore Center. (You can also select Start, Control Panel, and then click the Back Up Your Computer link under the System and Maintenance icon.) Vista displays the Backup and Restore Center shown in Figure 10.1. Click Back Up Files, and then enter your User Account Control (UAC) credentials when prompted.

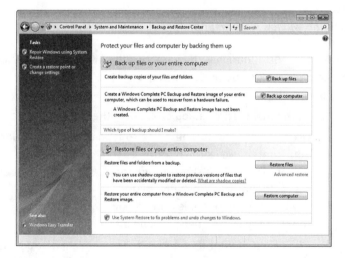

FIGURE 10.1
You can back up your computer and restore files using Vista's Backup and Restore Center.

■ Select Start, All Programs, Accessories, System Tools, Backup Status and Configuration. Vista displays the Backup Status and Configuration window shown in Figure 10.2. Click Set Up Automatic File Backup, and then enter your UAC credentials when prompted.

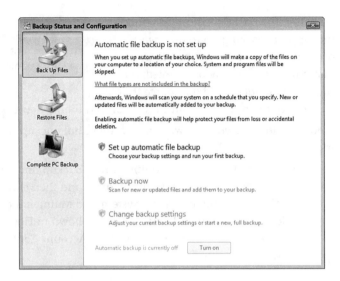

FIGURE 10.2

Vista displays this window when you run the Backup Status and Configuration command.

Either way, Vista launches the Back Up Files Wizard. Follow these steps to configure a network share as the backup location and activate Vista's Automatic File Backup feature:

1. In the first wizard dialog box, select the On a Network option.

2. Use the On a Network text box to type the network address of the share you want to use as the backup destination. Figure 10.3 shows an example. (Alternatively, click Browse to use the Browse for Folder dialog box to select the shared network folder.)

3. Click Next. If your user account doesn't have access to the network folder, the Connect to *Share* dialog box appears (where *Share* is the network address you typed in step 2).

4. Use the User Name and Password text boxes to type the credentials you need to access the shared folder, and then click OK.

> **note** The one exception in the list of file types to back up might be TV shows. Because most recorded TV shows produce multigigabyte files, you might have dozens or even hundreds of gigabytes of TV content. If most of these shows are ones you'll be deleting soon after you watch them, excluding them makes the backup perform faster and take up much less room on the network share. If you have important shows that you're saving, however, then by all means include them in the backup.

FIGURE 10.3

Activate the On a Network option, and then type the network address of the shared folder you want to use as the backup location.

5. If your system has multiple hard drives, the wizard asks you to select which of them you want to include in the backup. Deactivate the check box beside any drive you don't want to include in the backup (you can't exclude the system drive, however), and then click Next.

6. The next dialog box provides you with a long list of file types to back up, including documents, pictures, videos, and email. You probably want to leave all of these check boxes activated. Click Next when you're ready to continue.

7. The next wizard dialog box asks you to set up a backup schedule:

How Often   Select Daily, Weekly, or Monthly.

What Day   If you chose Weekly, select the day of the week you want the backups to occur; if you chose Monthly, select the day of the month you want the backups to occur.

What Time   Select the time of day you want the backup to run. (Choose a time when you won't be using your computer.)

8. Click Save Settings and Start Backup to save your configuration and launch the backup. Windows Backup lets you know that it will perform a full backup of your system now.

9. Click Yes.

10. When the backup is done, click Close.

The next time you run the Backup Status and Configuration command, the initial window shows you the backup status, when your system was last backed up, and when the next backup will occur. The window also sprouts several new options:

- **Back Up Now.** Click this option to rerun the entire backup.

- **Change Backup Settings.** Click this option to change your backup configuration by running through the Back Up Files Wizard's dialog boxes again.

- **Automatic Backup is Currently On.** Click the Turn Off button to disable the automatic file backup feature.

COMPLETE PC BACKUP

Perhaps even more useful than Vista's automatic file backup feature is its Complete PC Backup feature. As its name implies, Complete PC performs a backup of your entire system—what's known as a *system image* backup. This is extremely useful just in case your computer experiences a system crash that renders your hard disk or system files unusable. Without a system image backup, your only recourse in such a case is to start from scratch with either a reformatted hard disk or a new hard disk, reinstall Windows Vista, reinstall and reconfigure all your applications, and then restore your data from the most recent regular backup. In other words, you're looking at the better part of a day or, more likely, a few days, to recover your system. With a Complete PC backup, however, you can recover your system in just a couple of hours or so. That's the good news. The bad news is Vista gives you no way to perform a Complete PC backup to a network share; you must use a local hard drive or a set of writable DVDs.

Publishing a Windows Vista Calendar on the Network

By now you might have discovered Windows Calendar, a decent little program for managing your schedule. You can create appointments (both one-time and recurring), set up all-day events, schedule tasks, apply reminders to appointments and tasks, and view appointments by day, week, or month. This all works great for individuals, but a busy family needs to coordinate multiple schedules. The analog method for doing this is the paper calendar attached to the refrigerator by magnets. If you want to try something a bit more high tech, you can use Windows Calendar to publish a calendar to a network share. (Note that this is something that even the mighty Microsoft Outlook can't do. With Outlook's Calendar, you need to be on a Microsoft Exchange network to publish your calendar data.) You can configure the published calendar so that it gets updated automatically, which means the remote calendar always has current data. Your family members can then subscribe to the calendar to see your appointments (and optionally, your notes, reminders, and tasks).

First, start Windows Calendar using either of the following methods:

- Select Start, All Programs, Windows Calendar.
- In Windows Mail, select Tools, Windows Calendar, or press Ctrl+Shift+L.

Publishing Your Calendar

Here are the steps you need to follow in Windows Calendar to publish your calendar:

1. In the Calendars list, click the calendar you want to publish.

2. Select Share, Publish to open the Publish Calendar dialog box.

3. Use the Calendar Name text box to edit the calendar name, if necessary.

4. Use the Location to Publish Calendar text box to type the network address of the shared folder where you want to store the published calendar (see Figure 10.4). Alternatively, click Browse and then use the Browse for Files or Folders dialog box to select the network share, and then click OK.

> **caution** A bit later, you'll see that Windows Calendar gives you the option of sending an email message that tells people the network address of the shared calendar. Most email programs display this address as a link, which is convenient because the recipients can open the calendar just by clicking the link. However, if the network address includes spaces, the link stops at the first space, which means the link won't work properly. To avoid this problem, edit the calendar name to remove any spaces.

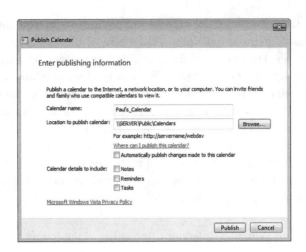

FIGURE 10.4

Use the Publish Calendar dialog box to publish your calendar to a shared network folder.

5. If you want Windows Calendar to update your calendar whenever you make changes to it, activate the Automatically Publish Changes Made to This Calendar check box. (If you leave this option deactivated, you can still publish your changes by hand, as described later; see "Working with Shared Calendars.")

6. In the Calendar Details to Include section, activate the check box beside each item you want in your published calendar: Notes, Reminders, and Tasks.

7 Click Publish. Windows Calendar publishes the calendar to the network share by creating a file in the iCalendar format (.ics extension) and copying that file to the share. Windows Calendar then displays a dialog box to let you know the operation was successful.

8. To let other people know that your calendar is shared and where it can be found, click Announce. (If you don't want to do this just now, you can send the invitation later on; see "Working with Shared Calendars," later in this chapter.) Windows Calendar creates a new email message that includes the following in the body (where *address* is the address of your published calendar; see Figure 10.5 for an example):

   You can subscribe to my calendar at *address*

9. Click Finish.

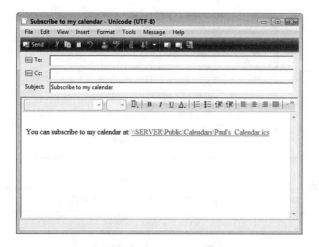

FIGURE 10.5
You can send an email message to let everyone know that you've published your calendar on the network.

Subscribing to a Calendar I: Using the Subscribe Message

How you subscribe to another person's published calendar depends on whether you receive a subscription invitation via email. If you have such a message, follow these steps to subscribe to the calendar:

1. Open the invitation message.

2. Click the link to the published calendar. Windows Mail asks you to confirm that you want to open the iCalendar file.

3. Click Open. If your user account doesn't have access to the network folder, the Connect to *Computer* dialog box appears (where *Computer* is the name of the computer where the calendar was published).

4. Use the User Name and Password text boxes to type the credentials you need to access the shared folder, and then click OK. Windows Calendar opens and displays the Import dialog box, shown in Figure 10.6.

> **tip** If the calendar address contains a space, you won't be able to click the link because it will be broken. In that case, select the address text and press Ctrl+C to copy it. Press Windows Logo+R (or select Start, All Programs, Accessories, Run) to open the Run dialog box, press Ctrl+V to paste the calendar address, and then click OK.

10

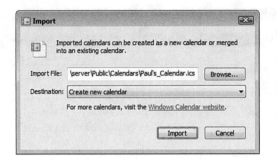

FIGURE 10.6

In the calendar subscription invitation message, click the link to import the calendar into Windows Calendar.

5. If you want to merge the published calendar into your own calendar, use the Destination list to select the name of your calendar; otherwise, the published calendar appears as a separate calendar.

6. Click Import. Windows Calendar adds the published calendar.

Subscribing to a Calendar II: Using Windows Calendar

If you don't have a subscription invitation message, you can still subscribe to a published calendar using Windows Calendar. Here are the steps to follow:

1. In Windows Calendar, select Share, Subscribe to open the Subscribe to a Calendar dialog box.

2. Use the Calendar to Subscribe To text box to type the address of the published calendar.

3. Click Next. Calendar subscribes you to the published calendar and then displays the Calendar Subscription Settings dialog box.

4. Edit the calendar name, if necessary.

5. Use the Update Interval list to select the interval at which you want Calendar to update the subscribed calendar: Every 15 Minutes, Every Hour, Every Day, Every Week, or No Update.

6. If you want to receive any reminders in the calendar, activate the Include Reminders check box.

7. If you also want to see the published calendar's tasks, activate the Include Tasks check box.

8. Click Finish. The published calendar appears in your Calendars list.

Working with Shared Calendars

After you publish one or more of your calendars and subscribe to one or more remote calendars, Windows Calendar offers a number of techniques for working with these items. Here's a summary:

- **Changing a calendar's sharing information.** When you select a published or subscribed calendar, the Details pane displays a Sharing Information section, and you use the controls in that section to configure the calendar's sharing options.

- **Publishing calendar changes.** If your published calendar isn't configured to automatically publish changes, you can republish by hand by selecting the calendar and then selecting Share, Sync.

- **Updating a subscribed calendar.** If you didn't configure an update interval for a subscribed calendar, or if you want to see the latest data in that calendar before the next update is scheduled, select the calendar and then select Share, Sync.

- **Synchronizing all shared calendars.** If you have multiple shared calendars (published and subscribed), you can synchronize them all at one time by selecting Share, Sync All.

- **Sending a published calendar announcement.** If you didn't send an announcement about your published calendar, or if you want to send the announcement to different people, select the calendar and then select Share, Send Publish E-Mail.

- **Stopping a published calendar.** If you no longer want other people to subscribe to your calendar, select it and then select Stop Publishing. When Calendar asks you to confirm, click Unpublish. (Note, however, that if you want your calendar file to remain on the network share, you first need to deactivate the Delete Calendar on Server check box.)

- **Stopping a subscribed calendar.** If you no longer want to subscribe to a remote calendar, select it and then press Delete. When Calendar asks you to confirm, click Yes.

Importing Pictures to a Network Share

In Chapter 9, you learned that you can set up one Vista machine as the storage area for all of your digital media. With images, for example, you could share the `Pictures` folder of whatever user account is on the Vista computer, and other computers could use the shared `Pictures` folder to store images.

You normally populate the shared `Pictures` folder by copying or moving images from a local computer. This is the best method if you only want to place some of your images on the network share.

However, you may find that you always place all of your images on the network share. If that's the case, you can save yourself a step by importing your images directly to the network. Windows Photo Gallery has an Import Pictures and Videos feature (select File, Import from Camera or Scanner) that enables you to import images from a digital camera or a document scanner. By default, Photo Gallery imports the images to a subfolder in your user profile's `Pictures` folder. To configure Photo Gallery to import the images directly to a network share, instead, follow these steps:

1. Select Start, All Programs, Windows Photo Gallery.

2. Select File, Options. The Windows Photo Gallery Options dialog box appears.

3. Select the Import tab.

4. Use the Settings For list to select the type of import you want to customize: Cameras, CDs and DVDs, or Scanners.

5. Click Browse to open the Browse for Folder dialog box.

6. Click Network to display the list of computers on your network.

7. Click the computer that contains the shared folder you want to use.

8. Select the network share you want to use.

9. Click OK. The network address appears in the Import To list, as shown in Figure 10.7.

10. Repeat steps 4 through 9 to customize the other import types, if necessary.

11. Click OK to put the new options into effect.

> **tip**
> If you want the other import types to store images in the same network share, you can skip steps 5 through 9. Instead, you can pull down the Import To list and select the shared folder.

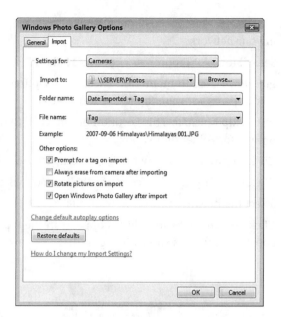

FIGURE 10.7
You can configure Photo Gallery to import pictures to a network share, as shown here in the
Import To list.

Ripping Audio CDs to a Network Share

Of all the digital media we watch and listen to, music seems to be the one
most in demand. After all, if someone has already taken the trouble to rip an
audio CD (that is, copy the CD's tracks to digital files on a computer), it
becomes easy for another person to play that CD on his own computer. This is
particularly true if you're using Windows Media Player to share your music
library, which gives other Media Player users easy access to that library.

→   For the details about setting up Media Player library sharing, **see** "Sharing Your Media Player
Library," **p. 207**.

As with images, getting music files onto a network share is a two-step process:
Rip the audio CD tracks, and then copy or move the resulting digital music
files to the network share. And, as with images, you can also configure Vista
to combine these two tasks into a single step. In this case, that involves configuring Windows Media Player to rip your audio CDs straight to the network
share.

Here are the steps to follow to change Media Player's rip location to a shared folder on your network:

1. Select Start, All Programs, Windows Media Player.

2. Pull down the Rip menu and select More Options. The Options dialog box appears with the Rip Music tab selected.

3. In the Rip Music to This Location group, click Change to open the Browse for Folder dialog box.

4. Click Network to display the list of computers on your network.

5. Click the computer that contains the shared folder you want to use.

6. Select the network share you want to use.

7. Click OK. The network address appears in the Rip Music to This Location group, as shown in Figure 10.8.

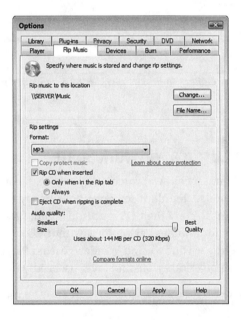

FIGURE 10.8

You can configure Media Player Gallery to rip audio CDs to a network share, as shown here.

8. Click OK to put the new setting into effect.

Recording TV Shows to a Network Share

I mentioned in the previous section that after you've ripped an audio CD, *someone* on the network will want to hear it. A close second in the digital media popularity contest is recorded TV. In fact, recorded TV is more problematic than digital audio because anybody with a CD drive can rip an audio CD, but recording a TV program requires specialized hardware, not to mention access to a broadcast signal.

> **note** You might think that you could also share the Media Player library on the computer that records the TV shows. Unfortunately, that won't work because Media Player doesn't include recorded TV shows as part of its media sharing feature.

→ For a discussion about the hardware needed to record TV, **see** "Understanding Digital Media Hardware," **p. 196.**

When you record TV in Windows Media Center, the program stores the resulting files—which use the Microsoft Recorded TV Show file type with the `.dvr-ms` extension—in the following folder (where `%SystemDrive%` is the drive on which Vista is installed, usually drive C:):

`%SystemDrive%\Users\Public\Recorded TV`

If you want to give other people access to your recorded TV shows, by far the easiest way to go about this is to share the `Recorded TV` folder.

If, for some reason, you can't share the `Recorded TV` folder, your only other option is to move or copy the recorded TV files to whatever computer wants to view them. As with ripping music (see "Ripping Audio CDs to a Network Share," earlier), this extra step is a hassle, particularly because recorded TV files are often multigigabyte behemoths that can take quite a while to transfer. A better solution is to record TV shows directly to a network share. Unfortunately, this is not as simple as tweaking a folder value, because Media Center has no such setting. However, by modifying some Media Center services and Registry settings, you can get it done.

Before getting started, you should first create a subfolder on whatever network computer you want to use to store the recorded

> **caution** Recording a TV show is incredibly bandwidth intensive, so the modification in this section stretches your home network to its limit. So although it's possible to record shows to the network on a 100Mbps wired or 54Mbps wireless connection, for best results, you really should do this only on a network that uses 1Gbps wired connections, an 802.11n wireless connection, or a 200Mbps powerline connection.

10

TV and to share that subfolder. For best results, use a share name without spaces, such as RecordedTV.

Now you need to follow these steps to configure the Media Center computer that records TV to save those recordings to the network share you just created:

1. On the Media Center computer, log on with a user who uses the Administrator account type.

2. Make sure this same user has full access to the network share where you want to save the recording.

→ For the details about changing user permissions, **see** "Setting Sharing Permissions on Shared Folders," **p. 315**.

3. On the Media Center computer, select Start, right-click Computer, and click Manage. The *User Account Control* (UAC) dialog box appears.

4. Enter your UAC credentials to continue. The Computer Management snap-in appears.

5. Select Services and Applications, Services.

6. Double-click the Windows Media Center Extender Service to open the service's property sheet.

7. Display the Log On tab.

8. In the This Account text box, type the name of the user account from step 1.

9. Type the user's password in the Password and Confirm Password text boxes.

10. Click OK. (If you see a dialog box confirming that the user has been granted Log On as Service rights, click OK.)

11. Repeat steps 6 through 10 for the Windows Media Center Receiver Service and the Windows Media Center Scheduler Service.

12. Because these two services in step 11 are started, in each case Windows warns you that you must stop and restart the service to put the new user into effect. To do that, for each of those services, select it in the Services list, click the Stop link, and then click the Start link.

13. Press Windows Logo+R (or select Start, All Programs, Accessories, Run) to open the Run dialog box, type regedit, and click OK. The User Account Control dialog box appears.

14. Enter your UAC credentials to continue. Vista loads the Registry Editor.

15. Double-click HKEY_LOCAL_MACHINE.

16. Double-click SOFTWARE.

17. Double-click Microsoft.

18. Double-click Windows.

19. Double-click CurrentVersion.

20. Double-click Media Center.

21. Double-click Service.

22. Click Recording.

23. Double-click the RecordPath setting and change its value to the network address of the folder you want to use to store the recorded TV.

> **caution** The Registry Editor gives you access to the Windows Vista Registry, which is a repository for vital data and settings related to Windows Vista and your programs. Improperly modifying anything in the Registry can have disastrous consequences, so only make the changes specified in these steps. Do not change or delete anything else in the Registry.

24. If you don't see a WatchedFolders setting, select Edit, New, String Value, type **WatchedFolders**, and press Enter.

25. Double-click the WatchedFolders setting and change its value to the network address of the folder you want to use to store the recorded TV. Figure 10.9 shows the resulting Registry values.

26. Reboot the Media Center computer.

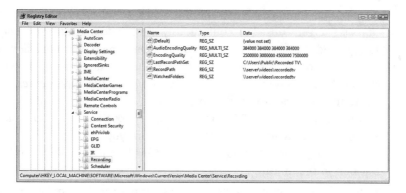

FIGURE 10.9

To get Media Center to record to the network, you need to make a couple of Registry tweaks.

When you return to Windows, all future Media Center TV recordings will go straight to the network share.

Setting Up a Network-Based Slideshow

When you upload a new set of digital photos from a recent vacation, event, or photo session, the first thing you probably do is open the `Pictures` folder (or whatever subfolder you used to stored the images) and then double-click the first image to open in the Windows Photo Gallery previewer. From there, you click the Next button (or press the Right arrow key) to scroll through the images, perhaps occasionally clicking Previous (or pressing the Left arrow key) to go back.

This hands-on approach to viewing your pictures is fine, but you might sometimes prefer to sit back and let Windows Vista do the work. That means loading the images into one of Vista's various slideshow features, each of which scrolls through the images automatically, often giving you some control over the speed of the show.

By default, Vista's slideshow features assume you want to view the images in your user profile's `Pictures` folder. If you have images on a network share that you prefer to see, instead, you need to tweak the slideshow settings. The next three sections show you how to do this.

Running a Screensaver Slideshow from the Network

Today's LCD monitors don't suffer from *burn-in*, permanent damage to areas of a CRT screen caused by continuously displaying a particular image over a long period. Not that LCDs are immune from screen problems, however. If your screen displays the same image constantly (such as, say, the Windows Vista Sidebar), you may end up with a problem called *persistence*, where the constant image persists onscreen as a faint version of the original. Fortunately, although CRT monitor burn-in is permanent, LCD monitor persistence is usually temporary: When you turn your monitor off at the end of the day, the persistent image is usually gone by the time you turn the monitor back on in the morning.

Unfortunately, persistence is *not* always temporary. You paid good money for your monitor, so it's probably best to play it safe and prevent persistence by configuring a screensaver to kick in after a specified period of computer idle time. Windows Vista offers a number of different screensavers that display wild patterns, a text message, or the Windows logo. However, Vista also offers a Photos screensaver that displays a slideshow of images from a folder. The default is the `Pictures` folder, but you can follow these steps to adjust the Photos screensaver to grab its images from a network share:

1. Right-click the desktop, click Personalize, and then click Screen Saver. (Alternatively, select Start, Control Panel, Appearance and Personalization, Change Screen Saver.) Vista displays the Screen Saver Settings dialog box.

2. In the Screen Saver list, select Photos.

3. Click Settings to open the Photos Screen Saver Settings dialog box.

4. Select the Use Pictures and Videos From option.

5. Click Browse to open the Browse for Folder dialog box.

6. Click Network to display the list of computers on your network.

7. Click the computer that contains the shared folder you want to use.

8. Select the network share you want to use.

9. Click OK. The network address appears under the Use Pictures and Videos From option, as shown in Figure 10.10.

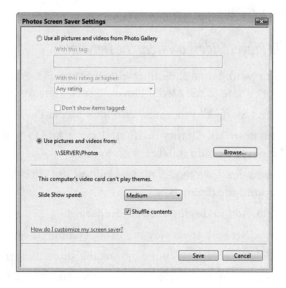

FIGURE 10.10

You can configure the Photos screensaver to display images from a network share, as shown here.

10. Use the Slide Show Speed list to select the speed at which you want the images to appear.

11. If you don't want the image to appear randomly, deactivate the Shuffle Contents check box.

12. Click Save to return to the Screen Saver Settings dialog box.

13. Use the Wait box to specify the number of minutes of computer idle time that must pass before the screensaver kicks in.

14. If you want Vista to display the Welcome screen when you exit the screensaver, activate the On Resume, Display Logon Screen check box.

15. Click OK to put the new screen saver into effect.

Running a Slideshow from the Network

Using network-based images in the Photos screensaver is a great way to prevent LCD persistence problems, but it's not very convenient when you want to view a slideshow because you have to wait until the screensaver kicks in, and when it does you have no way to control the slideshow.

Fortunately, Windows Vista gives you several different ways to start and control a slideshow without having to use a screensaver. The next three sections provide the details.

Running a Media Player Slideshow from the Network

To run a network-based slideshow within Media Player, you first have to add the network share to the Media Player library. Here are the steps involved:

1. Select Start, All Programs, Windows Media Player.

2. Pull down the Library menu and select Add to Library. Media Player displays the Add to Library dialog box.

3. If you don't see the Monitored Folders list, click Advanced Options to expand the dialog box.

4. Click Add to display the Add Folder list.

5. Click Network to display the list of computers on your network.

6. Click the computer that contains the shared folder you want to use.

7. Select the network share you want to use.

9. Click OK. The network address appears in the Monitored Folders list, as shown in Figure 10.11.

10. Click OK. Media Player begins adding the contents of the Photos share to the library.

11. Click Close.

FIGURE 10.11
To run a network-based Media Player slideshow, first add the network share to the Monitored Folders list.

With the network share added to Media Player, pull down Media Player's Library menu and select Pictures. Open the Library branch and select Folder to see an icon for the network share (see Figure 10.12). Click the network share, and then click Play.

FIGURE 10.12
Select Pictures, Library, Folder to see an icon for the network share that you added earlier.

Running a Photo Gallery Slideshow from the Network

To run a network-based slideshow from Photo Gallery, you first have to add the network share by following these steps:

1. Select Start, All Programs, Windows Photo Gallery.
2. Select File, Add Folder to Gallery. The Add Folder to Gallery dialog box appears.
3. Click Network to display the list of computers on your network.
4. Click the computer that contains the shared folder you want to use.
5. Select the network share you want to use.
6. Click OK. Photo Gallery asks you to confirm that you want to add the folder.
7. Click Add. Photo Gallery confirms that it has added the folder.
8. Click OK.

To start the slideshow, open Photo Gallery's Folders branch, select the network share, and then click the Play Slide Show button (see Figure 10.13; you can also press F11).

Network share

Play Slide Show

FIGURE 10.13
Select the network share, and then click Play Slide Show.

Running a Folder Slideshow from the Network

Instead of launching Photo Gallery to launch your slideshow, you can configure the network share to launch the slideshow directly. To do this, you must configure the shared network folder with a special template that customizes the folder to display image-related features, including a Slide Show button.

Follow these steps to customize the network share to use a picture folder template:

1. Open the folder containing the network share.

2. Right-click the network share folder, and then click Properties to open the folder's Properties window.

3. Display the Customize tab.

4. In the Use This Folder as a Template list, select Picture and Videos, as shown in Figure 10.14. This template gives the folder the same features as Vista's `Pictures` folder.

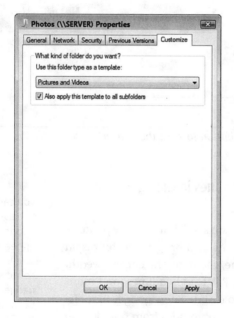

FIGURE 10.14

Apply the Pictures and Videos template to the shared network folder.

5. If you also want Vista to apply this template to all the subfolders in the network share, click to activate the Also Apply This Template to All Subfolders check box.

6. Click OK.

You can now open the network share and click Slide Show in the taskbar, as shown in Figure 10.15.

Slide Show

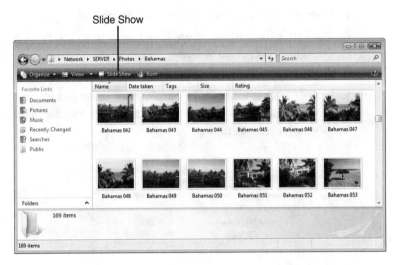

FIGURE 10.15
Click the Slide Show button to start the network-based slideshow.

Display Network Images in the Slide Show Gadget

Windows Vista's Sidebar is a new feature that holds one or more gadgets for displaying the time, the date, the current weather, stock data, RSS feed headlines, and more. There's also a Slide Show gadget that displays a series of images from a folder that you can choose. The default folder is Pictures, but you can configure the gadget to display images from a network share.

Follow these steps to configure the Slide Show gadget to use a network share:

note If you don't have the Sidebar onscreen, you can display it by selecting Start, All Programs, Accessories, Windows Sidebar. The Sidebar appears on the right side of the screen, and the default gadget collection includes the Slide Show gadget. (It usually appears between the Clock gadget and the Feed Headlines gadget.) If you don't see the Slide Show gadget, right-click the Sidebar, and then click Add Gadgets to open the gadgets gallery; then double-click the Slide Show gadget.

1. Right-click the Slide Show gadget and then click Options. The Slide Show dialog box appears.

2. Click the ... button to the right of the Folder list. The Browse for Folder dialog box appears.

3. Click Network to display the list of computers on your network.

4. Click the computer that contains the shared folder you want to use.

5. Select the network share you want to use.

6. Click OK. The Photos share appears in the Folder list, as shown in Figure 10.16.

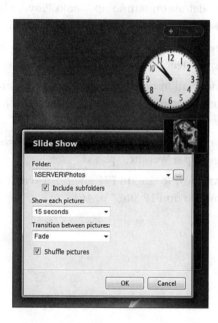

FIGURE 10.16
You can configure the Slide Show gadget to use images from a shared network folder.

7. Configure any other Slideshow options you want to use (such as the time to show each picture and the transition to use between pictures).

8. Click OK to put the new options into effect.

From Here

- For the steps required to connect to a standard wireless network, **see** "Making Wireless Network Connections," **p. 113.** (Chapter 4)

- To learn more about wired connections, **see** Chapter 6, "Managing Network Connections," **p. 139.**

- To learn more about wireless connections, **see** Chapter 7, "Managing Wireless Network Connections," **p. 157.**

- For a discussion about the hardware needed to record TV, **see** "Understanding Digital Media Hardware," **p. 196.** (Chapter 9)

- For the details on setting up Media Player library sharing, **see** "Sharing Your Media Player Library," **p. 207.** (Chapter 9)

- For the details on Meeting Space, **see** Chapter 12, "Collaborating with Windows Meeting Space," **p. 255.**

- For information about Remote Desktop Connection and Internet connections to your network, see Chapter 16, "Making Remote Network Connections," **p. 365.**

- To learn how to run a website from Windows Vista, see Chapter 19, "Setting Up a Website," **p. 431.**

- To learn how to run an FTP site from Windows Vista, see Chapter 20, "Setting Up an FTP Site," **p. 461.**

10

11

Working with Network Files Offline

I n Chapter 16, "Making Remote Network Connections," you learn how to connect to computers on your network using an Internet connection. This is very useful if you're away from your network and need to grab a file or two or just check a fact in some document. However, what do you do if there's no Internet connection available? In that case, there's nothing you can do to get connected to your network. Still, with a bit of advance planning on your part, you can do the next best thing: You can take a bit of the network with you.

This is possible using a Windows Vista feature known as *offline files*. These are network files or folders that Vista has copied to a special folder on your computer. When you disconnect from the network—that is, when you go *offline*—the files and folders remain on your computer, so you can view and even edit the files any time you like. When you reconnect to the network—that is, when you go online—you can synchronize your offline files with the network originals.

IN THIS CHAPTER

- Activating the Offline Files Feature

- Making a File or Folder Available for Offline Use

- Changing the Amount of Disk Space Used by Offline Files

- Prohibiting a Network Folder from Being Made Available Offline

- Encrypting Offline Files

- Working with Network Files While You're Offline

- Synchronizing Your Offline Files

- Dealing with Synchronization Conflicts

- From Here

This chapter shows you how to enable offline files, work with files offline, and synchronize the files to keep everything up-to-date. Note, however, that not all versions of Windows Vista come with the Offline Files feature. You only see this feature if you have Vista Business, Enterprise, or Ultimate.

→   For the details on making remote connections to your network, **see** "Connecting to a Remote Desktop via the Internet," **p. 380**.

Activating the Offline Files Feature

Most Vista systems should have offline files enabled by default. However, it's a good idea to check to make sure that your system has them enabled. Here are the steps to follow:

1. Select Start, Control Panel to open the Control Panel window.

2. Click Network and Internet to open the Network and Internet window.

3. Click Offline Files. Vista opens the Offline Files dialog box, shown in Figure 11.1.

FIGURE 11.1

Click Enable Offline Files to activate the Offline Files feature.

4. Click the Enable Offline Files button. (If you see the Disable Offline Files button instead, offline files are enabled, so click Cancel.) The User Account Control dialog box appears.

5. Enter your User Account Control (UAC) credentials to continue.

6. Click OK. Vista prompts you to restart your computer to put the new setting into effect.

7. Click Yes. Vista restarts your computer.

Making a File or Folder Available for Offline Use

With the Offline Files feature turned on, you're ready to make network files or folders available offline. First, decide what data you need to take with you. Remember that the more files you make available offline, the longer it will take to synchronize everything later, and the more disk space the files will take up on your system. (Note, however, that Vista places a ceiling on the amount of disk space that offline files can use; see "Changing the Amount of Disk Space Used By Offline Files," next.)

When you've decided which files and folders you want to use offline, follow these steps to set them up for offline use:

1. Use Windows Explorer to open the folder that contains the shared network files or folders that you want to use offline.

2. Select the files or folders you want to use offline.

3. Right-click any selected folder, and click Always Available Offline.

4. Windows Vista synchronizes the files or folders for offline use. While the initial synchronization occurs, Vista displays the Always Available Offline dialog box. If you're using quite a few files offline, the synchronization might take a long time. If so, click Close to hide the Always Available Offline dialog box.

> **tip** If your right mouse button doesn't work, press Alt to display the menu bar, and then select File, Always Available Offline.

When you make a file or folder available offline, Vista changes the object's Offline Availability property to `Always Available`, and it adds the Sync Center icon to the object's regular icon, as shown in Figure 11.2. Note, too, the Sync button in the task pane, which enables you to quick synchronize an offline file or folder; see "Synchronizing Your Offline Files," later in this chapter.

> **tip** A quick way to disconnect is to open a folder set up for offline use and then click Work Offline in the task pane.

Sync Center icon

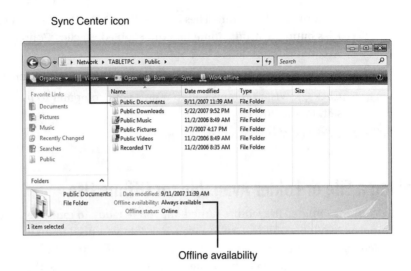

Offline availability

FIGURE 11.2

An offline file or folder shows Always Available *in the Offline Availability property, and the Sync Center icon on its regular icon.*

When the initial synchronization finishes, you can disconnect from the network and work with the files offline.

Changing the Amount of Disk Space Used by Offline Files

I mentioned earlier that you want to be a bit careful about the amount of data you choose to work with offline because synchronizing large amounts of data can take quite a while, and each offline file and folder takes up some disk space on your own computer. Fortunately, just in case you go overboard, Vista puts a limit on the amount of disk space that it uses for both the offline files themselves and for temporary offline files. (Temporary offline files are local copies of network files that you've used recently. Vista keeps these files cached automatically so that you can use them offline if you need them.)

The default limits on the disk space used by offline files and temporary offline files imposed by Vista depend on the size of your hard drive and the amount of free space on that drive. (More specifically, it depends on the size and free space of the hard drive where Windows Vista is installed.) In general, the larger the hard drive and the more free space it has, the greater the percentage of disk space that Vista sets aside for offline data. The usual limits are between 10% and 25% of the total disk space. For example, on a 15GB drive, if Vista sets a limit of 10% of total disk space, you have 1.5GB available for both types of offline files; similarly, on a 200GB drive, if Vista sets a limit of about 25% of total disk space, you have 50GB available for both types of offline files.

You can check your current limits, and optionally adjust them if you find them to be too high or too low, by following these steps:

1. Select Start, Control Panel to open the Control Panel window.

2. Click Network and Internet to open the Network and Internet window.

3. Under Offline Files, click the Manage Disk Space Used By Your Offline Files link. Vista opens the Offline Files dialog box and displays the Disk Usage tab. As shown in Figure 11.3, this tab tells you the amount of disk space you're currently using for offline files and for the offline files cache, and it also tells you the current limits for both types.

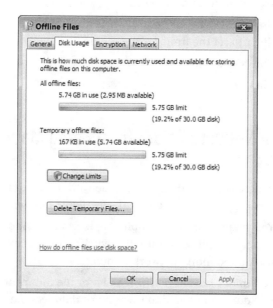

FIGURE 11.3

The Disk Usage tab shows you the disk space used by your offline files as well as the disk space limits.

4. Click Change Limits. The User Account Control dialog box appears.

5. Enter your UAC credentials. The Offline Files Disk Usage Limits dialog box appears, as shown in Figure 11.4.

FIGURE 11.4
Use the Offline Files Disk Usage Limits dialog box to adjust the maximum disk space used by offline and temporary offline files.

   6. Use the Maximum Amount of Space All Offline Files Can Use slider to set the limit for offline files.

   7. Use the Maximum Amount of Space Temporary Offline Files Can Use slider to set the limit for the offline files cache.

   8. Click OK to return to the Offline Files dialog box.

   9. Click OK.

Prohibiting a Network Folder from Being Made Available Offline

You may occasionally come across a network folder or file that you don't want some users on your network to make available offline:

   ■ You might want to prohibit people from making a recorded TV folder available offline because the synchronization would take too long and use up too many network resources.

   ■ You might have a network folder or file that contains private or sensitive data, and you don't want that data leaving the office.

   ■ You might want to do extensive work on the files in a particular folder, and so you don't want others making changes to those files while offline.

For these and similar reasons, Windows Vista enables you to prohibit a user from making a particular network folder available offline. This means that when the user navigates to the network folder or file, Vista doesn't display the Always Available Offline command, so the user can't make the object available offline.

Here are the steps to follow:

1. Log on to the computer of the user for whom you want to set up the restriction. Ideally, you should log on with an Administrator-level account.

2. Press Windows Logo+R (or select Start, All Programs, Accessories, Run) to open the Run dialog box.

3. Type `gpedit.msc` and click OK. The User Account Control dialog box appears.

4. Enter your UAC credentials to continue. The Group Policy Object Editor appears.

5. Select User Configuration, Administrative Templates, Network, Offline Files.

6. Double-click the Prohibit 'Make Available Offline' for These Files and Folders option.

7. Click the Enabled option.

8. Click Show to open the Show Contents dialog box.

9. Click Add to open the Add Item dialog box.

10. In the Enter the Name of the Item to be Added text box, type a name that describes the file or folder you're going to prohibit.

11. In the Enter the Value of the Item to be Added text box, type the network address of the folder or file you want to prohibit (see Figure 11.5).

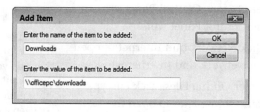

FIGURE 11.5

Specify the network address of the file or folder that you don't want to be made available offline.

12. Click OK to return to the Show Contents dialog box.

13. Repeat steps 9–12 to add any other files or folders that you want to prohibit.

14. Click OK to return to the Prohibit 'Make Available Offline' for These Files and Folders dialog box.

15. Click OK.

Encrypting Offline Files

In the previous section, I mentioned that one of the reasons you'd want to prohibit a file or folder from being made available offline is that it might contain private or sensitive data that you don't want leaving your home or office. That's sensible because a thief could easily steal your notebook and might be able to access the sensitive data. However, it's a problem if you really need to work with that data while you're offline.

To work around this problem, you can encrypt your offline files, which scrambles the file contents so that no snoop can read them unless he can log on to your computer using your Vista account. Because that's unlikely (I'm assuming here that your account is protected by a strong password, which it should be if you're working with sensitive data), your data is safe.

caution Of course, when you're logged in to Vista, you should never leave your notebook unattended. Not only does this make it easy for someone to make off with your computer, it also defeats the purpose of encryption because the thief will already be logged on.

Follow these steps to encrypt your offline files:

1. Select Start, Control Panel to open the Control Panel window.

2. Click Network and Internet to open the Network and Internet window.

3. Under Offline Files, click Encrypt Your Offline Files to open the Offline Files dialog box with the Encryption tab displayed, shown in Figure 11.6.

4. Click Encrypt. Vista encrypts the offline files.

note After Vista encrypts the offline files, it displays the Encrypting File System icon in the taskbar. You should back up your encryption key to a removable media, such as a USB thumb drive, external hard drive, or even a floppy disk, as soon as possible. To do this, click the Back Up Your File Encryption Key message to open the Encrypting File System dialog box, and then click Back Up Now to launch the Certificate Export Wizard.

FIGURE 11.6

Use the Encryption tab to encrypt your offline files for added security.

     5. Click OK.

Working with Network Files While You're Offline

After you disconnect from your network, you can start working with your offline files just as though you were still connected to the network. Windows Vista gives you two ways to go about this:

- You can access the offline files via the Sync Center.
- You can access the offline files by leaving the remote computer's folder window open.

The next couple of sections provide the details.

Working with Offline Files via the Sync Center

The Sync Center is Vista's home base for information that you want to keep synchronized, particularly offline files. To open the Sync Center and view your offline files, follow these steps:

    1. Select Start, Control Panel to open the Control Panel window.

    2. Click Network and Internet to open the Network and Internet window.

3. Click Sync Center. Vista opens the Sync Center window.

4. Click View Sync Partnerships (although this is selected by default). You see the Offline Files folder, as shown in Figure 11.7.

FIGURE 11.7

Use Vista's Sync Center to view and work with your offline files.

4. Double-click Offline Files. The Sync Center displays your sync partnership details, as shown in Figure 11.8.

5. Double-click a sync partnership to open the offline files in a folder window.

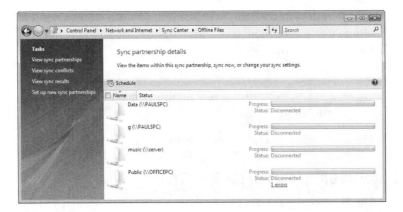

FIGURE 11.8

Double-click a sync partnership to see your offline files.

Now you can open and edit the files just as though you were connected to the network.

Working with Offline Files via the Remote Computer

If you leave the remote computer's folder open when you disconnect, you can use that folder to navigate the offline files directly. Figure 11.8 shows a folder for a network PC, but the computer itself is disconnected from the network (as shown by the Network icon in the notification area). As you saw earlier, the objects available offline display the Offline Files icon superimposed on their regular icon and, when you

tip After you disconnect, you can't navigate to a remote computer's folder via Start, Network because Vista will tell you that you aren't connected to a network. Besides leaving the remote computer's folder window open when you disconnect, you can also type the remote computer's network address into the Run dialog box or the Windows Explorer Address bar.

select an offline object, the Details pane shows Offline (not connected) as the Offline Status (see Figure 11.9).

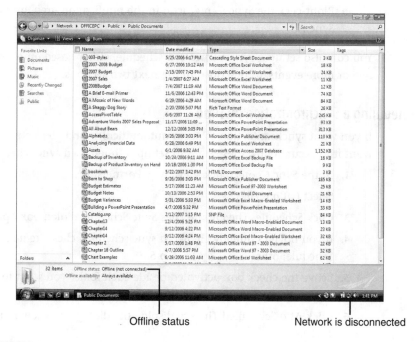

Offline status   Network is disconnected

FIGURE 11.9

A shared network folder displayed offline.

Synchronizing Your Offline Files

When you reconnect to the network, Windows Vista automatically synchronizes the files. This means that Windows Vista does two things: First, it updates your local copy of an offline folder by creating copies of any new or changed files in the shared network folder. Second, it updates the shared network folder with the files you changed while you were offline. This synchronization occurs automatically when you log on to the network and when you log off the network. You can also synchronize the offline files yourself. You have four choices:

- Open the shared network folder and click Sync in the task pane.
- Open the Sync Center, click View Sync Partnerships, double-click Offline Files, select the offline folder, and click Sync.
- Open the Sync Center, click View Sync Partnerships, double-click Offline Files, and click Sync All.
- Right-click the Sync Center icon in the notification area, and click Sync All.

You can also set up a synchronization schedule, either based on a time or on one or more events, as described in the next two sections.

Scheduling a Synchronization by Time

If you want synchronization to occur automatically, and you know when you want it to occur, follow these steps to set up a time-based sync schedule:

1. In the Sync Center, click View Sync Partnerships.
2. Select Offline Files.
3. Click Schedule. The Offline Files Sync Schedule dialog box appears.
4. If you haven't already created a sync schedule, click Create a New Sync Schedule; otherwise, skip to step 5.
5. Leave the check box activated beside each folder you want to include in the synchronization, and click Next.
6. Click At a Scheduled Time to display the dialog box shown in Figure 11.10.
7. Use the Start On controls to specify the date and time when you want synchronization to begin.

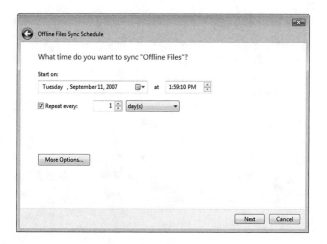

FIGURE 11.10

Use this dialog box to set up a basic sync schedule.

8. Use the Repeat Every controls to specify the numbers of minutes, hours, days, weeks, or months you want to occur between synchronizations.

9. Click More Options to see the More Scheduling Options dialog box with the following options (see Figure 11.11.):

Start Sync Only If: The Computer Is Awake. Leave this check box activated to ensure that the synchronization occurs only if the computer isn't in Standby or Hibernate mode.

Start Sync Only If: The Computer Has Been Idle for at Least X Minutes/Hours. Activate this check box to tell Vista to synchronize only when you're not using your computer. Use the spin box to set the amount of idle time that must occur before the sync begins.

Start Sync Only If: The Computer Is Running on External Power. Activate this check box to avoid running the synchronization when your portable computer is running on batteries.

Stop Sync If: The Computer Wakes Up from Being Idle. Activate this check box to have Vista abandon the sync if you start using your computer.

Stop Sync If: The Computer Is No Longer Running on External Power. Activate this check box to have Vista stop the sync if you switch your portable computer to battery power.

11

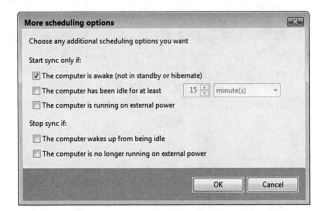

FIGURE 11.11

Use this dialog box to set up a more advanced sync schedule.

10. Click OK.

11. Click Next.

12. Type a name for the schedule.

13. Click Save Schedule.

Scheduling a Synchronization by Event

If you want the synchronization to occur automatically, and you know when you want the synchronization to occur, follow these steps to set up a time-based sync schedule:

1. In the Sync Center, click View Sync Partnerships.

2. Select Offline Files.

3. Click Schedule. The Offline Files Sync Schedule dialog box appears.

4. If you haven't already created a sync schedule, click Create a New Sync Schedule; otherwise, skip to step 5.

5. Leave the check box activated beside each folder you want to include in the synchronization, and click Next.

6. Click On an Event or Action to display the dialog box shown in Figure 11.12.

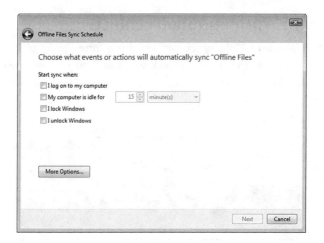

FIGURE 11.12

Use this dialog box to synchronize offline files based on one or more events.

7. Specify the events or actions that trigger the sync by activating one or more of the following check boxes:

   I Log On to My Computer. Activate this check box to start the sync when you log on.

   My Computer Is Idle for *X* Minutes/Hours. Activate this check box to start the sync when your computer has been idle for the number of minutes or hours that you specify.

   I Lock Windows. Activate this check box to start the sync when you lock your computer.

   I Unlock Windows. Activate this check box to start the sync when you unlock your computer.

8. Click More Options to see the More Scheduling Options dialog box (described in the previous section), select your options, and then click OK.

9. Click Next.

10. Type a name for the schedule.

11. Click Save Schedule.

> **note** You lock your computer either by selecting Start, Lock, or by pressing Windows Logo+L.

Dealing with Synchronization Conflicts

When Windows Vista synchronizes your offline files, it might find that a file has changed both on the network share and on your offline computer. In that case, the Sync Center icon displays a Sync Conflicts Have Occurred message (see Figure 11.13).

FIGURE 11.13

You see this message when a file has been changed both locally and offline.

Here's what you do:

1. Click the Sync Conflicts Have Occurred message to open the Sync Center.

2. Click View Sync Conflicts. The Sync Center displays a list of the conflicts.

3. Select the conflict you want to work with.

4. Click Resolve. Vista displays a Resolve Conflict dialog box similar to the one shown in Figure 11.14.

5. Click the version you want to keep, or click Keep Both Versions to have the offline version saved under a modified filename.

> **note** If the Sync Conflicts Have Occurred message no longer appears, you can either right-click the Sync Center icon and then click View Sync Conflicts, or you can open the Sync Center and click the View Sync Conflicts link.

FIGURE 11.14
Use the Resolve Conflict dialog box to tell Vista how you want it to handle a file that has been changed both locally and offline.

From Here

- For the steps required to connect to a standard wireless network, **see** "Making Wireless Network Connections," **p. 113**.

- To learn more about wired connections, **see** Chapter 6, "Managing Network Connections," **p. 139**.

- To learn more about wireless connections, **see** Chapter 7, "Managing Wireless Network Connections," **p. 157**.

- For the details on making remote connections to your network, **see** "Connecting to a Remote Desktop via the Internet," **p. 380**.

Collaborating with Windows Meeting Space

IN THIS CHAPTER

■ Working with the People Near Me Service

■ Configuring Windows Meeting Space

■ Launching Windows Meeting Space

■ Joining an Existing Meeting

■ Starting Your Own Meeting

■ Sending a Meeting Invitation

■ Handling a Meeting Invitation

■ Sharing a Handout

■ Starting a Shared Session

■ Controlling the Shared Session

■ Ending the Shared Session

■ From Here

Y ou saw earlier in this book (see Chapter 8, "Accessing and Sharing Network Resources") that creating a network enables users to share things with each other: an Internet connection, a device such as a printer, and of course files and folders. When you access a computer's shared resources you are, in a sense, working with those resources at a remove, as though you were reaching through the network pipes to grab the resource and use it for yourself for a while.

A much different form of network sharing involves setting up a computer as a Remote Desktop host. In this case, you can then use Vista's Remote Desktop Connection software to connect to that computer's desktop and operate the computer just as though you were sitting down in front of it. In that case, it's more like you sent yourself through the network pipes to work with the remote computer directly. You learn how to do this in Chapter 16, "Making Remote Network Connections."

→   For the details on making remote desktop connections, **see** "Connecting to the Remote Desktop," **p. 373**.

What these two scenarios have in common is that it's just *you* using the resource: It's just you working with the files from the shared network folder, and it's just you operating the remote machine's desktop. In other words, although you can use both of these techniques to accomplish some task for another person—you can, say, proofread a shared document or configure a Windows setting on the remote computer—you do that task by yourself and the other person only sees the results of your labors after you've completed the task. There is, in short, no direct collaboration going on.

That's a shame because it seems like collaboration—two or more people viewing or working on something at the same time—should be at the heart of what networks are all about.

Fortunately, the Windows Vista programmers haven't completely ignored collaboration. First, they did away with the old—and, truth be told, rather stale—tool called NetMeeting that waved the collaboration flag in previous versions of Windows. In its stead, they created a program called Windows Meeting Space that uses new technology and a new approach to make collaboration easier and more intuitive. With Meeting Space, collaboration involves setting up a meeting on one computer and sending out invitations to other people on the network. When users join a meeting, they can collaborate in three main ways:

- **Demonstrate a specific program.** This involves running the program on the computer that's hosting the meeting. This enables the other people in the meeting to watch what happens as the meeting host uses the program. This is a great way to demonstrate a particular technique that you want the others to learn.

- **Work together on a document.** This involves running a program on the computer that's hosting the meeting and using that program to open a document. The person who starts the shared sessions initially has control over the document, but that person can pass control to any participant. This enables multiple people to add to, edit, and format a document.

- **Demonstrate any action.** This involves sharing the desktop of the computer that's hosting the meeting. From there, the other participants see any action that's performed on the host computer. This is a great way to demonstrate multiple techniques.

This chapter gives you a complete look at Windows Meeting Space, from signing in to creating and joining shared sessions to performing the collaborative tasks I mentioned earlier.

Working with the People Near Me Service

Before you can use Windows Meeting Space, you must first configure and sign in to the People Near Me service, which is new to Windows Vista. People Near Me is a network service that looks for other users on your network who are also signed in to People Near Me. Users can then launch programs that support People Near Me and use those programs to contact those other users. For example, a computer game might use People Near Me to invite a nearby user to join the game. In Vista, the only program that supports People Near Me is Windows Meeting Space.

note Windows Meeting Space is available in all versions of Windows Vista. Note, however, that Vista Home Basic users can only view the shared sessions created by other people. They can't initiate shared sessions, and they can't take over a shared session.

Signing In to People Near Me

To use Windows Meeting Space, you must first sign in to People Near Me. You do this either by starting Windows Meeting Space (see "Launching Windows Meeting Space," later in this chapter) or directly via the Control Panel, as described in the following steps:

1. Select Start, Control Panel to open the Control Panel window.

2. Click the Network and Internet link to open the Network and Internet window.

3. Under People Near Me, click the Sign In or Out of People Near Me link. Vista displays the People Near Me dialog box with the Sign In tab displayed.

4. Select the Sign In to People Near Me option, as shown in Figure 12.1.

5. Click OK. The first time you sign in, the Set Up People Near Me dialog box appears.

6. You can configure People Near Me later on (see "Setting People Near Me Options," later in this chapter), so for now just click OK. Vista displays the User Account Control dialog box.

7. Enter your User Account Control (UAC) credentials to continue.

note However, it *is* worth noting that the Set Up People Near Me dialog box displays the People Near Me privacy policy, which states that the People Near Me feature discloses only your name, your computer name, and your computer's IP address.

12

FIGURE 12.1

In the People Near Me dialog box, use the Sign In tab to sign in to the service.

Windows Vista adds the People Near Me icon to the notification area, as shown in Figure 12.2. As you see in the sections that follow, this icon gives you a quicker way to perform certain People Near Me tasks, and it also shows your current status (Signed In or Signed Out) when you hover your cursor over the icon (as shown in Figure 12.2).

People Near Me icon

FIGURE 12.2

When you sign in to People Near Me, Vista adds the People Near Me icon to the notification area.

Working with Trusted Contacts

By default, anyone who is signed in to People Near Me can contact anyone else signed in to People Near Me on the same network. That's not a problem at home or in a small office, but it could be a security concern in a public location such as an airport or coffee shop that offers Wi-Fi service. To plug this security hole, you can configure People Near Me to work with only *trusted contacts*. A trusted contact is a person in your Vista Contacts list with whom you've exchanged contact information that includes a digital certificate that verifies the other person's identity.

Unfortunately, exchanging contact data in such a way that each of you becomes a trusted contact for the other isn't straightforward in Windows Vista. The next two sections show you the correct way to perform this exchange.

Configuring Windows Mail to Not Convert Contact Attachments to vCard

The standard format for exchanging contact information is vCard. However, the vCard format provides less information than the Contact format used by Vista's Contacts folder. In particular, vCard files don't include the digital certificate data that Vista requires to set up someone as a trusted contact. Therefore, before you proceed any further, it's a good idea to configure Windows Mail not to convert contact attachments from the Contact format to the vCard format. Here are the steps to follow:

1. In Windows Mail, select Tools, Options to open the Options dialog box.

2. Select the Advanced tab.

3. In the Contact Attachment Conversion group, select the Leave Contact Attachments in Contact Format option, as shown in Figure 12.3.

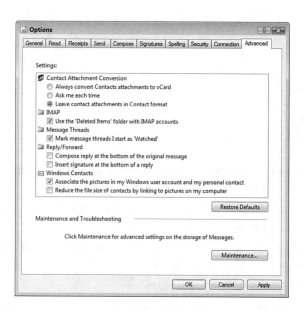

FIGURE 12.3

For best results when exchanging contact data, prevent Windows Mail from converting contact attachments to the vCard format.

4. Click OK to put the new setting into
effect.

Sending Your Contact Data to Another Person

When you first sign in to People Near Me, the
service adds a digital certificate to your personal contact file. To verify this, follow these steps:

1. Select Start, and then select your username at the top of the Start
menu. Vista opens your main user profile folder.

2. Double-click the Contacts icon to open your Contacts.

3. Select the contact that corresponds to your Vista username. You should
see Trusted Contact in the Details pane, as shown in Figure 12.4.

FIGURE 12.4
Select your contact and look for Trusted Contact *in the Details pane.*

Now you're ready to send your contact data to another user. Here are the
steps to follow to send the data using Windows Mail:

1. In Windows Mail, select File, New, Mail Message (or click the Create
Mail button).

2. Use the To box to enter the address of the person to whom you want
your contact information sent.

3. Type a subject for the message.

4. Select Insert, File Attachment to display the Open dialog box.

5. Navigate to the Contacts folder (in the Address bar, click your username and then double-click Contacts).

6. Select your contact file.

7. Click Open.

8. Type a message, if needed.

9. Select File, Send Message (or press Alt+S or click the Send button).

> **tip** If you already have the Contacts folder open, another way to create the attachment is to drag your contact file from the Contacts folder and drop it inside the message window.

Adding Another Person as a Trusted Contact

When you receive someone else's contact data, you need to add that data to your Contacts folder. Here's how it's done:

1. In Windows Mail, select the message that contains the contact data.

2. In the preview pane, click the Paperclip icon and then click the name of the file. The Mail Attachment dialog box appears.

3. Click Open. Windows Mail opens the contact in a Properties dialog box.

4. In the Summary tab, click Add to My Contacts. Vista confirms that it has added the contact.

5. Click OK. The contact data appears.

6. Click OK.

You should now confirm that the new contact is set up as a trusted contact. Open the Contacts folder, select the new contact, and then look for Trusted Contact in the Details pane, as shown in Figure 12.5.

Setting People Near Me Options

Before you use People Near Me extensively, you might consider setting a few options. In particular, if you've gone to the trouble of setting up your trusted contacts as described in the previous two sections, you'll want to configure People Near Me to only allow invitations from those trusted contacts.

> **tip** You can open the Contacts folder from Windows Mail by selecting Tools, Windows Contacts. You can also press Ctrl+Shift+C or click the Contacts button.

12

FIGURE 12.5

In the Contacts folder, select the new contact and look for Trusted Contact *in the Details pane.*

Here are the steps to follow:

1. Select Start, Control Panel to open the Control Panel window.

2. Click the Network and Internet link to open the Network and Internet window.

3. Under People Near Me, click the Change People Near Me Settings link. Vista displays the People Near Me dialog box with the Settings tab displayed, as shown in Figure 12.6.

4. The User Information group has two settings:

   ■ **Type the Name You Want Other People to See.** Use this text box to type the name that you want to expose to other People Near Me users. The default is your Vista username, but you can enter a different name if you like.

   ■ **Make My Picture Available.** Activate this check box to send your picture to other People Near Me users. Again, the default is your Vista user account picture. You can also click Change Picture to send a different picture. (Note, however, that this also changes the picture associated with your Vista user account.)

> **tip** A quicker way to get to the Settings tab is to double-click the People Near Me icon in the notification area. (You can also right-click the icon and then click Settings.)

FIGURE 12.6

In the People Near Me dialog box, use the Settings pane to configure the People Near Me service.

5. The Invitations group has two settings:

   ▓ **Allow Invitations From.** Use this list to select who you want to receive invitations from:

Anyone	This is the default value, and it means that all People Near Me users can send you invitations.
Trusted Contacts	Select this item if your prefer to work only with your trusted contacts.
No One	Select this item if you prefer not to receive invitations at all.

   ▓ **Display a Notification When an Invitation Is Received.** When this check box is activated (as it is by default), the People Near Me icon displays a fly-out message when an invitation comes in. If you prefer not to be interrupted by these messages, deactivate this check box.

6. By default, you're signed in to People Near Me automatically each time you log on to Windows Vista. If you prefer to sign on manually, deactivate the Sign Me In Automatically When Windows Starts check box.

7. Click OK to put the new settings into effect.

Signing Out of People Near Me

If you don't want to receive invitations for a while, or if you no longer want to use People Near Me, you need to sign out. Here are the steps to follow:

tip A quicker way to sign out of People Near Me is to right-click the People Near Me icon in the notification area, and then click Sign Out. When you're ready to sign in again, right-click the People Near Me icon and then click Sign In.

1. Select Start, Control Panel to open the Control Panel window.

2. Click the Network and Internet link to open the Network and Internet window.

3. Under People Near Me, click the Sign In or Out of People Near Me link. Vista displays the People Near Me dialog box with the Sign In tab displayed.

4. Select the Sign Out of People Near Me option.

5. Click OK. Vista signs you out of People Near Me.

Configuring Windows Meeting Space

With People Near Me configured, you're ready to start collaborating with your nearby network neighbors. To begin at the beginning (as the king in *Alice in Wonderland* recommended), you need to configure Windows Meeting Space so that it works properly over your network. Specifically, the Meeting Space data must be allowed to pass through the Windows Firewall, which means there must be Windows Firewall exceptions for three services: Peer to Peer Collaboration Foundation, Distributed File System Replication, and Network Projection.

Fortunately, Meeting Space can configure these firewall exceptions for you automatically. Here are the steps to follow:

1. Select Start, All Programs, Windows Meeting Space. The first time you do this, the Windows Meeting Space Setup dialog box appears, as shown in Figure 12.7.

2. Click Yes, Continue Setting Up Windows Meeting Space. The User Account Control dialog box appears.

12

3. Enter your UAC credentials to continue. Meeting Space creates the exceptions for you automatically. If you're not currently signed in to People Near Me, the People Near Me dialog box appears.

4. Click OK.

FIGURE 12.7
The first time you start Windows Meeting Space, the program offers to configure the Windows Firewall exceptions that it requires to function properly.

Launching Windows Meeting Space

Besides performing the one-time Meeting Space firewall configuration, the steps in the previous section also launched Meeting Space itself. Subsequent launches of the program are simpler, as the following steps show:

1. Select Start, All Programs, Windows Meeting Space. If you're not currently signed in to People Near Me, the People Near Me dialog box appears.

2. Adjust the People Near Me settings, as desired.

3. Click OK.

The Windows Meeting Space window appears, as shown in Figure 12.8. From here, you either start a new collaboration meeting or join an existing meeting, as described in the rest of this chapter.

12

FIGURE 12.8
Use the Windows Meeting Space window to start and join collaboration meetings.

Joining an Existing Meeting

When you launch Meeting Space, the program shows a list of the existing meetings. If you don't see any meetings, wait a while and then click the Update List link to refresh the list of meetings. If you didn't receive an invitation to a meeting, here are the steps to follow to join an existing meeting:

1. In the Meeting Space window, click Join a Meeting Near Me. Windows Meeting Space displays a list of running meetings, as shown in Figure 12.9.

2. Click the meeting you want to join. Windows Meeting Space prompts you to enter the meeting password.

3. Type the password and press Enter. Windows Meeting Space verifies your password and then joins the meeting.

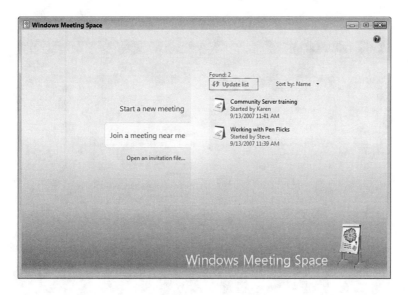

FIGURE 12.9
Click Join a Meeting Near Me to see a list of the running meetings.

Starting Your Own Meeting

If you want to demonstrate one of your programs, share your desktop, or collaborate on one of your documents, you need to start your own meeting. Here are the steps to follow:

1. Click Start a New Meeting to display the controls shown in Figure 12.10 (which shows the controls already filled in).

2. Use the Meeting Name text box to type a descriptive name for the meeting.

3. Use the Password text box to type a password that users must enter to join the meeting.

4. Click the Create a Meeting button (see Figure 12.10) or press Enter. Meeting Space starts the new meeting, as shown in Figure 12.11.

12

Create a Meeting

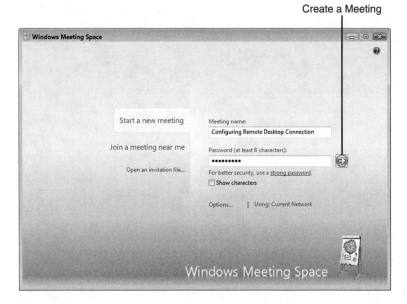

FIGURE 12.10

Click Start a New Meeting to begin defining your meeting.

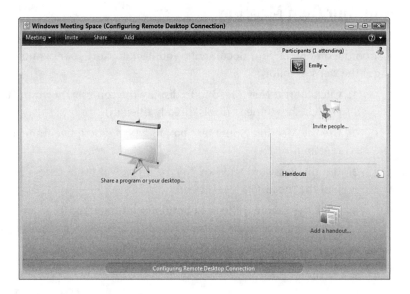

FIGURE 12.11

Meeting Space with a newly created meeting.

Sending a Meeting Invitation

Collaboration is, by definition, something that requires two or more people, so creating a new meeting is just the first step. You could wait for other people to notice your meeting in Meeting Space's Join a Meeting Near Me section. However, that's problematic because assuming others know the correct password (for example, you might institute a common password for all meetings), you have no control over who joins the meeting and, more important, you can't control when they join. A good meeting consists of just the people you want attending and starts when you want it to. To ensure this, you should send out invitations to the people you'd like in your meeting. The next couple of sections provide the details.

Sending a Meeting Invitation Using People Near Me

Here are the steps to follow to send an invitation to people who are signed in to People Near Me:

1. Click Invite in the menu bar or click the Invite People icon. The Invite People dialog box appears, as shown in Figure 12.12.

FIGURE 12.12
Use the Invite People dialog box to choose who you want to invite to your meeting.

2. Activate the check box beside each person you want to invite.
3. Click Send Invitations.

Sending a Meeting Invitation via Email

The list of users you see in the Invite People dialog box consists of those people signed in to People Near Me on your network. If you want others to attend, you can send them an email message. Here are the steps to follow to send an invitation via email:

1. Click Invite in the menu bar or click the Invite People icon to open the Invite People dialog box.

2. Click Invite Others to display the dialog box shown in Figure 12.13.

FIGURE 12.13

Click Send an Invitation in E-mail to invite people to your meeting using an email message.

3. Click Send an Invitation in E-mail. Meeting Space creates a new email message, includes a Windows Meeting Space invitation file as an attachment, and adds instructions to the message body (see Figure 12.14).

4. Use the To box to enter the addresses of the people you want to invite to your meeting.

5. (Optional) Edit the subject of the message.

6. (Optional) Edit the message body.

7. Select File, Send Message (or press Alt+S or click the Send button).

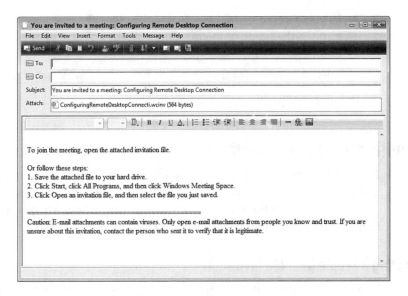

FIGURE 12.14

Meeting Space creates an email message that includes an invitation file and instructions for using it.

Creating an Invitation File

If there are people on your network who you want to invite to your meeting, but those people are not part of People Near Me and you don't know (or don't want to use) their email addresses, you can still invite them to your meeting. In this case, you need to create a Windows Meeting Space invitation file, which you can then put on the network in a shared folder. The users would then use Meeting Space to open the invitation file (as described later; see "Opening an Invitation File").

Here are the steps to follow to create an invitation file:

1. Click Invite in the menu bar or click the Invite People icon to open the Invite People dialog box.

2. Click Invite Others to display the dialog box shown earlier in Figure 12.13.

3. Click Create an Invitation File. The Save As dialog box appears.

> **tip** For best results, save the invitation file in a shared network folder that you know is accessible by the people you want to invite.

4. Use the File Name text box to edit the filename, if desired. (The default name is the name of the meeting, without any spaces or illegal file-name characters.)

5. Select a location for the invitation file.

6. Click Save.

Handling a Meeting Invitation

To get in on a meeting where you don't know the password, you need to accept an invitation that comes your way. How you do this depends on whether you receive the information through People Near Me or via an invitation file, as described in the next two sections.

Handling a People Near Me Invitation

When you receive an invitation via the People Near Me service, you first see a notification message from the People Near Me icon. The structure of this message depends on whether the user is a trusted contact.

If the user is not a trusted contact, you see the following message, as shown in Figure 12.15:

```
Someone is inviting you to use Windows Meeting Space.
```

FIGURE 12.15

When a People Near Me meeting invitation first arrives, you see this message if the invitation comes from a person who is not a trusted contact.

Click View (or wait a few seconds and then click the Invitation Details taskbar button), and you see the Invitation Details dialog box shown in Figure 12.16.

The invitation is slightly different if it comes from a trusted contact. In this case, you first see the following message (where *User* is the person's People Near Me name; see Figure 12.17):

```
User is inviting you to use Windows Meeting Space.
```

FIGURE 12.16

The Invitation Details dialog box for an invitation that came from a person who is not a trusted contact.

FIGURE 12.17

When a People Near Me meeting invitation first arrives, you see this message if the invitation comes from a person who is a trusted contact.

Again, click View (or wait a few seconds and then click the Invitation Details taskbar button) to display the Invitation Details dialog box. The trusted contact version looks like the dialog box shown in Figure 12.18.

Either way, you now have three choices:

Accept   Click this button to join the meeting. This also loads Windows Meeting Space, and you then enter the meeting password.

Decline   Click this button to refuse the invitation.

Dismiss   Click this button to do nothing.

As people accept the invitations, their People Near Me name appears in the Windows Meeting Space Participants list.

FIGURE 12.18
The Invitation Details dialog box for an invitation that came from a person who is a trusted contact.

Opening an Invitation File

If you receive an invitation file attached to an email message, or if an invitation file exists in a shared network folder, follow these steps to use the file to join the meeting:

1. How you begin depends on where the invitation file resides:

   - If you saved the invitation file attachment to a folder on your system or if the invitation file resides on a shared network folder, use Windows Explorer to open the folder and then double-click the invitation file.

   - If the invitation file only resides as an email attachment, open the message, double-click the attachment, and then click Open.

2. In the Meeting Space window that appears, type the password, as shown in Figure 12.19.

3. Click the Join a Meeting button (see Figure 12.19).

Join a Meeting

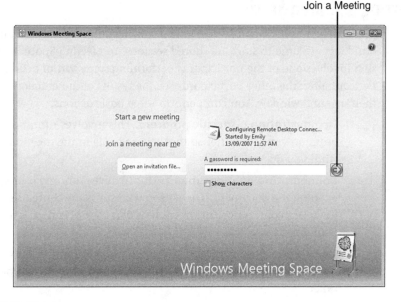

FIGURE 12.10
Click Start a New Meeting to begin defining your meeting.

Sharing a Handout

Before getting to the presentation, you might have some notes, instructions, background material, or other type of handout that you want to share with each participant. You do this by following these steps:

1. Click Add in the menu bar or click the Add a Handout icon. Meeting Space tells you the handouts will be copied to each computer.

2. Click OK. The Select Files to Add dialog box appears.

3. Select the file you want to use as a handout.

4. Click Open. The file appears immediately in the Handouts area, which shows the filename and the name of the person who added it.

caution You can share any type of file you want as a handout. However, remember that the remote users will be able to view and work with the handout file only if they have an application installed that's associated with the handout's file type.

12

Starting a Shared Session

When all your participants have joined the meeting and you've shared your handouts, it's time to start the shared sessions. In Meeting Space, a shared session involves one of the participants performing some sort of action on his or her computer; the other participants see the results of those actions within their meeting window. You can perform three basic actions:

- **Demonstrating a specific program.** This involves running the program on your computer so that other people in the meeting can watch what you do.

- **Collaborating on a document.** This involves running a program and opening the document. The person who starts the shared session initially has control over the document, but control can pass to any participant.

- **Demonstrating any action.** This involves sharing your desktop, which means that the other participants see anything you do on your computer.

Follow these steps to start a shared session:

1. If you're going to demonstrate a specific program or collaborate on a document, start the program or open the document.

2. Click Share in the menu bar. Meeting Space asks whether you want the other participants to see your desktop.

3. Click OK. The Start a Shared Session dialog box appears.

4. You have three choices:

    - To share a program, select the program from the list of running applications.

    - To share a document, select Browse for a File to Open and Share.

    - To share your desktop, select Desktop.

5. Click Share.

6. If you are sharing a document, the Open dialog box appears. Select the document, and then select Open.

caution Vista might automatically switch to a different color scheme if one of the participating computers can't handle your current color scheme. For example, if you're running the Aero scheme and a participating computer is running only Vista Basic, Vista switches to Basic.

tip To present your handout, right-click the handout and click Share to Meeting.

Controlling the Shared Session

After you begin a shared session, the Meeting Space window displays a You are sharing X message, where X is the object you're sharing. You also see two links:

■ **Show Me How My Shared Sessions Looks on Other Computers.** Click this link to see your shared session from the point of view of a remote computer.

■ **Stop Sharing.** Click this link to shut down the shared session.

Vista also displays a You are sharing message as well as the meeting title in a title bar across the top of the desktop, as shown in Figure 12.20. You can use the controls in this bar as follows:

■ Click Pause Shared Session to stop the shared session temporarily.

■ Click Give Control and then click a participant's name to give that person control of the shared session.

■ Click Give Control, Take Control (or press Windows Logo+Esc) to resume control of the shared session.

■ Click Options, Show Windows Meeting Space Window to switch to the Windows Meeting Space window.

■ Click the Stop button to stop the shared session.

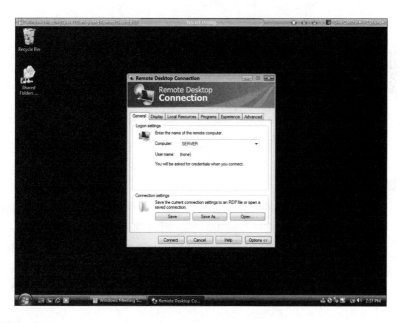

12

FIGURE 12.20

This bar appears at the top of your desktop after you start a shared session.

Figure 12.21 shows what the shared session looks like on a remote computer.

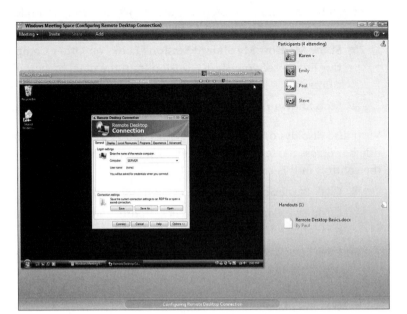

FIGURE 12.21

The presentation as seen on a remote computer.

Ending the Shared Session

When the shared session is over, click the Stop Sharing link in the Meeting Space window or click the Stop Sharing button in the session title bar. If you don't want to share anything else, select Meeting, Leave Meeting, or close the Meeting Space window.

From Here

- For information about shared network resources, **see** Chapter 8, "Accessing and Sharing Network Resources," **p. 171**.

- To learn more about network security, **see** Chapter 14, "Implementing Network Security," **p. 313**.

- For the details on making connections to network desktops, **see** "Connecting to the Remote Desktop," **p. 373**.

Securing Your Network

13 Securing Windows Vista

14 Implementing Network Security

15 Implementing Wireless Security

Securing Windows Vista

Securing a network is often a complex bit of business because it always requires a multipronged approach. First, you need to secure network objects such as shared folders and make adjustments to Windows Firewall to allow (or block) certain networking services, programs, and ports; I cover these aspects of securing your network in Chapter 14, "Implementing Network Security." Second, if you have a wireless component to your network, you have an inherently nonsecure setup because wireless data is almost always broadcast beyond your home or office; I cover securing your wireless network in Chapter 15, "Implementing Wireless Security." That would seem to cover everything, but network security is a "weakest link" proposition—your network is only as secure as the least secure network computer. That is, all your security precautions are for naught if you have a computer on your network that uses a weak password (or no password at all), or contains malware such as a virus, Trojan horse, or spyware. So the first step in securing your network is securing the network clients. This chapter takes you through the main security features of Windows Vista.

IN THIS CHAPTER

- Understanding Vista's Security Groups
- Understanding User Account Control
- Implementing Parental Controls
- Building a Strong Password
- Checking Your Computer's Security Settings
- Thwarting Spyware with Windows Defender
- Protecting Yourself Against Email Viruses
- Protecting Yourself Against Phishing Scams
- From Here

Understanding Vista's Security Groups

A *security group* is an object defined with a specific set of permissions and rights that determine what actions members of the group can perform. Any user added to a group is automatically granted that group's permissions and rights. Security for Windows Vista user accounts is handled mostly (and most easily) by assigning each user to a particular security group.

Although Vista comes with a relatively large number of security groups, there are actually only two groups that you need to work with:

Administrators   Members of this group have complete control over the computer (although see "Understanding User Account Control," next), meaning they can access all folders and files and install and uninstall programs (including legacy programs) and devices. They can also create, modify, and remove user accounts; install Windows updates, service packs, and fixes; use Safe mode; repair Windows; take ownership of objects; and more. The built-in Administrator account and the user account you created during the Windows Vista setup process are part of the Administrators group.

Users   Members of this group (also known as Standard Users) can access files only in their own folders and in the computer's shared folders. They can also change their account's password and picture, and they run programs and install programs that don't require administrative-level rights.

Each user is also assigned a user profile that contains all the user's folders and files, as well as the user's Windows settings. The folders and files are stored in %SystemDrive%\Users*user*, where %SystemDrive% is the drive on which Vista is installed (usually C:\), and *user* is the username; for the current user, this folder is designated by the %UserProfile% variable. This location contains a number of subfolders that hold the user's document folders (Documents, Pictures, Music, and so on), desktop icons and subfolders (Desktop), Internet Explorer favorites (Favorites), contacts (Contacts), saved searches (Searches), and more.

Understanding User Account Control

I mentioned earlier that administrators can do *anything* to a Windows machine. This includes potentially harmful activities such as installing programs, adding devices, updating device drivers, installing updates and patches, changing Registry settings, and running administrative tools. These are potentially harmful because if a malware program gets on your computer, it will attempt to give itself Administrator-level permissions and, if it's successful, the program can do all kinds of damage to your system and to other computers on the network. On the other hand, you can't simply ban these potentially harmful activities, because each one of them is also potentially useful.

Understanding the Least-Privileged User

So all this leads to the most fundamental security conundrum: How do you give users the flexibility and power of activities such as installing programs and devices, and at the same time prevent viruses and other malware from performing the same activities? Windows Vista's answer to this problem is called User Account Control (UAC). UAC uses a principle called the *least-privileged user*, which is defined as an account level that has no more permissions than it requires.

In Windows Vista, the least-privileged user concept arrives in the form of a new account type called the Standard User. This means that Vista has three basic account levels:

Administrator account	This built-in account can do anything to the computer, but it's turned off by default in Vista.
Administrators group	Members of this group (except the Administrator account) run as standard users but are able to elevate their privileges when required just by clicking a button in a dialog box (see the next section). Use this group for your own account and for people who are experienced computer users and who you believe are responsible.
Standard Users group	These are the least-privileged users, although they, too, can elevate their privileges when needed. However, they require access to an administrator password to do so. Use this group for people who are inexperienced users, particularly younger children, or for people with moderate experience but who are not yet responsible enough to merit inclusion in the Administrators group.

13

Elevating Privileges

This idea of elevating privileges is at the heart of Vista's new security model. If you're a member of the Administrators group (except the Administrator account, as described in the previous section), you run with the privileges of a standard user for extra security. When you attempt a task that requires administrative privileges, Vista prompts for your consent by displaying a User Account Control dialog box similar to the one shown in Figure 13.1. Click Continue to permit the task to proceed. If this dialog box appears unexpectedly, it's possible that a malware program is trying to perform some task that requires administrative privileges; you can thwart that task by clicking Cancel instead.

caution After you've used Vista for a while, the temptation may be to quickly click Continue each time the User Account Control dialog box shows up. I strongly urge you to fight this temptation with all your might! The thin thread that separates a secure Vista machine from a compromised one is your attention. That is, when the User Account Control dialog box appears, it's important that you pay attention to the text in the dialog box. Is it a program or service that you know you're starting or that you're already working with? If not, click Cancel. Did the dialog box appear right after you initiated some task, or did it just show up out of the blue? If it was the latter, click Cancel.

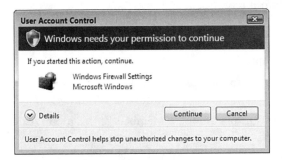

FIGURE 13.1

When an administrator launches a task that requires administrative privileges, Windows Vista displays this version of the User Account Control dialog box to ask for consent.

If you're running as a standard user and attempt a task that requires administrative privileges, Vista uses an extra level of protection. That is, instead of just prompting you for consent, it prompts you for the credentials of an

administrator, as shown in Figure 13.2. If your system has multiple administrator accounts, each one is shown in this dialog box. Type the password for
any administrator account shown, and then click Submit. Again, if this dialog
box shows up unexpectedly, it might be malware, so you should click Cancel
to prevent the task from going through.

FIGURE 13.2

*When a standard user launches a task that requires administrative privileges, Windows Vista
displays this version of the User Account Control dialog box to ask for administrative credentials.*

Note, too, that in both cases Windows Vista switches to Secure Desktop mode,
which means that you can't do anything else with Vista until you give your
consent or credentials or cancel the operation. Vista indicates the secure desktop by darkening everything on the screen except the User Account Control
dialog box.

Is there any way to tell when the User Account Control dialog box will show
up? In most cases, yes. Vista usually adds a Security icon beside a link or
other control that requires elevated permissions. Figure 13.3 shows a few
examples.

13

These tasks require elevation

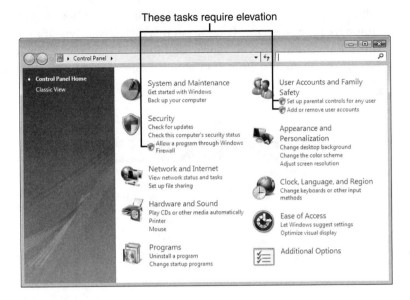

FIGURE 13.3
Vista displays a security icon beside links and other controls that initiate actions that require elevated permissions.

Implementing Parental Controls

If you're working with a home network, chances are that you have children who share your computer or who have their own computer. Either way, it's smart to take precautions regarding the content and programs that they can access. Locally, this might take the form of blocking access to certain programs (such as your financial software), using ratings to control which games they can play, and setting time limits on when the computer is used. If the computer has Internet access, you might also want to allow (or block) specific sites, block certain types of content, and prevent file downloads.

All this sounds daunting, but Windows Vista's Parental Controls make things a bit easier by offering an easy-to-use interface that lets you set all the aforementioned options and lots more.

> **note** Parental Controls are available in the Home Basic, Home Premium, and Ultimate editions of Windows Vista.

Setting Up User Accounts for the Kids

Before you configure Parental Controls, you need to create a Standard User account for each child who uses the computer. Here are the steps to follow:

1. Select Start, Control Panel, Add or Remove User Accounts. The User Account Control dialog box appears.

2. Enter your UAC credentials to continue. Vista displays the Manage Accounts window.

3. Click Create a New Account. The Create New Account window appears.

4. Type the name for the account. The name can be up to 20 characters and must be unique on the system.

5. Make sure the Standard User option is activated, as shown in Figure 13.4.

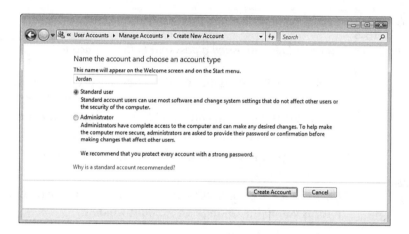

FIGURE 13.4

When you create an account for a child, be sure to select the Standard User option.

6. Click Create Account. Vista sets up the new account and returns you to the Manage Accounts window.

7. Click the account you just created to open the Change an Account window.

8. Click Create a Password to open the Create Password window, shown in Figure 13.5.

> **note** A strong password is the first line of defense when it comes to local computer security. Before setting up a password for an account, check out the section "Building a Strong Password," later in this chapter.

13

FIGURE 13.5
Use the Create Password window to assign a password to the new account.

9. Use the New Password and Confirm New Password text boxes to type a password for the account. (Make sure it's a password that the child can remember. If you think your child is too young to remember a password, skip to step 12 to bypass this portion of the procedure.)

10. Use the Type a Password Hint text box to type a hint for remembering the password.

11. Click Create Password. Vista adds the password to the account and returns you to the Change an Account window.

12. Click Manage Another Account

13. Repeat steps 3–12 to add standard user accounts for all your kids.

Turning On Parental Controls and Activity Reporting

With the kids' accounts in place, you get to Parental Controls using either of the following methods:

caution The password hint is text that Vista displays in the Welcome screen if you type an incorrect password. Because the hint is visible to anyone trying to log on to your machine, make the hint as vague as possible but still useful to you if you forget your password.

- If you still have the Manage Accounts window open, click Set Up Parental Controls.
- Select Start, Control Panel, Set Up Parental Controls.

Enter your UAC credentials to get to the Parental Controls window, and then click the user you want to work with to get to the User Controls window.

You should activate two options here (see Figure 13.6):

Parental Controls   Click On, Enforce Current Settings. This enables the Windows Vista Web Filter, and the Time Limits, Games, and Allow and Block Specific Programs links in the Settings area.

Activity Reporting   Click On, Collect Information About Computer Usage. This tells Vista to track system events such as blocked logon attempts and attempted changes to user accounts, the system date and time, and system settings.

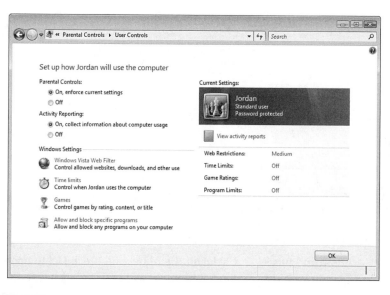

FIGURE 13.6

The User Controls window enables you to set up web, time, game, and program restrictions for the selected user.

The Windows Settings section has four links that you use to set up the controls on the selected user. Two of these are security related—Windows Vista Web Filter and Allow and Block Specific Programs—so I discuss them in the next two sections.

Securing the Web

In the User Controls window, click Windows Vista Web Filter to display the Web Restrictions page, shown in Figure 13.7. Make sure the Block Some Websites or Content option is activated.

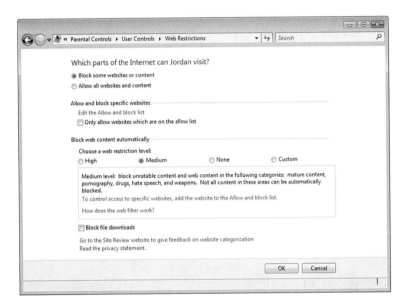

FIGURE 13.7

Use the Web Restrictions window control web surfing actions for the selected user.

You can control websites, web content, and file downloads:

Allow and Block Specific Websites	Click Edit the Allow and Block List to open the Allow Block Webpages window. For each safe site that the user can visit, type the website address and click Allow to add the site to the Allowed Websites list; for each unsafe site that the user can't visit, type the website address and click Block to add the site to the Blocked Websites list. Because there are so many possible sites to block, consider activating the Only Allow Websites Which Are on the Allow List check box.

Block Web Content
Automatically

Select the option you want to use to restrict site content: High, Medium, None, or Custom. If you select the Custom Web restriction level, Vista adds a number of check boxes that enable you to block specific content categories (such as Pornography, Mature Content, and Bomb Making).

Block File
Downloads

Activate this check box to prevent the user from downloading files via the web browser.

Allowing Only Specific Programs

If you want your kids to use only the programs that you specify (for example, games and other software suitable for children), follow these steps to configure Parental Controls accordingly:

1. In the User Controls window, click Allow and Block Specific Programs to display the Application Restrictions page.

2. Select the *User* Can Only Use the Programs I Allow option (where *User* is the name of the user you're working with). Vista then populates the Check the Programs That Can Be Used list with the applications on your computer, as shown in Figure 13.8.

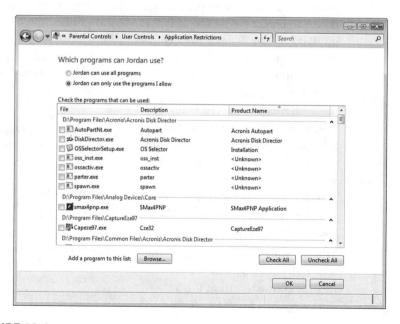

FIGURE 13.8

Use the Application Restrictions window control web surfing actions for the selected user.

3. Activate the check boxes for the programs you want to allow the person to use.

4. Click OK.

Building a Strong Password

With Vista's focus on improved security, it seems strange that the Administrator-level account you create when you first install Vista (or first start your new Vista computer) doesn't require a password. If you didn't bother assigning a password to this account, you should fix this gaping security hole as soon as possible. In fact, it's a good idea to assign passwords to *all* your user accounts on *all* your network computers.

However, it's not enough to just use any old password. You can improve the security of Vista—and, hence, of your entire network—by making each password *strong* enough that it is impossible to guess and is impervious to software programs designed to try different password combinations. Ideally, you want to build a password that provides maximum protection while still being easy to remember. Here are some guidelines you can follow to create a strong password:

- **Use passwords that are at least eight characters long.** Shorter passwords are susceptible to programs that just try every letter combination. You can combine the 26 letters of the alphabet into about 12 million different 5-letter word combinations, which is no big deal for a fast program. If you bump things up to 8-letter passwords, however, the total number of combinations rises to 200 *billion*, which would take even the fastest computer quite a while. If you use 12-letter passwords, as many experts recommend, the number of combinations goes beyond mind-boggling: 90 *quadrillion*, or 90,000 trillion!

- **Mix up your character types.** The secret to a strong password is to include characters from the following categories: lowercase letters,

> **tip** How will you know whether the password you've come up with fits the definition of *strong*? One way to find out is to submit the password to an online password complexity checker. (If you're the least bit paranoid about these things, consider submitting a password that's only similar to the one you want to use.) I recommend Microsoft's (http://www.microsoft.com/athome/security/privacy/password_checker.mspx), but a Google search on "password complexity checker" will reveal many others.

uppercase letters, numbers, and symbols. If you include at least one character from three (or, even better, all four) of these categories, you're well on your way to a strong password.

- **Don't be too obvious.** Because forgetting a password is inconvenient, many people use meaningful words or numbers so that their password will be easier to remember. Unfortunately, this means that they often use extremely obvious things such as their name, the name of a family member or colleague, their birth date, or Social Security number, or even their system username. Being this obvious is just asking for trouble.

- **Don't use single words.** Many crackers break into accounts by using "dictionary programs" that just try every word in the dictionary. So, yes, *xiphoid* is an obscure word that no person would ever guess, but a good dictionary program will figure it out in seconds flat. Using two or more words in your password (or pass phrase, as multiword passwords are called) is still easy to remember, and would take much longer to crack by a brute-force program.

- **Use a misspelled word.** Misspelling a word is an easy way to fool a dictionary program. (Make sure, of course, that the resulting arrangement of letters doesn't spell some other word.)

- **Try using acronyms.** One of the best ways to get a password that appears random but is easy to remember is to create an acronym out of a favorite quotation, saying, or book title. For example, if you've just read *The Seven Habits of Highly Effective People*, you could use the password T7HoHEP.

- **Don't write down your password.** After going to all this trouble to create an indestructible password, don't blow it by writing it on a sticky note and then attaching it to your keyboard or monitor! Even writing it on a piece of paper and then throwing the paper away is dangerous. Determined crackers have been known to go through a company's trash looking for passwords. (This is known in the trade as *dumpster diving*.) Also, don't use the password itself as your Windows Vista password hint.

- **Don't tell your password to anyone.** If you've thought of a particularly clever password, don't suddenly become unclever and tell someone. Your password should be stored in your head alongside all those "wasted youth" things you don't want anyone to know about.

13

■ **Change your password regularly.** If you change your password often (say, once a month or so), even if some skulker does get access to your account, at least he'll have it for only a relatively short period.

Checking Your Computer's Security Settings

Most of Windows Vista's security settings are turned on out of the box. However, security is such an important topic that you shouldn't take anything for granted. The following three sections take you through four Vista security settings that are worth taking the time to double-check: Windows Firewall, Windows Defender, Automatic Updates, and User Account Control.

Making Sure Windows Firewall Is Turned On

Your network probably connects to the Internet using a *broadband*—cable modem or Digital Subscriber Line (DSL)—service. This means that you have an always-on connection, so there's a much greater chance that a malicious hacker could find your computer and have his way with it. You might think that with millions of people connected to the Internet at any given moment, there would be little chance of a "script kiddy" finding you in the herd. Unfortunately, one of the most common weapons in a black-hat hacker's arsenal is a program that runs through millions of IP addresses automatically, looking for live connections. The fact that many cable systems and some DSL systems use IP addresses in a narrow range compounds the problem by making it easier to find always-on connections.

When a cracker finds your address, he has many avenues from which to access your computer. Specifically, your connection uses many different ports for sending and receiving data. For example, File Transfer Protocol (FTP) uses ports 20 and 21, web data and commands typically use port 80, email uses ports 25 and 110, the domain name system (DNS) uses port 53, and so on. In all, there are dozens of these ports, and each one is an opening through which a clever cracker can gain access to your computer.

As if that weren't enough, attackers can check your system for the installation of some kind of Trojan horse or virus. (Malicious email attachments sometimes install these programs on your machine.) If the hacker finds one, he can effectively

> **tip** An easy way to make sure your Vista machine is fully protected is to display the Security Center. Select Start, Control Panel, and then, under Security, click the Check This Computer's Security Status link.

take control of your machine (turning it into a *zombie computer*) and either wreak havoc on its contents or use your computer to attack other systems.

Again, if you think your computer is too obscure or worthless for someone else to bother with, think again. Hackers probe a typical computer connected to the Internet for vulnerable ports or installed Trojan horses at least a few times every day. If you want to see just how vulnerable your computer is, several good sites on the Web can test your security:

- **Gibson Research (Shields Up).** http://grc.com/default.htm
- **DSL Reports.** http://www.dslreports.com/secureme_go
- **HackerWhacker.** http://www.hackerwhacker.com

The good news is that Windows Vista comes with Windows Firewall, which is a personal firewall that can lock down your ports and prevent unauthorized access to your machine. In effect, your computer becomes invisible to the Internet (although you can still surf the Web and work with email normally).

Windows Firewall is activated by default in Windows Vista. However, it pays to be safe, so here are the steps to follow to ensure that it's turned on:

1. Select Start, Control Panel to open the Control Panel window.
2. Click Security to open the Security window.
3. Click Turn Windows Firewall On or Off. The User Account Control dialog box appears.
4. Enter your UAC credentials. The Windows Firewall Settings dialog box appears.
5. Make sure the On option is activated, as shown in Figure 13.9.
6. Click OK.

Making Sure Windows Defender Is Turned On

Malware is the generic term for malicious software such as viruses and Trojan horses. The worst malware offender by far these days is *spyware*, which is generally defined as any program that surreptitiously monitors a user's computer activities—particularly the typing of passwords, PINs, and credit card numbers—or harvests sensitive data on the user's computer and then sends that information to an individual or a company via the user's Internet connection (the so-called *back channel*) without the user's consent.

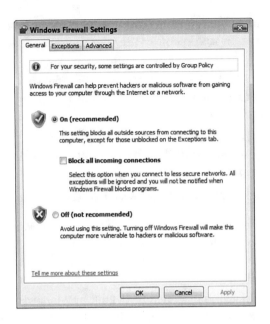

FIGURE 13.9

To ensure safe computing, make sure Windows Firewall is turned on.

You might think that having a robust firewall between you and the bad guys would make malware a problem of the past. Unfortunately, that's not true. These programs piggyback on other legitimate programs that users actually *want* to download, such as file-sharing programs, download managers, and screensavers. A *drive-by download* is the download and installation of a program without a user's knowledge or consent. This relates closely to a *pop-up download*—the download and installation of a program after the user clicks an option in a pop-up browser window, particularly when the option's intent is vaguely or misleadingly worded.

To make matters even worse, most spyware embeds itself deep into a system, and removing it is a delicate and time-consuming operation beyond the abilities of even some experienced users. Some programs actually come with an Uninstall option, but it's nothing but a ruse, of course. The program appears to remove itself from the system, but what it actually does is a *covert reinstall*—it surreptitiously reinstalls a fresh version of itself when the computer is idle.

All this means that you need to buttress your firewall with an antispyware program that can watch out for these unwanted programs and prevent them from getting their hooks into your system. In previous versions of Windows, you needed to install

tip For a list of known programs and sites that install malware, see stopbadware.org.

a third-party program. However, Windows Vista comes with an antispyware program named Windows Defender.

Follow these steps to ensure that Windows Defender is configured to defend your computer from spyware:

1. Start Windows Defender using any of the following methods:

   - Select Start, All Programs, Windows Defender.

   - Select Start, Control Panel, Security, Windows Defender.

   - Double-click the Windows Defender icon in the taskbar's notification area (although this icon usually appears only when Windows Defender needs your attention).

2. Select Tools.

3. Select Options. Windows Defender displays the Options window, shown in Figure 13.10.

> **tip** Many security experts recommend installing multiple antispyware programs on the premise that one program may miss one or two examples of spyware, but two or three programs are highly unlikely to miss any. So, in addition to Windows Defender, you might also consider installing antispyware programs such as Lavasoft Ad-Aware (http://www.lavasoft.com) and PC Tools Spyware Doctor (http://www.pctools.com).

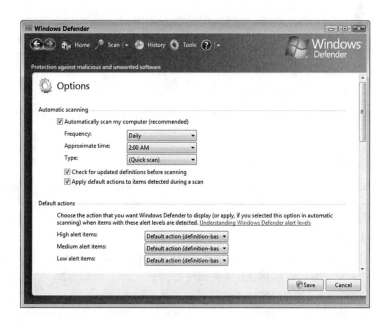

FIGURE 13.10

Make sure Windows Defender is configured to automatically scan your system for spyware.

4. Make sure the Automatically Scan My Computer check box is activated.

5. Scroll down to the bottom of the window, as shown in Figure 13.11.

6. Make sure the Use Real-Time Protection check box is activated.

7. Click Save. The User Account Control dialog box appears.

8. Enter your UAC credentials.

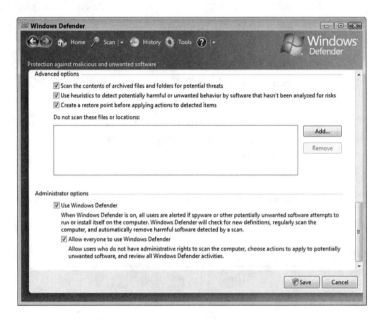

FIGURE 13.11
Make sure Windows Defender is configured to monitor your system for spyware activity.

Controlling Automatic Updates

Microsoft is constantly working to improve Windows Vista with bug fixes, security patches, new program versions, and device driver updates. All of these new and improved components are available online, so you should check for updates and patches often.

The main online site for Windows Vista updates is the Windows Update website, which you load into Internet Explorer by selecting Start, All Programs, Windows Update. You should visit this site regularly to look for crucial new components that can make Windows Vista more reliable and more secure.

Windows Vista also comes with a vastly improved automatic updating feature, which can download and install updates automatically. If you prefer to know what's happening with your computer, it's possible to control the automatic updating by following these steps:

note To view the updates installed on your computer, click the View Installed Updates link.

1. Select Start, Control Panel to open the Control Panel window.

2. Select Security to open the Security window.

3. Select Turn Automatic Updating On or Off. The Change Settings window appears, as shown in Figure 13.12.

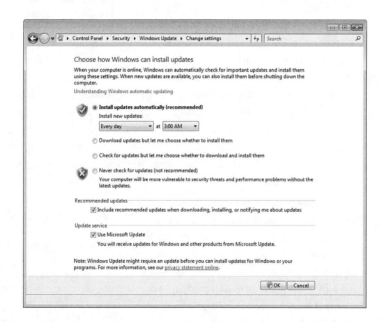

FIGURE 13.12

Use the Change Settings window to configure Vista's automatic updating.

13

4. Activate one of the following options to determine how Windows Vista performs the updating:

   Install Updates Automatically. This option tells Windows Vista to download and install updates automatically. Windows Vista checks for new updates on the date (such as every day or every Sunday) and time you specify. For example, you might prefer to choose a time when you won't be using your computer.

Download Updates, But Let Me Choose Whether to Install Them. If you activate this option, Windows Vista checks for new updates and then automatically downloads any updates that are available. Windows Vista then displays an icon in the notification area to let you know that the updates are ready to install. Click the icon to open the View Available Updates window and see the list of updates. If you see an update that you don't want to install, deactivate its check box.

Check for Updates But Let Me Choose Whether to Download and Install Them. If you activate this option, Windows Vista checks for new updates and then, if any are available, displays an icon in the notification area to let you know that the updates are ready to download. Click the icon to see the list of updates. If you see an update that you don't want to download, deactivate its check box. Click Start Download to initiate the download. When the download is complete, Windows Vista displays an icon in the notification area to let you know that the updates are ready to install. Click the icon, and then click Install to install the updates.

Never Check for Updates. Activate this option to prevent Windows Vista from checking for new updates. If you choose this option, be sure to check for new updates at least once a week. The easiest way to do this is to select Start, Control Panel, click the Check For Updates link under Security, and then click Check For Updates.

5. Click OK. The User Account Control dialog box appears.

6. Enter your UAC credentials.

caution To go into effect, some updates require your computer to reboot. In such cases, if you activate the Automatic option, Windows Vista will automatically reboot your system. This could lead to problems if you have open documents with unsaved changes or if you need a particular program to be running at all times. You can work around these problems by saving your work constantly and by putting any program you need running in your Startup folder.

tip An update that you choose not to install still appears in the View Available Updates window. If you'd prefer not to see that update, right-click the update, click Hide Update, enter your UAC credentials, and then click Cancel. If you later want to unhide the update, display the Windows Update window and click the Restore Hidden Updates link. In the Restore Hidden Updates window, activate the update's check box, click Restore, and then enter your UAC credentials.

Making Sure User Account Control Is Turned On

As you saw earlier, User Account Control is the centerpiece of Vista's new security approach (see "Understanding User Account Control"). Of course, this is undermined completely if User Account Control is turned off. Follow these steps to ensure UAC is activated in Vista:

1. Select Start, Control Panel to open the Control Panel window.

2. Select User Accounts and Family Safety.

3. Select User Accounts.

4. Select the Turn User Account Control On or Off. The User Account Control dialog box appears.

5. Enter your UAC credentials. The Turn User Account Control On or Off window appears, as shown in Figure 13.13.

FIGURE 13.13
Make sure User Account Control is turned on.

6. Make sure the Use User Account Control check box is activated.

7. Click OK.

Making Sure the Administrator Account Is Disabled

Windows Vista creates an Administrator account when it's first installed. This account is all-powerful on Windows Vista, so the last thing you want is for some malicious user to gain control of the system with Administrator access. Fortunately, Vista disabled the Administrator account by default. However, it's worth taking a few minutes now to ensure that the Administrator account is disabled on your Vista machines. Here are the steps to follow:

13

1. Select Start, right-click Computer, and then click Manage. The User Account Control dialog box appears.

2. Enter your UAC credentials to continue. The Computer Management snap-in appears.

3. Open the System Tools, Local Users and Groups, Users branch.

4. Double-click the Administrator account to open the Administrator Properties dialog box.

> **tip** You can open the Local Users and Groups snap-in directly by pressing Windows Logo+R (or by selecting Start, All Programs, Accessories, Run) to open the Run dialog box, typing `lusrmgr.msc`, and then clicking OK. (You can also select Start, type `lusrmgr.msc` in the Search box, and then click the lusrmgr icon when it appears.)

5. Make sure the Account Is Disabled check box is activated, as shown in Figure 13.14.

FIGURE 13.14

For the Administrator account, make sure the Account Is Disabled check box is activated.

6. Click OK.

Thwarting Spyware with Windows Defender

As you saw earlier in this chapter (see "Making Sure Windows Defender Is Turned On") Windows Defender protects your computer from spyware in two ways. It can scan your system for evidence of installed spyware programs (and remove or disable those programs, if necessary), and it can monitor your system in real time to watch for activities that indicate the presence of spyware (such as a drive-by download or data being sent via a back channel).

For the scanning portion of its defenses, Windows Defender supports three different scan types:

Quick Scan   This scan checks just those areas of your system where it is likely to find evidence of spyware. This scan usually takes just a couple of minutes. This scan is the default, and you can initiate one at any time by clicking the Scan link.

Full Scan   This scan checks for evidence of spyware in system memory, all running processes, and the system drive (usually drive C:), and it performs a deep scan on all folders. This scan might take 30 minutes or more, depending on your system. To run this scan, pull down the Scan menu and click Full Scan.

Custom Scan   This scan checks just the drives and folders that you select. The length of the scan depends on the number of locations you select and the number of objects in those locations. To run this scan, pull down the Scan menu and click Custom Scan, which displays the Select Scan Options page shown in Figure 13.15. Click Select, activate the check boxes for the drives you want scanned, and then click OK. Click Scan Now to start the scan.

note Black-hat hackers have one foot in your digital door already because they know that every Windows Vista machine comes with an account named Administrator. If you've disabled the Administrator account, you almost certainly have no worries. However, you can close the door completely on malicious intruders by taking away the one piece of information they know: the name of the account. By changing the account name from Administrator to something completely unobvious, you add an extra layer of security to Windows Vista. In the Computer Management window's System Tools, Local Users and Groups, Users branch, right-click the Administrator account, click Rename, type the new account name, and then press Enter. The Guest account also has an obvious and well-known name, so if you've enabled the Guest account, be sure to rename it, too.

13

FIGURE 13.15

In the Scan menu, select Custom Scan to see the Select Scan Options page.

Protecting Yourself Against Email Viruses

By far the most productive method for viruses to replicate is the humble email message. The list of email viruses and Trojan horses is a long one, but most of them operate more or less the same way: They arrive as a message attachment, usually from someone you know. When you open the attachment, the virus infects your computer and then, without your knowledge, uses your email client and your address book to ship out messages with more copies of itself attached. The nastier versions also mess with your computer by deleting data or corrupting files.

You can avoid infection by one of these viruses by implementing a few commonsense procedures:

- Never open an attachment that comes from someone you don't know.

- Even if you know the sender, if the attachment isn't something you're expecting, there's a good change that the sender's system is infected. Examine the message text to see if it makes sense in the context of your relationship with that person, and isn't just some generic message such as Check this out! (or something similar). Also, examine the attachment filename. If the message text says a picture is attached and the filename ends with a graphics extension (such as .jpg or .bmp), then it's probably okay; if the filename ends with an executable extension (such as .exe. .bat. or .vbs), then definitely don't open it. If you're not sure, write back and con-firm that the sender emailed the message.

- Some viruses come packaged as scripts hidden within messages that use the Rich Text (HTML) format. This means that the virus can run just by your viewing the message! If a message looks suspicious, don't open it; just delete it. (Note that you'll need to turn off the Windows Mail Preview pane before deleting the message. Otherwise, when you highlight the message, it appears in the Preview pane and sets off the virus. Select View, Layout, deactivate the Show Preview Pane check box, and click OK.)

caution It's particu-larly impor-tant to turn off the Preview pane before displaying Windows Mail's Junk E-Mail folder. Because many junk messages also carry a virus payload, your chances of initiat-ing an infection are highest when working with messages in this folder.

- Install a top-of-the-line antivirus program, particularly one that checks incoming email. In addition, be sure to keep your antivirus program's virus list up-to-date. As you read this, there are probably dozens, maybe even hundreds, of morally challenged scumnerds designing even nastier viruses. Regular updates will help you keep up. Here are some security suites to check out:

    Norton Internet Security (http://www.symantec.com/index.jsp)

    McAfee Internet Security Suite (http://mcafee.com/us)

    Avast! Antivirus (http://www.avast.com/)

    AVG Internet Security (http://free.grisoft.com/)

In addition to these general procedures, Windows Mail also comes with its own set of virus protection features. Here's how to use them:

1. In Windows Mail, select Tools, Options.

2. Display the Security tab.

3. In the Virus Protection group, you have the following options:

    Select the Internet Explorer Security Zone to Use. You use the secu-rity zones to determine whether to allow active content inside an HTML-format message to run:

    - **Internet Zone.** If you choose this zone, active content is allowed to run.

- **Restricted Sites Zone.** If you choose this option, active content is disabled. This is the default setting and the one I recommend.

Warn Me When Other Applications Try to Send Mail as Me. As I mentioned earlier, it's possible for programs and scripts to send email messages without your knowledge. This happens by using Simple MAPI (Messaging Application Programming Interface) calls, which can send messages via your computer's default mail client—and it's all hidden from you. With this check box activated, Windows Mail displays a warning dialog box when a program or script attempts to send a message using Simple MAPI.

tip What do you do if you want to send a file that's on the Windows Mail unsafe file list and you want to make sure that the recipient will be able to open it? The easiest workaround is to compress the file into a `.zip` file—a file type not blocked by Windows Mail, Outlook, or any other mail client that blocks file types. Note that you may have to rename the file to change the extension to, say, `.zix` if your recipient's firm blocks ZIP files for security reasons. In that case, be sure to tell the recipient about the rename so that he can reverse it once the file gets through.

Do Not Allow Attachments to Be Saved or Opened That Could Potentially Be a Virus. With this check box activated, Windows Mail monitors attachments to look for file types that could contain viruses or destructive code. If it detects such a file, it disables your ability to open and save that file, and it displays a note at the top of the message to let you know about the unsafe attachment.

FILE TYPES DISABLED BY WINDOWS MAIL

Internet Explorer's built-in Unsafe File list defines the file types that Windows Mail disables. That list includes file types associated with the following extensions: `.ad`, `.ade`, `.adp`, `.bas`, `.bat`, `.chm`, `.cmd`, `.com`, `.cpl`, `.crt`, `.exe`, `.hlp`, `.hta`, `.inf`, `.ins`, `.isp`, `.js`, `.jse`, `.lnk`, `.mdb`, `.mde`, `.msc`, `.msi`, `.msp`, `.mst`, `.pcd`, `.pif`, `.reg`, `.scr`, `.sct`, `.shb`, `.shs`, `.url`, `.vb`, `.vbe`, `.vbs`, `.vsd`, `.vss`, `.vst`, `.vsw`, `.wsc`, `.wsf`, `.wsh`.

4. Click OK to put the new settings into effect.

Protecting Yourself Against Phishing Scams

Phishing refers to creating a replica of an existing web page to fool a user into submitting personal, financial, or password data. The term comes from the fact that Internet scammers are using increasingly sophisticated lures as they "fish" for users' financial information and password data. The most common ploy is to copy the web page code from a major site—such as AOL or eBay—and use it to set up a replica page that appears to be part of the company's site. (This is why another name for phishing is spoofing.) Phishers send out a fake email with a link to this page, which solicits the user's credit card data or password. When a recipient submits the form, it sends the data to the scammer and leaves the user on an actual page from the company's site so that he or she doesn't suspect a thing.

A phishing page looks identical to a legitimate page from the company because the phisher has simply copied the underlying source code from the original page. However, no spoof page can be a perfect replica of the original. Here are five things to look for:

- **The URL in the Address bar.** A legitimate page will have the correct domain (such as aol.com or ebay.com), whereas a spoofed page will have only something similar (such as aol.whatever.com or blah.com/ebay).

- **The URLs associated with page links.** Most links on the page probably point to legitimate pages on the original site. However, some links might point to pages on the phisher's site.

- **The form-submittal address.** Almost all spoof pages contain a form into which you're supposed to type whatever sensitive data the phisher seeks from you. Select View, Source, and look at the value of the `<form>` tag's `action` attribute. The form submits your data to this address. Clearly, if the form is not sending your data to the legitimate domain, you're dealing with a phisher.

- **Text or images that aren't associated with the trustworthy site.** Many phishing sites are housed on free web hosting services. However, many of these services place an advertisement on each page, so look for an ad or other content from the hosting provider.

> **note** With some exceptions (see the following discussion of domain spoofing), the URL in the Address bar is usually the easiest way to tell whether a site is trustworthy. For this reason, Internet Explorer 7 makes it impossible to hide the Address bar in all browser windows, even simple pop-ups.

13

■ **Internet Explorer's Lock icon in the status bar and Security Report area.** A legitimate site would transmit sensitive financial data only using a secure HTTPS connection, which Internet Explorer indicates by placing a Lock icon in the status bar and in the Address bar's new Security Report area. If you don't see the Lock icon on a page that asks for financial data, the page is almost certainly a spoof.

If you watch for these things, you'll probably never be fooled into giving up sensitive data to a phisher. However, it's often not as easy as it sounds. For example, some phishers employ easily overlooked domain-spoofing tricks such as replacing the lowercase letter *L* with the number 1, or the uppercase letter *O* with the number 0. Still, phishing sites don't fool most experienced users, so this isn't a big problem for them.

Making Sure Internet Explorer's Phishing Filter Is Turned On

Novice users, on the other hand, need all the help they can get. They tend to assume that if everything they see on the Web looks legitimate and trustworthy, it probably is. And even if they're aware that scam sites exist, they don't know how to check for telltale phishing signs. To help these users, Internet Explorer 7 comes with a new tool called the Phishing Filter. This filter alerts you to potential phishing scams by doing two things each time you visit a site:

■ Analyzes the site content to look for known phishing techniques (that is, to see whether the site is *phishy*). The most common of these is a check for domain spoofing. This common scam also goes by the names *homograph spoofing* and the *lookalike attack*. Internet Explorer 7 also supports Internationalized Domain Names (IDN), which refers to domain names written in languages other than English, and it checks for *IDN spoofing*, domain name ambiguities in the user's chosen browser language.

■ Checks a global database of known phishing sites to see whether it lists the site. This database is maintained by a network of providers such as Cyota, Inc., Internet Identity, and MarkMonitor, as well as by reports from users who find phishing sites while surfing. According to Microsoft, this "URL reputation service" updates several times an hour with new data.

It's a sign of the phishing times that Internet Explorer comes with the Phishing Filter activated by default. To make sure, follow these steps:

13

1. In Internet Explorer, select Tools, Phishing Filter.
2. If you see a command named Turn On Automatic Website Checking, select that command to open the Microsoft Phishing Filter dialog box (see Figure 13.16).

FIGURE 13.16

Make sure Internet Explorer 7's Phishing Filter is activated.

3. Select the Turn On Automatic Phishing Filter option.
4. Click OK.

Here's how the Phishing Filter works:

■ If you visit a site that Internet Explorer knows is a phishing scam, it changes the background color of the Address bar to red and displays a Phishing Website message in the Security Report area. It also blocks navigation to the site by displaying a separate page telling you that the site is a known phishing scam. A link is provided to navigate to the site, if you so choose.

note The Security Report area is another Internet Explorer 7 security innovation. Clicking whatever text or icon appears in this area produces a report on the security of the site. For example, if you navigate to a secure site, you see the lock icon in this area. Click the lock to see a report that shows the site's digital certificate information.

13

■ If you visit a site that Internet Explorer thinks is a potential phishing scam, it changes the background color of the Address bar to yellow and displays a `Suspicious Website` message in the Security Report area.

Figure 13.17 shows Internet Explorer 7 displaying a warning about a known phishing site.

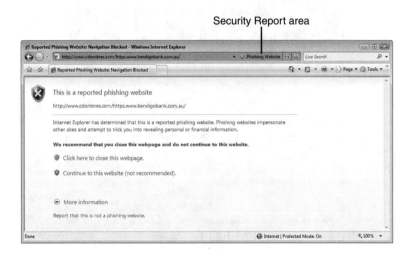

FIGURE 13.17

If Internet Explorer 7 detects a known phishing site, it displays `Phishing Website` *in the Security Report area and blocks access to the site.*

For a suspected phishing site, click the `Suspicious Website` text, and Internet Explorer displays a security report. If you're sure that this is a scam site, report it to improve the database of phishing sites and prevent others from giving up sensitive data. You should also send a report if you're sure that the site is *not* being used for phishing, because that improves the database, too. To report a site, either click the Report link in the security report or select Tools, Phishing Filter, Report This Website. This opens the Phishing Filter Feedback page.

Making Sure Windows Mail Phishing Protection Is Turned On

Most phishing attempts come via email, so it makes sense for the email program to be the first line of defense. Windows Mail does this by recognizing phishing messages, displaying a warning about such messages, and disabling their links. Follow these steps to ensure this phishing protection is turned on:

1. In Windows Mail, select Tools, Junk E-mail Option to open the Junk E-mail Options dialog box.

2. Select the Phishing tab.

3. Make sure the Protect My Inbox From Messages With Potential Phishing Links check box is activated, as shown in Figure 13.18.

FIGURE 13.18

Make sure that Windows Mail's phishing protection is activated.

4. If you'd prefer that Windows Mail automatically move suspected phishing messages to the Junk Mail folder, activate the Move Phishing E-mail to the Junk Mail Folder check box.

5. Click OK.

From Here

▪ For information about securing your network, **see** Chapter 14, "Implementing Network Security," **p. 313**.

▪ For ideas on securing your wireless network, **see** Chapter 15, "Implementing Wireless Security," **p. 335**.

▪ For the details on making connections to network desktops, **see** "Connecting to the Remote Desktop," **p. 373**.

13

14

Implementing Network Security

I f you have just one computer and you're the only person who uses it, your setup is inherently secure. True, if your computer contains sensitive or personal data, you probably still want to password-protect your account just in case, say, your computer gets stolen. Other than that, you need not worry too much about security.

When you join your computer to a network that contains multiple users, your setup is no longer secure. Assuming you're sharing at least a folder or two, the nature of a network means that other people have access to that information. If you want to control not only who has access to your data, but also what those users can do with the data, you need to implement a few network security precautions. Of course, other users inadvertently seeing data they shouldn't is one problem, but an outsider gaining unauthorized access to the network is quite another. Fortunately, you can take steps to minimize this sort of intrusion. This chapter takes you through a few useful techniques for securing your network.

IN THIS CHAPTER

- Deactivating the Sharing Wizard
- Setting Sharing Permissions on Shared Folders
- Setting Security Permissions on Shared Folders
- Hiding Your Shared Folders
- Disabling the Hidden Administrative Shares
- Removing Stored Remote Desktop Credentials
- Preventing Users from Logging On at Certain Times
- Hiding the Usernames in the Logon Screen
- Running the Baseline Security Analyzer on Your Network
- From Here

Remember that your network is only as secure as its client computers, so be sure to read the tips and techniques for making Vista more secure in Chapter 13, "Securing Windows Vista." Also, if you have wireless network connections, find out how to secure them in Chapter 15, "Implementing Wireless Security."

> **tip** You can open the Folder Options dialog box from any folder window. Select Organize, Folder and Search Options. You can also select Start, type **fol** in the Search box, and then click Folder Options when it appears in the search results.

Deactivating the Sharing Wizard

Back in Chapter 8, "Accessing and Sharing Network Resources," you learned how to use the File Sharing Wizard to apply simple permissions to folders that you're sharing with the network. If you've used Windows XP in the past, you no doubt noticed that the File Sharing Wizard is at least an improvement over XP's useless Simple File Sharing feature, and it certainly makes it easy to apply basic permissions, which novice users appreciate. However, Vista has a larger range of permissions and other sharing features, and these can make your network shares more secure. To work with these features, you need to deactivate the File Sharing Wizard.

→   For the details on using the File Sharing Wizard, **see** "Sharing a Resource with the File Sharing Wizard," **p. 190**.

Here are the steps to follow to turn off the File Sharing Wizard:

1. Select Start, Control Panel, to open the Control Panel window.
2. Select Appearance and Personalization.
3. Select Folder Options to open the Folder Options dialog box.
4. Display the View tab.
5. Deactivate the Use Sharing Wizard check box, as shown in Figure 14.1.
6. Click OK.

14

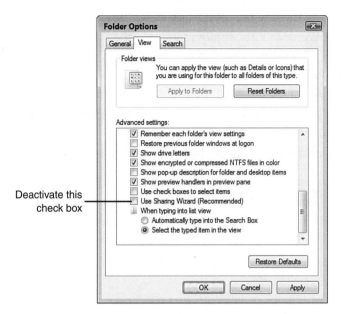

Deactivate this
check box

FIGURE 14.1
In the Folder Options dialog box, deactivate the Use Sharing Wizard check box.

Setting Sharing Permissions on Shared Folders

With the File Sharing Wizard no longer active, you can now share a folder with advanced permissions. You use these permissions to decide who has access to the folder and what those users can do with the folder. You can also apply advanced permissions to entire security groups rather than individual users. For example, if you apply permissions to the Administrators group, those permissions automatically apply to each member of that group.

→   Before continuing, make sure you have a user account set up for each person who will access the share; **see** "Creating User Accounts for Sharing," **p. 189**.

Follow these steps to share a folder with advanced permissions:

1. Select Start, and then click your username to open your user profile folder.

2. Click the folder you want to share. If you want to share a subfolder or file, instead, open its folder and then click the subfolder or file.

14

3. Click the Share button in the task pane. Windows Vista displays the object's Properties sheet with the Sharing tab selected.

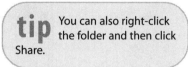

tip You can also right-click the folder and then click Share.

4. Click Advanced Sharing. The User Account Control dialog box appears.

5. Enter your UAC credentials to continue. The Advanced Sharing dialog box appears.

6. Activate the Share This Folder check box, as shown in Figure 14.2.

FIGURE 14.2

Activate the Share This Folder check box.

7. By default, Vista uses the folder name as the share name. If you prefer to use a different name, edit the Share Name text box.

8. In a small network, it's unlikely you'll need to restrict the number of users who can access this resource, so you're probably safe to leave the Limit the Number of Simultaneous Users To spin box value at 10.

9. Click Permissions to display the Permissions for *Share* dialog box, where *Share* is the share name you specified in step 7.

10. Select the Everyone group in the Group or User Names list, and then click Remove.

note As the name implies, the Everyone user refers to every user. It's always best to remove this user so that you can apply permissions to specific users and groups.

11. Click Add to display the Select Users or Groups dialog box.

12. In the Enter the Object Names to Select text box, type the name of the user or users you want to give permission to access the shared resource (separate multiple user-names with semicolons). Click OK when you're done.

> **tip** If you're not sure about the spelling of a user or group name, click Advanced to open an advanced version of the Select Users or Groups dialog box, and then click Find Now. Vista displays a list of all the available users and groups. Click the name you want to use, and then click OK.

13. Select a user in the Group or User Names list.

14. Using the Permissions list (see Figure 14.3), you can allow or deny the following permissions:

Read   Gives the group or user the ability only to read the contents of a folder or file. The user can't modify those contents in any way.

Change   Gives the group or user read permission and allows the group or user to modify the contents of the shared resource.

Full Control Gives the group or user change permission and allows the group or user to take ownership of the shared resource.

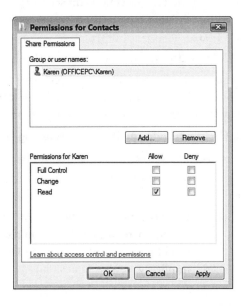

FIGURE 14.3
Use the Permissions dialog box to specify file permissions for the shared resource.

15. Repeat steps 11–14 to add and configure other users or groups.

16. Click OK to return to the Advanced Sharing dialog box.

17. Click OK to return to the Sharing tab.

18. Click Close to share the resource with the network.

Setting Security Permissions on Shared Folders

If you want even more control over the use of your shared resources across the network, you should also set NTFS security permissions on the folder. Security permissions are similar to sharing permissions, except that you get a longer list of permissions for each group or user.

Here are the steps to follow to set security permissions on a shared folder:

1. Select Start, and then click your user name to open your user profile folder.

2. Right-click the folder you want to work with, and then click Properties to open the folder's Properties dialog box.

3. Select the Security tab.

4. Select the group or user you want to work with.

5. Click Edit to open the Permissions for *Folder* dialog box, where *Folder* is the name of the folder. As you can see in Figure 14.4, this dialog box is similar to the dialog box you saw earlier for sharing permissions (see Figure 14.3).

6. Click Add to display the Select Users or Groups dialog box.

7. In the Enter the Object Names to Select text box, type the name of the user or users you want to give permission to access the shared resource (separate multiple usernames with semicolons).

8. Click OK to return to the Permissions dialog box.

9. Select a user in the Group or User Names list.

10. Using the Permissions list, you can allow or deny the following permissions:

    Full Control Users can perform any of the actions listed. Users can also change permissions. You should allow this permission level for yourself and for experienced users you trust implicitly.

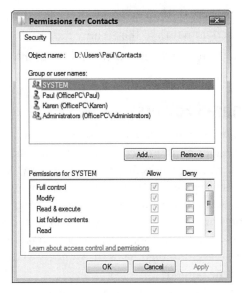

FIGURE 14.4

Use this version of the Permissions dialog box to specify security permissions for the shared resource.

Modify	Users can view the folder contents, open files, edit files, create new files and subfolders, delete files, and run programs. You should allow this level for experienced users whom you don't want to give the capability to change permissions.
Read and Execute	Users can view the folder contents, open files, and run programs.
List Folder Contents	Users can view the folder contents. You should disallow this level for users whom you want to keep the folder contents a secret.
Read	Users can open files, but cannot edit them. You should allow this level for inexperienced users to prevent those users from making changes to your data.
Write	Users can create new files and subfolders, and open and edit existing files.
Special Permissions	Advanced settings for permissions, auditing, ownership, and effective permissions.

14

11. Repeat steps 6–10 to add and configure other users or groups.

12. Click OK to return to the Security tab.

13. Click OK to put the new security settings into effect.

Hiding Your Shared Folders

Setting up user accounts with strong passwords and then applying shared-folder permissions on those accounts are the necessary network security tasks, and in most small networks they're also sufficient for achieving a decent level of security. However, when it comes to securing your network, a healthy dose of paranoia is another good "tool" to have at hand. For example, the properly paranoid network administrator doesn't assume that no one will ever infiltrate the network, just the opposite: The admin assumes that someday someone *will* get access, and then he or she wonders what can be done in that case to minimize the damage.

One of the first things these paranoid administrators do (or should do) is hide what's valuable, private, or sensitive. For example, if you have a shared folder named, say, Confidential Documents, you're simply *begging* a would-be thief to access that share. Yes, you could rename the share to something less inviting, but the thief may chance upon it anyway. To prevent this, it's possible to share a resource *and* hide it at the same time.

Even better, hiding a shared folder is also extremely easy to do: When you set up the shared resource, add a dollar sign ($) to the end of the share name. For example, if you're setting up drive F: for sharing, you could use F$ as the share name. This prevents the resource from appearing in the list of resources when you open a remote computer from the Network window.

To show you how this works, check out Figure 14.5. In the Properties dialog box for drive F:, you see that the drive is shared with the following path:

\\Officepc\f$

That is, the drive is shared on the computer named OfficePC with the name F$. However, in the folder window, you can see that drive F doesn't appear in the list of resources shared by OfficePC.

> **caution** Hiding shares will work for the average user, but a savvy snoop will probably know about the $ trick. Therefore, you should set up your hidden shares with nonobvious names.

Drive F doesn't appear in the
computer's list of shared resources

Drive F is set up as a hidden share (F$)

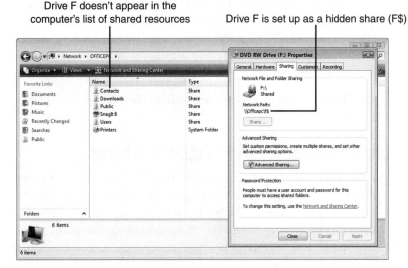

FIGURE 14.5

Hidden shared resources (such as drive F: shown here) don't appear in the computer's list of shared resources.

How do you connect to a hidden share? You need to know the name of the shared resource, of course, which enables you to use any of the following techniques:

- Select Windows Logo+R (or select Start, All Programs, Accessories, Run) to open the Run dialog box, type the network path for the hidden resource, and click OK. For example, to display the hidden share F$ on OfficePC, you would enter this:

```
\\officepc\f$
```

- In a command prompt session, type **start**, a space, the network path, and then press the Enter key. For example, to launch the hidden share F$ on OfficePC, you would enter this:

```
start \\officepc\f$
```

- Use the Map Network Drive command, as described in Chapter 8. In the Map Network Drive dialog box, type the UNC path for the hidden share in the Folder text box.

→ For the details on mapping a shared folder, **see** "Mapping a Network Folder to a Local Drive Letter," **p. 177**.

14

■ For a hidden shared printer, follow the instructions for accessing a shared printer in Chapter 8 and, when Vista begins searching for available printers, click The Printer That I Want Isn't Listed. In the Find a Printer By Name or TCP/IP Address dialog box, type the network path to the hidden printer in the Select a Shared Printer by Name text box.

→ For information about using a network printer, **see** "Accessing a Shared Printer," **p. 182**.

Disabling the Hidden Administrative Shares

I mentioned in the previous section that you can add $ to a share name to hide the share, and that it was a good idea to also modify the share name to something not easily guessable by some snoop. Note, however, that Windows Vista sets up certain hidden shares for administrative purposes, including one for drive C: (C$) and any other hard disk partitions you have on your system. Windows Vista also sets up the following hidden shares:

Share	Shared Path	Purpose
ADMIN$	%SystemRoot%	Remote administration
IPC$	N/A	Remote interprocess communication
print$	%SystemRoot%\System32\spool\ drivers	Access to printer drivers

To see these shares, select Start, All Programs, Accessories, Command Prompt to open a command prompt session, type **net share**, and press Enter. You see a listing similar to this:

```
Share name    Resource                              Remark
-------------------------------------------------------------------------
C$            C:\                                   Default share
D$            D:\                                   Default share
ADMIN$        C:\WINDOWS                            Remote Admin
IPC$                                                Remote IPC
print$        C:\System32\spool\drivers             Printer Drivers
Public        C:\Users\Public
```

So although the C$, D$, and ADMIN$ shares are otherwise hidden, they're well known, and they represent a small security risk should an intruder get access to your network.

To close this hole, you can force Windows Vista to disable these shares. Here are the steps to follow:

1. Press Windows Logo+R (or select Start, All Programs, Accessories, Run) to open the Run dialog box.

2. Type **regedit**, and then click OK. The User Account Control dialog box appears.

3. Enter your UAC credentials to continue. Windows Vista opens the Registry Editor.

4. Open the HKEY_LOCAL_MACHINE branch.

5. Open the SYSTEM branch.

6. Open the CurrentControlSet branch.

7. Open the Services branch.

8. Open the LanmanServer branch.

9. Select the Parameters branch.

10. Select Edit, New, DWORD (32-bit) Value. Vista adds a new value to the Parameters key.

11. Type **AutoShareWks** and press Enter. (You can leave this setting with its default value of 0.)

12. Restart Windows Vista Server to put the new setting into effect.

> **caution** Remember that the Registry contains many important settings that are crucial for the proper functioning of Vista and your programs. Therefore, when you are working with the Registry Editor, don't make changes to any settings other than the ones I describe in this section.

> **caution** Some programs expect the administrative shares to be present, so disabling those shares may cause those programs to fail or generate error messages. If that happens, enable the shares by opening the Registry Editor and either deleting the AutoShareWks setting or changing its value to 1.

Once again, select Start, Command Prompt to open a command prompt session, type **net share**, and press Enter. The output now looks like this:

```
Share name   Resource                    Remark
-------------------------------------------------------------------------
IPC$                                     Remote IPC
print$       C:\System32\spool\drivers   Printer Drivers
Public       C:\Users\Public
```

Removing Stored Remote Desktop Credentials

When you log on to a network computer using Remote Desktop Connection (see Chapter 16, "Making Remote Network Connections"), the logon dialog box includes a check box named Remember My Credentials, as shown in Figure 14.6. If you activate this check box, Windows Vista won't prompt you to enter a password when you connect to the computer in the future.

→ To learn how to log on with Remote Desktop Connection, **see** "Connecting to the Remote Desktop," **p. 313**.

FIGURE 14.6

Remote Desktop Connection enables you to save your logon credentials.

That's certainly convenient, but it's a gaping security hole because it enables anyone who can access your computer to also access the remote computer's desktop. Therefore, it's never a good idea to activate the Remember My Credentials check box.

However, what if you activated that option earlier? Fortunately, you're not stuck because Windows Vista gives you a way to "unremember" those credentials.

Here are the steps to follow:

1. Press Windows Logo+R (or select Start, All Programs, Accessories Run) to open the Run dialog box.

2. Type **control userpasswords2** and select OK. The User Account Control dialog box appears.

> **caution** The General tab of the Remote Desktop Connection dialog box (select Start, All Programs, Accessories, Remote Desktop Connection) has a check box named Always Ask for Credentials. (You may need to click the Options button to see it.) You might think that you can protect the connection by activating this check box. However, Windows Vista is still saving the credentials, and all someone has to do to use them is deactivate the Always Ask for Credentials check

3. Enter your UAC credentials to continue. The User Accounts dialog box appears.

4. Select the Advanced tab.

5. Click Manage Password. Vista displays the Stored User Names and Passwords dialog box, shown in Figure 14.7.

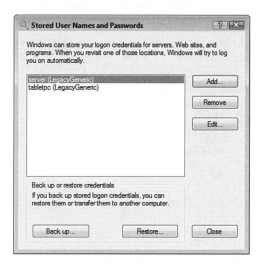

FIGURE 14.7

Remote Desktop Connection enables you to save your logon credentials.

6. Select the credentials you want to delete.

7. Click Remove. Vista tells you that the logon information will be deleted.

8. Click OK.

9. Repeat steps 6–8 to remove other saved credentials.

10. Click Close.

Preventing Users from Logging On at Certain Times

If you've set up user accounts so that other people on your network can access your

> **tip** Another way to remove saved Remote Desktop Connection credentials is to select Start, All Programs, Accessories, Remote Desktop Connection. In the Remote Desktop Connection dialog box, click Options to expand the dialog box, select the General tab, and then click the Delete link in the Logon Settings group. Click Yes when Remote Desktop Connection asks you to confirm.

14

computer, by default those users can view and use your shares any time of day. That's not usually a problem, but there may be situations where you want to prevent users from logging on at certain times. For example, if you work with a particular shared folder each afternoon, you might not want users accessing that folder until you're done.

Windows Vista enables you to specify the days of the week and hours of the day that a particular user is allowed to log on to your system. When the user attempts to access your computer over the network outside of those hours, he or she sees a dialog box similar to the one shown in Figure 14.8.

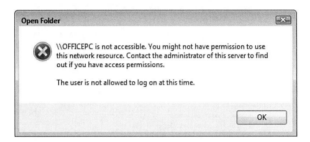

FIGURE 14.8
If you've set up logon hours for a user, that person sees a dialog box similar to this when attempting to log on outside of those hours.

The next couple of sections show you how to work with this feature.

Setting a User's Logon Hours

Unfortunately, Windows Vista doesn't have a dialog box or other interface that you can use to set logon hours for a user. Instead, you must use a command prompt session where you enter a command using the following general syntax:

```
net user username /times:day1,times1;day2,times2,...
```

username	The name of the user account you want to work with.
day1, day2	The day of the week that the user is allowed to log on. You can spell out the days, but it's quicker to use the following codes (case doesn't matter): Su, M, T, W, Th, F, and Sa. You can also specify a range of days, such as M-F (for Monday to Friday).

14

time1, *time2*   For a given day, the time range that the user is allowed to log on. The range syntax is *start-end*, where *start* is the beginning of the logon hours and *end* is the end of the logon hours. You can either use 24-hour notation or 12-hour notation, although the latter means you must also specify AM and PM.

> **tip**
> If you've previously set a user's logon hours, you may decide later to remove those restrictions. To give a user access at all times, use the all parameter:
>
> ```
> net user katy /times:all
> ```
>
> To give a user no access, use no parameters:
>
> ```
> net user Jordan /times:
> ```

Here are some examples:

```
net user karen /times:M-F,9AM-5PM
net user steve /times:M,18-24
net user emily /times:Sa,10PM-6PM; Su,12PM-6PM
```

Follow these steps to specify logon hours for a user:

1. Select Start, All Programs, Accessories.
2. Right-click Command Prompt, and then click Run as Administrator. The User Account Control dialog box appears.
3. Enter your UAC credentials to continue. Vista opens a command prompt session.
4. Type your **net user /times** command and press Enter. The NET USER command responds with The command completed successfully.
5. Repeat step 4 to specify all the logon hours you want to implement.
6. Type **exit** and press Enter to close the command prompt session.

Automatically Logging Off a User When the Logon Hours Expire

By default, Windows Vista does nothing if a user is currently logged on to your computer and that person's logon hours expire.

In other words, there's nothing to prevent a teenager from hanging out online all night instead of doing homework! To fix this, you can configure Vista to automatically log off the user when the account's logon hours are over. Here are the steps to follow:

> **note**
> These steps require the Local Security Policy snap-in, which is only available with Vista Business, Vista Enterprise, and Vista Ultimate.

14

1. Press Windows Logo+R (or select Start, All Programs, Accessories Run) to open the Run dialog box.

2. Type `secpol.msc` and click OK. The Local Security Policy window appears.

3. Open the Security Settings, Local Policies, Security Options branch.

4. Double-click the Network Security: Force Logoff When Logon Hours Expire policy.

5. Click the Enabled option, as shown in Figure 14.9.

FIGURE 14.9

Enable the Network Security: Force Logoff When Logon Hours Expire policy.

6. Click OK.

Hiding the Usernames in the Logon Screen

When you log on to Windows Vista, the logon screen always displays icons for each user account, and each icon shows the name of the account, as shown in Figure 14.10. It's unlikely that a malicious user would gain physical access to the computer in your home or office, but it's not impossible. If that happens, the hacker has an important advantage because he knows the names of all your user accounts.

FIGURE 14.10

The Windows Vista logon screen shows the names of the computer's user accounts.

Fortunately, you can plug this security breach by following these steps:

1. Press Windows Logo+R (or select Start, All Programs, Accessories, Run) to open the Run dialog box.

2. Type **secpol.msc** and then click OK. The User Account Control dialog box appears.

3. Enter your credentials to continue. The Local Security Policy window appears.

4. Open the Security Settings, Local Policies, Security Options branch.

5. Double-click the Interactive Logon: Do Not Display Last User Name policy.

> **note** These steps require the Local Security Policy snap-in, which is only available with Vista Business, Vista Enterprise, and Vista Ultimate.

14

6. Click the Enabled option.

7. Click OK to put the new setting into effect.

The next time you start your computer, the username no longer appears in the logon screen, as shown in Figure 14.11.

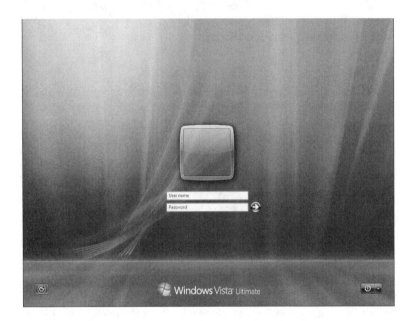

FIGURE 14.11

With the Do Not Display Last User Name policy enabled, the Windows Vista logon screen no longer shows the names of the computer's user accounts.

Running the Baseline Security Analyzer on Your Network

Microsoft regularly finds security vulnerabilities in components such as Internet Explorer and Windows Media Player. Fixes for these problems are usually available via Windows Update. That's fine if you're just trying to keep a single computer patched, but it can be a big problem when you're juggling security updates for multiple machines on your home network.

To ensure that not only *your* computer is safe, but *all* the Windows machines on your network, you should download and regularly run the Microsoft Baseline Security Analyzer (MBSA). This tool not only scans for missing security patches, it also looks for things such as weak passwords and other

Windows vulnerabilities. Best of all, you can configure MBSA to scan every computer in your workgroup, so you always know the current security update status of every machine.

To begin, download the tool from the following Microsoft TechNet site:

```
http://www.microsoft.com/technet/security/tools/mbsahome.mspx
```

Look for a link to the latest version. As I write this, version 2.1, which supports Windows Vista machines, is in beta testing, but there should be a release version by the time you get there. (The expected release time frame is the third quarter of 2007.)

After you download MBSA, install it on one of your network computers. It runs on Windows Vista, but you can also install it on machines running Windows 2000 SP4, Windows Server 2003, Windows Home Server, or Windows XP.

After MBSA is installed, follow these steps to use it:

1. Select Start, All Programs, Microsoft Baseline Security Analyzer 2.1. (You can also double-click the Microsoft Baseline Security Analyzer 2.1 icon on the desktop.) The User Account Control dialog box appears.

2. Enter your UAC credentials to continue. The program's Welcome screen appears.

3. Click Scan Multiple Computers.

4. Use the Domain Name text box to enter your network's workgroup name, as shown in Figure 14.12. (Alternatively, use the IP Address Range controls to specify the starting and ending IP addresses that you want to scan.)

5. Use the Options check boxes to specify the security components you want to check. For most scans, you should leave all the options activated.

6. Click Start Scan. The program checks all the computers on your network and displays a report on each system's security (and usually offers remedies for any vulnerability it finds). Figure 14.13 shows a sample report.

14

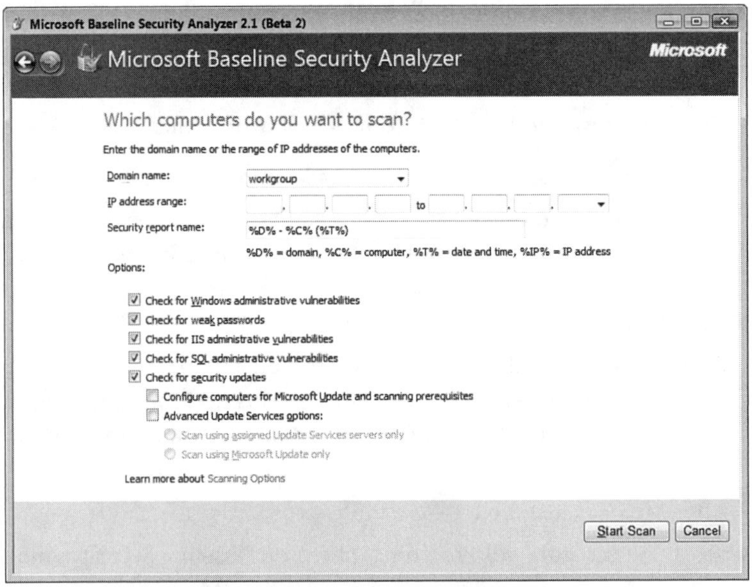

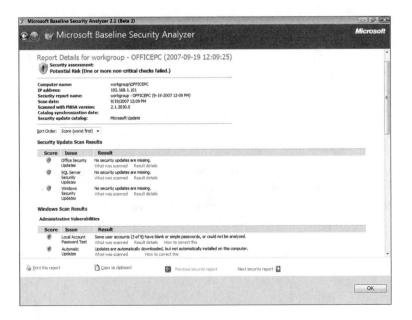

FIGURE 14.12

To scan your entire network, type your workgroup name in the Domain Name text box.

FIGURE 14.13

A sample report generated by Microsoft Baseline Security Analyzer.

From Here

- For the details on mapping a shared folder, **see** "Mapping a Network Folder to a Local Drive Letter," **p. 177**.

- For information about using a network printer, **see** "Accessing a Shared Printer," **p. 182**.

- You need to create a user account for each person who will access a share; **see** "Creating User Accounts for Sharing," **p. 189**.

- For the details on using the File Sharing Wizard, **see** "Sharing a Resource with the File Sharing Wizard," **p. 190**.

- Your network is only as secure as its client computers, so be sure to make each of your Vista machines as secure as possible; **see** Chapter 13, "Securing Windows Vista," **p. 281**.

- If you have wireless network connections to secure, **see** Chapter 15, "Implementing Wireless Security," **p. 335**.

- To learn how to log on with Remote Desktop Connection, **see** "Connecting to the Remote Desktop," **p. 373**.

Implementing Wireless Security

IN THIS CHAPTER

- Specifying a New Administrative Password

- Positioning the Access Point for Maximum Security

- Encrypting Wireless Signals with WPA

- Disabling Network SSID Broadcasting

- Changing the Default SSID

- Enabling MAC Address Filtering

- From Here

Computer veterans may be familiar with the term *wardialing*, a black-hat hacker technique that involves automatically calling thousands of telephone numbers to look for any that have a modem attached. (You might also know this term from the 1983 movie *War Games*, now a classic in computer cracking circles. In the movie a young cracker, Matthew Broderick, uses wardialing to look for games and bulletin board systems. However, he inadvertently ends up with a direct connection to a high-level military computer that gives him control over the U.S. nuclear arsenal. Various things hit the fan after that.) Modems are becoming increasingly rare these days, so wardialing is less of a threat than it used to be.

That doesn't mean we're any safer, however. Our houses and offices may no longer have modems, but many of them have a relatively recent bit of technology: a wireless network. So now wardialing has given way to *wardriving*, where a cracker drives through various neighborhoods with a portable computer or another device set up to look for available wireless networks. If the miscreant finds a nonsecured network, he uses it for free Internet access (such a person is called a *piggybacker*) or to cause mischief with shared network resources. The hacker may then do a little *warchalking*, using chalk to place a special symbol on the sidewalk or other surface that indicates there's a nonsecure wireless network nearby.

15

Crackers engage in all these nefarious deeds for a simple reason: Wireless networks are less secure than wired ones. That's because the wireless connection that enables you to access the network from the kitchen or the conference room can also enable an intruder from outside your home or office to access the network.

Fortunately, you can secure your wireless network against these threats with a few simple tweaks and techniques, as you'll see in this chapter.

> **tip** The most effective technique for securing your wireless access point (AP) is also the simplest: Turn it off if you won't be using it for an extended period. If you're going out of town for a few days, or if you're going on vacation for a week or two, shut down the access point and you're guaranteed that no wardriver will infiltrate your network.

Specifying a New Administrative Password

By far the most important configuration chore for any new router is to change the default logon password (and username, if your router requires one). Note that I'm talking here about the administrative password, which is the password you use to log on to the router's setup pages. This password has nothing to do with the password you use to log on to your Internet service provider (ISP) or to your wireless network.

Changing the default administrative password is particularly crucial if your router also includes a wireless AP because a nearby malicious hacker can see your router. This means that the intruder can easily access the setup pages just by navigating to one of the common router addresses—usually http://192.168.1.1 or http://192.168.0.1—and then entering the default password, which for most routers is well known or easy to guess. The next few sections show you how to modify the administrative password for various routers.

Belkin

Here are the steps to follow to change the administrative password on most Belkin routers:

1. Log on to the router's setup pages.

2. Under the Utilities section, click the System Settings link to display the System Settings page, shown in Figure 15.1.

3. Use the Type In Current Password text box to type the existing administrative password.

> **note** On most Belkin routers, the default administrative password is blank.

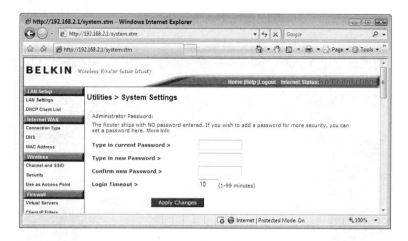

FIGURE 15.1

On most Belkin routers, use the System Settings page to change the administrative password.

4. Use the Type In New Password and Conform New Password text boxes to specify the new administrative password.

5. Click Apply Changes.

D-Link

For most D-Link routers, follow these steps to change the administrative password:

1. Log on to the router's setup pages.

2. Click the Tools tab.

3. Click Admin to display the Administrator Settings page, shown in Figure 15.2.

4. Use the Login Name text box to specify a new username.

5. Use the New Password and Confirm Password text box to specify the new password.

6. Click Save Settings. The router saves the new settings.

7. Click Continue.

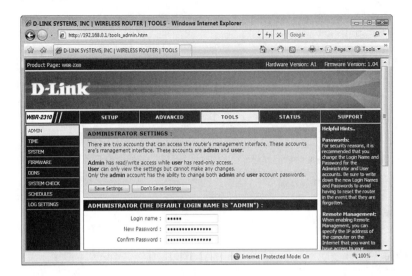

FIGURE 15.2

On your D-Link router, use the Administrator Settings page to change the administrative password.

Linksys

Here are the steps to follow to change the administrative password on most Linksys routers:

1. Log on to the router's setup pages.

2. Click the Administration tab.

3. Click the Management subtab to display the page shown in Figure 15.3.

FIGURE 15.3

On most Linksys routers, use the Administration/Management page to change the administrative password.

4. Use the Password and Re-enter to Confirm text boxes to specify the new administrative password.

5. At the bottom of the page, click Save Settings. The router reports that the Settings are successful.

6. Click Continue.

Netgear

Follow these steps to modify the administrative password on most Netgear routers:

1. Log on to the router's setup pages.

2. In the Maintenance section, click the Set Password link. The Set Password page appears, as shown in Figure 15.4.

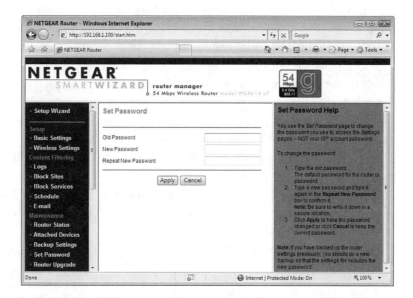

FIGURE 15.4

On most Netgear routers, use the Set Password page to change the administrative password.

3. Use the Old Password text box to type the current administrative password.

4. Use the New Password and Repeat New Password text boxes to specify the new administrative password.

5. Click Apply.

> **note** On most Netgear routers, the default administrative password is password.

Positioning the Access Point for Maximum Security

Almost all wireless network security problems stem from a single cause: wireless signals that extend outside of your home or office. This is called *signal leakage*, and if you can minimize the leakage, you're well on your way to having a secure wireless network. Of course, this assumes that a wardriver is using a standard antenna to look for wireless signals. That may be true in some cases, but many wardrivers use super-powerful antennas that offer many times the range of a regular antenna. There is, unfortunately, nothing you can do to hide your signal from such hackers. However, it's still worthwhile to reposition your access point to minimize signal leakage since this will help thwart those hackers using regular antennas.

Unfortunately, minimizing signal leakage isn't that easy because in most network setups there are a couple of constraints on the position of the wireless AP:

■ If you're using the wireless AP as your network router, you need the device relatively close to your broadband modem so that you can run ethernet cable from the modem's ethernet or LAN port to the router's Internet or WAN port.

■ If you're using the wireless AP as your network switch, you need the device relatively close to your computers with ethernet network interface cards (NICs) so that you can run ethernet cable from the NICs to the switch's RJ-45 jacks.

However, even working within these constraints, in almost all cases you can position the wireless AP away from a window. Glass doesn't obstruct radio frequency (RF) signals, so they're a prime source for wireless leakage. If your wireless AP must reside in a particular room, try to position it as far away as possible from any windows in that room.

> **note** You might think that your wireless network signals extend at most just a few feet outside of your home or office. I thought so too, but then one day I was looking at Vista's list of available wireless networks, and I saw a network where the service set identifier (SSID) was the house address, and that house was *four* houses down from us!

In an ideal world, you should position the wireless AP close to the center of your house or building. This will ensure that the bulk of the signal stays in the building. If your only concern is connecting the router to a broadband modem, consider asking the phone or cable company to add a new jack to a central room (assuming the room doesn't have one already). Then, if it's feasible, you could used wired connections for the computers and devices in that room, and wireless connections for all your other devices. Of course, if your office (or, less likely, your home) has ethernet wiring throughout, it should be easier to find a central location for the wireless AP.

tip If you find a more central location for your wireless AP, test for signal leakage. Unplug any wireless-enabled notebook and take it outside for a walk in the vicinity of your house. View the available wireless networks as you go, and see whether your network shows up in the list.

caution Many wireless APs come with an option to extend the range of the wireless signal. Unless you really need the range extended to ensure some distant device can connect to the AP, you should disable this option.

Encrypting Wireless Signals with WPA

Wardrivers usually look for leaking wireless signals so that they can piggyback on the Internet access. They may just be freeloading on your connection, but they may also have darker aims, such as using your Internet connection to send spam or download pornography.

However, some wardriving hackers are interested more in your data. They come equipped with *packet sniffers* that can pick up and read your network packets. Typically, these crackers are looking for sensitive data such as passwords and credit card numbers.

Therefore, it's absolutely crucial that you enable encryption for wireless data so that an outside user who picks up your network packets can't decipher them. Older wireless networks use a security protocol called Wired Equivalent Privacy, or WEP, that protects wireless communications with (usually) a 26-character security key. That sounds impregnable, but unfortunately there were serious weaknesses in the WEP encryption scheme, and now software exists that can crack any WEP key in minutes, if not seconds.

In newer wireless networks, WEP has been superseded by Wi-Fi Protected Access, or WPA, which is vastly more secure than WEP. WPA uses most of the IEEE 802.11i wireless security standard, and WPA2 implements the full standard. WPA2 Personal requires a simple pass phrase for access (so it's suitable for homes and small offices), and WPA2 Enterprise requires a dedicated authentication server. Be sure to use the strongest encryption that your equipment supports.

The next few sections show you how to change the encryption properties in several popular wireless APs.

Belkin

Here are the steps to follow to change the encryption settings on most Belkin routers:

1. Log on to the router's setup pages.

2. In the Wireless section, click the Security link to display the Security page.

3. Select an encryption type. The setup page refreshes to show the encryption options associated with the type you selected. For example, Figure 15.5 shows the options associated with the WPA2 Only type.

caution Unfortunately, encryption is a "lowest common denominator" game. That is, if you want to use a strong encryption standard such as WPA2, *all* your wireless devices must support WPA2. If you have a device that only supports WEP, you either need to drop your encryption standard down to WEP, or you need to replace that device with one that supports the stronger standard. (You might also be able to upgrade the existing device; check with the manufacturer.) Note that some APs come with a setting that enables you to support both WPA and WPA2 devices.

FIGURE 15.5

On your Belkin router's Security page, select an encryption type to see the associated encryption settings.

4. For WPA or WPA2, you should select Password (PSK) as the Authentication option, and Passphrase as the Password (PSK) option.

5. Use the Password (PSK) text box to specify the password or pass phrase required to connect to the AP.

6. Click Apply Changes.

note PSK is short for *pre-shared key*, which refers in general to the sharing of some secret information with a person so that person can use the information later on (which is why this system is also sometimes called *shared secret*). In the case of WPA, the shared secret is the password or pass phrase that you give to your users so that they can connect to the wireless AP.

D-Link

For most D-Link routers, follow these steps to change the encryption settings:

1. Log on to the router's setup pages.

2. Click the Setup tab.

3. Click Wireless Settings to display the Wireless Network page.

4. In the Wireless Security Mode section, use the Security Mode list to select an encryption type. The setup page refreshes to show the encryption options associated with the type you selected. For example, Figure 15.6 shows the options that appear when you select Enable WPA2 Wireless Security.

5. In the Cipher Type list, select either TKIP (Temporal Key Integrity Protocol) or AES (Advanced Encryption Standard). Note that AES is slightly stronger than TKIP, but either one is certainly good enough for a small network.

6. In the Personal/Enterprise list, select Personal.

7. Use the Passphrase and Confirm Passphrase text boxes to specify the password or pass phrase required to connect to the AP.

8. Click Save Settings. The router saves the new settings.

9. Click Continue.

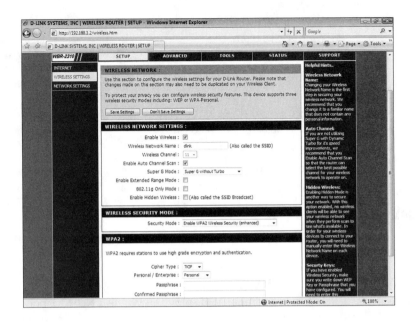

FIGURE 15.6
On your D-Link router, use the Wireless Network page to change the encryption settings.

Linksys

Here are the steps to follow to change the encryption settings on most Linksys routers:

1. Log on to the router's setup pages.

2. Click the Wireless tab.

3. Click the Wireless Security subtab.

4. Use the Security Mode list to select an encryption type. The setup page refreshes to show the encryption options associated with the type you selected. For example, Figure 15.7 shows the options that appear when you select WPA2 Personal.

5. Select a WPA Algorithm (AES or TKIP+AES).

6. Use the WPA Shared Key text box to specify the password or pass phrase required to connect to the AP.

7. Click Save Settings. The router reports that the Settings are successful.

8. Click Continue.

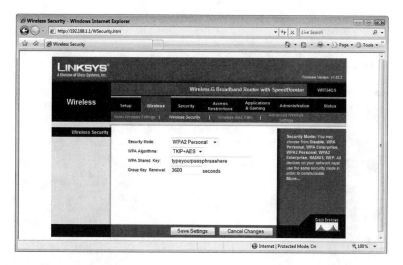

FIGURE 15.7

On most Linksys routers, use the Wireless Security page to change the encryption settings.

Netgear

Follow these steps to modify the encryption settings on most Netgear routers:

1. Log on to the router's setup pages.

2. In the Setup section, click the Wireless Settings link. The Wireless Settings page appears.

3. In the Security Options group, select an encryption type. The Wireless Settings page refreshes to show the encryption options associated with the type you selected. For example, Figure 15.8 shows the options that appear when you select WPA2-PSK (AES).

4. Use the Passphrase text box to specify the password or pass phrase required to connect to the AP.

5. Click Apply.

Changing the Wireless Connection Security Properties

If you change your wireless AP encryption method as described in the previous sections, you also need to update each wireless Vista computer to use the same form of encryption. Here are the steps to follow to modify the security properties for a wireless connection:

FIGURE 15.8

On most Netgear routers, use the Wireless Settings page to change the encryption settings.

1. Select Start, Control Panel to open the Control Panel window.

2. Under Network and Internet, click the View Network Status and Tasks link to open the Network and Sharing Center.

3. In the Tasks list, click Manage Wireless Network. Vista displays the Manage Wireless Networks window.

4. Double-click the network for which you modified the encryption. Vista opens the network's Wireless Network Properties dialog box.

5. Select the Security tab, shown in Figure 15.9.

6. Change the following three settings, as needed:

Security Type	Select the encryption standard you're now using on the wireless AP.
Encryption Type	Select the type of encryption used by the AP.
Network Security Key	Type your shared key.

7. Click OK.

FIGURE 15.9

Use the Security tab to match the network connection's security properties with the new encryption settings on the wireless AP.

Disabling Network SSID Broadcasting

Windows Vista sees your wireless network because the AP broadcasts the network's SSID. However, Windows remembers the wireless networks that you have successfully connected to (as described in Chapter 7, "Managing Wireless Network Connections"). Therefore, after all of your computers have accessed the wireless network at least once, you no longer need to broadcast the network's SSID. And so, you should use your AP setup program to disable broadcasting and prevent others from seeing your network.

➔   For more information about how Vista remembers wireless networks, **see** "Opening the Manage Wireless Networks Window," **p. xxx**. (Chapter 7)

However, you should know that when previously authorized devices attempt to connect to a nonbroadcasting network, they include the network's SSID as part of the probe requests they send out to see whether the network is within range. The SSID is sent in unencrypted text, so it would be easy for a snoop

15

with the right software (easily obtained from the Internet) to learn the SSID. If the SSID is not broadcasting to try to hide a network that is unsecure or uses an easily breakable encryption protocol, such as WEP, hiding the SSID in this way actually makes the network *less* secure.

Of course, *you* aren't trying to hide an unsecure network, right? From the previous section, you should now have WPA or WPA2 encryption enabled. So in your case, disabling SSID broadcasting either keeps your security the same or improves it:

caution Okay, there *is* one scenario where hiding your SSID can make your wireless network *less* secure. If a cracker detects that you've disabled SSID broadcasting, he might think you've done it because you've got something particularly important or sensitive to hide, so he might pull out all the stops to crack your network. How likely is this? Not very. Most crackers want easy targets, and most neighborhoods supply them, so unless a snoop *knows* that you're hiding something juicy, he'll almost certainly move on to a less-secure network.

■ If a cracker detects your nonbroad-casting SSID, you're no worse off.

■ If the snoop doesn't have the necessary software to detect your nonbroad-casting SSID, he won't see your network, so you're more secure.

So as long as your wireless signals are encrypted with WPA or WPA2, you should disable SSID broadcasting.

The next few sections show you how to disable SSID broadcasting in several popular wireless APs.

Belkin

Here are the steps to follow to disable SSID broadcasting on most Belkin routers:

1. Log on to the router's setup pages.

2. In the Wireless section, click the Channel and SSID link to display the Channel and SSID page.

3. For the ESSID Broadcast option, select Disable, as shown in Figure 15.10.

4. Click Apply Changes.

FIGURE 15.10

On most Belkin routers, use the Channel and SSID page to disable SSID broadcasting.

D-Link

For most D-Link routers, follow these steps to disable SSID broadcasting:

1. Log on to the router's setup pages.

2. Click the Setup tab.

3. Click Wireless Settings to display the Wireless Network page.

4. In the Wireless Network Settings group, activate the Enable Hidden Wireless check box, as shown in Figure 15.11.

5. Click Save Settings. The router saves the new settings.

6. Click Continue.

Linksys

Here are the steps to follow to disable SSID broadcasting on most Linksys routers:

1. Log on to the router's setup pages.

2. Click the Wireless tab.

3. Click the Basic Wireless Settings subtab.

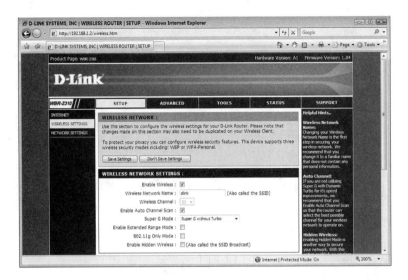

FIGURE 15.11

On your D-Link router, use the Wireless Network page to disable SSID broadcasting.

> **4.** For the Wireless SSID Broadcast setting, select Disable, as shown in Figure 15.12.

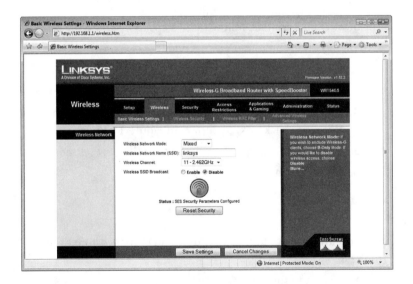

FIGURE 15.12

On most Linksys routers, use the Basic Wireless Settings page to disable SSID broadcasting.

5. Click Save Settings. The router reports that the Settings are successful.

6. Click Continue.

Netgear

Follow these steps to disable SSID broadcasting on most Netgear routers:

1. Log on to the router's setup pages.

2. In the Advanced section, click the Wireless Settings link. The Advanced Wireless Settings page appears.

3. Click to deactivate the Enable SSID Broadcast check box, as shown in Figure 15.13.

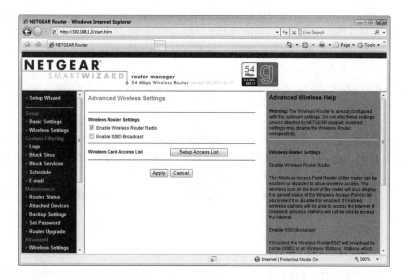

FIGURE 15.13

On most Netgear routers, use the Advanced Wireless Settings page to disable SSID broadcasting.

4. Use the Old Password text box to type the current administrative password.

5. Use the New Password and Repeat New Password text boxes to specify the new administrative password.

6. Click Apply.

Changing the Default SSID

Even if you disable broadcasting of your network's SSID, users can still attempt to connect to your network by guessing the SSID. All wireless APs come with a predefined name, such as linksys, dlink, or default, and a would-be intruder will attempt these standard names first. Therefore, you can increase the security of your network by changing the SSID to a new name that is difficult to guess.

> **note** Another good reason to change the default SSID is to prevent confusion with other wireless networks in your area. If Vista's list of available wireless networks includes two (or more) networks named, say, linksys, how will you know which one is yours?

Even if you're broadcasting your wireless network's SSID, it's still a good idea to change the default SSID. Because in most cases the default SSID includes the name of the manufacturer, the SSID gives a would-be intruder valuable information on the type of AP you're using. In some cases, the default SSID offers not only the name of the manufacturer, but also information about the specific model (for example, belkin54g), which is of course even more useful to a cracker.

Finally, changing the default SSID is at the very least a small sign that you know what you're doing. One of the hallmarks of inexperienced users is that they don't change default settings because they're afraid of breaking something. If a wardriver sees a wireless network that's still using a default SSID, he's likely to think that he's dealing with an inexperienced user, so he'll be more likely to try to infiltrate the network.

The next few sections show you how to change the default SSID in several popular wireless APs.

Belkin

Here are the steps to follow to change the default SSID on most Belkin routers:

1. Log on to the router's setup pages.
2. In the Wireless section, click the Channel and SSID link to display the Channel and SSID page, shown in Figure 15.14.
3. Use the SSID text box to type the new SSID.
4. Click Apply Changes.

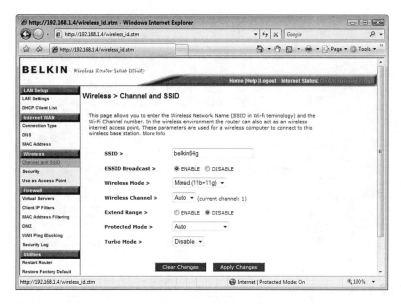

FIGURE 15.14

On most Belkin routers, use the Channel and SSID page to change the default SSID.

D-Link

For most D-Link routers, follow these steps to change the default SSID:

1. Log on to the router's setup pages.
2. Click the Setup tab.
3. Click Wireless Settings to display the Wireless Network page, shown in Figure 15.15.
4. In the Wireless Network Settings group, edit the Wireless Network Name text box.
5. Click Save Settings. The router saves the new settings.
6. Click Continue.

Linksys

Here are the steps to follow to change the default SSID on most Linksys routers:

1. Log on to the router's setup pages.
2. Click the Wireless tab.
3. Click the Basic Wireless Settings subtab to open the Basic Wireless Settings page, shown in Figure 15.16.

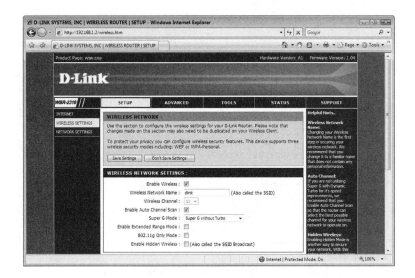

FIGURE 15.15
On your D-Link router, use the Wireless Network page to change the default SSID.

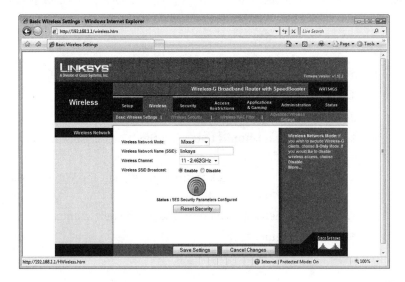

FIGURE 15.16
On most Linksys routers, use the Basic Wireless Settings page to change the default SSID.

4. Edit the Wireless Network Name (SSID) text box.

5. At the bottom of the page, click Save Settings. The router reports that the `Settings are successful`.

6. Click Continue.

Netgear

Follow these steps to modify the default SSID on most Netgear routers:

1. Log on to the router's setup pages.

2. In the Setup section, click the Wireless Settings link. The Wireless Settings page appears, as shown in Figure 15.17.

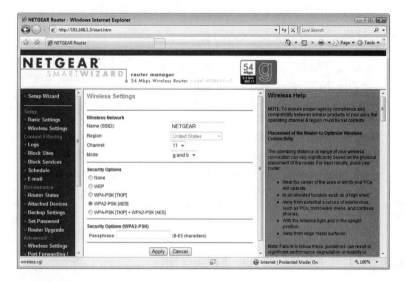

FIGURE 15.17

On most Netgear routers, use the Wireless Settings page to change the default SSID.

3. Use the Name (SSID) text box to edit the SSID.

4. Click Apply.

Enabling MAC Address Filtering

The *MAC* (*Media Access Control*) *address* is the physical address of a network adapter. This is unique to each adapter, so you can enhance security by setting up your AP to use MAC address filtering. This feature means that the AP only accepts connections from a list of MAC addresses that you specify. If a hacker tries to connect to your network using a NIC that has a MAC address not on the list, the AP denies the connection.

Unfortunately, MAC address filtering isn't a particularly robust form of security. The problem is that wireless network packets use a nonencrypted header that includes the MAC address of the device sending the packet! So any reasonably sophisticated cracker can sniff your network packets, determine the MAC address of one of your wireless devices, and then use special software to spoof that address so that the AP thinks the hacker's packets are coming from an authorized device.

Does this mean you shouldn't bother configuring a MAC address filter? Not at all. For one thing, even if a savvy wardriver can fool your wireless AP into thinking his device is authorized, the hacker still has to get past your other security layers. For another, not every cracker out there uses sophisticated tools such as packet sniffers and MAC address spoofing software, so your filter will at least thwart those would-be intruders.

note Another way to find out the MAC address of your wireless network adapter is to select Start, All Programs, Accessories, Command Prompt to open a command prompt session. Type the following command and press Enter:

```
ipconfig /all
```

Find the data for the wireless adapter and look for the `Physical Address` value.

Getting the MAC Address of Your Wireless NIC

The good news about MAC address filtering is that most modern APs come with a feature that displays a list of the devices currently connected to the AP and enables you to quickly add the MAC addresses of those devices to the AP's MAC address filter. Just in case your access point doesn't come with this feature, here are the steps to follow in Windows Vista to determine the MAC address of your wireless NIC:

tip While we're on the subject of wireless NICs, this is as good a place as any to talk about security updates. Wireless NIC vendors occasionally find security vulnerabilities in their NIC device drivers, and they issue patches and driver upgrades to fix those security holes. You should check the manufacturer's website from time to time to see whether any updates are available for your NIC.

1. Select Start, Control Panel to open the Control Panel window.
2. Under Network and Internet, click the View Network Status and Tasks link to open the Network and Sharing Center.
3. In the Tasks list, click Manage Network Connections.
4. Double-click the wireless connection to open the Status dialog box.
5. Click Details to open the Network Connection Details dialog box.
6. Make a note of the Physical Address value (see Figure 15.18), which is the same as the MAC address.

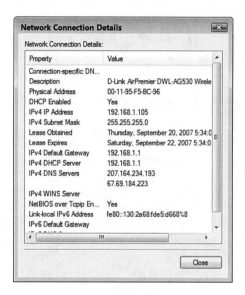

FIGURE 15.18

In the Network Connection Details dialog box, the wireless NIC's MAC address is given by the Physical Address value.

7. Click Close.

The next few sections show you how to configure MAC address filtering in several popular wireless APs.

Belkin

Here are the steps to follow to set up MAC address filtering on most Belkin routers:

1. Log on to the router's setup pages.

2. In the Firewall section, click the MAC Address Filtering link to display the MAC Address Filtering page, shown in Figure 15.19.

3. Click Enable.

4. Use the MAC Address table to type the MAC addresses for each device.

5. Click Apply Changes.

tip If you're using the Belkin router as a Dynamic Host Configuration Protocol (DHCP) server, the DHCP Client List will show the devices connected to the AP, and this list can save you tons of time when setting up your MAC address filter. For each device in the list, select the device, select an ID number in the second list, and then click Copy To.

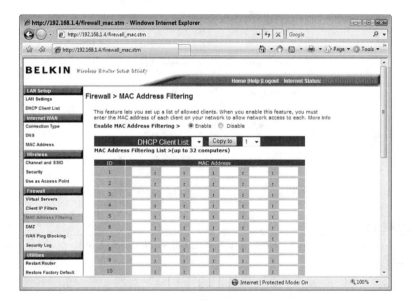

FIGURE 15.19

On most Belkin routers, use the MAC Address Filtering page to set up MAC address filtering.

D-Link

For most D-Link routers, follow these steps to configure MAC address filtering:

1. Log on to the router's setup pages.

2. Click the Advanced tab.

3. Click Network Filter to display the MAC Filtering page.

4. In the Configure MAC Filtering Below list, select Turn MAC Filtering ON and ALLOW Computers Listed to Access the Network, as shown in Figure 15.20.

5. In the MAC Address column, use the text boxes to type the MAC addresses for each device.

> **tip** If you're using the D-Link access point as a DHCP server, the AP populates the DHCP Client List boxes with the names of the devices connected to the AP. For each connected device, select the device in one of the lists and then click the << button to add the device's MAC address to the corresponding MAC Address text box. Figure 15.20 shows the MAC Filtering page with some MAC addresses added in this way.

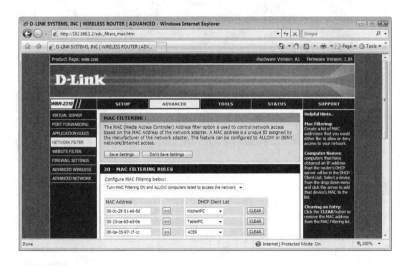

FIGURE 15.20

On your D-Link router, use the MAC Filtering page to configure MAC address filtering.

6. Click Save Settings. The router saves the new settings.

7. Click Continue.

Linksys

Here are the steps to follow to set up MAC address filtering on most Linksys routers:

1. Log on to the router's setup pages.
2. Click the Wireless tab.
3. Click the Wireless MAC Filter subtab to display the Wireless MAC Filter page.
4. Click the Enable option.
5. Click the Permit Only PCs Listed to Access the Wireless Network, as shown in Figure 15.21.

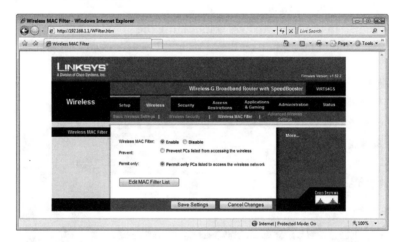

FIGURE 15.21

On most Linksys routers, use the Wireless MAC Filter page to set up MAC address filtering.

6. Click Edit MAC Filter List to open the MAC Address Filter List window.
7. Use the text boxes to type the MAC addresses for each device.
8. At the bottom of the page, click Save Settings. The router reports that the Settings are successful.
9. Click Continue.

> **tip** If you're using the Linksys router as a DHCP server, click the Wireless Client MAC List button. For each connected device shown, click the check box in the Enable MAC Filter column, and then click Update Filter List. The AP then populates the MAC Address Filter List for you automatically. Click Save Settings.

Netgear

Follow these steps to configure up MAC address filtering on most Netgear routers:

note To see a list of MAC addresses for the devices connected to the Netgear AP, click the Attached Devices link in the Maintenance section.

1. Log on to the router's setup pages.

2. In the Advanced section, click the Wireless Settings link to display the Advanced Wireless Settings page.

3. Click Setup Access List to open the Wireless Card Access List page.

4. Click to activate the Turn Access Control On check box.

5. Click Add to open the Wireless Card Access Setup page.

6. Use the Device Name text box to type the name of the device.

7. Use the MAC Address text box to type the device's MAC address.

8. Click Add. The AP adds the device name and MAC address to the Wireless Card Access List page, as shown in Figure 15.22.

FIGURE 15.22

On most Netgear routers, use the Wireless Card Access List page to configure MAC address filtering.

9. Repeat steps 4–7 to add other device MAC addresses.

10. Click Apply.

From Here

- For more information about how Vista remembers wireless networks, **see** "Opening the Manage Wireless Networks Window," **p. 158**.

- Your network is only as secure as its client computers, so be sure to make each of your Vista machines as secure as possible; **see** Chapter 13, "Securing Windows Vista," **p. 281**.

- For other network security techniques, **see** Chapter 14, "Implementing Network Security," **p. 313**.

- To learn how to log on with Remote Desktop Connection, **see** "Connecting to the Remote Desktop," **p. 373**.

Advanced Networking with Windows Vista

16 Making Remote Network Connections

17 Monitoring Your Network

18 Troubleshooting Network Problems

19 Setting up a Website

20 Setting up an FTP Site

Glossary of Networking Terms

Making Remote Network Connections

One of the big advantages to having a network is that you can set up shared folders for other people to access, and you can access the shared folders that other people have set up. This is so much easier than trying to share data using less-direct means, such as the old "sneak-ernet" solution. (That is, place the files on a memory card or other removable media, walk the card over to the other computer—sneakers are optional—and then insert the card in the other computer.)

Shared folders are great, but there are plenty of problems they can't solve:

■ A program you need is installed on a remote computer, but not on your computer. For example, you might want to open or edit a document in a shared folder, but only the remote computer has a program that's capable of opening that document.

■ A remote computer has data that's impossible or difficult to share. For example, you may need to read or respond to an email message that you received on the remote computer, or you might need to visit an Internet site that you've set up as a favorite in Internet Explorer on the remote computer.

IN THIS CHAPTER

■ Setting Up the Remote Computer as a Host

■ Installing Remote Desktop on an XP Client Computer

■ Connecting to the Remote Desktop

■ Disconnecting from the Remote Desktop

■ Connecting to a Remote Desktop via the Internet

■ Using Dynamic DNS to Access Your Network

■ From Here

■ A remote computer contains data you need, but that data resides in a folder that hasn't been shared.

To solve these and similar problems, you need to go beyond shared folders and establish a more powerful connection to the remote computer. That is, you need to connect to the remote machine's desktop, which enables you to open folders, run programs, edit documents, and tweak settings. In short, anything you can do while physically sitting in front of the other computer you can do remotely from your own computer. As you see in this chapter, Windows Vista's Remote Desktop feature enables you to connect to a computer's desktop over the network. It's also possible to configure your network to allow you to make a Remote Desktop connection over the Internet. This is a great way to give yourself access to your home computer while you're traveling with a laptop.

You might think that operating another computer remotely would be too slow to be useful. However, the responsiveness of the remote session depends a great deal on the speed of the connection. For a LAN connection, an Ethernet (10Mbps) connection or 802.11b (11Mbps) wireless connection is just too slow, whereas a Fast Ethernet (100Mbps) or 802.11g (54Mbps) connection will give you adequate performance for most tasks. If you want to play games or perform other graphics-intensive tasks, you really need a Gigabit Ethernet (1Gbps) connection or an 802.11n (248Mbps) wireless connection. Over the Internet, don't even bother connecting with dial-up; instead, you need a cable or Digital Subscriber Line (DSL) broadband (1Mbps or better) link, and even then you'll want to avoid large files and heavy-duty graphic tasks.

Setting Up the Remote Computer as a Host

Remote Desktop is easy to configure and use, but it does require a small amount of prep work to ensure trouble-free operation. Let's begin with the remote computer, also called the *host* computer. The next few sections tell you how to set up a machine to act as a Remote Desktop host.

Windows Versions That Can Act as Hosts

The first thing you need to know is that not all versions of Windows can act as Remote Desktop hosts:

■ With Vista, the only versions that support Remote Desktop are Vista Business, Vista Enterprise, and Vista Ultimate.

- If you want to use a Windows XP computer as the host, you can use any version except XP Home.

Setting Up User Accounts on the Host

For security reasons, not just anyone can connect to a remote computer's desktop. By default, Windows gives permission to connect remotely to the host to the following:

- The user who is currently logged on to the host machine
- Members of the host's Administrators and Remote Desktop Users groups

Note, however, that all of these users must have password-protected accounts to use Remote Desktop.

For anyone else, if you want to give a person permission to connect to the host remotely, you first need to set up an account for the username with which you want that person to connect from the client, and you must assign a password to this account.

→   To learn how to set up a user account in Windows Vista, **see** "Creating User Accounts for Sharing," **p. xxx**. (Chapter 8)

Configuring Vista to Act as a Remote Desktop Host

If the host machine is running Vista Business, Enterprise, or Ultimate, you have to do three things to prepare the computer for its Remote Desktop hosting duties:

- Disable automatic Sleep mode.
- Allow Remote Desktop through the Windows Firewall.
- Activate the Remote Desktop service.

Disabling Automatic Sleep Mode

Most Vista machines are configured to go into Sleep mode after one hour of inactivity. Sleep is a low-power mode that turns everything off except power to the memory chips, which store the current desktop configuration. When you turn the machine

> **note** All we're doing here is disabling the feature that puts your computer into Sleep mode automatically after a period of inactivity. If need be, you can still put the computer into Sleep mode manually by selecting Start and clicking the Sleep button.

back on, the desktop and your open programs and documents appear within a few seconds. However, remote clients won't be able to connect to the host if it's in Sleep mode, so you have to disable this feature.

Here are the steps to follow:

1. Select Start, Control Panel to open the Control Panel window.

2. Select System and Maintenance to open the System and Maintenance window.

3. Under Power Options, click the Change When the Computer Sleeps link. Vista opens the Edit Plan Settings window.

4. In the Put the Computer to Sleep list, select Never, as shown in Figure 16.1.

> **tip** Another way to get to the Edit Plan Settings window is to select Start, type **power** in the Search box, and then click Power Options in the search results. In the Power Options window, click the Change When the Computer Sleeps link.

FIGURE 16.1
On the Remote Desktop host, turn off the feature that automatically puts the computer into Sleep mode.

5. Click Save Changes.

Configuring a Windows Firewall Exception for Remote Desktop

By default, Windows Firewall doesn't allow Remote Desktop connections. This is a sensible security precaution because connecting to someone's desktop gives you nearly complete control over that PC. To enable remote connections, you must configure a Windows Firewall exception for Remote Desktop.

Here are the steps you need to follow:

1. Select Start, Control Panel to open the Control Panel window.

2. Under Security, click the Allow a Program Through Windows Firewall link. The User Account Control dialog box appears.

3. Enter your User Account Control (UAC) credentials to continue. Vista opens the Windows Firewall Settings dialog box with the Exceptions tab displayed.

4. Activate the check box beside Remote Desktop, as shown in Figure 16.2.

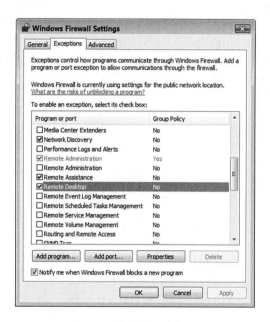

FIGURE 16.2

To enable remote connections, activate the Remote Desktop check box.

5. Click OK. Vista enables the firewall exception for Remote Desktop.

Activating the Remote Desktop Service

Now follow these steps to activate the Remote Desktop service:

1. Select Start, Control Panel to open the Control Panel window.

2. Click System and Maintenance to open the System and Maintenance window.

3. Under System, click the Allow Remote Access link. The User Account Control dialog box appears.

4. Enter your UAC credentials to continue. Vista opens the System Properties dialog box with the Remote tab displayed, as shown in Figure 16.3.

> **tip** Another way to open the System Properties dialog box with the Remote tab displayed is to select Start, right-click Computer, click Properties to open the System window, and then click the Remote Settings link. Alternatively, press Windows Logo+R (or select Start, All Programs, Accessories, Run) to open the Run dialog box, type `systempropertiesremote` (or `control sysdm.cpl,,5`), and click OK. With either method, you need to enter your UAC credentials to continue.

FIGURE 16.3

On the remote host, select an option in the Remote Desktop group to enable remote connections to the computer's desktop.

5. In the Remote Desktop group, you have two choices:

   Allow Connections from Computers Running Any Version of Remote Desktop. Select this option if you want people running previous versions of Remote Desktop to be able to access the host.

   Allow Connections Only from Computers Running Remote Desktop with Network Level Authentication. Select this option if you only want the most secure form of Remote Desktop access. In this case, Vista checks the client computer to see whether its version of Remote Desktop supports Network Level Authentication (NLA). NLA is an authentication protocol that authenticates the user before making the Remote Desktop connection. NLA is built in to every version of Windows Vista, but is not supported on older Windows systems.

6. If you didn't add more users earlier, skip to step 9. Otherwise, click Select Users to display the Remote Desktop Users dialog box.

7. Click Add to display the Select Users dialog box, type the username, and click OK. (Repeat this step to add other users.)

8. Click OK to return to the System Properties dialog box.

9. Click OK.

Configuring XP to Act as a Remote Desktop Host

You may want to connect your Vista computer to the desktop of a remote XP machine. If the host machine is running any version of XP except XP Home, here are the steps to follow to set it up to host Remote Desktop sessions:

1. Log on to the XP computer as an administrator.

2. Select Start, Control Panel to open the Control Panel window.

3. Double click the System icon to open the System Properties dialog box.

4. Display the Remote tab.

5. In the Remote Desktop group, activate the Allow Users to Connect Remotely to This Computer check box, as shown in Figure 16.4.

> **tip** Another way to get to the System Properties dialog box and its Remote tab is to select Start, right-click My Computer, click Properties, and then select the Remote tab. Alternatively, you can display the Remote tab directly by pressing Windows Logo+R (or selecting Start, Run) to open the Run dialog box, typing **control sysdm.cpl,,6**, and clicking OK.

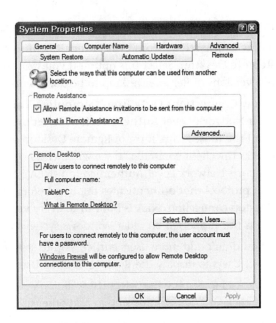

FIGURE 16.4
In XP, the Allow Users to Connect Remotely to This Computer check box must be activated to enable Remote Desktop sessions on the computer.

6. If you didn't add more users earlier, skip to step 9. Otherwise, click Select Remote Users to display the Remote Desktop Users dialog box.

7. Click Add to display the Select Users dialog box, type the username, and click OK. (Repeat this step to add other users.)

8. Click OK to return to the System Properties dialog box.

9. Click OK.

Installing Remote Desktop on an XP Client Computer

A computer that connects to a remote computer's desktop is said to be a Remote Desktop *client*. To act as a client, the computer must have the Remote Desktop Connection software installed. Remote Desktop Connection is installed by default in all versions of Windows Vista, but some versions of XP don't come with the program installed. However, you can install the Remote Desktop Connection software from the Windows XP CD (if you have one):

1. Insert the Windows XP CD and wait for the Welcome to Microsoft Windows XP screen to appear.

2. Click Perform Additional Tasks.

3. Click Set Up Remote Desktop
   Connection.

> **note** You can also download the latest client software from Microsoft:
>
> www.microsoft.com/
> windowsxp/downloads/tools/
> rdclientdl.mspx
>
> You can also use this client if you're running Windows XP and don't have access to the XP install disc.

Connecting to the Remote Desktop

With your Windows Vista or Windows XP
computer set up to act as a Remote
Desktop host, you've ready to make the
connection, as described in the next two
sections.

Making a Basic Connection

Remote Desktop Connection comes with a large number of advanced connection options and settings. If you don't want to bother with those advanced features right now, you can connect to the host in just a few steps. On the Vista client computer, you make a basic connection to the host computer's desktop by following these steps:

1. Select Start, All Programs, Accessories, Remote Desktop Connection. The Remote Desktop Connection dialog box appears.

2. In the Computer text box, type the name or the IP address of the host computer, as shown in Figure 16.5.

FIGURE 16.5

In the Remote Desktop Connection dialog box, type the name or the IP address of the remote host computer.

3. Click Connect. Windows Vista prompts you to enter your security credentials.

4. In Windows Vista, type the user-name and password of the host account you want to use for the logon, and then click OK. (Note that in subsequent logons, you only need to type the password.)

Making an Advanced Connection

The basic remote connection from the pre-vious section may be all you need to use for your remote sessions. However, Remote Desktop Connection comes with many set-tings that enable you to configure options such as the size of the remote desktop screen, whether your Windows keyboard shortcuts (such as Alt+Tab) apply to the remote computer or your computer, and much more.

> **note** If you're using Windows XP to connect to a Vista host, select Start, All Programs, Accessories, Communications, Remote Desktop Connection to open the Remote Desktop Connection window. Type the host computer name or IP address, and then click Connect. When the Vista logon screen appears, click the icon of the user account with which you want to connect, type the account's password, and press Enter to complete the connection.

Here are the steps to follow to use these settings to make an advanced connec-tion to the host computer's desktop:

1. Select Start, All Programs, Accessories, Remote Desktop Connection. (In XP, select Start, All Programs, Accessories, Communications, Remote Desktop Connection.) The Remote Desktop Connection dialog box appears.

2. In the Computer text box, type the name or the IP address of the host computer.

3. Click Options to expand the dialog box to the version shown in Figure 16.6.

4. The General tab offers the following additional options:

Computer	The name or IP address of the remote computer.
User Name	(Windows XP only) The username you want to use to log in to the host computer.
Password	(Windows XP only) The password to use to log on to the host computer.
Domain	(Windows XP only) Leave this text box blank.

FIGURE 16.6

Click the Options button to expand the dialog box so that you can customize Remote Desktop.

Save (Windows Vista only)   Click this button to have Vista remember your current settings so that you don't have to type them again the next time you connect. This is useful if you only connect to one remote host.

Save As   Click this button to save your connection settings to a Remote Desktop (.rdp) file for later use. This is convenient if you regularly connect to multiple hosts.

Open   Click this button to open a saved .rdp file.

caution You may need to be a bit careful if the remote host is currently using a higher resolution than the one you select using the Remote Desktop Size slider. When you make the connection, Vista will change the host's screen resolution to the lower setting, and then when you disconnect from the host Vista will return the resolution to the higher setting. However, some video cards don't react well to these resolution switches, and they cause the running programs to think they're still operating at the lower resolution. To work around this, try to use the same resolution both locally and remotely. If you can't do that, minimize all the open windows before making the connection (if possible).

5. The Display tab offers three options for controlling the look of the Remote Desktop window:

Remote Desktop Size	Drag this slider to set the resolution of Remote Desktop. Drag the slider all the way to the left for a 640×480 screen size; drag the slider all the way to the right to have Remote Desktop take up the entire client screen, no matter what resolution the host is currently using.
Colors	Use this list to set the number of colors used for the Remote Desktop display. Note that if the number of colors on either the host or the client is fewer than the value you select in the Colors list, Windows uses the lesser value.
Display the Connection Bar When in Full Screen Mode	When this check box is activated, the Remote Desktop Connection client displays a connection bar at the top of the Remote Desktop window, provided you selected Full Screen for the Remote Desktop Size setting. You use the connection bar to minimize, restore, and close the Remote Desktop window. If you find that the connection bar just gets in the way, deactivate this check box to prevent it from appearing.

6. The Local Resources tab offers three options for controlling certain interactions between the client and host:

Remote Computer Sound	Use this list to determine where Windows plays the sounds generated by the host. You can play them on the client (if you want to hear what's happening on the host), on the host (if you want a user sitting at the host to hear the sounds), or not at all (if you have a slow connection).
Keyboard	Use this list to determine which computer is sent special Windows key combinations—such as Alt+Tab and Ctrl+Esc—that you press on the client keyboard. You can have the key combos sent to the client, to the host, or to the host only when you're running the Remote Desktop window in full-screen mode. What happens if you're sending key combos to one computer and you need to use a particular

key combo on the other computer? For such situations, Remote Desktop offers several keyboard equivalents, outlined in the following table:

Windows Key Combo	Remote Desktop Equivalent
Alt+Tab	Alt+Page Up
Alt+Shift+Tab	Alt+Page Down
Alt+Esc	Alt+Insert
Ctrl+Esc or Windows Logo	Alt+Home
Print Screen	Ctrl+Alt+– (numeric keypad)
Alt+Print Screen	Ctrl+Alt++ (numeric keypad)

Local Devices and Resources
Leave the Printers check box activated to display the client's printers in the host's Printers and Faxes window. The client's printers appear with the syntax `Printer (from COMPUTER)`, where `Printer` is the printer name and `COMPUTER` is the network name of the client computer. In Vista, leave the Clipboard check box activated to use the client's Clipboard during the remote session. In XP, you can also connect disk drives and serial ports, which I describe in the next step.

7. In Vista, click More to see the Remote Desktop Connection dialog box. Use the following check boxes to configure more client devices and resources on the host. (Click OK when you have finished.)

Smart Cards Leave this check box activated to access the client's smart cards on the host.

Serial Ports Activate this check box to make any devices attached to the client's serial ports (such as a barcode scanner) available while you're working with the host.

> **tip** Here are three other useful keyboard shortcuts that you can press on the client computer and have Windows send to the host:
>
> Ctrl+Alt+End Displays the Windows Security dialog box. This is equivalent to pressing Ctrl+Alt+Delete, which Windows always applies to the client computer.
>
> Alt+Delete Displays the active window's Control menu.
>
> Ctrl+Alt+Break Toggles the Remote Desktop window between full-screen mode and a regular window.

Drives	Activate this check box to display the client's hard disk partitions and mapped network drives in the hosts Computer (or My Computer) window. (You can also open the branch to activate the check boxes of specific drives.) The client's drives appear in the window's Other group with the syntax D on $Computer$, where D is the drive letter and $Computer$ is the network name of the client computer.
Supported Plug and Play Devices	Activate this check box to make some of the client's Plug and Play devices, such as media players and digital cameras, available to the host. (You can also open the branch to activate the check boxes of specific devices.)

8. Use the Programs tab to specify a program to run on connection. Activate the Start the Following Program on Connection check box, and then use the Program Path and File Name text box to specify the program to run. After connecting, the user can work with only this program, and when he quits the program, the session also ends.

9. Use the Experience tab (the Vista version is shown in Figure 16.7) to set performance options for the connection. Use the Choose Your Connection Speed to Optimize Performance drop-down list to set the appropriate connection speed. Because you're connecting over a network, you should choose the LAN (10 Mbps or higher) option. Depending on the connection speed you choose, one or more of the following check boxes will be activated. (The faster the speed, the more check boxes Windows activates.)

Desktop Background	Toggles the host's desktop background on and off.
Font Smoothing	(Windows Vista only) Toggles the host's font smoothing on and off.
Desktop Composition	(Windows Vista only) Toggles the host's desktop composition engine on and off.
Show Contents of Window While Dragging	Toggles the display of window contents when you drag a host window with your mouse.
Menu and Windows Animation	Toggles on and off the animations that Windows normally uses when you pull down menus or minimize and maximize windows.
Themes	Toggles the host's current visual theme on and off.
Bitmap Caching	Improves performance by not storing frequently used host images on the client computer.

FIGURE 16.7

Use the Experience tab to set performance options for the connection.

10. Click Connect. Windows Vista prompts you to enter your security credentials.

11. In Windows Vista, type the username and password of the host account you want to use for the logon, and then click OK. (Note that in subsequent logons, you only need to type the password.) In Windows XP, click the icon of the user account with which you want to connect, type the account's password, and press Enter to complete the connection.

12. If you activated the Disk Drives or Serial Ports check boxes in the Local Resources tab, a security warning dialog box appears. If you're sure that making these resources available to the remote computer is safe, activate the Don't Prompt Me Again for Connections to This Remote Computer check box. Click OK.

Working with the Connection Bar

The remote desktop then appears on your computer. If you chose to work in full-screen mode, move the cursor to the top of the screen to see the connection bar, shown in Figure 16.8.

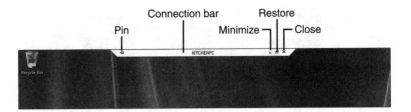

FIGURE 16.8

After you've connected and the remote computer's desktop appears on your screen, move the cursor to the top of the screen to see the connection bar.

If you want the connection bar to appear all the time, click to activate the Pin button. If you need to work with your own desktop, you have two choices:

■ Click the connection bar's Minimize button to minimize the Remote Desktop window.

■ Click the connection bar's Restore button to display the Remote Desktop window.

Disconnecting from the Remote Desktop

When you finish with the Remote Desktop session, you have two choices for disconnecting:

■ To shut down the host's running programs and windows, use the host desktop to select Start, Log Off.

■ To leave the programs and windows open on the host, click the Close button in the connection bar. Windows displays a dialog box to let you know that your remote session will be disconnected. Click OK.

Connecting to a Remote Desktop via the Internet

Connecting to a Remote Desktop host over your network is easy to set up and fast, but your local area network might not always be so local. If you're traveling, what do you do if you want to connect to your desktop or to the desktop of some computer on your network? This is possible, but it requires some care to ensure that you don't open up your computer or your network to Internet-based hackers.

→ To learn more about what constitutes a strong password, **see** "Building a Strong Password," **p. 292**.

To configure your system to allow Remote Desktop connections via the Internet, you need to perform these general steps (I explain each step in more detail in the sections that follow):

1. Configure Remote Desktop to use a listening port other than the default.

2. Configure Windows Firewall to allow TCP connections through the port you specified in step 1.

3. Determine the IP address of the Remote Desktop host or your network's router.

> **caution** Besides the security precautions I present in this section, you should also set up your accounts with robust passwords, as described in Chapter 13, "Securing Windows Vista." Using Remote Desktop over the Internet means that you open up a small window on your network that is at least visible to others on the Net. To ensure that other Internet users cannot exploit this hole, a strong password is a must.

4. Configure your network router (if you have one) to forward data sent to the port specified in step 1 to the Remote Desktop host computer.

5. Use the IP address from step 3 and the port number from step 1 to connect to the Remote Desktop host via the Internet.

Changing the Listening Port

Your first task is to modify the Remote Desktop software on the host computer to use a listening port other than 3389, which is the default port. This is a good idea because there are hackers on the Internet who use port scanners to examine Internet connections (particularly broadband connections) for open ports. If the hackers see that port 3389 is open, they could assume that it's for a Remote Desktop connection, so they try to make a Remote Desktop connection to the host. They still have to log on with an authorized username and password, but knowing the connection type means they've cleared a very large hurdle.

To change the Remote Desktop listening port, follow these steps:

1. Press Windows Logo+R (or select Start, All Programs, Accessories, Run) to open the Run dialog box.

2. Type **regedit**, and then click OK. The User Account Control dialog box appears.

3. Enter your UAC credentials to continue. Windows Vista opens the Registry Editor.

4. Open the HKEY_LOCAL_MACHINE branch.

5. Open the SYSTEM branch.

6. Open the CurrentControlSet branch.

7. Open the Control branch.

8. Open the TerminalServer branch.

9. Select the WinStations branch.

10. Select the RDP-Tcp branch.

caution I would be remiss if I didn't remind you the Vista's Registry contains settings that are vitally important for both Vista and your installed programs. Therefore, when you're working with the Registry Editor, don't make changes to any keys or settings other than the ones I describe in this section.

11. Double-click the PortNumber setting to open the Edit DWORD (32-bit) Value dialog box.

12. Select the Decimal option.

13. Replace the existing value (3389) with some other number between 1024 and 65536, as shown in Figure 16.9.

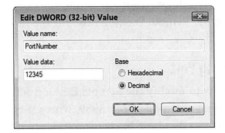

FIGURE 16.9

Replace port 3389 with another number between 1024 and 65536.

14. Click OK.

15. Reboot the computer to put the new port setting into effect.

Configuring Windows Firewall

Now you have to configure Windows Firewall to allow data to pass through the port you specified in the previous section. Here are the steps to follow:

1. Select Start, Control Panel to open the Control Panel window.

2. Under Security, click the Allow a Program through Windows Firewall link. The User Account Control dialog box appears.

3. Enter your UAC credentials to continue. Vista opens the Windows Firewall Settings dialog box with the Exceptions tab displayed.

4. Click Add Port to display the Add a Port dialog box.

5. Use the Name text box to type a name for the unblocked port (such as *Remote Desktop Alternate*).

6. In the Port Number text box, type the port number you specified in the previous section.

7. Make sure that the TCP option is activated, as shown in Figure 16.10.

16

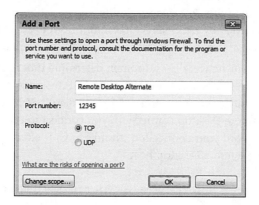

FIGURE 16.10

Configure a Windows Firewall exception for the new Remote Desktop listening port.

8. Click OK to return to the Windows Firewall Settings dialog box.

9. Click OK to put the firewall exception into effect.

Determining the Host IP Address

To connect to a remote desktop via the Internet, you need to specify an IP address rather than a computer name. (Although see "Using Dynamic DNS to Access Your Network," later in this chapter, for a way to avoid using IP addresses.) The IP address you use depends on your Internet setup:

■ If the Remote Desktop host computer connects directly to the Internet and your Internet service provider (ISP) supplied you with a static IP address, connect using that address.

- If the host computer connects directly to the Internet but your ISP supplies you with a dynamic IP address each time you connect, use the IPCONFIG utility to determine your current IP address. (That is, select Start, All Programs, Accessories, Command Prompt to get to the command line, type **ipconfig**, and press Enter.) Make note of the IPv4 Address value returned by IPCONFIG (you might need to scroll the output up to see it) and use that address to connect to the Remote Desktop host.

> **tip** Another way to determine your router's external IP address is to navigate to any of the free services for determining your current IP. Here are two:
>
> WhatISMyIP (http://www.whatismyip.com)
> DynDNS (http://checkip.dyndns.org)

- If your network uses a router, determine that router's external IP address by examining the router's status page. See Chapter 3, "Configuring Your Router," for the details. When you set up your Remote Desktop connection, you connect to the router, which will then forward your connection (thanks to your efforts in the next section) to the Remote Desktop host.

→ To learn how to view the status page in some popular routers, **see** "Checking the Router Status," **p. 90**.

Setting Up Port Forwarding

If your network uses a router, you need to configure it to forward data sent to the port specified in step 1 to the Remote Desktop host computer. This is *port forwarding*, and the steps you follow depend on the device. The next few sections show you how to configure port forwarding on some popular routers.

Belkin

Here are the steps to follow to configure port forwarding on most Belkin routers:

1. Under Firewall, click the Virtual Servers link to display the Virtual Servers page.

2. In the first LAN IP Address text box, type the last three digits of the Remote Desktop host's IP address.

3. In the Protocol Type list, select TCP.

4. In LAN Port text box, type the Remote Desktop listening port you specified earlier.

5. In Public Port text box, type the Remote Desktop listening port you
specified earlier.

6. Activate the Enable check box. Figure 16.11 shows a Belkin router configured to forward port 12345 to the computer with the address
192.168.1.110.

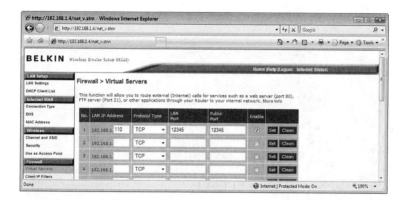

FIGURE 16.11

On most Belkin routers, use the Virtual Servers page to configure port forwarding.

7. Click Set. The Belkin router applies the new setting.

D-Link

For most D-Link routers, follow these steps to configure port forwarding:

1. Click the Advanced tab.

2. Click Port Forwarding to open the Port Forwarding Rules page.

3. In the first rule, activate the check box.

4. In the Name text box, type a name
for the rule, such as **RDP** or **Remote
Desktop**.

5. In the IP Address text box, type the
IP address of the Remote Desktop
host's IP address.

> **tip** If the Remote Desktop
> host computer appears
> in the Computer Name list, select
> the computer and then click <<
> to automatically add the host's IP
> address.

6. In Port column, use the Start text box to type the Remote Desktop listening port you specified earlier.

7. In Port column, use the End text box to type the Remote Desktop listening port you specified earlier.

8. In the Traffic Type list, select TCP. Figure 16.12 shows a D-Link router configured to forward port 12345 to the computer with the address 192.168.1.110.

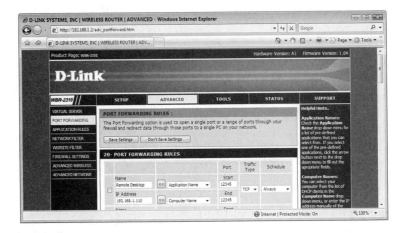

FIGURE 16.12

On your D-Link router, use the Port Forwarding Rules page to configure port forwarding.

9. Click Save Settings. The router saves the new settings.

10. Click Continue.

Linksys

Here are the steps to follow to configure port forwarding on most Linksys routers:

1. Click the Applications & Gaming tab.

2. Click the Port Range Forward subtab to display the Port Range Forward page.

3. In the Application text box, type a name for the rule, such as **RDP** or **Remote Desktop**.

4. Use the Start text box to type the Remote Desktop listening port you specified earlier.

5. Use the End text box to type the Remote Desktop listening port you specified earlier.

6. In the Protocol list, select TCP.

7. In the IP Address text box, type the last three digits of the Remote Desktop host's IP address.

8. Activate the Enable check box. Figure 16.13 shows a Linksys router configured to forward port 1235 to the computer with the address 192.168.1.110.

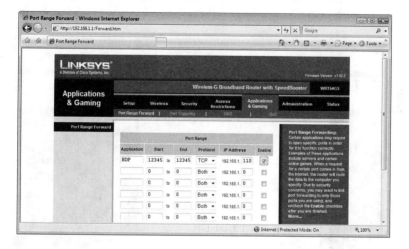

FIGURE 16.13
On most Linksys routers, use the Port Range Forward page to configure port forwarding.

9. At the bottom of the page, click Save Settings. The router reports that the Settings are successful.

10. Click Continue.

Netgear

Follow these steps to configure port forwarding on most Netgear routers:

1. In the Advanced section, click the Port Forwarding / Port Triggering link. The Port Forwarding / Port Triggering page appears.

2. Select the Port Forwarding option.

3. Click Add Custom Service to display the Ports - Custom Services page.

4. Use the Service Name text box to type a name for the rule, such as **RDP**.

5. In the Service Type list, select TCP.

6. Use the Starting Port text box to type the Remote Desktop listening port you specified earlier.

7. Use the Ending Port text box to type the Remote Desktop listening port you specified earlier.

8. Use the Server IP Address text boxes to enter the IP address of the Remote Desktop host. Figure 16.14 shows a Netgear router configured to forward port 1235 to the computer with the address 192.168.1.110.

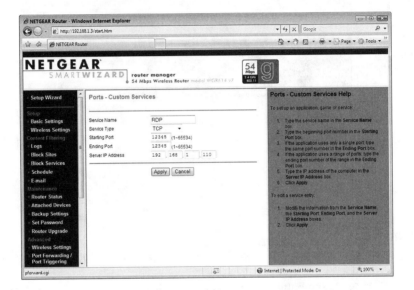

FIGURE 16.14
On most Netgear routers, use the Port Forwarding / Port Triggering page to configure port forwarding.

9. Click Apply. The router adds the service to the Port Forwarding / Port Triggering page.

Connecting Using the IP Address and New Port

You're now ready to make the connection to the Remote Desktop host via the Internet. Here are the steps to follow:

1. Connect to the Internet.

2. Select Start, All Programs, Accessories, Remote Desktop Connection. The Remote Desktop Connection dialog box appears.

3. In the Computer text box, type the external IP address of the router or remote computer and the alternative port you specified in step 1, separated by a colon. Figure 16.15 shows an example.

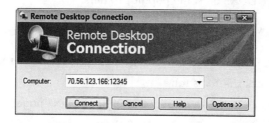

FIGURE 16.15

In the Remote Desktop Connection dialog box, type the external IP address, a colon, and then the new Remote Desktop listening port.

4. Set up your other Remote Desktop options as needed. For example, click Options, display the Experience tab, and then select the appropriate connection speed, such as Modem (28.8 Kbps), Modem (56 Kbps), or Broadband (128 Kbps–1.5 Mbps).

5. Click Connect.

Using Dynamic DNS to Access Your Network

If you want to use Remote Desktop via the Internet regularly, constantly monitoring your dynamic IP address can be a pain, particularly if you forget to check it before heading out of the office. A useful solution is to sign up with a dynamic DNS (DDNS) service, which supplies you with a static domain name. The service also installs a program on your computer that monitors your IP address and updates the service's DDNS servers to point your domain name to your IP address. Here are some DDNS services to check out:

DynDNS (http://www.dyndns.org)

TZO (http://www.tzo.com)

No-IP.com (http://www.no-ip.com)

D-Link (http://www.dlinkddns.com)

However, you may not want to rely on a program to keep your network external IP address and your domain name synchronized. For example, you may want to turn off the computer when you're away from home or the office. In that case, most routers offer a DDNS feature that will handle this for you. You specify your DDNS provider, your domain name, and your logon data, and the router does the rest. The next few sections show you how to configure DDNS on some popular routers.

> **tip** If you use either D-Link DDNS service or DynDNS, select the appropriate service from the list and then click << to automatically add the service address.

D-Link

For most D-Link routers, follow these steps to configure DDNS:

1. Click the Tools tab.
2. Click DDNS to display the Dynamic DNS page.
3. Activate the Enable DDNS check box.
4. Use the Server Address text box to type the address of your DDNS provider.
5. Use the Host Name text box to type your domain name.
6. Use the Username, Password, and Verify Password text boxes to type the logon data for your account with the DDNS provider. Figure 16.16 shows a completed version of the Dynamic DNS page.

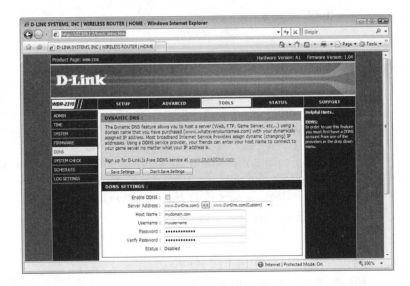

FIGURE 16.16
On your D-Link router, use the Dynamic DNS page to configure dynamic DNS.

7. Click Save Settings. The router saves the new settings.

8. Click Continue.

Linksys

Here are the steps to follow to configure DDNS on most Linksys routers:

1. Click the Setup tab.

2. Click the DDNS subtab.

3. In the DDNS Service list, select either DynDNS.org or TZO.com. Note that how you proceed from here depends on the service you choose. The rest of these steps assume you're using DynDNS.org.

4. Use the User Name and Password text boxes to type the logon data for your account.

5. Use the Host Name text box to type your domain name. Figure 16.17 shows a completed version of the DDNS page.

FIGURE 16.17

On most Linksys routers, use the DDNS page to configure dynamic DNS.

6. Click Save Settings. The router reports that the `Settings are successful`.

7. Click Continue.

Netgear

Follow these steps to configure dynamic DNS on most Netgear routers:

> **note** My Netgear router only supports DynDNS. Yours may support other services.

1. In the Advanced section, click the Dynamic DNS link. The Dynamic DNS page appears.

2. Activate the Use a Dynamic DNS Service check box.

3. Use the Service Provider to select a DDNS service.

4. Use the Host Name text box to type your domain name.

5. Use the Username and Password text boxes to type the logon data for your account with the DDNS provider. Figure 16.18 shows a completed version of the Dynamic DNS page.

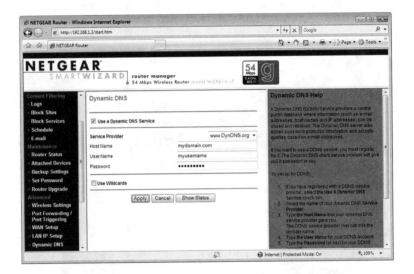

FIGURE 16.18

On most Netgear routers, use the Dynamic DNS page to configure dynamic DNS.

6. Click Apply.

From Here

■ To learn how to view the status page in some popular routers, **see** "Checking the Router Status," **p. 90**.

■ For the details on setting up a user account in Windows Vista, **see** "Creating User Accounts for Sharing," **p. 189**.

■ To learn more about what constitutes a strong password, **see** "Building a Strong Password," **p. 292**.

■ For other ethernet network security techniques, **see** Chapter 14, "Implementing Network Security," **p. 313**.

■ For other wireless network security techniques, **see** Chapter 15, "Implementing Wireless Security," **p. 335**.

16

Monitoring Your Network

IN THIS CHAPTER

- Monitoring Network Performance
- Monitoring Shared Folders
- From Here

If you're the unofficial administrator of your home or small office network, I imagine you're already saddled with a fairly long to-do list of network chores: adding and upgrading network devices, configuring your router, adding and maintaining users, creating passwords, adding shared folders, setting permissions, and on and on. The last thing you probably need is yet another set of chores tacked on to that list. Well, sorry, but I'm afraid I'm going to do just that in this chapter as I show you how to monitor three aspects of your network: performance, shared folders, and users.

The good news is that none of the monitoring tasks you learn about in this chapter are activities you need to do very often. In all cases, in fact, you may need to perform the monitoring chores only once in a while, or on an as-needed basis. For example, you might want to check your network performance now to get a baseline for comparison, then you might want to check it again only if the network feels slow or if you upgrade your equipment.

Remember, however, that even a network with just a few computers is still a fairly large and unwieldy beast that requires a certain amount of vigilance to keep things running smoothly. Therefore, it's worth it to keep an eye on the network to watch for things going awry.

Monitoring Network Performance

By far the most important aspect of your network that you should monitor is the network's performance. A network's job is to transfer data, and if your data is getting transferred at a rate that's substantially slower than it should be, you and your users won't be happy *or* productive.

The easiest way to check network performance is to check the current status of wired and wireless network connections (see Figure 17.1). I explained how to do this in Chapter 5, "Working with Vista's Basic Network Tools and Tasks." In particular, you want to look at the Speed value: If it says, for example, that you have a 100Mbps connection but you thought you were using Gigabit Ethernet equipment, you need to check that equipment.

→   To learn how to view the status of a network connection, **see** "Viewing the Current Network Status," **p. 123**.

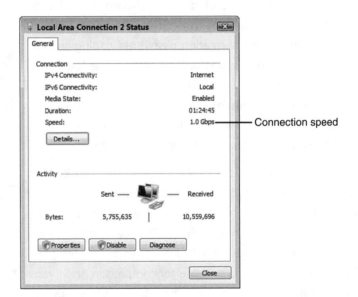

FIGURE 17.1

In the Status dialog box for your network connection, check the Speed value to ensure your connection is operating at the correct rate.

Monitoring Network Performance with Task Manager

The Task Manager utility is excellent for getting a quick overview of the current state of the system, and it offers a couple of tools that help you monitor your network. To get Task Manager onscreen, follow these steps:

1. Press Ctrl+Alt+Delete. Vista displays its security window.

2. Select Start Task Manager.

If your network feels sluggish, it could be that the remote computer you're working with is sharing data slowly or that network traffic is exceptionally high. To see whether the latter situation is the cause of the problem, you can check out the current *network utilization* value, which is the percent of available bandwidth that your network adapter is currently using.

To check network utilization, display Task Manager's Networking tab, shown in Figure 17.2. Use the graph or the Network Utilization column to monitor the current network utilization value. Notice that this value is a percentage. This means that the utilization is a percentage of the bandwidth shown in the Link Speed column. So, for example, if the current network utilization is 10% and the Link Speed value is 1Gbps, the network is currently using about 100Mbps bandwidth.

The Network Utilization value combines the data sent by the computer and the data received by the computer. If the utilization is high, it's often useful to break down the data stream into the separate sent and received components. To do that, select View, Network Adapter History, and then select Bytes Sent (which displays as a red line on the graph) or Bytes Received (which displays as a yellow line on the graph).

If you're feeling ambitious or curious, you can view much more information than what you see in the default Networking tab. Follow these steps to add one or more columns to the view:

1. Select the View, Select Columns command. Task Manager displays the Select Columns dialog box, as shown in Figure 17.3. This dialog box offers a long list of networking measures that you can monitor.

17

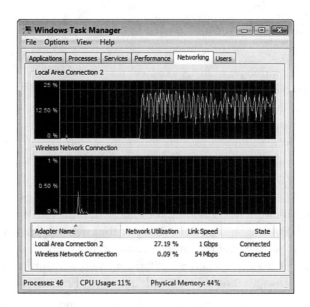

FIGURE 17.2

Use Task Manager's Networking tab to check the current network utilization percentage.

FIGURE 17.3

Use the Select Columns dialog box to choose which values you want to monitor in the Networking tab.

2. Activate the check box of a value that you want to monitor.

3. Repeat step 2 for each value you want to add to the networking tab.

4. Click OK.

tip By default, the Networking tab doesn't collect data when you're viewing some other Task Manager tab. If you prefer that the Networking tab always collect data, select Options, Tab Always Active.

Here's a summary of some of the more useful columns you can add:

Adapter Description	This column shows the description of the network adapter.
Network Utilization	This is the network utilization value.
Link Speed	This value shows the network adapter's connection speed.
State	This column displays the general state of the adapter.
Bytes Sent Throughput	This value shows the percentage of connection bandwidth used by traffic sent from Windows Vista.
Bytes Received Throughput	This value shows the percentage of connection bandwidth used by traffic received by Windows Vista.
Bytes Throughput	This value shows the percentage of connection bandwidth used by traffic both sent from and received by Windows Vista.
Bytes Sent	This column tells you the total number of bytes sent from Windows Vista over the network adapter during the current session (that is, since the last boot).
Bytes Received	This column tells you the total number of bytes received by Windows Vista over the network adapter during the current session.
Bytes	This column tells you the total number of bytes sent from and received by Windows Vista over the network adapter during the current session.
Bytes Sent Per Interval	This value shows the total number of bytes sent from Windows Vista over the network adapter during the most recent update interval. (For example, if the Update Speed value is set to Low, the display updates every 4 seconds, so the Bytes Sent Per Interval value is the number of bytes sent during the most recent 4-second interval.)

17

Bytes Received
Per Interval
This value shows the total number of bytes received by Windows Vista over the network adapter during the most recent update interval.

Bytes Per
Interval
This value shows the total number of bytes sent from and received by Windows Vista over the network adapter during the most recent update interval.

On your small network, you can use these measures to watch out for extreme values. That is, with normal network traffic, the values should never be either really small or really large for long periods. If you notice small (or zero) values for long periods, it could indicate that your computer isn't able to send or receive data; if you notice high values (particularly on the various "Throughput" measures, where "high" means values near 100%) for an extended time, it could indicate a software problem where a rogue application is bombarding your computer with data.

Monitoring Network Performance with Performance Monitor

For more advanced performance monitoring, Windows Vista offers the Performance Monitor tool, which you display by following these steps:

1. Select Start, Control Panel to open the Control Panel window.

2. Select System and Maintenance to open the System Maintenance window.

3. Select Administrative Tools to open the Administrative Tools window.

4. Double-click Reliability and Performance Monitor. The User Account Control dialog box appears.

5. Enter your UAC credentials to continue. Windows Vista displays the Reliability and Performance Monitor.

The Reliability and Performance branch displays the Resource Monitor, which is divided into six sections:

- **Resource Overview.** This section shows graphs of the data in the CPU, Disk, Network, and Memory sections.

- **CPU.** This section shows the percentage of CPU resources that your

tip You can also open the Reliability and Performance Monitor by pressing Windows Logo+R (or selecting Start, All Programs, Accessories, Run) to open the Run dialog box, typing **perfmon**, clicking OK, and then entering your UAC credentials when prompted. (Alternatively, select Start, type **perfmon** in the Search box, and then click perfmon in the search results.)

system is using. Click anywhere on the CPU bar to expand the section and show the percentage of resources that each running process is using.

▪ **Disk.** This section shows the total hard disk input/output transfer rate (disk reads and writes in kilobytes per second). Click anywhere on the Disk bar to expand the section to see the files involved in the current disk I/O operations.

▪ **Network.** This section shows the total network data-transfer rate (data sent and received in kilobits per second). Click anywhere on the Network bar to expand the section to see the remote computers and other processes involved in the current network transfers, as shown in Figure 17.4.

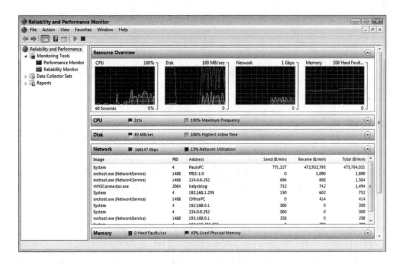

FIGURE 17.4
The new Reliability and Performance Monitor enables you to monitor various aspects of your system.

▪ **Memory.** This section shows the average number of hard memory faults per second and the percentage of physical memory used. Click anywhere on the Memory bar to expand the section to view the individual processes in memory.

▪ **Learn More.** This section contains links to the Reliability and Performance Monitor help files.

For more detailed network performance monitoring, select the Reliability and Performance Monitor, Monitoring Tools, Performance Monitor branch. The Performance Monitor appears, as shown in Figure 17.5.

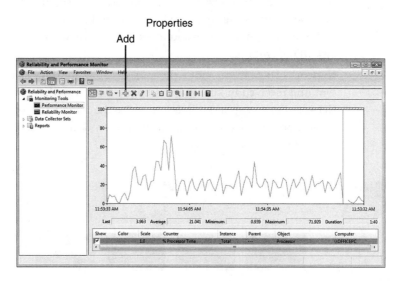

FIGURE 17.5
You can use Performance Monitor to keep an eye on your network performance.

Performance Monitor's job is to provide you with real-time reports on how various system settings and components are performing. Each item is called a *counter*, and the displayed counters are listed at the bottom of the window. Windows Vista shows just one counter at first—the % Processor Time, which tells you the percentage of time the processor is busy. However, as you see in the next section, you can add more counters to monitor what you want. Each counter is assigned a different colored line, and that color corresponds to the colored lines shown in the graph. Note, too, that you can get specific numbers for a counter— the most recent value, the average, the minimum, and the maximum—by clicking a counter and reading the boxes just below the graphs.

tip By default, Performance Monitor samples the performance data every second. To change the sample interval, right-click Performance Monitor and then select Properties. (You can also press Ctrl+Q or click the Properties button in the toolbar, pointed out in Figure 17.5.) In the Performance Monitor Properties dialog box, display the General tab, and modify the value in the Sample Every X Seconds text box. Click OK to put the new sample interval into effect.

The idea is that you should configure Performance Monitor to show the processes you're interested in (such as current network bandwidth) and then keep Performance Monitor running while you perform your normal chores. By examining the Performance Monitor readouts from time to time, you gain an appreciation of what is typical on your system. Then, if you run into performance problems, you can check Performance Monitor to see whether you've run into any bottlenecks or anomalies.

Adding Performance Counters

To add another setting to the Performance Monitor window, follow these steps:

1. Right-click Performance Monitor and then click Add Counters. (You can also press Ctrl+I or click the Add button in the toolbar; see Figure 17.5.) The Add Counters dialog box appears

2. Double-click the counter category you want to work with.

3. Select the counter you want. If you need more information about the object, activate the Show Description check box.

4. If the counter has multiple instances (see Figure 17.6), select the instance you want from the Instances of Selected Object List. (For example, if you choose Network Interface as the performance object and your system has multiple network interface cards, you need to choose which NIC you want to monitor. You can also usually select <All Instances> to monitor the total of all the instances.)

5. Click Add. Performance Monitor places the counter in the Added Counters list.

6. Repeat steps 2–5 to add any other counters you want to monitor.

7. Click OK.

> **tip**
>
> The graph is only useful if you can see the results properly. Unfortunately, sometimes the scale of the graph isn't appropriate for the numbers generated by a particular counter. The default scale is from 0 to 100; so if a counter regularly generates numbers larger than 100, all you'll see is a straight line across the top of the graph. Similarly, if a counter regularly generates very small numbers, the counter's graph will be a straight line across the bottom of the graph.
>
> To fix this, you can change the scale used by the Performance Monitor graph. Right-click Performance Monitor, and then select Properties. (You can also press Ctrl+Q or click the Properties button in the toolbar.) In the Performance Monitor Properties dialog box, display the Graph tab and modify the values in the Maximum and Minimum text boxes. I also find that activating the Horizontal Grid check box helps you to interpret the graph. Click OK to put the new settings into effect.

17

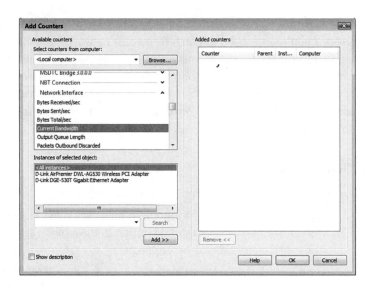

FIGURE 17.6
Use the Add Counters dialog box to add more counters to Performance Monitor.

Understanding Network Performance Counters

In the Add Counters dialog box, the Network Interface category has the network performance counters you want to work with. There are quite a few here, some of which monitor the same things as the Task Manager statistics I mentioned earlier. Fortunately, only a few of the performance objects are truly useful for your Windows Vista network, and in most situations you need only track a few counters to monitor the network performance. Here's my list of the most useful Network Interface counters:

Current Bandwidth	This counter tells you the current network bandwidth, in bits per second. For example, a 1Gbps connection shows as 1,000,000,000,000.
Bytes Total/Sec	This counter tells you the total number of bytes received and bytes sent over the network connection per second. (This is the sum of the Bytes Received/Sec and Bytes Sent/Sec values.) Multiply this value by 1,024 to calculate the number of bits per second that are passing through the adapter. Under load (say, while streaming media), the result should be close to the Current Bandwidth value. If it's substantially less, you have a network bottleneck.

Packets Outbound Errors	This counter shows the number of network packets that could not be sent because of errors. Errors are normally rare, so if you're seeing packet errors, it could indicate a problem. You may need to update the remote computer's NIC device driver, or it could mean that the NIC has a problem and needs to be replaced.
Packet Received Errors	This counter shows the number of network packets that could not be received because of errors. Seeing errors here may mean that you need to update your computer's NIC device driver, or it could mean that your NIC needs to be replaced.

Monitoring Shared Folders

Windows Vista comes with a snap-in tool called Shared Folders that enables you to monitor various aspects of the folders that you've shared with the network. For example, for each shared folder, you can find out the users who are connected to the folder, how long they've been connected, and the files they have open. You can also disconnect users from a shared folder or close files that have been opened on a shared folder. The next few sections provide the details.

Launching the Shared Folders Snap-In

To get started, you need to open the Shared Folders snap-in. Here are the steps to follow:

1. Press Windows Logo+R (or select Start, All Programs, Accessories, Run) to open the Run dialog box.

2. In the Open text box, type `fsmgmt.msc`.

3. Click OK. The User Account Control dialog box appears.

4. Enter your UAC credentials. Windows Vista opens and the Shared Folders snap-in appears.

note A snap-in is a component that works with Vista's Microsoft Management Console (MMC) program. This program creates a console into which different mini-programs can be "snapped in." If you want to take a look at MMC, press Windows Logo+R (or select Start, All Programs, Accessories, Run) to open the Run dialog box, type `mmc`, and click OK. In the Console window that appears, select File, Add/Remove Snap-in (or press Ctrl+M) to see the list of available snap-ins.

5. Select the System Tools, Shared Folders branch.

Viewing the Current Connections

To see a list of the users connected to any Windows Vista shared folder, select Shared Folders, Sessions. Figure 17.7 shows an example. For each user, you get the following data:

User	The name of the user.
Computer	The name of the user's computer. If Windows Vista doesn't recognize the computer, it shows the machine's IP address, instead.
Type	The type of network connection. Windows Vista always shows this as Windows (even if the user is connected from a Mac or from Linux).
Open Files	The number of open files in the shared folders.
Connected Time	The amount of time that the user has been connected to the remote computer.
Idle Time	The amount of time that the user has not been actively working on the open files.
Guest	Whether the user logged on using the Guest account.

Refresh

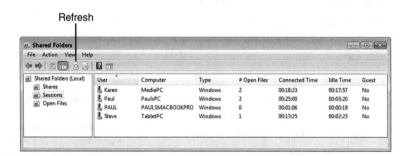

FIGURE 17.7

The Sessions folder shows the users currently connected to shared folders on the remote computer.

Viewing Connections to Shared Folders

The Shared Folders snap-in also makes it possible for you to view the connections to Windows Vista by its shared folders. To get this display, select Shared Folders, Shares. As you can see in Figure 17.8, this view provides the following information:

> **note** To ensure that you're always viewing the most up-to-date information, regularly select the Action, Refresh command or click the Refresh toolbar button (pointed out in Figure 17.7).

Share Name	The name of the shared folder. Note that the list includes the Windows Vista hidden shares.
Folder Path	The drive or folder associated with the share.
Type	The type of network connection, which Windows Vista always shows as Windows.
# Client Connections	The number of computers connected to the share.
Comment	The description of the share.

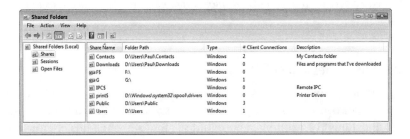

FIGURE 17.8
The Shared Folders snap-in can display a server's connections by its shared folders.

Viewing Open Files

The Shared Folders snap-in can also display the files that are open on the Windows Vista shares. To switch to this view, select System Tools, Shared Folders, Open Files. Figure 17.9 shows the result. Here's a summary of the columns in this view:

Open File	The full pathname of the file.
Accessed By	The name of the user who has the file open.

> **tip** You can also use the Shares branch to work with the shared folders. For example, select a share and then select Actions, Open to display the folder. You can also select Action, Properties to modify the share name, description, and permissions of the selected share. Finally, you can also select Action, Stop Sharing to turn off sharing on the selected folder.

Type	The type of network connection, which Windows Vista always shows as Windows.
# Locks	The number of locks on the file.
Open Mode	The permissions the user has over the file.

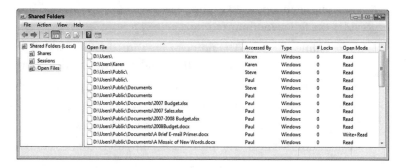

FIGURE 17.9
The Shared Folders snap-in can also display a remote computer's open files in its shared resources.

Closing a User's Session or File

Although in the interest of network harmony you'll want to let users connect and disconnect as they please, at times you might need to boot someone off a machine. For example, you might see that someone has obtained unauthorized access to a share. To disconnect that user, follow these steps:

1. In the Shared Folders snap-in, select Shared Folders, Sessions.

2. Right-click the name of the user you want to disconnect.

3. Click Close Session. Windows Vista asks you to confirm.

4. Click Yes.

Similarly, you'll usually want to let users open and close files themselves so that they don't lose information. However, you might find that a user has a particular file open and you would prefer that the user not view that file (for example, because you want to work on the file yourself or because the file contains information you

caution If you have a file in a shared folder and you don't want other users to see that file, it makes more sense to either move the file to a protected folder or change the permissions on the file's current folder.

don't want the user to see). To close a file opened by a user, follow these steps:

1. In the Shared Folders snap-in, select Shared Folders, Open Files.

2. Right-click the name of the file you want to close.

3. Click Close Open File. Windows Vista asks you to confirm.

4. Click Yes.

note The remote user doesn't see a warning or any other indication that you're closing the file. For example, if the user is playing a music file, that file just stops playing and can't be started again (except by closing all open shared files and folders and starting a new session).

From Here

- To learn how to view the status of a network connection, **see** "Viewing the Current Network Status," **p. 123**.

- For the details on sharing folders, **see** "Sharing Resources with the Network," **p. 184**.

- If you detect a problem with your network, you'll need to do some troubleshooting; **see** Chapter 18, "Troubleshooting Network Problems," **p. 441**.

17

Troubleshooting Network Problems

As you've seen throughout this book, networking can be a complex, arcane topic that taxes the patience of all but the most dedicated wireheads (an affectionate pet name often applied to network hackers and gurus). There are so many hardware components to deal with (from the network adapter to the cable to the switch to the router) and so many layers of software (from the device drivers to the protocols to the redirectors to the network providers) that networks often seem like accidents looking for a place to happen.

If your network has become a "notwork" (some wags also refer to a downed network as a *nyetwork*), this chapter offers a few solutions that might help. I don't make any claim to completeness here, however; after all, most network ills are a combination of several factors and therefore are relatively obscure and difficult to reproduce. Instead, I just go through a few general strategies for tracking down problems and pose solutions for some of the most common network afflictions.

IN THIS CHAPTER

- Repairing a Network Connection
- Checking the Connection Status
- General Solutions to Network Problems
- Checking for Solutions to Problems
- Troubleshooting Using Online Resources
- Checking Connectivity with the PING Command
- Troubleshooting Cables
- Troubleshooting the NIC
- Troubleshooting Wireless Network Problems
- Reverting to an Earlier Configuration
- From Here

Repairing a Network Connection

If you came to Vista from Windows XP, you may have come across the latter's network Repair tool that did an okay job of repairing connectivity problems because most networking problems can be resolved by running the Repair tool's basic tasks: disconnecting, renewing the Dynamic Host Control Protocol (DHCP) lease, flushing various network caches, and then reconnecting.

Unfortunately, the Repair tool would all too often report that it couldn't fix the problem, which usually meant that the trouble existed at a level deeper in the network stack than the Repair tool could go. In an attempt to handle these more challenging connectivity issues, Vista comes with a completely redesigned Network Diagnostics tool that digs deep into all layers of the network stack to try to identify and resolve problems. Vista gives you several methods of launching the Network Diagnostic tool:

- Right-click the notification area's Network icon and then click Diagnose.
- In the Network and Sharing Center, click View Status, and then click Diagnose.
- If you lose a connection to a network share, Vista displays a Network Error dialog box to let you know. Click the Diagnose button.
- In the Network Connections window, click the broken connection, and then click Repair This Connection.

→ **See** "Opening the Network Connections Window," **p. 140**.

When you launch the diagnostics, Vista invokes the new Network Diagnostics Framework (NDF), a collection of tools, technologies, algorithms, programming interfaces, services, and troubleshooters. The NDF passes the specifics of the problem to the Network Diagnostics Engine (NDE), which then generates a list of possible causes. For each potential cause, the NDE launches a specific troubleshooter, which determines whether the aspect of networking covered by the troubleshooter could be creating the problem. For example, there are troubleshooters related to wireless connectivity, Transport Control Protocol (TCP) connections, address acquisition, and many more. In the end, the troubleshooters end up creating a list of possible solutions to the problem. If there is just one solution that can be performed automatically, the NDE attempts the solution. If there are multiple solutions (or a single solution that requires user input), you see a Windows Network Diagnostics dialog box similar to the one shown in Figure 18.1. Click the solution or follow the instructions that appear.

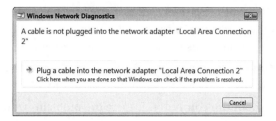

FIGURE 18.1

If Vista can't connect to a network or device, it displays this dialog box; you can click Diagnose to run the network diagnostics.

Checking the Connection Status

The first thing you should check when you suspect a network problem is Vista's Network icon. As I mentioned in Chapter 5, " Working with Vista's Basic Network Tools and Tasks," the Network icon changes depending on the current network state. To refresh your memory, three states indicate a problem:

➔ To learn how to view the status of a network connection, **see** "Viewing the Current Network Status," **p. 123**.

Connected without Internet access	This state means that you have access to the network, but your computer cannot access the Internet.
Error	This state means that you may have limited network connectivity.
Disconnected	This state means that you are completely cut off from the network.

General Solutions to Network Problems

Figuring out that a problem exists is one thing, but it's often quite another to come up with a fix for the problem. I discus a few solutions in later sections, but here are a few other general fixes you need to keep in mind:

▇ **Enable network discovery.** If you can't access your network, by far the most common cause is that you have Vista's network discovery feature turned off. Make sure network discovery is turned on, as described in Chapter 5.

➔ For the details on how to activate network discovery in Vista, **see** "Turning On Network Discovery," **p. 128**.

■ **Close all programs.** You can often fix flaky behavior by shutting down all your open programs and starting again. This is a particularly useful fix for problems caused by low memory or low system resources.

■ **Log off Windows Vista.** Logging off clears the RAM and so gives you a slightly cleaner slate than merely closing all your programs.

■ **Reboot the computer.** If there are problems with some system files and devices, logging off won't help because these objects remain loaded. By rebooting the system, you reload the entire system which is often enough to solve many computer problems.

■ **Turn off the computer and restart.** You can often solve a hardware problem by first shutting your machine off. Wait for 30 seconds to give all devices time to spin down, and then restart. This is called *power cycling* the computer.

■ **Power cycle the router.** If you're getting a network error or you can't access the Internet, the router may be at fault. Power off the router and then power it on again. Wait until the status lights stabilize and then try accessing the network.

■ **Power cycle the modem.** If you can't get Internet access, it could be a problem with your broadband modem. Power off the modem and then power it on again. Wait until the status lights stabilize and then try accessing the Internet.

■ **Check connections, power switches, and so on.** Some of the most common (and some of the most embarrassing) causes of hardware problems are the simple physical things: making sure that a device (for example, your router) is turned on; checking that cable connections (particularly between the NIC and router) are secure; and ensuring that insertable devices (such as a USB or PC Card NIC) are properly inserted.

■ **Revert to a working configuration.** If you could access the network properly in the past, you may be able to solve the problem by reverting your system to that working state. See "Reverting to an Earlier Configuration," later in this chapter.

■ **Upgrade the router's firmware.** Some network problems are caused by router bugs. If the manufacturer has corrected these bugs, the fixes will appear in the latest version of the router firmware, so you should upgrade to the new version, as described in Chapter 3, "Configuring Your Router."

→   To learn how to upgrade your router's firmware, **see** "Updating the Firmware," **p. 66**.

■ **Reset the router.** You can cause network problems by misconfiguring your router, or by the router's internal settings becoming corrupted somehow. Almost all routers come with a reset feature that enables you to return the router to its factory settings. Ideally the device comes with a Reset button that you can push; otherwise, you need access to the router's setup pages.

■ **Use the Help and Support Center.** Microsoft has greatly improved the quality of the Help system in Windows Vista. The Help and Support Center (select Start, Help and Support) is awash in articles and advice on using Windows Vista. However, the real strength of Help and Support is, in my opinion, the Support side. In the Help and Support Center home page, click Troubleshooting to see links for troubleshooting network problems.

Checking for Solutions to Problems

Microsoft constantly collects information about Vista from users. When a problem occurs, Vista usually asks whether you want to send information about the problem to Microsoft, and if you do, it stores these tidbits in a massive database. Engineers then tackle the "issues" (as they euphemistically call them) and hopefully come up with solutions.

One of Vista's most promising new features is Problem Reports and Solutions, and it's designed to make solutions available to anyone who goes looking for them. Vista keeps a list of problems your computer is having, so you can tell it to go online and see whether a solution is available. If there's a solution waiting, Vista will download it, install it, and fix your system.

Here are the steps to follow to check for solutions to problems:

1. Select Start, Control Panel to open the Control Panel window.

2. Select System and Maintenance.

3. Select Problem Reports and Solutions.

4. In the Problem Reports and Solutions window, click the Check for New Solutions link. Windows Vista begins checking for solutions.

5. If you see a dialog box asking whether you want to send more information about your problems, click Send Information.

6. If a solution exists for your computer, you'll see it listed in the Solutions to Install section of the Problem Reports and Solutions window. Click the solution to install it.

18

By default, when a problem occurs, Vista does two things:

■ It automatically checks for a solution to the problem.

■ It asks whether you want to send more information about the problem to Microsoft.

You can control this behavior by configuring a few settings:

1. In the Problem Reports and Solutions window, click Change Settings.

2. In the Choose How to Check for Solutions to Computer Problems window, click Advanced Settings to display the Advanced Settings for Problem Reporting window shown in Figure 18.2.

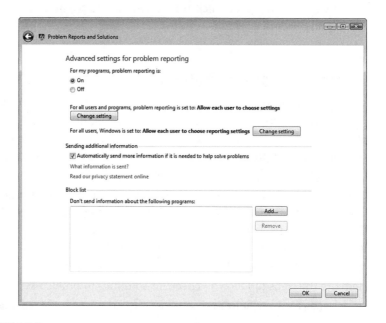

FIGURE 18.2

Use the Advanced Settings for Problem Reporting window to configure the Problem Reports and Solutions feature.

3. If you don't want to report problems at all on your user account, activate the Off option. Alternatively, you can configure problem reporting for all users of your computer. Click Change Setting beside the For All Users and Programs, Problem Reporting Is Set To, and then click one of the following options (when you're done, click OK and enter your User Account Control [UAC] credentials):

On. Activate this option to force all users to report problems

Off. Activate this option to force all user not to report problems

Allow Each User to Choose Settings. Activate this option (it's the default) to enable each user to turn problem reporting on or off

> **note** When you send extra troubleshooting information to Microsoft, you're only adding data about the problem to Microsoft's existing database of problems and solutions. It's unlikely a human being will ever see the data, so don't expect a response.

4. To configure problem reporting, click Change Setting beside For All Users, Windows Is Set To, and then click one of the following options (when you're done, click OK and enter your UAC credentials):

   Allow Each User to Choose Reporting Settings. Activate this options to enable the Automatically Send More Information If It Is Needed to Help Solve Problems check box.

   Ask Each Time a Problem Occurs. Activate this option to have Vista prompt each user to check box solutions and to send additional information about the problem.

   Automatically Check for Solutions. Activate this option (it's the default) to have Vista automatically check online for an existing solution to a problem.

   Automatically Check for Solutions and Send Additional Information, If Needed. Activate this option to have Vista automatically check online for an existing solution to a problem and to automatically send extra information about the problem.

5. If you want Vista to always send the extra troubleshooting information, activate the Automatically Send More Information If It Is Needed To Help Solve Problems check box.

6. If you don't want Vista to send information about a specific program, click Add, locate and select the program's executable file, and then click Open.

7. Click OK.

Troubleshooting Using Online Resources

The Internet is home to an astonishingly wide range of information, but its forte has always been computer knowledge. Whatever problem you have, there's a good chance that someone out there has run into the same thing, knows how to fix it, and has posted the solution on a website or newsgroup, or would be willing to share it with you if asked. True, finding what you need is sometimes difficult, and you often can't be sure how accurate some of the solutions are. However, if you stick to the more reputable sites and if you get second opinions on solutions offered by complete strangers, you'll find the online world an excellent troubleshooting resource. Here's my list of favorite online resources:

- **Microsoft Product Support Services.** This is Microsoft's main online technical support site. Through this site you can access frequently asked questions about Windows Vista, see a list of known problems, download files, and send questions to Microsoft support personnel: http://support.microsoft.com/.

- **Microsoft Knowledge Base.** The Microsoft Product Support Services site has links that enable you to search the Microsoft Knowledge Base, which is a database of articles related to all Microsoft products including, of course, Windows Vista. These articles provide you with information about Windows Vista and instructions on using Windows Vista features. But the most useful aspect of the Knowledge Base is for troubleshooting problems. Many of the articles were written by Microsoft support personnel after helping customers overcome problems. By searching for error codes or keywords, you can often get specific solutions to your problems.

- **Microsoft TechNet.** This Microsoft site is designed for IT professionals and power users. It contains a huge number of articles on all Microsoft products. These articles give you technical content, program instructions, tips, scripts, downloads, and troubleshooting ideas: http://www.microsoft.com/technet/.

- **Windows Update.** Check this site for the latest device drivers, security patches, service packs, and other updates: http://windowsupdate. microsoft.com/.

- **Microsoft Security.** Check this site for the latest information on Microsoft security and privacy initiatives, particularly security patches: http://www.microsoft.com/security/.

- **Vendor websites.** All but the tiniest hardware and software vendors maintain websites with customer support sections that you can peruse for upgrades, patches, workarounds, frequently asked questions, and sometimes chat or bulletin board features.

■ **Newsgroups.** There are computer-related newsgroups for hundreds of topics and products. Microsoft maintains its own newsgroups via the msnews.microsoft.com server (an account for which is automatically set up in Windows Mail), and

> **tip** You can also access Microsoft's Vista newsgroups via the Web:
>
> `http://windowshelp.microsoft.com/communities/newsgroups/en-us/default.mspx`

Usenet has a huge list of groups in the alt and comp hierarchies. Before asking a question in a newsgroup, be sure to search Google Groups to see whether your question has been answered in the past: http://groups.google.com/.

Checking Connectivity with the PING Command

As you might know, a submarine can detect a nearby object by using sonar to send out a sound wave and then seeing whether the wave is reflected. This is called *pinging* an object.

Windows Vista has a PING command that performs a similar function. PING sends out a special type of IP packet—called an *Internet Control Message Protocol (ICMP) echo packet*—to a remote location. This packet requests that the remote location send back a response packet. PING then tells you whether the response was received. In this way, you can check your network configuration to see whether your computer can connect with a remote host.

To use PING, first open a command-line session by selecting Start, All Programs, Accessories, Command Prompt. Here's a simplified version of the PING syntax:

```
ping [-t] [-n count]  target_name
```

-t   Pings the specified *target_name* until you interrupt the command.

-n *count*   Sends the number of echo packets specified by *count*. The default is 4.

target_name Specifies either the IP address or the hostname (a fully qualified domain name) of the remote host you want to ping.

18

Here's an example that uses PING on the Google.com domain:

```
C:\Users\Paul>ping google.com

Pinging google.com [64.233.187.99] with 32 bytes of data:

Reply from 64.233.187.99: bytes=32 time=43ms TTL=240
Reply from 64.233.187.99: bytes=32 time=42ms TTL=239
Reply from 64.233.187.99: bytes=32 time=43ms TTL=239
Reply from 64.233.187.99: bytes=32 time=42ms TTL=240

Ping statistics for 64.233.187.99:
    Packets: Sent = 4, Received = 4, Lost = 0 (0% loss),A
Approximate round trip times in milli-seconds:
    Minimum = 42ms, Maximum = 43ms, Average = 42ms
```

Here you see that each echo packet received a reply. If you can't connect to the remote host, `ping` returns a `Request timed out` message for each packet.

If you can't connect to a remote host, here are some notes on using PING to troubleshoot problems:

- First, check to see whether you can use PING successfully on the loopback address:

  `ping 127.0.0.1.`

  The only reason this PING would fail is if your computer doesn't have the Internet Protocol installed. However, all Vista machines have IP installed, and the option to uninstall it is disabled, so pinging the loopback address will almost certainly work. The only reason to include it in your troubleshooting is that if it doesn't work, it means you have a serious problem with your machine. Either revert to a working configuration (see "Reverting to an Earlier Configuration," later in this chapter), reinstall Windows Vista, or take your machine to a computer repair professional.

- Try using PING on your computer's IP address. (If you're using DHCP, run the IPCONFIG utility to get your current IP address.) If you don't get a successful echo, then your NIC may not be inserted properly or the device drivers may not be installed. See "Troubleshooting the NIC," later in this chapter.

- Now PING another computer on your network. If PING fails, check your cable or wireless connections.

■ The next test you should run is on your default gateway (that is, your router). If you can't successfully ping the router's internal IP address, you won't be able to access remote Internet sites. In this case, check the IP address you entered for the gateway, check the cable connections, and make sure the router is turned on. You may need to power cycle the router.

■ If you get this far, try using PING on the remote host you're trying to contact. If you're unsuccessful, check to make sure that you're using the correct IP address for the host. Try power cycling your broadband modem.

Troubleshooting Cables

If one of the problems discussed so far isn't the cause of your networking quandary, the next logical suspect is the cabling that connects the workstations. This section discusses cabling, gives you a few pointers for preventing cable problems, and discusses some common cable kinks that can crop up.

Although most large-scale cabling operations are performed by third-party cable installers, home setups are usually do-it-yourself jobs. You can prevent some cable problems and simplify your troubleshooting down the road by taking a few precautions and "ounce of prevention" measures in advance:

18

■ First and foremost, always buy the highest-quality cable you can find (for example, Category 5e or Category 6 or higher for twisted-pair cable). With network cabling, you get what you pay for.

■ Good-quality cable will be labeled. You should also add your own labels for things such as the source and destination of the cable.

■ To avoid electromagnetic interference, don't run cable near electronic devices, power lines, air conditioners, fluorescent lights, motors, and other electromagnetic sources.

■ Try to avoid phone lines because the ringer signal can disrupt network data carried over twisted-pair cable.

■ To avoid the cable being stepped on accidentally, don't run it under carpet.

■ To avoid people tripping over a cable (and possibly damaging the cable connector, the NIC port, or the person doing the tripping!), avoid high-traffic areas when laying the cable.

■ If you plan to run cable outdoors, use conduit or another casing material to prevent moisture damage.

■ Don't use excessive force to pull or push a cable into place. Rough handling can cause pinching or even breakage.

If you suspect cabling might be the cause of your network problems, here's a list of a few things to check:

■ **Watch for electromagnetic interference.** If you see garbage on a workstation screen or experience random packet loss or temporarily missing nodes, the problem might be electromagnetic interference. Check your cables to make sure that they are at least 6 to 12 inches from any source of electromagnetic interference.

■ **Check your connections.** Loose connections are a common source of cabling woes. Be sure to check every cable connection associated with the workstation that's experiencing network difficulty, including connections to the network adapter, router, switch, and so on.

■ **Check the lay of the line.** Loops of cable could be generating an electrical field that interferes with network communication. Try not to leave your excess cable lying around in coils or loops.

■ **Inspect the cable for pinching or breaks.** A badly pinched cable can cause a short in the wire, which could lead to intermittent connection problems. Make sure that no part of the cable is pinched, especially if the back of the computer is situated near a wall. A complete lack of connection with the network might mean that the cable's copper core has been severed completely and needs to be replaced.

Troubleshooting the NIC

After cabling, the NIC is next on the list of common sources of networking headaches. Here's a list of items to check if you suspect that Windows Vista and your NIC aren't getting along:

■ **Make sure that Windows Vista installed the correct NIC.** Windows Vista usually does a pretty good job of detecting the network card. However, a slight error (such as choosing the wrong transceiver type) can wreak havoc. Double-check that the NIC listed in Device Manager (see the next section) is the same as the one installed in your computer. If it's not, click Remove to delete it, run the Add Hardware Wizard, and choose your NIC manually.

- **Perform a physical check of the NIC.** Open the case and make sure that the card is properly seated in its slot.

- **Disable the motherboard NIC.** If you added a new NIC to replace the motherboard NIC that came with your computer, it could be that the original NIC is interfering with the

> **caution** Before touching any component inside a computer case, ground yourself to prevent electrostatic discharge. To ground yourself, touch any metal surface, such as the metal of the computer case.

new one. To work around this problem, shut down Vista, restart your computer, and access your computer's BIOS configuration program. There should be an option that enables you to disable the motherboard NIC.

- **Try a new NIC.** Try swapping out the NIC for one that you know works properly. (If the existing NIC is on the computer's motherboard, insert the working NIC in an open bus slot.) If that fixes the problem, you'll have to remove the faulty interface card (if possible) and insert a new one.

- **Get the latest driver.** Check with the manufacturer of the NIC to see whether it has newer Windows Vista drivers for the card. If so, download and install them, as described in the next section.

Viewing the NIC in Device Manager

Windows Vista stores all its hardware data in the Registry, but it provides Device Manager to give you a graphical view of the devices on your system. To display Device Manager, follow these steps:

1. Select Start, right-click Computer, and then click Properties in the shortcut menu. The System window appears.

2. In the Tasks list, click Device Manager. The User Account Control dialog box appears.

3. Enter your UAC credentials. Vista displays the Device Manager window.

> **tip** One quick way to go directly to Device Manager is to press Windows Logo+R (or select Start, All Programs, Accessories, Run) to open the Run dialog box, type `devmgmt.msc`, and click OK. Alternatively, select Start, type **dev** in the Search box, and then click Device Manager in the search results. Note, too, that you can also press Windows Logo+Pause/Break to display the System window, and then click Device Manager.

18

Device Manager not only provides you with a comprehensive summary of your system's hardware data, it also doubles as a decent troubleshooting tool. To see what I mean, check out the Device Manager window shown in Figure 18.3. See how the icon for the D-Link DGE-530T Gigabit Ethernet Adapter device has an exclamation mark superimposed on it? This tells you that there's a problem with the device.

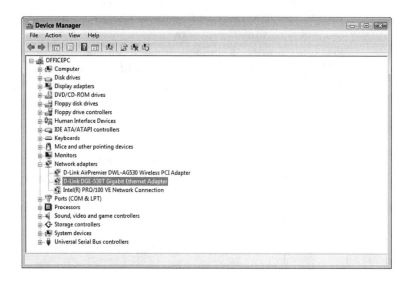

FIGURE 18.3

Device Manager uses icons to warn you if there's a problem with a device.

If you examine the device's properties, as shown in Figure 18.4, the Device Status area tells you a bit more about what's wrong. As you can see in Figure 18.4, the problem here is that the device won't start. Either try Device Manager's suggested remedy or click the Troubleshoot button to launch the hardware troubleshooter.

Device Manager uses three different icons to indicate the device's current status:

- A black exclamation mark (!) on a yellow field tells you that there's a problem with the device.

- A red *X* tells you that the device is disabled or missing.

> **note** Device Manager has several dozen error codes. See the following Microsoft Knowledge Base article for a complete list of the codes as well as solutions to try in each case: http://support.microsoft.com/kb/310123/.

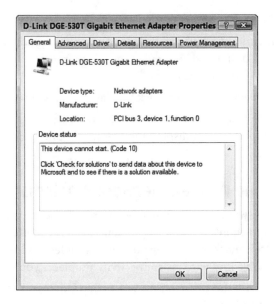

FIGURE 18.4

The Device Status area tells you if the device isn't working properly.

■ A blue *i* on a white field tells you that the device's Use Automatic Settings check box (on the Resources tab) is deactivated and that at least one of the device's resources was selected manually. Note that the device might be working just fine, so this icon doesn't indicate a problem. If the device isn't working properly, however, the manual setting might be the cause. (For example, the device might have a DIP switch or jumper set to a different resource.)

Updating the NIC Device Driver

If a device is flagged on your system but you don't notice any problems, you can usually get away with just ignoring the flag. I've seen lots of systems that run perfectly well with flagged devices, so this falls under the "If it ain't broke…" school of troubleshooting. The danger here is that tweaking your system to try and get rid of the flag can cause other—usually more serious—problems. Otherwise, a good next step is to get an updated device driver from the manufacturer and then install it.

note Remember, too, that just because the Device Status message says This device is working properly, it doesn't mean that the device is working flawlessly. Device Manager can only detect certain problems.

Follow these steps to update a device driver:

1. If you have a floppy disk or CD with the updated driver, insert the disk or CD. If you downloaded the driver from the Internet, decompress the driver file, if necessary.

2. In Device Manager, click the device you want to work with.

3. Select Action, Update Driver Software. (You can also open the device's property sheet, display the Driver tab, and click Update Driver.)

Troubleshooting Wireless Network Problems

Wireless networking adds a whole new set of potential snags to your troubleshooting chores because of problems such as interference, compatibility, and device ranges. Here's a list of a few troubleshooting items that you should check to solve any wireless connectivity problems you're having:

- **Repair the connection.** Vista's network repair tool seems to work particularly well for solving wireless woes, so you should always start with that (see "Repairing a Network Connection" earlier in this chapter).

- **Reboot and power cycle devices.** Reset your hardware by performing the following tasks, in order: log off Vista; restart your computer; power cycle your computer; power cycle the wireless access point; power cycle the broadband modem.

- **Check connections.** Make sure your wireless NIC is installed properly and that the antenna is attached securely.

- **Move the antenna.** If the wireless NIC antenna is on a cable, move the antenna to a higher position.

- **Check your notebook WLAN switch.** Many notebook computers come with a switch or program that turns the internal wireless NIC on and off. Make sure you haven't inadvertently turned the NIC off.

- **Look for interference.** Devices such as baby monitors and cordless phones that use the 2.4GHz radio frequency (RF) band can play havoc with wireless signals. Try either moving or turning off such devices if they're near your wireless NIC or wireless access point.

caution You should also keep your wireless NIC and access point well away from a microwave oven; microwaves can jam wireless signals.

■ **Change the channel.** You can configure your wireless access to broadcast signals on a specific channel. Sometimes one channel gives a stronger signal than another, so try changing the channel. You do this by logging on to the access point's configuration pages and looking for a setting that determines the broadcast channel.

■ **Check your range.** If you're getting no signal or a weak signal, it could be that your wireless NIC is too far away from the access point. You usually can't get much farther than about 115 feet away from an access point before the signal begins to degrade (230 feet if you're using 802.11n devices). Either move closer to the access point, or turn on the access point's range booster feature, if it has one. You could also install a wireless range extender.

■ **Check 802.11b/g/n compatibility.** For your wireless NIC to work properly with your wireless access point, both must use a compatible version of the wireless 802.11 standard. For example, if your NIC supports only 802.11n, but your access point supports only 802.11g, the two will not be able to connect.

■ **Reset the router.** As a last resort, reset the router to its default factory settings (see the device documentation to learn how to do this). Note if you do this you'll need to set up your network from scratch.

18

Reverting to an Earlier Configuration

Ideally, solving a problem will require a specific tweak to the system: a driver upgrade, a reboot, a firmware update. But sometimes you need to take more of a "big picture" approach to revert your system to some previous state in the hope that you'll leap past the problem and get your system working again. Windows Vista offers an easy method for doing this: System Restore. This feature can revert your system to a previous state. In this case, you want to revert your system to a state when you could access your network and the Internet.

To revert your system to a restore point, follow these steps:

1. Select Start, All Programs, Accessories, System Tools, System Restore. The User Account Control dialog box appears.

2. Enter your UAC credentials to display the System Restore dialog box.

3. The first System Restore dialog box offers two options:

Recommended Restore. Activate this option to restore Windows Vista to the restore point shown (which is usually the most recent restore point). Skip to step 4.

Choose a Different Restore Point. Activate this option to select from a list of restore points. Click Next to display the Chose a Restore Point dialog box, shown in Figure 18.5, and continue with step 3.

note By default, Windows Vista displays only the restore points from the previous five days. If you need to restore to an earlier date, activate the Show Restore Points Older Than 5 Days check box, as shown in Figure 18.5. Note that this check box only appears if you have at least one restore point that is more than five days old.

4. Click the restore point you want to use. There are five common types of restore points:

System. A restore point that Windows Vista creates automatically. For example, the System Checkpoint is the restore point that Vista creates each day or when you boot your computer.

Install. A restore point set prior to installing a program or update.

Manual. A restore point you create yourself.

Undo. A restore point set prior to a previous use of System Restore to revert the system to an earlier state.

Unknown. Any restore point that doesn't fit in the above categories.

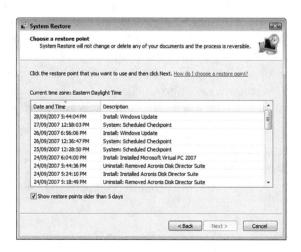

FIGURE 18.5

Use the Choose a Restore Point window to choose the restore point you want to revert to.

5. Click Next. If other hard disks are available in the restore point, Vista displays a list of the disks. Activate the check box beside each disk you want to include in the restore, and then click Next.

6. Click Finish. Vista asks you to confirm that you want your system restored.

7. Click Yes. System Restore begins reverting to the restore point. When it's done, it restarts your computer and displays a message telling you the results of the restore.

8. Click Close.

From Here

- To learn how to upgrade your router's firmware, **see** "Updating the Firmware," **p. 66**.

- To learn how to view the status of a network connection, **see** "Viewing the Current Network Status," **p. 123**.

- For the details on how to activate network discovery in Vista, **see** "Turning On Network Discovery," **p. 128**.

- To learn how to get the Network Connections window onscreen, **see** "Opening the Network Connections Window," **p. 140**.

- You can find some problems by monitoring the performance of your network; **see** "Monitoring Network Performance," **p. 396**.

18

Setting Up a Website

Windows Vista is definitely a client operating system, but it does have its server moments. For example, you've seen that Windows Vista acts as a kind of server when you set up a folder to be shared with the network. Similarly, Vista also acts as a kind of server when you use it to host an ad hoc wireless network and when you create a meeting using Windows Meeting Space.

However, these are only "server-like" applications. Surprisingly, there is a way that Vista can act as a full-fledged server: by running the built-in service called Internet Information Services (IIS) that enables Vista to serve web pages. Why bother? Here are just a few good reasons:

- You're running a home office or small office and you want to set up an internal website for your employees (that is called an *intranet*).

- You want to set up a simple site with photos and updates for friends and family to access.

- You don't want to pay a web hosting company to store your site.

- You want to learn web programming and need a server to practice on.

- You're already a web developer and you need a full-fledged server to test your applications.

IN THIS CHAPTER

- Understanding Internet Information Services
- Installing Internet Information Services
- Accessing Your Website
- Understanding the Default Website
- Adding Folders and Files to the Default Website
- Controlling and Customizing Your Website
- From Here

Yes, for at least some of these scenarios it's easier to use one of the many thousands of web hosting companies to put up your site. However, if you want complete control over the site, you need to roll up your sleeves and get hands on with IIS. Fortunately, as you see in this chapter, although IIS itself is tremendously complex, the basic features of IIS (which are all you need) aren't hard to grasp.

Understanding Internet Information Services

A *web server* is a computer that accepts and responds to remote requests for pages and other web content that are stored on the server. Most of these requests come from remote users running Internet Explorer, Firefox, Safari, or some other web browser. IIS is Microsoft's web server and, amazingly, they've made it available on some versions of Windows Vista. IIS runs the World Wide Web Publishing Service, which makes a default website available to anyone on your network (or, with a bit of tweaking, anyone on the Internet) who uses a web browser. You can add your own pages and folders to the default website, so you can serve almost any type of World Wide Web content from your Vista computer. IIS also comes with the IIS Management Console, which enables you to customize your website to get it set up the way you want.

I mentioned above that some versions of Windows Vista come with IIS. Specifically, you get IIS on Windows Vista Home Premium, Business, Enterprise, and Ultimate. However, the Home Premium version doesn't implement IIS in the same way as the other versions:

- Home Premium doesn't come with some high-end features such as advanced authentication.

- Home Premium doesn't offer remote administration of IIS.

- Home Premium doesn't include the FTP server (which I discuss in Chapter 20, "Setting Up an FTP Site").

- Home Premium is restricted to a maximum of three simultaneous data requests (compared to the limit of 10 simultaneous requests in the Business, Enterprise, and Ultimate versions).

> **note** Vista IIS 7's simultaneous data request limit is different than XP IIS 5.1's connection limit. With the connection limit of 10, when an eleventh user tried to access your site, he or she received a Server Too Busy error. With the simultaneous data request limit of 10 (3 in Home Premium), if an eleventh (or fourth) request comes in at the same time, that request is simply placed in a queue and is handled when the server is ready for it.

If you used IIS 5.1 on Windows XP, note that two major restrictions have been lifted from Vista's IIS 7: First, there is no maximum connection limit. XP IIS 5.1 had a connection limit of 10 users, but there is no such limit in Vista's IIS 7. Second, there is no website limit. XP IIS 5.1 allowed you to create just one website, but Vista's IIS 7 lets you create as many sites as you want.

Installing Internet Information Services

IIS 7 is a feature in the Home Premium, Business, Enterprise, and Ultimate versions of Vista, but it's not installed by default on any of them. To install it, you need to work through the following steps:

1. Select Start, Control Panel to open the Control Panel window.

2. Click Programs to open the Program window.

3. Under Programs and Features, click the Turn Windows Features On or Off link. The User Account Control dialog box appears.

4. Enter your UAC credentials. Vista displays the Windows Features dialog box, which takes a few moments to populate.

5. Click to activate the check box beside Internet Information Services. Vista selects the most commonly used IIS features. If you want to install these default features, skip to step 7.

6. Open the Internet Information Services branch, and then activate the check boxes beside each component you want to work with. Here are some suggestions:

   - **Web Management Tools, IIS Management Service.** Install this component to configure your web server from any other computer on your network.

   - **World Wide Web Services, Application Development Features.** The components in this branch represent the IIS programming features. If you're running IIS to build and test web applications, be sure to activate the check box for each development technology you require.

   - **World Wide Web Services, Security, Basic Authentication.** Install this component if you want to restrict website access to users who have a valid Windows username and password.

7. Click OK. Vista installs IIS 7.

19

Accessing Your Website

Although there's not much to see, the default website is ready for action as soon as you install IIS. To access the website from the computer running IIS, you can enter any of the following addresses into your web browser:

```
http://127.0.0.1/
http://localhost/
http://IPAddress/ (replace IPAddress with the IP address of the computer)
http://ComputerName/ (replace ComputerName with name of the computer)
```

Figure 19.1 shows the home page of the default IIS website that appears.

FIGURE 19.1

The default IIS 7 website home page.

Creating a Windows Firewall Exception for the Web Server

As things stand now, your new website will only work properly when you access it using a web browser running on the Windows Vista PC that's running IIS. If you try to access the site on any other computer (or from a location outside your network), you get an error message.

The problem is that the Windows Firewall on the Vista machine hasn't been configured to allow data traffic through the World Wide Web Services used by IIS. For your website to work from any remote location, you need to set up an exception for the World Wide Web Services in Windows Firewall. Here are the steps to follow:

1. Select Start, Control Panel to open the Control Panel window.

2. Under Security, click the Allow a Program through Windows Firewall link. The User Account Control dialog box appears.

> **note** HTTP is short for Hypertext Transport Protocol, the protocol used to exchange information on the World Wide Web.

3. Enter your UAC credentials. The Windows Firewall Settings dialog box appears.

4. Select the Exceptions tab.

5. Click to activate the check box beside the World Wide Web Services (HTTP) item, as shown in Figure 19.2.

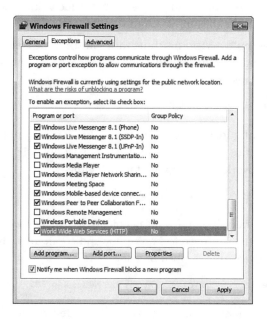

FIGURE 19.2

You need to configure Windows Firewall on the Vista machine to allow traffic over the World Wide Web Services.

6. Click OK to put the exception into effect.

Accessing Your Website Over the Network

With the Windows Firewall exception for the World Wide Web Services in place, you can now access the website from any remote computer on your network. You do this by launching your web browser and entering one of the following addresses:

```
http://IPAddress/ (replace IPAddress with the IP address of the IIS
computer)
http://ComputerName/ (replace ComputerName with name of the IIS computer)
```

Accessing Your Website Over the Internet

People on your network can now access your website, but you may also want to allow website access to people from outside your network (that is, from the Internet). To set this up, you must do three things:

1. Set up the Vista machine that's hosting the website with a permanent IP address, as described in Chapter 6, "Managing Network Connections."

→ **See** "Setting Up a Static IP Address," **p. 145**.

2. Configure your router to forward TCP traffic on port 80 to the IP address you specified in step 1. See Chapter 16, "Making Remote Network Connections," for the details.

→ **See** "Setting Up Port Forwarding," **p. 384**.

3. (Optional) If you want people to access your website using a domain name, you need to sign up for and configure a dynamic DNS (DDNS) service, as described in Chapter 16.

→ **See** " Using Dynamic DNS to Access Your Network," **p. 389**.

An Internet user can now access your website by entering the following addresses into a web browser:

```
http://IPAddress/ (replace IPAddress with your router's external IP
address)
http://DomainName/ (replace DomainName with your Dynamic DNS domain name)
```

→ To learn how to find out your router's external IP address, **see** "Checking the Router Status," **p. 90**.

Understanding the Default Website

As you saw earlier, the default website set up by IIS isn't much to look at. That's okay because a bit later you'll be adding plenty of your own content to the site. For now, the simplicity of the site is an advantage because it makes it easy for you to look around and see how the default site is constructed. This will help you down the road to customize the site and to add your own content.

> **tip** The Vista hard drive is usually the C: drive. If you're not sure, look for the drive icon that has the Windows flag superimposed on it. You may need to pull down the Views menu and select Large Icons or Tiles to see the flag.

Viewing the Default Website Folder

Let's begin by examining the folder that holds the website content:

1. Select Start, Computer to open the computer window.
2. Double-click the hard drive on which Windows Vista is installed.
3. Open the `inetpub` folder.
4. Open the `wwwroot` subfolder.

The `wwwroot` folder holds the IIS default website files, as shown in Figure 19.3

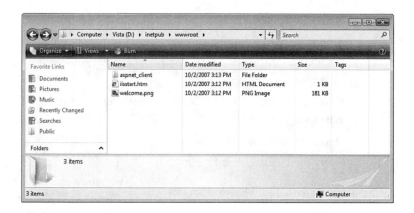

FIGURE 19.3

The contents of the IIS `wwwroot` *folder.*

The wwwroot folder has one subfolder (aspnet_client, which you can ignore) and two files:

iisstart.htm   This file contains the code that is used to display the home page you saw earlier in Figure 19.1.

welcome.png   This file is the image that you see in the home page.

tip You can also launch IIS Manager by pressing Windows Logo+R (or by selecting Start, All Programs, Accessories, Run) to open the Run dialog box, typing **inetmgr**, and clicking OK.

Viewing the Default Website with IIS Manager

The wwwroot folder enables you to examine the physical files and subfolders associated with the IIS default website. However, you probably won't often deal with the wwwroot folder (or any folder) directly when creating and configuring your own web pages and websites. Instead, you'll most often use a Microsoft Management Console snap-in called the IIS Manager.

To display this snap-in and the default IIS website, follow these steps:

1. Select Start, Control Panel to open the Control Panel window.

2. Click System and Maintenance.

3. Click Administrative Tools.

4. Double-click Internet Information Server (IIS) Manager. The User Account Control dialog box appears.

5. Enter your UAC credentials. The Internet Information Services (IIS) Manager window appears.

6. Open the *Computer* branch (where *Computer* is the name of your Windows Vista PC).

7. Open the Web Sites branch.

8. Select the Default Web Site branch.

IIS Manager gives you two ways to view the website files:

■ Click the Content View button to see the site contents. As you can see in Figure 19.4, you see the same subfolder and files as you saw earlier (see Figure 19.3) when you examined the contents of the wwwroot folder.

tip You can also use IIS Manager to open the website in your default web browser. In IIS Manager, open the *Computer*, Web Sites branch (where *Computer* is the name of the computer running IIS), select Default Web Site, and then click Browse in the Actions pane. (You can also right-click Default Web Site, and then click Browse in the shortcut menu.)

■ Click Features View to see a collection of icons associated with the site's features, as shown in Figure 19.5. Most of these are advanced features, so you'll be using only a small subset of them.

FIGURE 19.4

Click Content View to see the site's files and subfolders.

FIGURE 19.5

Click Features View to see icons associated with the site's features.

Much of the rest of this chapter shows you how to use IIS Manager to create and configure Windows Vista website content.

Adding Folders and Files to the Default Website

By far, the easiest way to set up your own web content in Windows Vista is to add that content to the existing default website. This requires no reconfiguration of the server, of IIS, of the Windows Vista firewall, of the client computers, or of the router. You simply add the content, and it's ready for browsing.

Setting Permissions on the Default Website Folder

Somewhat annoyingly, Windows Vista makes it difficult for you to modify the contents of the wwwroot folder. For example, if you copy a file to the folder, you need to enter your UAC credentials to allow the copy. Even worse, you get read-only access to the files, so if you edit a file you can't save your changes.

To avoid these hassles, you need to adjust the Security permissions on the wwwroot folder to give your Vista user account Full Control. Here are the steps to follow:

1. Select Start, Computer and navigate to the inetpub folder on your system drive.

2. Right-click the wwwroot folder, and then click Properties to open the folder's Properties dialog box.

3. Select the Security tab.

4. Click Edit. You may see the User Account Control dialog box.

5. Enter your UAC credentials. Vista displays the Permissions for wwwroot dialog box.

6. Click Add to display the Select Users or Groups dialog box.

7. In the Enter the Object Names to Select text box, type your username, and then click OK to return to the Permissions dialog box.

8. Select your username in the Group or User Names list.

9. In the Permissions list, under the Allow column, click to activate the Full Control check box, as shown in Figure 19.6.

10. Click OK to return to the Security tab.

11. Click OK to put the new security settings into effect.

note For a primer on Hypertext Markup Language (HTML) and Cascading Style Sheets (CSS), check out my book *The Complete Idiot's Guide to Creating a Website.* You can find out more about it at my own site located at http://www.mcfedries.com/.

caution Don't use spaces in the names of files (or folders) that you add to your website. Although Internet Explorer may display such pages successfully, other browsers may not.

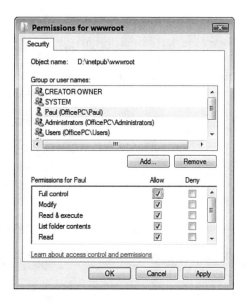

FIGURE 19.6

For hassle-free editing in the wwwroot *folder, give your user account Full Control permission.*

Adding a File to the Default Website

If you have just a few web content files that you want to add to the Windows Vista website, you can add them directly to the default website folder. First, create your web content file (HTML, ASP, or whatever). Here's a sample HTML file—which I've named HelloWorld.htm—that I'll use as an example:

```
<html>
<head>
<title>Hello World!</title>
</head>
<body>
<p>
<font style="size: 20pt; font-family:
Verdana; color: DarkBlue">
Hello Windows Vista World!
<font>
</p>
</body>
</html>
```

caution If your web content file references other files—for example, an HTML file that uses the `<img>` tag to reference an image file—be sure to copy those files to the wwwroot folder. You can either put the files in the root, or you can store them in a subfolder. For example, you might want to create a subfolder named images and use it to store your image files. If you store the files in subfolders, make sure you adjust the path in your code, as required. For example, if you place a file named HelloWorld.jpg in the images subfolder, you need to add the subfolder to the `<img>` tag, like so:

```
<img src="images\
HelloWorld.jpg" />
```

19

Next, save the file to the wwwroot folder.

Figure 19.7 shows the HelloWorld.htm file copied to the wwwroot folder, and Figure 19.8 shows the file displayed with Internet Explorer.

> **tip** A quick way to navigate to the wwwroot folder from IIS Manager is to open the *Computer*, Web Sites branch (where *Computer* is the name of the computer running IIS), select Default Web Site, and then click Explore in the Actions pane. (You can also right-click Default Web Site, and then click Explore in the shortcut menu.)

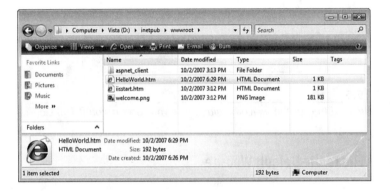

FIGURE 19.7
You can add individual files directly to the wwwroot *folder.*

FIGURE 19.8
The HelloWorld.htm *file displayed with Internet Explorer.*

Changing the Default Website Home Page

One of the first things you'll probably want to do with your new website is change the home page. To do that, you need to create a new HTML (or other web content) file in the wwwroot folder and give the file one of the following names:

```
default.htm
default.asp
index.htm
index.html
```

See "Setting the Website's Default Document," later in this chapter, to learn more about these special filenames. For example, here's some bare-bones HTML code that I've put in a file named default.htm:

```
<html>
<head>
<title>Home Page</title>
</head>
<body>
<p style="text-align: center">
<font style="size: 24pt; font-family: Verdana; color: Navy">
Welcome to Our Website!
<font>
</p>
</body>
</html>
```

Figure 19.9 shows default.htm added to the Default Web Site in IIS Manager, and Figure 19.10 shows the site's new home page in a web browser.

Adding a Folder to the Default Website

To add a folder to the Windows Vista default website, you have two choices:

■ Add the folder manually

■ Add the folder as a new virtual directory

The next two sections provide you with the details.

FIGURE 19.9

The default.htm *file added to the Default Web Site.*

FIGURE 19.10

The default.htm *file now appears as the website's home page.*

Adding a Folder Manually

Adding a folder to the Windows Vista default website is not all that different from adding a file. That is, you can create a new subfolder within the wwwroot folder, or copy or move an existing folder and paste it within wwwroot. To access web content within the new folder, tack the folder name and filename to the default website address. For example, if you create a subfolder named photos within the wwwroot folder, and the main page is named photos.htm, you access the content by entering the following address into the browser:

```
http://localhost/photos/photos.htm
```

Note that you can save some wear and tear on your typing fingers by changing the name of the main content file to one of the following:

```
default.htm
default.asp
index.htm
index.html
default.aspx
```

When you use one of these names, IIS displays the file by default if you don't specify a filename as part of the URL. For example, if you rename the `photos.htm` file to `default.htm`, you can access the file just by specifying the folder path in the URL:

```
http://localhost/photos/
```

I discuss default content files in more detail later in this chapter (see "Setting the Website's Default Document").

Adding a Folder as a New Virtual Directory

When you add a folder manually, IIS Manager detects the new folder and adds it to the folder content. (If you don't see the folder right away, switch to Content View, right-click Default Web Site, and then click Refresh.) However, you can also use IIS Manager to create a new folder within the default website. Here are the steps to follow:

1. In IIS Manager, open the *Computer*, Web Sites, Default Web Site branch (where *Computer* is the name of your Windows Vista PC).

2. Right-click Default Web Site and then click Add Virtual Directory. IIS Manager displays the Add Virtual Directory dialog box. Figure 19.11 shows a completed version of the dialog box.

3. Use the Alias text box to enter an alias for the virtual directory. The alias is the name that will appear in IIS Manager as a sub-branch of the Default Web Site.

4. To specify the location of the virtual directory, you have three choices:

   ■ If the folder exists and you know the full pathname (drive and folders), type it in the Physical Path text box.

   ■ If the folder exists and you're not sure of the full pathname (or it's too long to type), click the Browse (...) button, use the Browse for Folder dialog box to select the folder, and then click OK.

> **note** The alias doesn't have to be the same as the name of the virtual directory itself. For example, if you give the name `photos` to the new virtual directory, you could use something like `Photos Virtual Directory` as the alias.

FIGURE 19.11

Use the Add Virtual Directory dialog box to add a folder to your website using IIS Manager.

> ▦ If the folder doesn't exist, click Browse (…), use the Browse for Folder dialog box to select the folder within which you want the new folder to appear (for example, wwwroot), click Make New Folder, type the folder name, press Enter, and then click OK.

5. Click OK.

Figure 19.12 shows the Default Web Site in IIS Manager with the new virtual directory added.

FIGURE 19.12

The new virtual directory appears as part of the Default Web Site in IIS Manager.

Controlling and Customizing Your Website

At this point, you could use your website as is and just continue adding web pages, folders, and other content. However, IIS Manager offers a number of features and settings that enable you to control your website and to customize its look and feel. For example, you can stop and start the website, change the default name of the site, and specify the default content page. The rest of this chapter takes you through the most useful of these IIS Manager features.

Stopping Your Website

By default, when you start Windows Vista, the World Wide Web Publishing Service starts automatically, and that service automatically starts your website. This is reasonable behavior because in most cases you'll want your website available full time (that is, as long as the Vista computer is running). However, there might be occasions when you don't want your site to be available:

 ■ If you plan on making major edits to the content, you might prefer to take the site offline while you make the changes.

 ■ You might only want your website available at certain times of the day.

 ■ If you're developing a web application, certain changes may require that you stop and then restart the website.

For these and similar situations, you can stop the website. Here are the steps to follow:

  1. Open IIS Manager.

  2. Select *Computer*, Web Sites, Default Web Site (where *Computer* is the name of the computer running IIS).

  3. In the Actions pane, click Stop. (You can also right-click Default Web Site and then click Stop.) IIS Manager stops the website.

tip If you'd prefer that your website not start automatically when you log on to Windows Vista, select Default Web Site, and then click Advanced Settings in the Actions pane. (You can also right-click Default Web Site, and then click Advanced Settings.) In the Start Automatically setting, select False, and then click OK.

If you only want your website to not start the next time you launch Windows Vista, stop the site and then shut down Vista. When you next log on to Vista, your website won't start. Note, however, that if you then restart the website during the Vista session, the website will start automatically the next time you start Vista.

19

Restarting Your Website

When you're ready to get your website back online, follow these steps to restart it:

1. Open IIS Manager.

2. Select *Computer*, Web Sites, Default Web Site (where *Computer* is the name of the computer running IIS).

3. In the Actions pane, click Start. (You can also right-click Default Web Site and then click Start.) IIS Manager starts the website.

> **tip** If your website is stuck or behaving erratically, you can often solve the problem by stopping and restarting the site. However, instead of performing two separate operations—clicking Stop and then clicking Start—IIS Manager lets you perform both actions in one shot by clicking Restart.

Renaming the Default Website

The name Default Web Site is innocuous enough, I suppose, but it's a bit on the bland side. If you prefer to use a more interesting name, follow these steps to change it:

1. Open IIS Manager.

2. Open the *Computer*, Web Sites branch (where *Computer* is the name of the computer running IIS).

3. Right-click Default Web Site and then click Rename in the shortcut menu. IIS Manager adds a text box around the name.

4. Type the new name for the website.

5. Press Enter.

Changing the Website Location

By default, your website's home folder is the wwwroot folder, but that isn't necessarily permanent. You may decide to move the website to a different home folder, or you may decide to rename the existing folder. In either case, you must use IIS Manager to specify the new home folder. Here are the steps to follow:

1. Open IIS Manager.

2. Open the *Computer*, Web Sites branch (where *Computer* is the name of the computer running IIS).

> **caution** When you rename the site, the new name can be up to 259 characters long, but you must be sure to not use any of the following illegal characters:
> @ $ & = + | \ ; : " ' , < > / ?

3. Select Default Web Site.

4. In the Action pane, click Basic Settings to open the Edit Web Site dialog box, shown in Figure 19.13.

FIGURE 19.13

Use the Edit Web Site dialog box to change the site's home folder.

5. To specify the website's new home folder, you have three choices:

   ◾ If the folder exists and you know the full pathname (drive and folders), type it in the Physical Path text box.

   ◾ If the folder exists and you're not sure of the full pathname (or it's too long to type), click the Browse (...) button, use the Browse for Folder dialog box to select the folder, and then click OK.

   ◾ If the folder doesn't exist, click Browse (...), use the Browse for Folder dialog box to select the folder within which you want the new folder to appear, click Make New Folder, type the folder name, press Enter, and then click OK.

6. Click OK.

Setting the Website's Default Document

A normal website URL looks like the following:

```
http://name/folder/file
```

Here, *name* is a domain name or hostname, *folder* is a folder path, and *file* is the filename of the web page or other resource. Here's an example:

```
http://localhost/photos/default.htm
```

Intriguingly, you can view the same web page by entering the following address into the browser:

```
http://localhost/photos/
```

This works because IIS defines `default.htm` as one of its default document file-names. Here are the others:

```
default.asp
index.htm
index.html
iisstart.htm
default.aspx
```

This means that as long as a folder contains a file that uses one of these names, you can view the corresponding page without specifying the filename in the URL.

Note, too, that these default documents have an assigned priority, with `default.htm` having the highest priority, followed by `default.asp`, then `index.htm`, then `index.html`, then `iisstart.htm`, and finally `default.aspx`. This priority defines the order in which IIS looks for and displays the default document pages. That is, IIS first looks for `default.htm`; if that file doesn't exist in a folder, IIS next looks for `default.asp`, and so on.

For your own websites, you can add new default documents (for example, `default.html` and `index.asp`), remove existing default documents, and change the priority of the default documents. Here are the steps to follow:

1. Open IIS Manager.

2. Open the *Computer*, Web Sites branch (where *Computer* is the name of the computer running IIS).

3. Select Default Web Site.

4. Click Features View.

5. Double-click the Default Document icon. IIS Manager displays the Default Document page, shown in Figure 19.14.

6. To specify a new default document, type the filename in the File Name(s) text box, making sure you separate each name with a comma.

7. To delete a default document, select it in the File Name(s) text box and then press Delete.

8. To change the default document priority order, cut and paste the items in the File Name(s) text box.

9. In the Actions pane, click Apply to put the new settings into effect.

10. Click the Back button to return to the website's main page in IIS Manager.

FIGURE 19.14

Use the Default Document page to add, remove, and reorder a site's default content pages.

Working Without a Default Document

Using a default document is usually a good idea because it enables users to access your site without knowing the name of any file. However, for security reasons, you might want to allow access to the site only to users who know a specific filename on the site (for example, through a URL that you've provided). In that case, you have two choices:

- Don't include a file that uses one of the default document names.
- Disable the default documents.

Here are the steps to follow to disable default documents for your website:

1. Open IIS Manager.
2. Open the *Computer*, Web Sites branch (where *Computer* is the name of the computer running IIS).
3. Select Default Web Site.
4. Click Features View.
5. Double-click the Default Document icon to display the Default Document page.
6. In the Actions pane, click Disable. IIS Manager disables the default documents for the site.
7. Click the Back button to return to the website's main page in IIS Manager.

19

At this point, you may still have a security risk because it's possible that any anonymous user who surfs to the site without specifying a filename will see a listing of all the files and subfolders in the website's home folders! An example is shown in Figure 19.15.

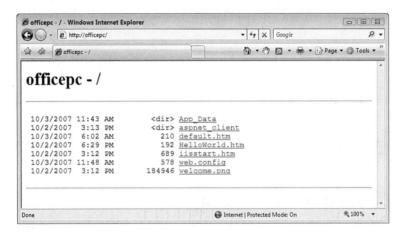

FIGURE 19.15

If you've disabled the default documents but directory browsing is enabled, anonymous users who don't specify a filename see a listing of the contents of the home folder.

This is called *directory browsing*, and it's normally disabled in IIS 7, but just to make sure, follow these steps:

1. Open IIS Manager.
2. Open the *Computer*, Web Sites branch (where *Computer* is the name of the computer running IIS).
3. Select Default Web Site.
4. Click Features View.
5. Double-click the Directory Browsing icon to display the Directory Browsing page.
6. In the Actions pane, look for the message `Directory browsing has been disabled`, as shown in Figure 19.16. If you see the message, skip to step 8.

> **note** In the directory listing shown in Figure 19.15, you see a file named `web.config`. This is a file created by IIS Manager to store some of the settings you've been working with so far, including the name and order of the default documents and whether default documents are enabled.

Look for this message

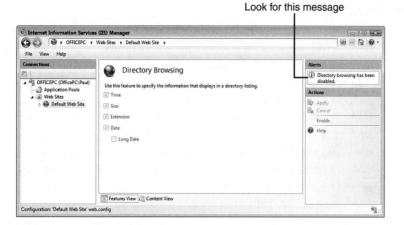

FIGURE 19.16

Make sure that your website has directory browsing disabled.

7. If you do not see the message, click the Disable link to disable directory browsing. IIS Manager disables directory browsing for the site.

8. Click the Back button to return to the website's main page in IIS Manager.

Now when an anonymous user surfs to your website without specifying a filename (and assuming you still have default documents disabled), that person sees the error message shown in Figure 19.17.

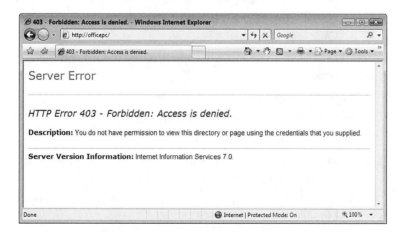

FIGURE 19.17

If you've disabled default documents and directory browsing, anonymous users who don't specify a filename see the error message shown here.

Disabling Anonymous Access

Earlier in the chapter I showed you how to give yourself Full Control permission on the wwwroot folder to make it easier (and in some cases possible) to add and edit content in that folder. When you access your website on the IIS computer using the http://localhost/, http://127.0.0.1/, or http://Computer/ addresses (where Computer is the name of the IIS computer), you access the site using your own user account. Everyone else on your network, and anyone who surfs to your site from the Internet (including you if you navigate to the site using http://IPAddress/, where IPAddress is your router's external IP address) accesses the site as an anonymous user. This means that IIS gives the person read-only access to the site without requiring a username and password, a technique called *anonymous authentication*.

However, you may have content that you want to restrict to people who have user accounts on Windows Vista. In that case, you need to disable anonymous access for the website and switch to *basic authentication*, which means IIS prompts each user for a username and password before allowing access to the site.

Follow these steps to disable anonymous access:

1. Open IIS Manager.
2. Open the *Computer*, Web Sites branch (where *Computer* is the name of the computer running IIS).
3. If you want to disable anonymous authentication on the entire site, select Default Web Site; if you want to disable anonymous authentication only on a specific folder within the site, open the Default Web Site branch and select the folder.
4. Click Features View.
5. Double-click the Authentication icon to display the Authentication page.
6. Select Anonymous Authentication.
7. In the Actions pane, click the Disable link.
8. Select Basic Authentication.
9. In the Actions pane, click the Enable link. The Authentication page should now appear as shown in Figure 19.18.
10. Click the Back button to return to the website's main page in IIS Manager.

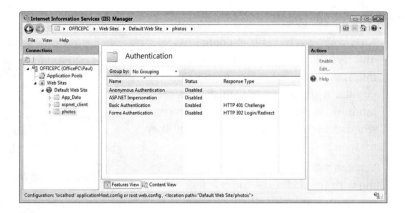

FIGURE 19.18

To secure your website or a folder within the website, disable anonymous authentication and enable basic authentication.

When an anonymous user attempts to access your website or website folder, he sees a Connect dialog box similar to the one shown in Figure 19.19. The user must enter a username and password for an account that exists on the Windows Vista machine that's running IIS.

FIGURE 19.19

With basic authentication enabled, users must enter a valid Windows Vista username and password to access the website or folder.

Viewing the Server Logs

After your web server is chugging along and serving pages to all and sundry, you might start to wonder which pages are popular with surfers and which ones are languishing. You might also want to know whether users are getting errors when they try to access your site.

You can tell all of this and more by working with the IIS logs. A log is a text file that records all the activity on your website, including the IP address and computer name (if applicable) of the surfer, the file that was served, the date and time the file was shipped to the browser, and the server return code (see the next Note box). For each server request, the log file writes a sequence of space-separated values, which makes it easy to import the file into a database or spreadsheet program for analysis.

tip Switching to basic authentication means that any user with a valid account on Windows Vista can access the website. What if there are one or more users with Windows Vista accounts that you do *not* want to view the website? In that case, you must adjust the security of the website's home folder directly. Use Windows Explorer to display the website's home folder, right-click the folder, and then click Properties. In the Security tab, click Edit, click Add, type the name of the user, and then click OK. Select the user, and then activate the Full Control check box in the Deny column. This tells Windows Vista not to allow that user to view the folder, thus barring the user from viewing the website.

The log files are stored in the \inetpub\logs\LogGiles\W3SVC1 folder of your Windows Vista system drive. (As you navigate to this folder, you may see one or two dialog boxes telling you that you don't have permission to open a particular folder. In each case, click Continue and enter your UAC credentials.)

Each filename takes the form u_*exyymmdd*.log, where *yy* is the two-digit year, *mm* is the two-digit month, and *dd* is the two-digit day. For example, the log for August 23, 2008, would be stored in u_ex080823.log. Figure 19.20 shows a typical log file.

At first glance, an IIS log file appears to be nothing but a jumble of letters, numbers, and symbols. However, there's a bit of method in the apparent madness. First, know that each line (that is, each line that doesn't begin with #) represents an object that IIS served. This could be a file, and image, or some other content on the website. Second, remember that each field is separated by a space. Third, notice the #Fields line, which appears from time to time in the log:

```
#Fields: date time s-ip cs-method cs-uri-stem cs-uri-query s-port
➥cs-username
c-ip cs(User-Agent) sc-status sc-substatus sc-win32-status
```

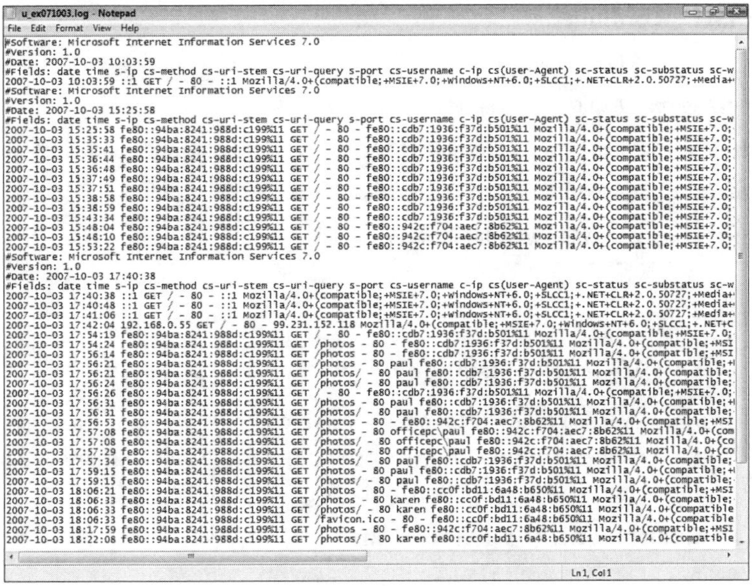

FIGURE 19.20
A typical IIS log file.

This line tells you the name of each log field. To help you make sense of what you're looking at, Table 19.1 gives you a summary of what you see in each field.

Table 19.1   A Description of the Fields Found in an IIS Log File

Field	Description
date	The date on which the item (file or folder) was served.
time	The time at which the item was served.
s-ip	The IP address of the computer that's running the web server.
cs-method	The method used to request the item. (This is almost always GET.)
cs-uri-stem	The name of the requested item.
cs-uri-query	The query used to generate the item request. (This will usually be blank, represented by a dash.)
s-port	The port used to exchange the data. (This will always be 80.)
cs-username	The name—and sometimes the computer name—of the authenticated user. You only see values in this field if you turn on basic authentication for the website or a folder.
c-ip	The IP address of the user who requested the item.

continues

Table 19.1   Continued

Field	Description
cs(User-Agent)	A string that identifies the user's web browser.
sc-status	A code that specifies whether the request was handled successfully and, if not, what the error was.
sc-substatus	A secondary error code if the request failed.
sc-win32-status	The Windows status during the request.

SERVER RETURN CODES

A sc-status code of 200 means the document was sent successfully to the browser. For unsuccessful operations, here's a summary of some of the return codes you'll find in the log:

Return Code	What It Means
204	File contains no content
301	File moved permanently
302	File moved temporarily
304	File not modified
400	Bad request
401	Unauthorized access
402	Payment required
403	Access forbidden
404	File not found
500	Internal server error
501	Service not implemented
502	Bad gateway
503	Service unavailable

From Here

■ To learn how to find out your router's external IP address, **see** "Checking the Router Status," **p. 90**.

■ For the details on configuring a Vista computer with a static IP address, **see** "Setting Up a Static IP Address," **p. 145**.

■ For information about configuring port forwarding in your router, **see** "Setting Up Port Forwarding," **p. 384**.

■ To learn about dynamic DNS, **see** "Using Dynamic DNS to Access Your Network," **p. 389**.

■ To learn how to use the IIS FTP server, **see** Chapter 20, "Setting Up an FTP Site," **p. 461**.

19

Setting Up an FTP Site

You saw in Chapter 19, "Setting Up a Website," that you can install Internet Information Services (IIS) 7 in most versions of Vista, which enables you to offer web content either locally on your intranet, or remotely via the Internet. This works great if all you have is web content to serve. However, what if you also have documents, archives, and other files that you want to make available for users to download? For example, you might have product information sheets, spreadsheets, ZIP files, or images that you want to offer. If you have just a few files, you can add them to your website and set up pages that contain links to the files. However, that's not practical if you're dealing with dozens or even hundreds of files.

A better solution is to use the Internet service that specializes in uploading and downloading files: File Transfer Protocol (FTP). With this service, an FTP server makes files available, and an FTP client selects some or all of those files and transfers them to the user's hard drive. The FTP client can be either a standalone FTP program or Vista's version of Windows Explorer.

IN THIS CHAPTER

■ Installing the FTP Publishing Service

■ Starting the FTP Publishing Service

■ Accessing Your FTP Site

■ Understanding the Default FTP Site

■ Adding Folders and Files to the Default FTP Site

■ Working with Your FTP Site

■ From Here

To make files available from your computer, you can use the FTP server that comes with some versions of Windows Vista. The FTP Server is part of the FTP Publishing Service, which creates a default FTP site that's available to anyone on your network (or, with a bit of tweaking, to anyone on the Internet) who uses an FTP client. You can add your own files and folders to the default FTP site, so you can make any kind of document or file available from your Vista computer. The FTP Publishing Service also comes with the FTP Management Console, which enables you to customize your FTP site to get it set up the way you want. This chapter provides you with the details for installing, starting, accessing, and configuring your Vista FTP site.

Installing the FTP Publishing Service

The FTP Server is part of the FTP Publishing Service, which is available in Vista Business, Enterprise, and Ultimate. Vista doesn't come with this service installed, so you need to install it by hand. Here are the steps to follow:

1. Select Start, Control Panel to open the Control Panel window.

2. Click Programs to open the Program window.

3. Under Programs and Features, click the Turn Windows Features On or Off link. The User Account Control dialog box appears.

4. Enter your UAC credentials. Vista displays the Windows Features dialog box, which takes a few moments to populate.

5. Open the Internet Information Services branch.

6. Click to activate the FTP Publishing Service check box.

7. Open the FTP Publishing Service branch.

8. Click to activate the FTP Management Console and FTP Server check boxes.

9. Click OK. Vista installs the FTP Publishing Service.

Starting the FTP Publishing Service

By default, Vista doesn't automatically start the FTP Publishing Service, so your FTP server isn't yet operational. So after the service is installed your first task should be to start it. Follow these steps:

1. Select Start, Control Panel to open the Control Panel window.

2. Click System and Maintenance.

3. Click Administrative Tools.

4. Double-click Services. The User Account Control dialog box appears.

5. Enter your UAC credentials. The Services console window appears.

6. Double-click the FTP Publishing Service. Vista displays the FTP Publishing Service Properties dialog box.

> **tip** You can also launch the Services console by pressing Windows Logo+R (or by selecting Start, All Programs, Accessories, Run) to open the Run dialog box, typing `services.msc`, and clicking OK.

7. In the Startup Type list, select Automatic as shown in Figure 20.1. This tells Vista to automatically start the service each time you log on.

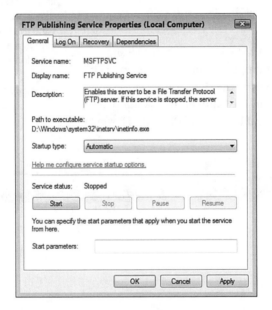

FIGURE 20.1

Configure the FTP Publishing Service to start automatically each time you log on to Vista.

8. Click Start. Vista starts the FTP Publishing Service.

9. Click OK.

10. Close the Services console.

Accessing Your FTP Site

The default FTP site is empty by default, but it's ready for action as soon as you start the FTP Publishing Service. To access the FTP site from the computer running the FTP server, you can enter any of the following addresses into your FTP client or Windows Explorer:

```
ftp://127.0.0.1/
ftp://localhost/
ftp://IPAddress/ (replace IPAddress with
the IP address of the computer)
ftp://ComputerName/ (replace
ComputerName with name of the computer)
```

Figure 20.2 shows the default FTP site which is empty because you haven't yet added files to the site. (You'll get to that a bit later in this chapter; see "Adding Folders and Files to the Default FTP site.")

> **tip** To enter an address in Windows Explorer, click an empty section of the Address bar, delete the address that appears, type the address you want to use, and then press Enter.

> **note** You might be wondering if you can enter the FTP site address in Internet Explorer. You can do that, but Internet Explorer 7 will only display a message that tells you to view the site using Windows Explorer, and that you can do this from Internet Explorer by selecting Page, Open FTP Site in Windows Explorer.

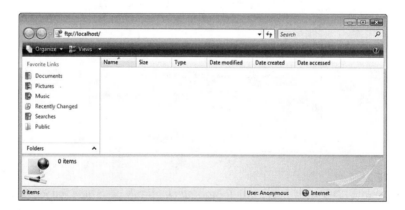

FIGURE 20.2
The default FTP site is empty at first.

Creating a Windows Firewall Exception for the FTP Server

The default FTP site works as advertised on the Vista computer that's running the FTP server. However, if you try to access the FTP site on any other computer (or from a location outside your network), you get an error message or the connection attempt just times out.

To fix this problem, you need to configure Windows Firewall on the Vista machine to allow data traffic through the FTP port (port 21). Specifically, you need to set up an exception for the FTP server in Windows Firewall. Here are the steps to follow:

1. Select Start, Control Panel to open the Control Panel window.

2. Under Security, click the Allow a Program Through Windows Firewall link. The User Account Control dialog box appears.

3. Enter your UAC credentials. The Windows Firewall Settings dialog box appears.

4. Select the Exceptions tab.

5. Click to activate the check box beside the FTP Server item, as shown in Figure 20.3.

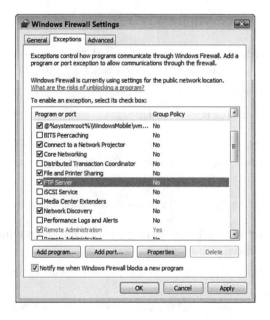

FIGURE 20.3

You need to configure Windows Firewall on the Vista machine to allow traffic through the FTP Server port.

6. Click OK to put the exception into effect.

Accessing Your FTP Site Over the Network

With the Windows Firewall exception for the FTP server in place, you can now access the FTP site from any remote computer on your network. You do this by launching Windows Explorer and entering one of the following addresses:

`ftp://IPAddress/` (replace `IPAddress` with the IP address of the FTP computer)

`ftp://ComputerName/` (replace `ComputerName` with name of the FTP computer)

Accessing Your FTP Site Over the Internet

People on your network can now access your FTP site, but you may also want to allow FTP site access to people from outside your network, that is, from the Internet. To set this up, you must do three things:

1. Set up the Vista machine that's hosting the FTP site with a permanent IP address, as described in Chapter 6, "Managing Network Connections."

→ **See** "Setting Up a Static IP Address," **p. 145**.

2. Configure your router to forward TCP traffic on port 21 to the IP address you specified in step 1. See Chapter 16, "Making Remote Network Connections," for the details.

→ **See** "Setting Up Port Forwarding," **p. 384**.

3. (Optional) If you want people to access your FTP site using a domain name, you need to sign up for and configure a dynamic DNS service, as described in Chapter 16.

→ **See** " Using Dynamic DNS to Access Your Network," **p. 389**.

An Internet user can now access your FTP site by entering the following addresses into a web browser:

`ftp://IPAddress/` (replace `IPAddress` with your router's external IP address)

`ftp://DomainName/` (replace `DomainName` with your Dynamic DNS domain name)

→ To learn how to find out your router's external IP address, **see** "Checking the Router Status," **p. 90**.

Understanding the Default FTP Site

The default FTP site is empty, as you've seen. Before you learn how to add files and folders to the FTP site, it's a good idea to take a quick look around so that you understand how the site works. This will help you down the road to customize the site and to add your own content.

> **tip** The Vista hard drive is usually the C: drive. If you're not sure, look for the drive icon that has the Windows flag superimposed on it. You may need to pull down the Views menu and select Large Icons or Tiles to see the flag.

Viewing the Default FTP Site Folder

Let's begin by examining the folder that holds the FTP site content:

1. Select Start, Computer to open the computer window.
2. Double-click the hard drive on which Windows Vista is installed.
3. Open the `inetpub` folder.
4. Open the `ftproot` subfolder.

The `ftproot` folder is where you store the files that you want to make available via the FTP server. Figure 20.4 shows the default `ftproot` folder which is, not surprisingly, empty.

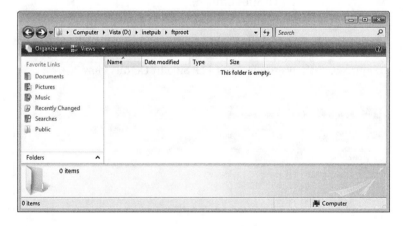

FIGURE 20.4

You use the `ftproot` *folder to store the files you want to make available through the FTP server.*

20

Viewing the Default FTP Site with IIS 6 Manager

If you read Chapter 19, you know that Vista's web server runs under IIS 7. However, Vista's FTP server actually runs under IIS 6. It's confusing, I know, but Vista does provide a separate console interface for IIS 6: the Internet Information Services (IIS) 6.0 Manager (which I'll call IIS 6 Manager from here on).

tip You can also launch IIS 6 Manager by pressing Windows Logo+R (or by selecting Start, All Programs, Accessories, Run) to open the Run dialog box, typing **inetmgr6**, and clicking OK.

To display this console and the default FTP site, follow these steps:

1. Select Start, Control Panel to open the Control Panel window.

2. Click System and Maintenance.

3. Click Administrative Tools.

4. Double-click IIS6 Manager. The User Account Control dialog box appears.

5. Enter your UAC credentials. The Internet Information Services (IIS) Manager window appears.

6. Open the *Computer* branch (where *Computer* is the name of your Windows Vista PC).

7. Open the FTP Sites branch.

8. Right-click Default FTP Site and then click either Explore (to see the site content in Details view) or Browse (to see the site content as icons).

Figure 20.5 shows the Default FTP Side in Details view.

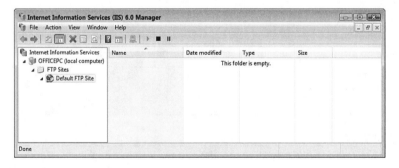

FIGURE 20.5
You can use IIS 6 Manager to view the Default FTP Site.

Much of the rest of this chapter shows you how to use IIS 6 Manager to create and configure Windows Vista FTP site content.

> **tip** You can also use IIS 6 Manager to open the FTP site in Windows Explorer. In IIS 6 Manager, open the *Computer*, FTP Sites branch (where *Computer* is the name of the computer running IIS), right-click Default FTP Site, and then click Open in the shortcut menu.

Adding Folders and Files to the Default FTP Site

By far, the easiest way to set up your own downloadable FTP content in Windows Vista is to add that content to the existing default FTP site. This requires no reconfiguration of the server, of IIS, of the Windows Vista Firewall, of the client computers, or of the router. You simply add the content, and it's ready for downloading.

Setting Permissions on the Default FTP Site Folder

Because the ftproot folder is on the Vista system drive but not in your user profile folder, working with files and folders within ftproot is difficult because of the default permissions that Vista imposes on the system drive. These permissions mean you need to enter your UAC credentials to copy or move files to the folder, or to delete files from the folder. Annoyingly, you get read-only access to the files; so if you edit a file, you can't save your changes. Even worse, it's hard to create new files because the Organize, New command only includes a single option: Folder.

To work around these problems, you need to adjust the Security permissions on the ftproot folder to give your Vista user account Full Control. Here are the steps to follow:

1. Select Start, Computer and navigate to the inetpub folder on your system drive.

2. Right-click the ftproot folder, and then click Properties to open the folder's Properties dialog box.

3. Select the Security tab.

4. Click Edit. You may see the User Account Control dialog box.

5. Enter your UAC credentials. Vista displays the Permissions for ftproot dialog box.

6. Click Add to display the Select Users or Groups dialog box.

> **tip** You can also get to the Security tab via IIS 6 Manager. Right-click Default FTP Site, and then click Permissions.

20

7. In the Enter the Object Names to Select text box, type your username, and then click OK to return to the Permissions dialog box.

8. Select your username in the Group or User Names list.

9. In the Permissions list, under the Allow column, click to activate the Full Control check box, as shown in Figure 20.6.

FIGURE 20.6

For easier editing and file maintenance in the ftproot *folder, give your user account Full Control permission.*

10. Click OK to return to the Security tab.

11. Click OK to put the new security settings into effect.

Adding a File to the Default FTP Site

To get some content on your FTP site, you need to copy existing files to the site, or create new files on the site. Note that you can perform both tasks using the ftproot folder directly, or by using IIS 6 Manager:

■ **Copying files to the FTP site.** In most cases you'll want to copy an existing file for use on the FTP site. Use Windows Explorer to locate the file you want to work with, right-click the file, and then click Copy.

Open either the ftproot folder or IIS 6 Manager's Default FTP Site, right-click an empty section of the folder, and then click Paste.

caution Don't use spaces in the names of files (or folders) that you add to your FTP site. Some FTP programs may not be able to work with such files.

- **Creating new files on the FTP site.** If you want to create content directly on the FTP site, first open either the ftproot folder or IIS 6 Manager's Default FTP Site, right-click an empty section of the folder, and then click New. In the submenu that appears, click the type of content you want to add. Type a name for the new file, press Enter, and then press Enter again to open the file for editing.

Adding a Folder to the Default FTP Site

To add a folder to the default FTP site, you have two choices:

- Add the folder manually
- Use the Virtual Directory Creation Wizard

The next two sections provide you with the details.

Adding a Folder Manually

Adding a folder to the Windows Vista default FTP site is not all that different from adding a file. That is, you can create a new subfolder within the ftproot folder, or copy or move an existing folder and paste it within ftproot. To access content within the new folder, tack the folder name and filename to the default FTP site address. For example, if you create a subfolder named archives within the ftproot folder, you access the content in that folder by entering the following address into the browser:

```
ftp://localhosct/archives/
```

Adding a Folder as a New Virtual Directory

When you add a folder manually, IIS 6 Manager detects the new folder and adds it to the folder content. (If you don't see the folder right away, right-click Default FTP Site, and then click Refresh.) However, you can also use IIS 6

Manager to create a new folder within the default FTP site. Here are the steps to follow:

note   The alias doesn't have to be the same as the name of the virtual directory itself. For example, if you give the name archives to the new virtual directory, you could use something like Archives Virtual Directory as the alias.

1. In IIS 6 Manager, open the *Computer*, FTP Sites, Default FTP Site branch (where *Computer* is the name of your Windows Vista PC).

2. Select Action, New, Virtual Directory. IIS 6 Manager launches the Virtual Directory Creation Wizard.

3. Click Next. The wizard asks you to enter an alias for the virtual directory.

4. Use the Alias text box to enter an alias for the virtual directory. The alias is the name that will appear in IIS 6 Manager as a sub-branch of the Default FTP Site.

5. Click Next. The wizard prompts you for the folder path.

6. You have three choices. (Click Next when you're done.)

   - If the folder exists and you know the full pathname (drive and folders), type it in the Path text box.

   - If the folder exists and you're not sure of the full pathname (or it's too long to type), click Browse, use the Browse for Folder dialog box to select the folder, and then click OK.

   - If the folder doesn't exist, click Browse, use the Browse for Folder dialog box to select the folder within which you want the new folder to appear, click Make New Folder, type the folder name, press Enter, and then click OK.

7. Activate the check boxes for the permissions you want to apply to the new folder. (see Figure 20.7); click Next when you're done.

   Read   Allows each user to view and download files from the folder. This is the default permission.

   Write   Allows each user to upload files to the folder and to modify files within the folder. Obviously, you only want to apply this potentially destructive permission in the rarest circumstances.

8. Click Finish.

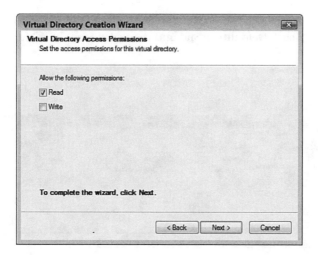

FIGURE 20.7
When you add a virtual directory using IIS 6 Manager, you can set permissions on that folder.

Working with Your FTP Site

The rest of this chapter takes you through a few useful techniques and tweaks that you might want to consider before putting your FTP site into production. For example, you might want to give the site a better name, change the site location, configure messages to display to users, and disable anonymous access for better security. The next few sections take you through these and other FTP site tasks.

Stopping Your FTP Site

Earlier in this chapter, I showed you how to set up the FTP Publishing Service to start automatically when you log on to Windows Vista. Starting this service also starts your FTP site, which makes the site available full time while your Vista machine is running. If you prefer to make the FTP site available at only certain times of the day, or if you want to make major changes to the site, you can stop the site from the IIS 6 Manager. Here are the steps to follow:

1. Open IIS 6 Manager.

2. Select *Computer*, FTP Sites, Default FTP Site (where *Computer* is the name of the computer running the FTP server).

20

3. Click the Stop button (pointed out in Figure 20.8); you can also right-click Default FTP Site and then click Stop. IIS 6 Manager stops the FTP site.

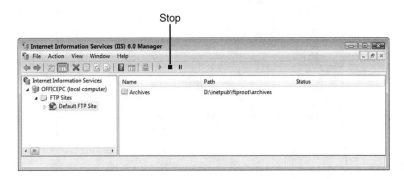

Stop

FIGURE 20.8

Click the Stop button to stop your FTP site.

Restarting Your FTP Site

If you stopped your FTP site in the previous section, here are the steps to follow to restart it:

1. Open IIS 6 Manager.

2. Select *Computer*, FTP Sites, Default FTP Site (where *Computer* is the name of the computer running the FTP server).

3. Click the Start button (pointed out in Figure 20.9; you can also right-click Default FTP Site and then click Start.) IIS 6 Manager restarts the FTP site.

caution If you stop the FTP site and then shut down Vista, when you next log on to Vista, your FTP site won't start automatically. (The FTP Publishing Service still starts, just not the site.) Note, however, that if you then restart the FTP site during the Vista session, the FTP site will start automatically the next time you start Vista.

tip If your FTP site is stuck or behaving erratically, you can often solve the problem by stopping and restarting the site.

20

Properties   Start

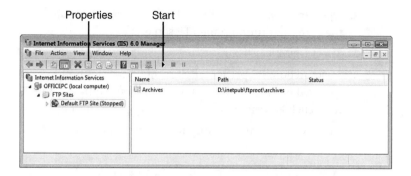

FIGURE 20.9

Click the Start button to restart your FTP site.

Renaming the Default FTP Site

As the administrator of your FTP site, you're the only person who sees the name Default FTP Site. So changing the name doesn't mean all that much, except that you might feel better by giving the site a less prosaic moniker. Here are the steps to follow to change the site name:

1. Open IIS 6 Manager.

2. Open the *Computer*, FTP Sites branch (where *Computer* is the name of the computer running the FTP server).

3. Right-click Default FTP Site, and then click Rename in the shortcut menu. IIS 6 Manager adds a text box around the name.

4. Type the new name for the FTP site.

5. Press Enter.

Changing the FTP Site Location

By default, your FTP site's home folder is `%SystemDrive%\inetpub\ftproot`, but you may prefer to move the home folder to a new location. For example, you might want the FTP site on a hard drive that has more free space.

Here are the steps to follow to use IIS 6 Manager to change the FTP site's home folder:

1. Open IIS 6 Manager.

> **caution** When you rename the site, you can use any combination of letters, numbers, and symbols up to a maximum of 259 characters.

20

2. Open the *Computer*, FTP Sites branch (where *Computer* is the name of the computer running the FTP server).

3. Select Default FTP Site.

4. Select Action, Properties, or click the Properties button in the toolbar (pointed out in Figure 20.9); you can also right-click the FTP site and then click Properties. The FTP site's property sheet appears.

5. Display the Home Directory tab, shown in Figure 20.10.

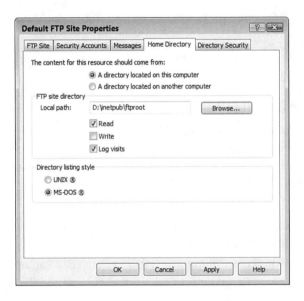

FIGURE 20.10

Use the Home Directory tab to change the FTP site's home folder.

6. To specify the FTP site's new home folder, you have three choices:

- If the folder exists and you know the full pathname (drive and folders), type it in the Local Path text box.

- If the folder exists and you're not sure of the full pathname (or it's too long to type), click the Browse (...) button, use the Browse for Folder dialog box to select the folder, and then click OK.

note You can change the FTP site location to a share on a network computer. In the Home Directory tab, select A Directory Located on Another Computer, and then use the Network Share text box to enter the network address for the share you want to use. Note that only users who have permission to view the share can access the FTP site (Windows Vista prompts for an authorized username and password).

- If the folder doesn't exist, click Browse (…), use the Browse for Folder dialog box to select the folder within which you want the new folder to appear, click Make New Folder, type the folder name, press Enter, and then click OK.

7. Click OK.

Displaying Messages to FTP Users

When you log on to an FTP site, you usually see one or more messages that welcome you to the site and provide information about the site. You can configure your own FTP site with these and other user messages. In fact, there are four types of messages you can set up:

- **Banner.** This is the message that appears to the user before he or she logs on to the FTP site.

- **Welcome.** This is the message that appears after the user has logged on to the FTP site.

- **Exit.** This is the message that appears when the user disconnects from the FTP site.

- **Maximum Connections.** This is the message that the user sees when the FTP site can't accept any new connections.

I should point out here that you only see these message if you use a stand-alone FTP program; you don't see the messages if you connect to the FTP site using Windows Explorer.

Here are the steps to follow to use IIS 6 Manager to set the FTP site messages:

1. Open IIS 6 Manager.

2. Open the *Computer*, FTP Sites branch (where *Computer* is the name of the computer running the FTP server).

3. Select Default FTP Site.

4. Select Action, Properties, or click the Properties button in the toolbar (pointed out in Figure 20.9); you can also right-click the FTP site and then click Properties. The FTP site's property sheet appears.

5. Display the Messages tab.

note In the Windows Vista FTP server, the maximum number of connections is 10. If you want to use a lower maximum (you can't set a higher one), open IIS 6 Manager, select the FTP site, click the Properties button, and then select the FTP Site tab. Use the Connections Limited To text box to enter the maximum number of connections, and then click OK.

20

6. Add your messages to the Banner, Welcome, Exit, and Maximum Connections text boxes. Figure 20.11 shows some example messages.

FIGURE 20.11

Use the Messages tab to configure user messages for your FTP site.

7. Click OK.

Figure 20.12 shows how the banner, welcome, and exit messages in Figure 20.11 appear in a standalone FTP program.

Disabling Anonymous Access

Earlier in the chapter I showed you how to give yourself Full Control permission on the ftproot folder to make it easier (and in some cases possible) to add and edit content in that folder. When you access your site on the same computer that's running the FTP server computer using the ftp://localhost/, ftp://127.0.0.1/, or ftp://Computer/ addresses (where Computer is the name of the FTP server computer), you access the site using your own user account. Everyone else on your network, and anyone who surfs to your site from the Internet (including you if you navigate to the site using ftp://IPAddress/, where IPAddress is your router's external IP address) accesses the site as an anonymous user. This means that the FTP server gives the person read-only access to the site without requiring a username and password, a technique called *anonymous authentication*.

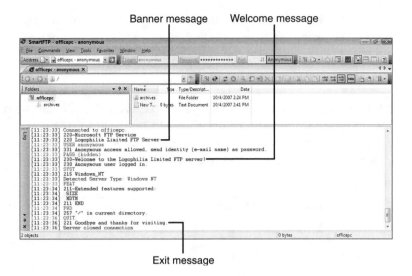

FIGURE 20.12

The banner and welcome messages as they appear in an FTP client.

However, you may have content that you want to restrict to people who have user accounts on Windows Vista. In that case, you need to disable anonymous access for the FTP site and switch to basic authentication, which means the FTP server prompts each user for a username and password before allowing access to the site.

Follow these steps to disable anonymous access:

1. Open IIS 6 Manager.

2. Open the *Computer*, FTP Sites branch (where *Computer* is the name of the computer running the FTP server).

3. Select Default FTP Site.

4. Select Action, Properties, or click the Properties button in the toolbar (pointed out in Figure 20.9); you can also right-click the FTP site and then click Properties. The FTP site's property sheet appears.

5. Display the Security Accounts tab.

6. Click to deactivate the Allow Anonymous Connections check box. IIS 6 Manager warns you that

caution The Vista FTP server has no way to encrypt the usernames and passwords as the users send them. So, it's theoretically possible for a malicious hacker to monitor traffic to and from your site and grab this logon data. Therefore, you should only use this technique on your local network, not over the Internet.

the logon data will be transmitted without encryption and asks you to confirm.

7. Click Yes.

8. Click OK.

When an anonymous user attempts to access your FTP site, he sees a Log On As dialog box similar to the one shown in Figure 20.13. The user must enter a username and password for an account that exists on the Windows Vista machine that's running the FTP server.

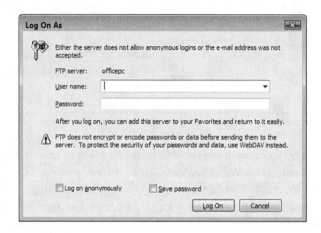

FIGURE 20.13

With anonymous connections disabled, users must enter a valid Windows Vista username and password to access the FTP site.

Securing an FTP Folder

By default, anonymous users can view and download the contents of any folder on the FTP site. What do you do if you have a folder that you do not want anonymous users to view? Disabling anonymous access is overkill in this situation because it applies to the entire site. A better solution is to set permissions on the folder that deny anonymous users the right to view its contents. Here are the steps to follow:

1. Open IIS 6 Manager.

2. Open the *Computer*, FTP Sites branch (where *Computer* is the name of the computer running the FTP server).

3. Open Default FTP Site.

4. Right-click the folder you want to protect, and then click Permissions. The property sheet for the folder appears, showing just the Security tab.

5. Click Edit to open the Permissions dialog box.

6. Click Add to open the Select Users or Groups dialog box.

7. Type IUSR_Computer, where Computer is the name of the computer running the FTP server. IUSR_Computer is the account that the FTP server uses for anonymous connections.

8. Click OK to return to the Permissions dialog box.

9. In the Group or User Names list, select the IUSR_Computer user.

> **tip** Switching to basic authentication means that any user with a valid account on Windows Vista can access the FTP site. What if there are one or more users with Windows Vista accounts that you do *not* want to view the FTP site? In that case, you must adjust the permissions on the FTP site directly. In IIS 6 Manager, right-click Default FTP Site, and then click Permissions. In the Security tab, click Edit, click Add, type the name of the user, and then click OK. Select the user, and then activate the Full Control check box in the Deny column. This tells Windows Vista not to allow that user to view the folder, thus barring the user from viewing the FTP site.

10. Activate the Full Control check box in the Deny column. This tells Windows Vista not to allow that user to view the folder.

11. Click OK. Vista asks you to confirm the Deny permissions.

12. Click Yes to return to the Security tab.

13. Click OK.

From Here

- To learn how to find out your router's external IP address, **see** "Checking the Router Status," **p. 90**.

- For the details on configuring a Vista computer with a static IP address, see "Setting Up a Static IP Address," **p. 145**.

- For information about configuring port forwarding in your router, **see** "Setting Up Port Forwarding," **p. 384**.

- To learn about dynamic DNS, **see** "Using Dynamic DNS to Access Your Network," **p. 389**.

- To learn how to use the IIS web server, **see** Chapter 19, "Setting Up a Website," **p. 431**.

20

Glossary of Networking Terms

10 Gigabit Ethernet   An *ethernet* standard that operates at 10*Gbps*. See also *100 Gigabit Ethernet, 10BASE-T, Fast Ethernet,* and *Gigabit Ethernet.*

100 Gigabit Ethernet   A future *ethernet* standard that will operate at 100*Gbps*. See also *10 Gigabit Ethernet, 10BASE-T, Fast Ethernet,* and *Gigabit Ethernet.*

10/100   Describes an *ethernet* device that supports both *10BASE-T* and *100BASE-T.*

10/100/1000   Describes an *ethernet* device that supports *10BASE-T, 100BASE-T,* and *1000BASE-T.*

10BASE-T   The original *ethernet* standard, which operated at 10Mbps. See also *10 Gigabit Ethernet, 100 Gigabit Ethernet, Fast Ethernet,* and *Gigabit Ethernet.*

100BASE-T   See *Fast Ethernet.*

1000BASE-T   See *Gigabit Ethernet.*

10GBASE-T   See *10 Gigabit Ethernet.*

802.3   The number associated with the ethernet standard as assigned by the Institute of Electrical and Electronics Engineers (IEEE).

802.11   The number associated with the wireless networking standard as assigned by the IEEE.

802.11a   An amendment to the 802.11 standard that operates in the 5.0GHz radio frequency band and offers a theoretical maximum data transmission speed of 54Mbps over a maximum range of about 75 feet.

802.11b   An amendment to the 802.11 standard that operates in the 2.4GHz radio frequency band and offers a theoretical maximum data transmission speed of 11Mbps over a maximum range of about 115 feet.

802.11g   An amendment to the 802.11 standard that operates in the 2.4GHz radio frequency band and offers a theoretical maximum data transmission speed of 54Mbps over a maximum range of about 115 feet.

802.11n   A future amendment to the 802.11 standard that operates in the 2.4GHz radio frequency band and offers a theoretical maximum data transmission speed of 248Mbps over a maximum range of about 230 feet.

8P8C   The networking purist's name for the connectors attached to the ends of network cables and for the corresponding ports on network devices; short for *8 Position 8 Contact*. See also *RJ-45*.

A

ad hoc wireless network—A wireless network configuration that allows for direct wireless *NIC*-to-*NIC* communication. See also *infrastructure wireless network*.

Address Resolution Protocol   A network protocol that handles the conversion of an *IP address* to a *MAC address* of a *network interface card*.

anonymous authentication   A security feature that gives a user access to an *IIS* website without requiring a username and password. See also *basic authentication*.

API   See *application programming interface*.

application layer   That portion (Layer 7) of the *OSI model* that provides the connection between the network and network-based applications such as email programs, web browsers, and FTP clients.

application programming interface   A set of procedures and other code that higher-level programs can call to perform lower-level functions.

ARP   See *Address Resolution Protocol*.

ARP cache   A memory location that improves network performance by temporarily storing addresses that have been resolved by the *Address Resolution Protocol*.

B

baseband   A communications medium (such as an *ethernet* cable) that only allows one signal at a time. See also *broadband*.

basic authentication   A security feature that gives a user access to an *IIS* website only if that person can provide an authorized Windows Vista username and password. See also *anonymous authentication*.

bps   Bits per second. The rate at which a *modem* or other communications device transmits data.

broadband   A communications medium that allows multiple simultaneous signals. See also *baseband*.

C

Category 3   A network cable specification that supports a maximum data transfer rate of 10*Mbps*. See also *Category 5*, *Category 5e*, and *Category 6*.

Category 5   A network cable specification that supports a maximum data transfer rate of 100*Mbps*. See also *Category 3*, *Category 5e*, and *Category 6*.

Category 5e   A network cable specification that supports a maximum data transfer rate of 1*Gbps*. See also *Category 3*, *Category 5*, and *Category 6*.

Category 6   A network cable specification that supports a maximum data transfer rate of 1*Gbps*. See also *Category 3*, *Category 5*, and *Category 5e*.

client   In a *client/server network*, a computer that uses the services and resources provided to the network by a *server*.

client/server network   A network model that splits the computing workload into two separate but related areas. On the one hand, you have users working at intelligent "front-end" systems called *clients*. In turn, these client machines interact with powerful "back-end" systems called *servers*. The basic idea is that the clients have enough processing power to perform tasks on their own, but they rely on the servers to provide them with specialized resources or services, or access to information that would be impractical to implement on a client (such as a large database). See also *peer-to-peer network*.

collision   In an *ethernet* data transfer, the error that occurs when two devices attempt to send *frames* over the network at the same time.

concentrator   See *hub*.

cone NAT   A type of *network address translation*. When a client with a specific *internal address* uses a port, all external hosts can communicate with the client by sending data through that port via the *external address*. See also *symmetric NAT*.

connection-oriented protocol   See *transport layer protocol*.

connectionless protocol   See *network layer protocol*.

covert reinstall   When a malicious program surreptitiously reinstalls a fresh version of itself when the computer is idle.

cracker   A computer *hacker* who performs illegal or unethical activities.

crossover cable   A network cable that reverses the position of the transmit and receive lines, which enables you to connect two computers directly via their *NIC* ports.

D

data link layer   The portion (Layer 2) of the *OSI model* that deals with the basic transfer of data from one part of the network to another.

data throughput   The collective term for network tasks involving client computers, users, and files.

datagram   An *IP packet*. The datagram header includes information such as the address of the *host* that sent the datagram and the address of the host that is supposed to receive the datagram.

demodulation   The conversion into digital data of an analog wave (a series of tones) transmitted over a telephone line. This conversion is performed by a *modem*. See also *modulation*.

device driver   A small software program that serves as an intermediary between hardware devices and the operating system. Device drivers encode software instructions into signals that the device understands, and, conversely, the drivers interpret device signals and report them to the operating system.

Device Manager   A snap-in that provides a graphical outline of all the devices on your system. It can show you the current configuration of each device (including the *IRQ, I/O ports,* and *DMA channel* used by each device). It even lets you adjust a device's configuration (assuming that the device doesn't require you to make physical adjustments to, say, a DIP *switch* or jumper). The Device Manager actually gets its data from, and stores modified data in, the *Registry*.

DHCP   See *Dynamic Host Configuration Protocol*.

DHCP lease   An agreement from a *DHCP server* that allows a client computer to use a specified *IP address* for a certain length of time, typically 24 hours.

DHCP server   A computer or device that dynamically assigns *IP addresses* to client computers.

digital media receiver   A device that can access a media stream being sent over a wired or wireless network connection and then play that stream through connected equipment such as speakers, audio receivers, or a TV.

DMR   See *digital media receiver*.

DNS   See *domain name system*.

Domain Name System   On the Internet, a hierarchical distributed database system that converts *hostnames* into *IP addresses*.

dotted-decimal notation   A format used to represent *IP addresses*. The 32 bits of the address are divided into quads of 8 bits, which are then converted into their decimal equivalent and separated by dots (for example, 205.208.113.1).

dotted-quad notation   See *dotted-decimal notation*.

drive-by download   The download and installation of a program without a user's knowledge or consent. See also *pop-up download*.

Dynamic Host Configuration Protocol   A system that manages the dynamic allocation of *IP addresses*.

E

ECN   See *Explicit Congestion Notification*.

edge router   An Internet-connected *router* that performs *network address translation* duties. See also *gateway*.

elevate   To enter credentials to increase a user's *permissions* level. See also *User Account Control*.

EPROM   Erasable programmable read-only memory; a memory chip often used to store *firmware*.

Ethernet   A *frame*-based *network architecture* that transmits data over twisted-pair wires. See also *10 Gigabit Ethernet*, *100 Gigabit Ethernet*, *10BASE-T*, *Fast Ethernet*, and *Gigabit Ethernet*.

Explicit Congestion Notification   A technology that enables your router to alert hosts that they are sending data too fast, and that they should throttle back the transmission.

external address   The IP address that a computer, router, or other device shows to the Internet. The conversion between the external address and the *internal address* is handled by *network address translation*.

F

Fast Ethernet   An *ethernet* standard that operates at 100Mbps. See also *10 Gigabit Ethernet, 100 Gigabit Ethernet, 10BASE-T,* and *Gigabit Ethernet.*

File Transfer Protocol   An Internet protocol that defines file transfers between computers. Part of the *TCP/IP* suite of protocols.

firmware   Programming code embedded in a device, often stored in an *EPROM* chip.

frame   A *packet* in an *ethernet* data transmission.

FTP   See *File Transfer Protocol.*

G

gateway   A network device such as a *router* that is set up as the sole connection point between a network and the Internet. See also *edge router* and *network address translation.*

Gb   See *gigabit.*

Gbps   *Gigabits* per second. This is the transmission speed unit used by *Gigabit Ethernet* networks.

gigabit   One billion bits, in the context of data communications. In the context of memory or data storage, a gigabit equals 1,073,741,824 bits.

Gigabit Ethernet   An *ethernet* standard that operates at 1*Gbps*. See also *10 Gigabit Ethernet, 100 Gigabit Ethernet, 10BASE-T,* and *Fast Ethernet.*

H

hacker   A computer enthusiast who is skilled in the use of computer systems. Most hackers are benign, but there are also "black hat" hackers who exploit system security breaches for nefarious ends (see also *cracker*), "white hat" hackers who, upon discovering a vulnerability in a computer system, alert the system vendor to the problem, and "gray hat" hackers who supply information about a security issue both to the vendor and to crackers.

header   Extra data attached to the beginning of a *frame* or *packet* that contains information about which machine sent the data, which machine is supposed to receive the data, and a few extra tidbits that let the receiving computer put all the original data together in the correct order and check for errors that might have cropped up during the transmission.

home theater PC   A PC that is designed to look more like a typical audio/video component than a computer. Also called a Media Center PC. See also *small form factor PC.*

hostname   The unique name of a network or Internet computer expressed as an English-language equivalent of an *IP address.*

hot spot   See *wireless hotspot.*

HTPC   See *home theater PC.*

HTTP   Hypertext Transfer Protocol, an Internet *protocol* that defines the format of *Uniform Resource Locator* addresses and how World Wide Web data is transmitted between a server and a browser. Part of the *TCP/IP* suite of protocols.

hub—A central connection point for network cables. They range in size from small boxes with six or eight RJ-45 connectors to large cabinets with dozens of ports for various cable types.

hypertext   In a World Wide Web page, an underlined word or phrase that takes you to a different website.

Hypertext Transport Protocol   See *HTTP.*

I-K

ICMP   See *Internet Control Message Protocol echo packet.*

IIS   See *Internet Information Server.*

infrastructure wireless network—A wireless network configuration that uses a wireless access point to receive and transmit signals from wireless computers. See also *ad hoc wireless network.*

internal address   The IP address that a computer, router, or other device uses on the local network. The conversion between the internal address and the *external address* is handled by *network address translation.*

Internet Control Message Protocol echo packet—A *packet* sent by the PING command to a remote computer that requests that the remote location send back a response packet. See also *ping.*

Internet Information Server   A service that implements a *web server* in Windows Vista's Home Premium, Business, Enterprise, and Ultimate versions.

Internet Protocol   A network layer protocol that defines the Internet's basic *packet* structure and its addressing scheme, and also handles routing of packets between *hosts*. See also *TCP/IP* and *Transmission Control Protocol*.

internetwork   A network that combines two or more *LANs* by means of a special device, such as a *bridge* or *router*. Internetworks are often called internets for short, but they shouldn't be confused with *the* Internet, the global collection of networks.

Intranet   The implementation of Internet technologies such as *TCP/IP* and World Wide Web servers for use within a corporate organization rather than for connection to the Internet as a whole.

IP   See *Internet Protocol.*

IP address   The unique address assigned to every *host* and *router* on the Internet. IP addresses are 32-bit values that are usually expressed in *dotted-decimal notation*. See also *hostname.*

IPX/SPX—Internet Packet eXchange/Sequenced Packet eXchange. IPX is a *network layer protocol* that addresses and routes *packets* from one network to another on an IPX *internetwork*. SPX, on the other hand, is a *transport layer protocol* that enhances the IPX protocol by providing reliable delivery. IPX/SPX is used by NetWare networks.

Kbps   One thousand bits per second (*bps*).

L

LAN   See *local area network.*

least privileged user   A user account level that has no more *permissions* than it requires.

local area network   A network in which all the computers occupy a relatively small geographical area, such as a department, office, home, or building. All the connections between computers are made via network cables.

local resource   Any peripheral, file, folder, or application that is either attached directly to your computer or resides on your computer's hard disk. See also *remote resource.*

M

MAC address   The Media Access Control address, which is the unique physical address assigned to a device such as a *network interface card* or *router*.

MAC address filtering   A security feature where a wireless access point only accepts connections from a list of authorized *MAC addresses*. If a hacker tries to connect to the network using a *NIC* that has a MAC address not on the list, the access point denies the connection

magic packet   The ethernet *packet* used to wake up a sleeping remote computer using *wake-on-LAN*. The magic packet is usually the hexadecimal constant FF FF FF FF FF FF followed by several repetitions of the computer's MAC address.

malware   The generic term for malicious software such as viruses, Trojan horses, and *spyware*.

Mb   See *megabit*.

Mbps   *Megabits* per second. This is the most common unit used to measure the transmission speed of *ethernet* networks.

Media Access Control address   See *MAC address*.

megabit   One million bits, in the context of data communications. In the context of memory or data storage, a megabit equals 1,048,576 bits.

modem   A device used to transmit data between computers via telephone lines. See also *modulation* and *demodulation*.

modulation   The conversion, performed by a *modem*, of digital data into an analog wave (a series of tones) that can be transmitted over a telephone line. See also *demodulation*.

Moore's law   Processing power doubles every 18 months (from Gordon Moore, cofounder of Intel).

motherboard   The computer's main circuit board, which includes connectors for the CPU, memory chips, hard drives, ports, expansion slots, controllers, and BIOS.

multimedia   The computer-based presentation of data using multiple modes of communication, including text, graphics, sound, animation, and video.

multithreading   A multitasking model in which multiple *threads* run simultaneously.

N

name resolution   A process that converts a *hostname* into an *IP address*. See *domain name system* and *Windows Internet Name Service*.

NAS   See *network attached storage*.

NAT   See *network address translation*.

NetBIOS   An API that handles the conversion between the network names of computers and their IP addresses.

NetBIOS name cache—A memory location used to improve network performance by storing names resolved by *NetBIOS*.

network   A collection of computers connected via special cables or other network media (such as infrared) to share files, folders, disks, peripherals, and applications.

network adapter   See *network interface card*.

network address translation   The process by which a *router* converts the public destination *IP address* specified with incoming Internet data to the private address of the network computer that requested the data. See also *gateway* and *routing table*.

network architecture   The hardware components that encompass a network, how those components connect together, and the methods those components use to send data from one part of the network to another.

network attached storage   A device that contains one or more hard drives and that plugs into a *switch* or router to enable computers on the network to store files on the device rather than on a network share.

network connection   A link to a remote resource, such as dial-up or broadband Internet service, dial-up or Internet-based virtual private networking, or ethernet or wireless networking.

network discovery   A Vista networking feature that, when turned on, means that you can see the other computers on your network and that the other computers can see yours.

network interface card   An adapter that usually slips into an expansion bus slot inside a *client* or *server* computer. (There are also external *NICs* that plug into parallel ports or PC Card slots, and internal NICs that are integrated into the system's *motherboard*.) The *NIC*'s main purpose is to serve as the connection point between the PC and the network. The *NIC*'s backplate (the portion of the *NIC* that you can see after the card is installed) contains one or more ports into which you plug a network cable.

network layer   That portion (Layer 3) of the *OSI model* which deals with how data is routed from one network location to another.

network layer protocol   A *protocol* in which no communications channel is established between nodes. Instead, the protocol builds each *packet* with all the information required for the network to deliver each packet and for the destination *node* to assemble everything. See also *Internet Protocol* and *transport layer protocol*.

network name   The unique name by which a computer is identified on the network.

Network News Transport Protocol   An Internet *protocol* that defines how Usenet newsgroups and postings are transmitted. Part of the *TCP/IP* suite of protocols.

network operating system   Operating system software that runs on a network *server* and provides the various network services for the network *clients*.

network redirector   A virtual *device driver* that lets applications find, open, read, write, and delete files on a remote drive.

network segment   A collection of network devices connected to a single *switch*.

network switch   See *switch*.

network utilization   The percent of available bandwidth that the computer's *network interface card* is currently using.

NIC   See *network interface card*.

NNTP   See *Network News Transport Protocol*.

node   A device connected to a network, such as a desktop computer, notebook, *router*, or *print server*.

nonunicast   A network *packet* exchanged between a single sender and multiple receivers. See also *unicast*.

NOS   See *network operating system*.

notification area   The box on the right side of the taskbar that Windows uses to display icons that tell you the current state of the system.

notwork   A network that is not working. Also called a *nyetwork*.

O

offline   Not connected to the network.

offline files   A Windows Vista feature that enables you to work with some network files and folders while you are *offline*.

Open Systems Interconnection model   See *OSI model*.

OSI model   A hierarchical, abstract description of the various aspects of network design. See *physical layer* (Layer 1), *data link layer* (Layer 2), *network layer* (Layer 3), *transport layer* (Layer 4), *session layer* (Layer 5), *presentation layer* (Layer 6), and *application layer* (Layer 7).

P-Q

P2P network   See *peer-to-peer network*.

packet   The data transfer unit used in network and *modem* communications. Each packet contains not only data, but also a *header*. In ethernet communications, each packet is usually called a *frame*.

Parkinson's law of data   Data expands to fill the space available for storage (from the original Parkinson's law: Work expands to fill the time available).

payload   In an *ethernet* data transfer, the part of the *frame* that includes a portion of the actual data being transferred.

peer-to-peer network   A network in which no one computer is singled out to provide special services. Instead, all the computers attached to the network have equal status (at least as far as the network is concerned), and all the computers can act as both *servers* and *clients*. See also *client/server network*.

permissions—Attributes applied to a user or *security group* that define the actions the user can take in a specified folder, usually a network share.

phishing   Creating a replica of an existing web page to fool a user into submitting personal, financial, or password data.

physical layer   The portion (layer 1) of the *OSI model* that deals with the technical specifications of networking hardware.

piggybacker   A *wardriver* who, if he finds a nonsecured network, uses it for free Internet access.

ping   To use the PING command to send an *Internet Control Message Protocol echo packet* to a remote location.

pop-up download   The download and installation of a program after the user clicks an option in a pop-up browser window, particularly when the option's intent is vaguely or misleadingly worded. See also *drive-by download*.

port forwarding   A router feature that forwards data sent to a specified port to the IP address of a network computer.

POST   At system startup, the POST detects and tests memory, ports, and basic devices such as the video adapter, keyboard, and disk drives. If everything passes, your system emits a single beep.

power cycle   To turn a device off, optionally wait 30 seconds for its components to spin down, and then turn the device back on.

Power-On Self Test   See *POST*.

powerline adapter   A networking device that you use to connect a computer to your network using the AC power lines in your home or office.

pre-shared key   A security system in which some secret information is shared with a person so that person can use the information later on. In the case of *WPA*, the shared secret is the password or passphrase that you pass along to your users so that they can connect to the wireless access point.

presentation layer   That portion (Layer 6) or the *OSI model* which deals with formatting, converting, or encrypting data received from the *session layer* so that it can be used by the *application layer*.

primary name   In a filename, the part to the left of the period.

print server   A printer connected directly to the network and so capable of being used by any computer on the network.

private IP address   The *IP address* used by your *router* on your local network. This address is usually either 192.168.1.1 or 192.168.0.1. See also *public IP address*.

process   A running instance of an executable program.

property sheet   A dialog box with controls that let you manipulate various properties of the underlying *object*.

protocol   A set of standards that defines the way information is exchanged between two systems across a network connection. See also *transport layer protocol* and *network layer protocol*.

PSK   See *pre-shared key*.

public IP address   The *IP address* that your ISP assigns dynamically to your router. See also *private IP address*.

R

redirector   A networking driver that provides all the mechanisms needed for an application to communicate with a remote device, including file reads and writes, print job submissions, and resource sharing.

Registry   A central repository that Windows Vista uses to store anything and everything that applies to your system's configuration. This includes hardware settings, object properties, operating system settings, and application options.

remote resource   Any peripheral, file, folder, or application that exists somewhere on the network. See also *local resource*.

repeater   A device that boosts a network cable's signal so that the length of the network can be extended. Repeaters are needed because copper-based cables suffer from attenuation—a phenomenon in which the degradation of the electrical signal carried over the cable is proportional to the distance the signal has to travel.

rip   To copy an audio CD's tracks to digital files on a computer.

RJ-45   The connectors attached to the ends of network cables and for the corresponding ports on network devices. Also: RJ45. See also *8P8C*.

router   A network device that uses *IP addresses* to route data from one part of the network to another, or between the network and the Internet.

routing   The process whereby *packets* travel from *host* to host until they eventually reach their destination.

routing table   A record of the *IP addresses* and network port numbers used by each device on the network, or by nearby routers on the Internet. The table is stored in and maintained by a *router*. See also *network address translation*.

S

security group—A security object that is defined with a specific set of *permissions*, and any user added to the group is automatically granted that group's permissions.

server   In a *client/server network*, a computer that provides and manages services (such as file and print sharing and security) for the users on the network.

service set identifier   The name of your wireless network.

session   The period between the initial connection between two network devices and the termination of that connection.

session layer   That portion (Layer 5) of the *OSI model* which deals with initiating, managing, and terminating connections between network devices.

SFF PC   See *small form factor PC*.

shielded twisted-pair   A *twisted-pair* cable shielded by a braided metal insulation to reduce interference problems. See also *unshielded twisted-pair*.

signal leakage   Wireless networking signals that extend outside of your home or office.

Simple Mail Transport Protocol   An Internet protocol that describes the format of Internet email messages and how those messages are delivered. Part of the *TCP/IP* suite of protocols.

small form factor PC   A computer that comes with a small case, particularly one designed for home theater setups. See also *home theater PC*.

SMTP   See *Simple Mail Transport Protocol*.

snagless   Describes an *RJ-45* connector that includes a rounded bit of rubber just behind or on either side of the plastic tab. The rubber helps the connector slide over any obstacles, thus preventing the plastic tab from snagging and breaking.

snap-in   A Microsoft Management Console tool that is wrapped in a Microsoft Common Console Document (.msc) file and can be added to the MMC interface.

sneakernet   A jocular way of referring to the "network" you use when you copy files from one computer to another by putting those files on a removable disk and walking that disk over to the other computer.

socket   In the *Transmission Control Protocol*, a communications channel between two *hosts* that consists of their *IP addresses* and *port numbers*.

spam   Unsolicited commercial email messages.

spyware   Any *malware* program that surreptitiously monitors a user's computer activities—particularly the typing of passwords, PINs, and credit card numbers—or harvests sensitive data on the user's computer, and then sends that information to an individual or a company via the user's Internet connection without the user's consent.

SSID   See *service set identifier*.

start topology   A network configuration where multiple network *nodes* are joined to a central connection point, such as a *switch* or *router*.

STP   See *shielded twisted-pair*.

subnet   A subsection of a network that uses related *IP addresses*.

subnet mask   A 32-bit value, usually expressed in *dotted-decimal notation*, that lets *IP* separate a network ID from a full *IP address* and thus determine whether the source and destination hosts are on the same network.

switch   A network device that connects multiple devices into a *network segment*, and that uses device *MAC addresses* to forward data from one part of the network segment to another, or across multiple network segments.

switched network   A network in which all the devices are connected via one or more *switches*.

switching table   A record of the *MAC addresses* and network port numbers used by each device on the network. The table is stored in and maintained by a *switch*.

symmetric NAT   A type of *network address translation*. When a client with a specific *internal address* uses a port to communicate with an external host, NAT creates a unique mapping for the internal address and port, and only that external host can use the mapping. If the client uses the same port to communicate with a different external host, an entirely new address/port mapping is created.

T

TCP   See *Transmission Control Protocol*.

TCP/IP   Transmission Control Protocol/Internet Protocol. TCP/IP is the lingua franca of most UNIX systems and the Internet as a whole. However, TCP/IP is also an excellent choice for other types of networks because it's routable, robust, and reliable.

TCP window   The amount of data that can be transmitted before the sending host must stop and wait for the receiving host to acknowledge that the data has been received. The bigger the TCP window, the better the performance of the connection. See also *window scaling*.

thread   A program task that can run independently of other tasks in the same program. In a spreadsheet, for example, you might have one thread for recalculating, another for printing, and a third for accepting keyboard input. See also *multithreading*.

topology   Describes how the various *nodes* that comprise a network—which include not only the computers, but also devices such as *hubs* and *bridges*—are connected.

Transmission Control Protocol—A *transport layer protocol* that sets up a connection between two *hosts* and ensures that data is passed between them reliably. If *packets* are lost or damaged during transmission, TCP takes care of retransmitting the packets. See also *Internet Protocol* and *TCP/IP*.

transport layer   That portion (Layer 4) of the *OSI model* which deals with ensuring that data is successfully and accurately transferred from one network location to another.

transport layer protocol   A *protocol* in which a virtual communications channel is established between two systems. The protocol uses this channel to send *packets* between *nodes*. See also *Transmission Control Protocol* and *network layer protocol*.

Trojan horse   A computer program that installs itself on a computer without authorization and that is designed to run surreptitiously on that system to steal sensitive data or perform other malicious activities. See also *virus*.

twisted-pair   An *ethernet* network cable that consists of four pairs of twisted copper wires that together form a circuit that can transmit data. See also *shielded twisted-pair* and *unshielded twisted-pair*.

U-V

UAC   See *User Account Control*.

UDP   See *User Datagram Protocol*.

unicast   A network *packet* exchanged between a single sender and a single receiver. See also *nonunicast*.

Uniform Resource Locator   An Internet addressing scheme that spells out the exact location of a net resource. Most URLs take the following form:

```
protocol://host.domain/directory/file.name
```

`protocol`	The TCP/IP protocol to use for retrieving the resource (such as HTTP or FTP)
`host.domain`	The domain name of the host computer where the resource resides
`directory`	The host directory that contains the resource
`file.name`	The filename of the resource

Universal Plug and Play   A technology that uses standards such as *TCP/IP*, *UDP*, and *HTTP* to make networking devices easier to manage and configure.

unshielded twisted-pair   A *twisted-pair* cable that has no insulation. See also *shielded twisted-pair*.

UPnP   See *Universal Plug and Play*.

uptime   The amount of time that some system has been running continuously since the last time the system was started.

URL   See *Uniform Resource Locator*.

User Account Control   A Windows Vista security feature that gives each user only the minimum level of *permissions* required to perform day-to-day tasks, and requires that the user *elevate* those permissions to perform tasks that might compromise the computer's security.

User Datagram Protocol   A standard protocol used for sending short bits of data called *datagrams*, a form of *packet*.

UTP   See *unshielded twisted-pair*.

virus   A computer program installed on a computer without authorization and designed to corrupt the system or to destroy data. See also *Trojan horse*.

W-Z

wake-on-LAN   A process that enables a *NIC* to wake up a computer when the NIC receives a special *ethernet* packet called a *magic packet*.

WAN   See *wide area network*.

warchalking   Using chalk to place a special symbol on the sidewalk or other surface that indicates there's a nonsecure wireless network nearby.

wardriver   A person who engages in *wardriving*. See also *piggybacker*.

wardriving   An activity where a person drives through various neighborhoods with a portable computer or another device set up to look for available wireless networks.

web server   A computer that accepts and responds to remote requests for pages and other web content that are stored on the server. See also *Internet Information Server*.

WEP   Wired Equivalent Privacy, an encryption standard that protects wireless communications with (usually) a 26-character security key. WEP has been superseded by *WPA* and *WPA2*.

Wi-Fi   The most common wireless networking technology. See also *802.11*.

wide area network   A network that consists of two or more *local area* networks or *internetworks* that are spaced out over a relatively large geographical area, such as a state, a country, or the entire world. The networks in a WAN typically are connected via high-speed fiber-optic phone lines, microwave dishes, or satellite links.

window scaling   A technology that modifies the size of the *TCP window* to achieve the optimum data transfer rate over *TCP*.

Windows Internet Name Service   A service that maps NetBIOS names (the names you assign to computers in the Identification tab of the Network properties sheet) to the *IP addresses* assigned via *DHCP*.

WINS   See *Windows Internet Name Service*.

wireless access point   A device that receives and transmits signals from wireless computers to form a wireless network.

wireless fidelity   See *Wi-Fi*.

wireless gateway   A *wireless access point* that has a built-in *router* to provide Internet access to all the computers on the network.

wireless hot spot   A public wireless network that shares an Internet connection, either free of charge or for a fee.

wireless range extender   A device used to boost signals going to and from a *wireless access point*.

WPA   Wi-Fi Protected Access, an encryption protocol that uses most of the IEEE 802.11i wireless security standard and protects wireless networks using a *pre-shared key*.

WPA2   Am encryption protocol that implements the full IEEE 802.11i wireless security standard. WPA2 Personal requires a simple *pre-shared key* pass phrase for access (so it's suitable for homes and small offices), whereas WPA2 Enterprise requires a dedicated authentication server.

Index

NUMBERS

10BASE-T Ethernet standard, 12

100BASE-T (Fast Ethernet) standard, 12

802.11a Wi-Fi standard, 41

802.11b Wi-Fi standard, 41

802.11g Wi-Fi standard, 42

802.11n Wi-Fi standard, 42-43

1000BASE-T (Gigabit Ethernet) standard, 13

A

AC outlets, powerline adapters, 32

ad hoc wireless networks, 40, 161

Add Counters dialog (Performance Monitor), 403

Add Network Location Wizard, adding remote folders to network locations, 181-182

Add Printer Wizard, adding shared printers to networks, 183

Address bar
network addresses, viewing, 175-176
phishing attacks, 307

administrative passwords, specifying in wireless networks, 336-337, 340

Administrator accounts, 283, 301-303

Administrator groups, 283
elevating privileges, 284
security groups, 282

ADSL (Asymmetric Digital Subscriber Line) broadband modems, 105

advanced Remote Desktop connections, 374-379

Allow and Block Specific Websites option (Web Restrictions page), 290

Allow Connections from Computers Running Any Version of Remote Desktop option (Remote Desktop), 371

Allow Connections Only from Computers Running Remote Desktop with Network Level Authentication option (Remote Desktop), 371

Allow This Device to Wake the Computer check box (User Account Control dialog), 153

Always Ask for Credentials check box (Remote Desktop Connection dialog), 324

Always Available Offline dialog (Offline Files feature), 239

announcements (calendars), sending, 221

anonymous access, disabling in
FTP sites, 478-481
IIS websites, 454-455

AntiSpyware (MS). *See* Windows Defender

antivirus software, 305

AP (Access Points)

infrastructure wireless networks, 40

WAP, 47-48

encryption, 343-346

firewalls, 50

purchasing, 56

router configuration, 49, 85-89

security, 336

signal leakage, 340

SSID broadcasting, 86

switches, 49

application layer (OSI model), 10

Application Restrictions page (Parental
Controls), 291

architectures (network)

Ethernet, 10

10BASE-T Ethernet standard, 12

100BASE-T (Fast Ethernet) standard, 12

1000BASE-T (Gigabit Ethernet) standard,
13

broadband modems, 107

DMR, 32

frames, 11

hardware buyer's guide, 32-37

MAC addresses, 11

NAS, 30

network cable, 11, 18-21, 34-35

NIC, 13-17, 33-34

payloads, 11

powerline adapters, 32

print servers, 31

routers, 24-28, 36-37

standards development, 13

switches, 22-24, 35-36

wireless networks, 157

ad hoc wireless networks, 40, 161

administrative passwords, 336-337, 340

configuring, 113-117, 163

disconnecting from, 117-118

DMR, 53

finders, 51

hardware buyer's guide, 53-57

hidden network connections, 159-160

infrastructure wireless networks, 40

interference, 426

Manage Wireless Networks window,
163-165

NIC, 44-47, 54-55, 356-357

packet sniffers, 341

piggybackers, 335

print servers, 52

radio transceivers, 40

range extenders, 50

removing, 170

renaming, 166-167

reordering, 167

resetting routers, 427

RF signals, 40

security, 165, 336-337, 340-348,
351-362

signal leakage, 340

signal ranges, 340

SSID, 159, 347-348, 351-355

troubleshooting, 426-427

user-specific connections, 168

WAP, 47-50, 56

warchalking, 335

wardriving, 335

Wi-Fi, 41-43

audio

audio cards, digital media hub requirements, 200

digital media hub connections, 205

television, audio receiver connectors,
203-204

authentication, IIS default websites,
454-455

Auto Crossover, switch support, 24, 36

automatic IP addressing, 142-143

Automatic Sleep mode, disabling, 367-368

automatic updates, configuring, 298-300

B

Back Up Files Wizard, 214-216

Backup and Restore Center, 213-216

Backup Status and Configuration command, 216

backups
  Complete PC Backup feature, 216
  encryption keys, 244
  networks
    Backup and Restore Center, 213-216
    NAS, 212
  system image backups, 216

Baseline Security Analyzer, 330-332

basic authentication, IIS default websites, 454-455

basic Remote Desktop connections, 373-374

Belkin routers
  administrative passwords, changing, 336
  broadband connections, configuring, 73
  DHCP routers, enabling in, 82
  encryption settings, changing, 342
  firmware, updating, 67
  IP addresses, changing, 64
  MAC address filtering, enabling, 358
  port forwarding, configuring, 384-385
  SSID
    changing default SSID, 352
    disabling broadcasting, 348
  status-checks, 90
  UPnP, enabling in, 78
  WAP configuration, 86

binary values, converting to decimal (IP addresses), 26

Block File Downloads option (Web Restrictions page), 291

Block Web Content Automatically option (Web Restrictions page), 291

blocking
  file downloads, 291
  web contents, 291
  websites, 290

Bluetooth, 44

boots (cable), 35

broadband connections, configuring in routers, 71-76

broadband modems, 105-108

browsing directories, 452

buses, SFF PCs, 197

buying
  AP, WAP, 56
  network cable, Ethernet networks, 34-35
  NIC, 33-34, 54-55
  routers, 36-37
  switches, 35-36

Bytes Total/Sec performance counter (Performance Monitor), 404

C

cable
  boots, 35
  broadband modem network configuration, 105-106
  network cable, 11
    crossover cable, 20-21
    purchasing, 34-35
    twisted-pair cable, 18-19
  network connections, 111
  OTA broadcasts signals, 199

snagless connectors, 35
troubleshooting, 421-422

cable broadband modems, network configuration, 105-106

CableCards, digital media hub requirements, 200

Calculator, converting binary values to decimal, 26

Calendar
publishing, 217-218
shared calendars, 221
subscribing to via
subscribe message, 219
Windows Calendar, 220

CDs, ripping to network shares, 223-224

Change Network Icon dialog (Network and Sharing Center), 136

Change Settings of This Connection command
Network Connections window, 148
User Account Control dialog, 142

Change Settings window
Check for Updates but Let Me Choose Whether to Download and Install Them option, 300
Download Updates, but Let Me Choose Whether to Install Them option, 300
Install Updates Automatically option, 299
Never Check for Updates option, 300
View Installed Updates link, 299

children, Parental Control, 286-288, 291

Choose a Connection Option dialog (Manage Wireless Networks window), 159

Choose a Different Restore Point option (System Restore), 428

closing programs as troubleshooting technique, 414

Collect Information About Computer Usage option (Parental Controls), 289

command-line, mapping folders at, 179

commands, network addresses as, 176

Complete PC Backup feature, 216

component connectors (television), 202

composite connectors (television), 202

computer names, changing (network configuration), 112-113

configuring
automatic updates, 298-300
broadband connections, routers, 71-76
DDNS for Remote Desktop, 389-392
files
as offline files, 239
sharing permissions, 315-319
networks
broadband modems, 105-108
cable layouts, 111
changing computer names, 112-113
changing workgroup names, 112-113
installing internal NIC, 98-104
router connections, 108-109
switch connections, 110
wireless networks, 113-117
port forwarding, Remote Desktop, 384-387
Remote Desktop hosts
via Vista, 368-371
via Windows XP, 371
routers, WAP, 85-89
slideshows, 228-230
static IP addresses, 145
assigning, 147-148
displaying DNS addresses, 146-147
updates, 298-300
user accounts, Remote Desktop hosts, 367
WAP, routers, 85-89

Windows Firewall
  exceptions for Remote Desktop, 368-369
  FTP server exceptions for FTP default sites, 464
  in Remote Desktop, 382
  web server exceptions for IIS default websites, 434-435
Windows Mail, disabling contact attachment conversions to vCards, 259
Windows Meeting Space, 264

Connect Automatically When This Network Is In Range check box (Manage Wireless Networks window), 164

Connect Even If the Network Is Not Broadcasting check box (Manage Wireless Networks window), 164

Connect to a More Preferred Network If Available check box (Manage Wireless Networks window), 164

Connect to a Network command (Network icon), 122

Connect to a Network dialog, 114-118

Connected with Internet access status indicator (Network icon), 123

Connected without Internet access status indicator (Network icon), 123

connecting routers, 60

connection bar (Remote Desktop), 379

connections (network)
  disabling, 154-155
  IP addresses
    automatic IP addressing, 142-143
    displaying current IP addresses, 143-144
    static IP addresses, 145-148
  MAC addresses, finding, 149
  PING command, checking via, 419-420
  renaming, 141
  status checks, 413-414
  troubleshooting, 412
  waking up computers via, 151-154

contacts (trusted)
  adding people as, 261
  attachments, disabling conversions to vCards, 259
  sending data to other people, 260

Content View (IIS Manager), 438

Control Panel, configuring Parental Controls, 289

converting binary values to decimal (IP addresses), 26

cooling systems
  digital media hub requirements, 198
  HTPC, 198

covert reinstalls (spyware), 296, 486

CPU section (Resource Monitor), 400

crossover cable, 20-21

Current Bandwidth performance counter (Performance Monitor), 404

Custom Scan (Windows Defender), 303

Customize Network Settings dialog (Network and Sharing Center), 136

customizing networks, 135-136

D

D-Link routers
  administrative passwords, changing, 337
  broadband connections, configuring, 74
  DDNS configuration, 390
  DHCP routers, enabling in, 83
  encryption settings, changing, 343
  firmware, updating, 68
  IP addresses, changing, 64
  MAC address filtering, enabling, 359
  port forwarding, configuring, 385-386
  SSID
    changing default SSID, 353
    disabling broadcasting, 349
  status-checks, 91

UPnP, enabling in, 78
WAP configuration, 87-88

data storage
digital media hub requirements, 198
NAS, backing up to, 212

DDNS (Dyanmic DNS), configuring for Remote Desktop, 389-392

decimals, converting binary values to (IP addresses), 26

default FTP sites
accessing, 464
disabling anonymous access, 478-481
via Internet, 466
via networks, 466
files, adding to, 470
folders
adding to, 471-472
changing location of, 475-476
securing, 480
ftproot folder
setting permissions, 469-470
viewing, 467
messages, displaying, 477-478
renaming, 475
restarting, 474
stopping, 473-474
viewing via IIS Manager, 468
Windows Firewall exceptions, creating, 464

default website folder (IIS), 437
default home pages, changing, 443
files, adding to, 441-442
folders, adding to, 443-445
permissions, setting, 440

Defender (Windows), 297, 303

deleting wireless network connections, 170

Details view (Network window), 130

device drivers
internal NIC, installing in, 98-100
updating, 425-426

Device Manager
internal NIC installations, checking, 104
NIC, viewing in, 423-424

DHCP (Dynamic Host Configuration Protocol)
broadband connections, router configuration, 72
IP addresses, 27
servers, enabling in routers, 81-85

Diagnose and Repair command (Network icon), 123

digital audio receiver connectors, digital media hub connections, 204

digital media hubs
computers
audio card requirements, 200
CableCards, 200
cooling system requirements, 198
HDTV requirements, 200
HTPCs, 196
keyboard requirements, 200
memory requirements, 199
network card requirements, 200
processor requirements, 198-199
SFF PCs, 197
storage requirements, 198
tv tuner requirements, 199
upgrade requirements, 196
video card requirements, 199
DMR, 204
television
audio receiver connectors, 203-204
component connectors, 202
DVI connectors, 203
HDMI connectors, 203
HDTV requirements, 201
NTSC requirements, 201-202
S-Video connectors, 202

UPnP devices, 205

Xbox 360 connections, 205-206

directory browsing, 452

Disable This Network Device command (Network Connections window), 154

disabling

Administrator accounts, 301-303

anonymous access

FTP sites, 478-481

IIS websites, 454-455

Automatic Sleep mode, 367-368

default documents in IIS websites, 451-453

file types in Windows Mail, 306

network connections, 154-155

SSID broadcasting, 347-348, 351

Disconnect From command (Network icon), 122

Disconnect option (Connect to a Network dialog), 118

Disconnected icons (Network Connections window), 141

Disconnected status indicator (Network icon), 124

disconnecting from

mapped network folders, 180

Remote Desktop, 380

wireless networks, 117

Disk section (Resource Monitor), 401

disk space, adjusting for offline files, 240-242

Disk Usage tab (Offline Files feature), 241-242

Display tab (Remote Desktop Connection dialog), 376

displaying

messages to FTP sites, 477-478

network images in Slide Show gadget, 234

DMR (Digital Media Receivers), 204

Ethernet networks, 32

wireless DMR, 53

DNS (Domain Name Systems), static IP addresses, 146-147

Do Not Allow Attachments to Be Saved or Opened That Could Potentially Be a Virus option (Virus Protection group), 306

domain-spoofing, 308

domains, 135

dotted-quad notation, IP addresses, 26

Download Updates, but Let Me Choose Whether to Install Them option (Change Settings window), 300

downloading

drive-by downloads, 296

files, blocking, 291

Internet Connectivity Evaluation tool, 94

pop-up downloads, 296, 494

Drives check box (Remote Desktop Connection dialog), 378

DVI (Digital Visual Interface) connectors (television), 203

dynamic IP addresses, 26

E

echo packets (ICMP), 419

ECN (Explicit Congestion Notification), routers, 94

email

sending meeting invitations via (Windows Meeting Space), 270

viruses, 304-305

Windows Mail, Virus Protection group, 305

encryption

backups, 244

offline files, 244

wireless networks
  WEP, 341
  WPA, 341-346
  WPA2, 341-344

Encryption tab (Offline Files feature), 244

Enforce Current Settings option (Parental Controls), 289

Error status indicator (Network icon), 124

Ethernet networks, 10
  10BASE-T Ethernet standard, 12
  100BASE-T (Fast Ethernet) standard, 12
  1000BASE-T (Gigabit Ethernet) standard, 13
  broadband modems, 107
  DMR, 32
  frames, 11
  hardware buyer's guide, 32-37
  MAC addresses, 11
  NAS, 30
  network cable, 11
    crossover cable, 20-21
    purchasing, 34-35
    twisted-pair cable, 18-19
  NIC, 13
    motherboard NIC, 14
    network adapters, 16
    PC Card NIC, 17
    purchasing, 33-34
    USB NIC, 16
  payloads, 11
  powerline adapters, 32
  print servers, 31
  routers
    as firewalls, 27
    IP addresses, 24-26
    purchasing, 36-37
    as switches, 28
  standards, development of, 13
  switches, 22-24, 35-36

Experience tab (Remote Desktop Connection dialog), 378-379

Explorer (Internet)
  lock icon, phishing attacks, 308
  Phishing Filter, 308-310
  Security Report area, 309-310

F

fans (cooling systems)
  digital media hub requirements, 198
  HTPC, 198

Fast Ethernet (100BASE-T) standard, 12

Features View (IIS Manager), 439

Feedback page (Phishing Filter), 310

files
  downloading, blocking, 291
  FTP sites, adding to, 470
  IIS websites, adding to, 441-442
  sharing
    activating, 185-186
    File Sharing setting (Sharing and Discovery section), 185-186
    File Sharing Wizard, 190-192, 314
    hiding shared files, 320-323
    permissions, 315-319
    viewing shared files, 192
  storing, NAS, 30

filtering
  MAC addresses, 356-362
  Phishing Filter (Internet Explorer), 308-310

finding MAC addresses, 149

firewalls
  routers as, 27
  WAP, 50
  Windows Firewall
    FTP default sites, 464
    IIS default websites, 434-435

Remote desktop exceptions, 368-369

verifying activation, 295

firmware

defining, 43

routers

updating in, 66-70

upgrading in, 414

folders

FTP sites, adding to, 471-472

IIS websites, adding to, 443-445

mapping

at command-line, 179

creating mapped network folders, 177-178

disconnecting mapped network folders, 180

Public Folder Sharing, 186

remote folders, creating network locations for, 180-182

shared folders

File Sharing Wizard, 190-192

mapping to local drive letters, 177-180

monitoring, 405-409

Public Folder Sharing, 188

viewing, 192

form-submittal addresses, phishing attacks, 307

frames, Ethernet networks, 11

FTP Publishing Service

automatically starting, 463

default FTP sites

accessing, 464

adding files to, 470

adding folders to, 471-472

changing folder location, 475-476

disabling anonymous access, 478-481

displaying messages, 477-478

renaming, 475

restarting, 474

securing FTP folders, 480-481

setting permissions, 469-470

stopping, 473-474

viewing, 467

ftproot folder

setting permissions, 469-470

viewing, 467

installing, 462

launching, 462-463

FTP servers, Windows Firewall, 464

FTP sites

accessing, 464-466

annonymous access, disabling, 478-481

files, adding to, 470

folders

adding to, 471-472

changing folder location, 475-476

securing, 480

ftproot folder

setting permissions, 469-470

viewing, 467

messages, displaying, 477-478

renaming, 475

restarting, 474

stopping, 473-474

viewing via IIS Manager, 468

Windows Firewall exceptions, creating, 464

ftproot folder (FTP default websites), 467-470

Full Control permissions, 318

Full Scan (Windows Defender), 303

Full System Scan (Windows Defender), 303

G - H

games, Xbox 360 digital media hub connections, 205-206

General tab (Remote Desktop Connection dialog), 374

Gigabit Ethernet (1000BASE-T) standard, 13

Group Policy Object Editor, Prohibit 'Make Available Offline' option, 243

handouts, sharing in meetings (Windows Meeting Space), 275

HDCP (High-Bandwidth Digital Content Protection), 199

HDMI (High-Definition Multimedia Interface) connectors (television), 203

HDTV (High-Definition TV)
CableCards, 200
digital media hub requirements, 201

Help and Support Center, 415

Help Topics section (Resource Monitor), 401

Hibernate mode, 151

hidden network connections, wireless networks, 159-160

hiding
shared folders, 320-323
usernames in logon screen, 328-330

home pages, changing in IIS default websites, 443

homograph spoofing, 308

hot spot finders. *See* **wireless networks, finders**

hot spots (Wi-Fi), 43

HTPC (Home Theater PCs), 196-198

I

ICMP (Internet Control Message Protocol), echo packets, 419

icons
network icons, changing, 182
Network Locations group, adding to, 180-182

IDN (International Domain Name) spoofing, 308

IIS (Internet Information Services)
installing, 433
maximum connection limits, 433
simultaneous data request limits, 432
Vista versions of, 432
website limits, 433
websites
accessing, 434-436
adding files to, 441-442
adding folders to, 443-445
basic authentication, 454-455
changing default home pages in, 443
changing folder location, 448
configuring Windows Firewall exceptions, 434-435
default website folder, 437, 440-445
disabling anonymous access, 454-455
disabling default documents, 451-453
limits, 433
renaming, 448
restarting, 448
setting default documents, 449-450
stopping, 447
viewing server logs, 456-458
viewing via IIS Manager, 438
wwwroot folder, 437, 440-445
Windows Firewall, configuring IIS default website exceptions, 434-435
Windows XP restrictions, 433

IIS Manager
Content View, 438
default FTP sites
adding files to, 470
adding folders to, 471-472
changing folder location, 475-476
disabling anonymous access, 478-481
displaying messages, 477-478
renaming, 475
restarting, 474

securing FTP folders, 480

stopping, 473-474

viewing, 468

Features View, 439

launching, 438

websites

basic authentication, 454-455

changing folder location, 448

disabling anonymous access, 454-455

disabling default documents, 451-453

renaming, 448

restarting, 448

setting default documents, 449-450

stopping, 447

viewing default websites, 438

viewing server logs, 456-458

images

network images, displaying in Slide Show gadget, 234

network shares, importing to, 222

phishing attacks, 307

infrastructure wireless networks, 40

Install Updates Automatically option (Change Settings window), 299

installing

covert reinstalls (spyware), 296, 486

device drivers, internal NIC, 98-100

FTP Publishing Service, 462

IIS, 433

internal NIC, network configuration, 98-104

Internet Connectivity Evaluation tool, 95

Remote Desktop clients via Windows XP, 372-373

interference (wireless networks), 426

interlaced scanning (television), 202

internal NIC (network interface cards)

device driver installation, 98-100

installing, 100-104

wireless networks, 44

Internet

default FTP sites, accessing, 466

IIS websites, accessing, 436

Remote Desktop connections, 380

changing listening ports, 381

configuring port forwarding, 384-387

configuring Windows Firewall, 382

determining host IP addresses, 383-384

host IP addresses, new port connections, 388-389

Internet Connectivity Evaluation Tool

downloading, 94

installing, 95

Multiple Simultaneous Connection States test, 94

Network Address Translation Type test, 93

operating, 95

router tests, 93-95

TCP High Performance test, 94

Traffic Congestion test, 94

UPnP Support test, 94

Internet Explorer

lock icon, phishing attacks, 308

Phishing Filter, 308-310

Security Report area, 309-310

Invitation Details dialog (People Near Me dialog), 272-273

invitation files

creating, 271-272

opening, 274

Invite People dialog (People Near Me dialog)

creating invitation files, 271

sending invitations to meetings, 269

IP addresses

assigning, 26

automatic IP addressing, 142-143

binary values, converting to decimal, 26

current addresses, displaying, 143-144

DHCP, 27
dotted-quad notation, 26
dynamic IP addresses, 26
private IP addresses, 27
public IP addresses, 26
Remote Desktop hosts
    determining in, 383-384
    new port connections, 388-389
routers, 24-26
    accessing setup pages, 61
    changing in, 63-64
static IP addresses, 145-148

J - K - L

Junk E-Mail folder (Windows Mail), 305

keyboards, digital media hub requirements, 200

kids, Parental Control (security), 286-288,
291

LCD (liquid crystal display) monitors, 228

least-privileged users (UAC), 283

links (Web), phishing attacks, 307

Linksys routers
    administrative passwords, changing, 338
    broadband connections, configuring, 75
    DDNS configuration, 391
    DHCP routers, enabling in, 83-84
    encryption settings, changing, 344
    firmware, updating, 69-70
    IP addresses, changing, 64
    MAC address filtering, enabling, 360
    port forwarding, configuring, 386
    SSID
        changing default SSID, 353
        disabling broadcasting, 349-351
    status-checks, 91

UPnP, enabling in, 79
WAP configuration, 88-89

List Folder Contents permissions, 319

listening ports, changing in Remote
Desktop, 381

local drives, mapping shared folders to,
177-180

Local Resources tab (Remote Desktop
Connection dialog), 376-377

lock icon (Internet Explorer), phishing
attacks, 308

logging off Vista as troubleshooting technique, 414

logon hours, user accounts
    automatically logging off users when
        hours expire, 327-328
    setting for, 326-327

logon screen, hiding usernames, 328-330

lookalike attacks, 308

M

MAC (Media Access Control) addresses
    Ethernet networks, 11
    filtering, 356-362
    finding, 149
    NIC, finding in, 356-357

magic packets, NIC, 153

Mail (Windows)
    file types, disabling, 306
    Junk E-mail folder, turning on/off
        Preview pane, 305
    phishing protection, turning on/off, 310
    Virus Protection group, 305-306

malware, 295, 491

Manage Wireless Networks window, 158
    ad hoc connections, 161
    Choose a Connection Option dialog,
        Manually Connect to a Wireless
        Network command, 159

configurging automatic connections in, 163

Connect Automatically When This Network Is In Range check box, 164

Connect Even If the Network Is Not Broadcasting check box, 164

Connect to a More Preferred Network If Available check box, 164

hidden network connections, 159-160

removing wireless network connections, 170

renaming networks, 166-167

reordering networks, 167

Save This Network check box, 163

Security tab, 165

Set Up a Wireless Ad Hoc Network dialog, 161

Start This Connection Automatically check box, 163

storing wireless networks in, 163

user-specific wireless network connections, 168

Manually Connect to a Wireless Network command (Choose a Connection Option dialog), 159

Map area (Network and Sharing Center), 127

Map Network Drive dialog, creating mapped network folders, 177-178

mapping
mapped network folders
creating, 177-178
disconnecting, 180
mapping at command line
shared folders to local drive letters, 177-180

maximum connection limits (IIS), 433

MBSA (Microsoft Baseline Security Analyzer), 330-331

Media Player (Windows)
media sharing, 207-209
slideshow operation, 230-231

Meeting Space (Windows)
configuring, 264
handouts, sharing in meetings, 275
invitation files, creating, 271-272
joining meetings, 266
launching, 264-265
People Near Me dialog, 257
Invitation Details dialog, 272-273
Invite People dialog, 269-271
receiving invitations to meetings, 272-273
sending invitations to meetings, 269
setting options, 262-263
signing out of, 264
trusted contacts, 259-261
receiving invitations
opening invitation files, 274
People Near Me, 272-273
sharing handouts in meetings, 275
sending invitations to meetings
People Near Me, 269
via Email, 270
shared sessions
controlling, 277-278
ending, 278
starting, 276
starting meetings, 267

memory, digital media hub requirements, 199

Memory section (Resource Monitor), 401

Microsoft AntiSpyware. *See* Windows Defender

Microsoft Knowledge Base website, 418

Microsoft Product Support Services website, 418

Microsoft Security website, 418

Microsoft TechNet website, 418

MIMO (multiple-input multiple-output) technology, 802.11 Wi-Fi standard, 42

modems
  broadband modems, 105-108
  power cycling, 414

Modify permissions, 319

monitoring
  network performance, 396
    Performance Monitor, 400-403
    Task Manager, 397-400
  shared folders
    closing user sessions/files, 408-409
    launching Shared Folders snap-in, 405
    viewing current connections, 406
    viewing open files, 407-408
    viewing Vista connections, 407

monitors
  LCD monitors, 228
  slideshows
    running from Media Player, 230-231
    running from network shares, 233
    running from Photo Gallery, 232
    screensaver slideshows, 228-230

motherboard NIC (Network Interface Cards), 14, 47

multichannel analog audio receiver connectors, digital media hub connections, 204

multimedia. *See* digital media hubs

Multiple Simultaneous Connection States test (Internet Connectivity Evaluation Tool), 94

N

naming
  IIS default websites, 448
  networks, 136
    network connections, 141
    wireless networks, 166-167

NAS (Network-Attached Storage)
  backing up to, 212
  Ethernet networks, 30

NAT (Network Address Translation), 93

NDF (Network Diagnostics Framework), 412

Netgear routers
  administrative passwords, changing, 339
  broadband connections, configuring, 75-76
  DDNS configuration, 392
  DHCP routers, enabling in, 84-85
  encryption settings, changing, 345
  firmware, updating, 70
  IP addresses, changing, 66
  MAC address filtering, enabling, 361-362
  port forwarding, configuring, 387
  SSID
    changing default SSID, 355
    disabling broadcasting, 351
  status-checks, 92
  UPnP, enabling in, 79-81
  WAP configuration, 89

network adapters, 16

Network Address Translation Type test (Internet Connectivity Evaluation Tool), 93

network addresses
  Address bar, viewing in, 175-176
  as commands, 176
  opening shared resources from, 176

Network and Sharing Center, 123-125
  Change Network Icon dialog, 136
  Customize Network Settings dialog, 136
  launching, 126-127
  Map area, 127
  Network area, 127
  Network Diagnostic tool, 412
  network discovery, turning on/off, 129
  Network Map, 132

Sharing and Discovery section, 128
  File Sharing setting, 185-186
  Password Sharing setting, 187
  Printer Sharing setting, 187
  Public Folder Sharing setting, 186-188
Tasks pane, 128
View Network Computers and Devices option, viewing shared resources, 172
View Status link, 133

network cable, 11
boots, 35
crossover cable, 20-21
puchasing, 34-35
snagless connectors, 35
twisted-pair cable
  RJ-11 jacks, 19
  RJ-45 jacks, 19
  STP, 18-19, 34
  UTP, 19, 34

network cards, digital media hub requirements, 200

Network Connection Details dialog (Network Connections window), 134, 149

Network Connections window
Change Settings of This Connection command, 148
Disable This Network Device command, 154
Disconnected icons, 141
Network Connection Details dialog, 149
User Account Control dialog
  Allow This Device to Wake the Computer check box, 153
  Change Settings of This Connection command, 142
View Status of This Connection command, 144-146
Wired icons, 140
Wireless icons, 141

Network Diagnostic tool (Network Center), 412

network discovery, turning on/off, 128-129, 413

Network icon
Connect to a Network command, 122
Diagnose and Repair command, 123
Disconnect From command, 122
Network and Sharing Center command, 123
right-clicking, 122
status indicators, 123
Turn Off Notification of New Networks command, 122
Turn On Activity Animation command, 122
turning on/off, 124

network layer (OSI model), 10

Network Locations group, adding icons to, 180-182

Network Map (Network and Sharing Center), 132

Network section (Resource Monitor), 401

Network window
Details view, 130
opening, 130
routers, accessing setup pages, 62

networking interface
Network Center, Network Diagnostic tool, 412
Windows Meeting Space
  configuring, 264
  controlling shared sessions, 277-278
  creating invitation files, 271-272
  ending shared sessions, 278
  joining meetings, 266
  launching, 264-265
  People Near Me dialog, 257, 262-264, 269-273
  receiving invitations to meetings, 272-274

sending invitations to meetings, 269-270

sharing handouts in meetings, 275

starting meetings, 267

starting shared sessions, 276

networks

backing up to

Backup and Restore Center, 213-216

NAS, 212

configuring

broadband modems, 105-108

cable layouts, 111

changing computer names, 112-113

changing workgroup names, 112-113

installing internal NIC, 98-104

router connections, 108-109

switch connections, 110

wireless networks, 113-117

connections

automatic IP addressing, 142-143

checking via PING command, 419-420

disabling, 154-155

displaying current IP addresses, 143-144

finding MAC addresses, 149

renaming, 141

status checks, 413-414

static IP addresses, 145-148

troubleshooting, 412

waking up computers via, 151-154

*wireless networks. **See** networks, wireless networks*

customizing, 135-136

default FTP sites, accessing, 466

domains, 135

Ethernet, 10

10BASE-T Ethernet standard, 12

100BASE-T (Fast Ethernet) standard, 12

1000BASE-T (Gigabit Ethernet) standard, 13

broadband modems, 107

DMR, 32

frames, 11

hardware buyer's guide, 32-37

MAC addresses, 11

NAS, 30

network cable, 11, 18-21, 34-35

NIC, 13-17, 33-34

payloads, 11

powerline adapters, 32

print servers, 31

routers, 24-28, 36-37

standards development, 13

switches, 22-24, 35-36

icons, changing, 136

IIS websites, accessing, 436

names, changing, 136

offline files, 242-243

performance monitoring, 396

Performance Monitor, 400-403

Task Manager, 397-400

private networks, 135

public networks, 135

segments, 23

shares

importing pictures to, 222

recording television to, 225-227

ripping CDs to, 223-224

slideshows, running from, 233

troubleshooting, 412-414

type of, changing, 136

wireless networks, 157

ad hoc wireless networks, 40, 161

administrative passwords, 336-337, 340

configuring, 113-117, 163

disconnecting from, 117-118

DMR, 53

finders, 51

hardware buyer's guide, 53-57

hidden network connections, 159-160

infrastructure wireless networks, 40

interference, 426

Manage Wireless Networks window, 163-165

NIC, 44-47, 54-55, 356-357

packet sniffers, 341

piggybackers, 335

print servers, 52

radio transceivers, 40

range extenders, 50

removing, 170

renaming, 166-167

reordering, 167

resetting routers, 427

RF signals, 40

security, 165, 336-337, 340-348, 351-362

signal leakage, 340

signal ranges, 340

SSID, 159, 347-348, 351-355

troubleshooting, 426-427

user-specific connections, 168

WAP, 47-50, 56

warchalking, 335

wardriving, 335

Wi-Fi, 41-43

Never Check for Updates option (Change Settings window), 300

newsgroups, troubleshooting resources, 419

NIC (Network Interface Cards), 13

device drivers
    installing internal NIC, 98-100
    updating, 425-426

Device Manager, viewing in, 423-424

internal NIC
    checking installations, 104
    device driver installation, 98-100
    installing, 100-104

MAC addresses, finding, 149

magic packets, 153

Motherboard NIC, 14

network adapters, 16

PC Card NIC, 17

purchasing, 33-34

troubleshooting, 422-423

USB NIC, 16

wake-on-LAN feature, 153

wireless NIC
    finding MAC addresses of, 356-357
    internal NIC, 44
    motherboard NIC, 47
    PC NIC, 45
    purchasing, 54-55
    USB NIC, 45

NTSC (National Television System Committee), digital media hub requirements, 201-202

O

offline files

accesing via
    remote computers, 247
    Sync Center, 245

configuring files as, 239

disk space, adjusting, 240-242

enabling, 238

encryption, 244

prohibiting network files from being, 242-243

synchronizing
    scheduling by event, 250-251
    scheduling by time, 248-250
    troubleshooting conflicts, 252

Offline Files feature

Always Available Offline dialog, 239

Disk Usage tab, 241-242

enabling, 238

Encryption tab, 244

OSI (Open System Interconnection) model, 10

OTA (Over-The-Air) broadcast signals, 199

P

Packet Received Errors performance counter (Performance Monitor), 405

packet sniffers, 341

Packets Outbound Errors performance counter (Performance Monitor), 405

Parental Controls, 286-288
Collect Information About Computer Usage option, 289
configuring, 289
Enforce Current Settings option, 289
Settings area
Application Restrictions page, 291
Web Restrictions page, 290

Password Sharing setting (Sharing and Discovery section), 187-189

passwords
administrative passwords, specifying in wireless networks, 336-337, 340
Parental Controls, 288
sharing, 187-189
strong passwords, building, 292-293

payloads, Ethernet networks, 11

PC NIC (Network Interface Cards), 17, 45

PCI cards, SFF PCs, 197

PCI slots, internal NIC installation, 101-102

People Near Me dialog (Windows Meeting Space), 257
Invitation Details dialog, 272-273
Invite People dialog
creating invitation files, 271
sending invitations to meetings, 269
options, setting, 262-263
receiving invitations to meetings, 272-273
sending invitations to meetings, 269
signing out of, 264

trusted contacts
adding people as, 261
disabling attachment conversions to vCards, 259
sending data to other people, 260

performance, monitoring in networks, 396
Performance Monitor, 400-403
Task Manager, 397-400

Performance Monitor
Add Counters dialog, 403
network performance, monitoring, 400-403
performance counters
adding, 403
Bytes Total/Sec, 404
Current Bandwidth, 404
Packet Received Errors, 405
Packets Outbound Errors, 405

peripherals
keyboards, digital media hub requirements, 200
monitors
persistence, 228
running slideshows from Media Player, 230-231
running slideshows from network shares, 233
running slideshows from Photo Gallery, 232
screensaver slideshows, 228-230

permissions
default website folders, setting in, 440
file sharing, configuring security permissions, 315-319
FTP sites, setting for, 469-470
Full Control, 318
List Folder Contents, 319
Modify, 319
Read and Execute, 319
Read, 319

Special Permissions, 319
Write, 319
wwwroot folder, setting in, 440

persistence (LCD monitors), 228

phishing, 307, 494
domain-spoofing, 308
homograph spoofing, 308
IDN spoofing, 308
lookalike attacks, 308
Phishing Filter (Internet Explorer), 308-310
phishing protection (Windows Mail), turning on/off, 310

Photo Gallery
importing pictures to network shares, 222
slideshows, running, 232

piggybackers, 335

PING command, checking network connections, 419-420

PnP (Plug and Play), 378. *See also* UPnP (Universal Plug and Play)

pop-up downloads, 296, 494

port forwarding, configuring in Remote Desktop, 384-387

ports
Auto Crossover, switch support, 24, 36
Remote Desktop connections
changing listening ports, 381
new port connections, 388-389
Serial Ports check box (Remote Desktop Connection dialog), 377
uplink ports, 23

power cycling, modems/routers, 414

powerline adapters, Ethernet networks, 32

PPPoE broadband connections, router configuration, 72

PPTP broadband connections, router configuration, 72

presentation layer (OSI model), 10

Preview pane (Windows Mail), turning on/off, 305

Printer Sharing setting (Sharing and Discovery section), 187

printers
print servers
Ethernet networks, 31
wireless print servers, 52
shared printers, 187
accessing, 182-183
activating, 185-186

private IP addresses, 27

private networks, 135

privileges (user accounts)
Administrator accounts, 283
Administrator groups, 283-284
Standard User groups, 283-285

Problem Reports and Solutions, 415-417

processors, digital media hub requirements, 198-199

Programs tab (Remote Desktop Connection dialog), 378

progressive scanning (television), 202

Prohibit 'Make Available Offline' option (Group Policy Object Editor), 243

PSK (Pre-Shared Keys), 343

Public Folder Sharing setting (Sharing and Discovery section), 186-188

public IP addresses, 26

public networks, 135

publishing calendars, 217-218, 221

purchasing
AP, WAP, 56
network cable, Ethernet networks, 34-35
NIC, 33-34, 54-55
routers, 36-37
switches, 35-36

Q - R

Quick Scan (Windows Defender), 303

radio transceivers, wireless networks, 40

Read and Execute permissions, 319

Read permissions, 319

rebooting computers as troubleshooting technique, 414

Recommended Restore option (System Restore), 428

recording television to network shares, 225-227

registering broadband modems, 107-108

Reliability and Performance Monitor

  Add Counters dialog, 403

  network performance, monitoring, 400-403

  performance counters, 403-405

  Resource Monitor, 400-401

remote computers, accessing offline files, 247

Remote Desktop

  advanced connections, 374-379

  Allow Connections from Computers Running Any Version of Remote Desktop option, 371

  Allow Connections Only from Computers Running Remote Desktop with Network Level Authentication option, 371

  basic connections, 373-374

  clients, Windows XP installation of, 372-373

  connection bar, 379

  DDNS, configuring, 389-392

  disconnecting from, 380

  hosts

    configuring user accounts, 367

    determining IP addresses, 383-384

    IP address, new port connections, 388-389

    Vista configuration of, 367-368, 371

    Windows support for, 366-367

    Windows XP configuration of, 371

  Internet connections, 380

    changing listening ports, 381

    configuring port forwarding, 384-387

    configuring Windows Firewall, 382

    determining host IP addresses, 383-384

    host IP addresses, new port connections, 388-389

  listening ports, changing, 381

  port forwarding, configuring, 384-387

  service activation, 370-371

  stored credentials, removing, 324

  Windows Firewall

    configuring, 382

    exceptions, 368-369

Remote Desktop Connection dialog

  Always Ask for Credentials check box, 324

  Display tab, 376

  Drives check box, 378

  Experience tab, 378-379

  General tab, 374

  Local Resources tab, 376-377

  Programs tab, 378

  Serial Ports check box, 377

  Smart Cards check box, 377

  Supported Plug and Play Devices check box, 378

remote folders, creating for network locations, 180-182

removing wireless network connections, 170

renaming

  FTP sites, 475

  IIS default websites, 448

  networks, 136

    network connections, 141

    wireless networks, 166-167

reordering wireless networks, 167

Report link (Phishing Filter), 310

resetting routers, 415

Resolve Conflict dialog (Sync Center), 252

Resource Monitor (Reliability and Performance Monitor), 400-401

Resource Overview section (Resource Monitor), 400

restarting
  computers as troubleshooting techniques, 414
  FTP sites, 474
  IIS websites, 448

RF (Radio Frequencies)
  WAP, 86
  wireless networks, 40

ripping CDs, network shares, 223-224

RJ-11 jacks, twisted-pair cable, 19

RJ-45 jacks
  routers, 28
  switches, 22
  twisted-pair cable, 19

routers
  Belkin routers
    changing administative passwords, 336
    changing default SSID, 352
    changing encryption settings, 342
    configuring port forwarding, 384-385
    disabling SSID broadcasting, 348
    enabling MAC address filtering, 358
  broadband connections, configuring, 71-76
  connecting, 60
  D-Link routers
    changing administative passwords, 337
    changing default SSID, 353
    changing encryption settings, 343
    configuring port forwarding, 385-386
    DDNS configuration, 390

    disabling SSID broadcasting, 349
    enabling MAC address filtering, 359
  DHCP servers, enabling in, 81-85
  ECN, 94
  Ethernet networks, 24-28
  firewalls, 27
  firmware
    updating, 66-70
    upgrading, 414
  IP addresses, 24-25
    accessing setup pages, 61
    assigning, 26
    changing, 63-64
  Linksys routers
    changing administative passwords, 338
    changing default SSID, 353
    changing encryption settings, 344
    configuring port forwarding, 386
    DDNS configuration, 391
    disabling SSID broadcasting, 349-351
    enabling MAC address filtering, 360
  Netgear routers
    changing administative passwords, 339
    changing default SSID, 355
    changing encryption settings, 345
    configuring port forwarding, 387
    DDNS configuration, 392
    disabling SSID broadcasting, 351
    enabling MAC address filtering, 361-362
  network connections, 108-109
  power cycling, 414
  purchasing, 36-37
  resetting, 415, 427
  RJ-45 jacks, 28
  routing tables, 24
  setup pages, accessing via
    IP addresses, 61
    Network window, 62
  status-checks, 90-92
  switches, 28

testing, Internet Connectivity Evaluation Tool, 93-95

UPnP, enabling in, 77-78, 81

WAP, 49, 85-89

routing tables, 24

S

S-Video connectors (television), 202

Save This Network option

Connect to a Network dialog, 116

Manage Wireless Networks window, 163

scheduling offline file synchronization

by event, 250-251

by time, 248-250

troubleshooting conflicts, 252

screensaver slideshows, 228-230

security

Administrator groups, 282

Baseline Security Analyzer, 330-331

drive-by downloads, 296

file sharing permissions, configuring, 318-319

FTP site folders, 480

Internet Explorer

Phishing Filter, 308-310

Report link, 310

Security Report area, 309

malware, 295, 491

Microsoft Security, 418

offline files, encryption, 244

Parental Controls, 286-288

Application Restrictions page, 291

Collect Information About Computer Usage option, 289

configuring, 289

Enforce Current Settings option, 289

Web Restrictions page, 290

passwords, building strong passwords, 292-293

phishing, 307, 494

domain-spoofing, 308

homograph spoofing, 308

IDN spoofing, 308

lookalike attacks, 308

Phishing Filter (Internet Explorer), 308-310

phishing protection (Windows Mail), turning on/off, 310

pop-up downloads, 296, 494

spyware, 295-296

testing, web resources, 295

user accounts

automatically logging off users when hours expire, 327-328

setting logon hours, 326-327

User groups, 282

usernames, hiding in logon screen, 328-330

Windows Defender, 297, 303

wireless networks

AP, 336

changing default SSID, 352-355

changing security properties, 346

disabling SSID broadcasting, 347-348, 351

filtering MAC addresses, 356-362

finding NIC MAC addresses, 356-357

minimizing signal leakage, 340

packet sniffers, 341

piggybackers, 335

signal leakage, 340

signal ranges, 340

speciying administrative passwords, 336-337, 340

warchalking, 335

wardriving, 335

WEP, 341

WPA, 341-346

WPA2, 341-344

wireless networks, 335

Security Report area (Internet Explorer), 309-310

Security tab (Manage Wireless Networks window), 165

Select Columns dialog (Task Manager), 397-400

Select Drives and Folders scan (Windows Defender), 303

Select Scan Options page (Windows Defender), 303

Select the Internet Explorer Security Zone to Use option (Virus Protection group), 305-306

Serial Ports check box (Remote Desktop Connection dialog), 377

server logs
 field descriptions list, 457-458
 IIS default websites, 456-458
 return codes list, 458

servers
 print servers
  Ethernet networks, 31
  wireless print servers, 52
 web servers. *See* IIS (Internet Information Services)

session layer (OSI model), 10

Set Up a Wireless Ad Hoc Network dialog (Manage Wireless Networks window), 161

Settings area (Parental Controls)
 Application Restrictions page, 291
 Web Restrictions page, 290

setup pages (routers), accessing via
 IP addresses, 61
 Network window, 62

SFF (Small Form Factor) PCs, 197

shared folders
 monitoring
  closing user sessions/files, 408-409
  launching Shared Folders snap-in, 405

  viewing current connections, 406
  viewing open files, 407-408
  viewing Vista connections, 407
 monitoring, 405
 problems with, 365-366

Shared Folders snap-in
 launching, 405
 open files, viewing, 407-408
 user sessions/files, closing, 408-409
 Vista shared folder connections, viewing, 407

shared resources
 calendars, 221
 file-sharing, 185-186, 190-192
 folders
  mapping to local drive letters, 177-180
  Public Folder Sharing, 186-188
  running slideshows from, 233
  sharing via File Sharing Wizard, 190-192
 media, Windows Media Player 11, 207-209
 network addresses, 175-176
 passwords
  creating user accounts for, 189
  Password Sharing, 187
 printers
  accessing, 182-183
  activating sharing, 185-186
  Printer Sharing, 187
 viewing, 172-174, 192

shared sessions
 controlling, 277-278
 ending, 278
 starting, 276

Sharing and Discovery area (Network and Sharing Center), 128
 File Sharing setting, 185-186
 Password Sharing setting, 187
 Printer Sharing setting, 187
 Public Folder Sharing setting, 186-188

sharing files
   File Sharing setting (Sharing and
      Discovery section), 185-186
   File Sharing Wizard
      disabling, 314
      sharing files via, 190-192
   hiding shared files, 320
      connecting to folders, 321-322
      disabling hidden administrative shares,
      322-323
   permissions, configuring, 315-319

Sidebar, Slide Show gadget, 234

signal leakage (wireless networks), 340

signal ranges (wireless networks), 340

simultaneous data request limits (IIS),
432

single-channel analog audio receiver
connectors, digital media hub connec-
tions, 203

Sleep mode, 151, 367-368

Slide Show gadget (Sidebar), displaying
network images in, 234-235

slideshows
   Media Player, running from, 230-231
   network shares, running from, 233
   network-based slideshows, configuring,
      228-230
   Photo Gallery, running from, 232
   screensaver slideshows, 228-230

Smart Cards check box (Remote Desktop
Connection dialog), 377

snagless connectors, 35

Special Permissions permissions, 319

spoofing, 307-308

spyware
   convert reinstalls, 296, 486
   defining, 295
   drive-by downloads, 296
   pop-up downloads, 296, 494
   Uninstall options, 296

SSID (Service Set Identifiers)
   broadcasting, disabling, 347-348, 351
   default SSID, changing, 352-355
   WAP, 86
   wireless networks, 159

Standard User groups, 282-285

star topologies, 23

Start This Connection Automatically
option
   Connect to a Network dialog, 116
   Manage Wireless Networks window, 163

static broadband connections, router con-
figuration, 72

static IP addresses
   assigning, 147-148
   configuring, 145-147

status indicators (Network icon), 123

status-checks, routers, 90-92

storing data
   digital media hub requirements, 198
   NAS
      backing up to, 212
      Ethernet networks, 30

STP (Shielded Twisted-Pair) cable, 18-19,
34

streaming media, DMR, 32

subscribing to Calendar via
   subscribe message, 219
   Windows Calendar, 220

Supported Plug and Play Devices check
box (Remote Desktop Connection dia-
log), 378

Suspicious Website messages (Security
Report area), 310

switches
   Auto Crossover support, 24, 36
   Ethernet networks, 22-24
   network connections, 110
   network segments, 23

purchasing, 35-36
RJ-45 jacks, 22
routers as, 28
switching tables, 23
uplink ports, 23
WAP, 49

switching tables, 23

Sync Center
offline files
accessing, 245
synchronizing, 248-252
Resolve Conflict dialog, 252
Sync Conflicts Have Occurred error message, 252

synchronizing
offline files
scheduling by event, 250-251
scheduling by time, 248-250
troubleshooting conflicts, 252
shared calendars, 221

system image backups, 216

System Restore, 428-429

T

Task Manager
network performance, monitoring, 397-400
Select Columns dialog, 397-400

Tasks pane (Network and Sharing Center), 128

TCP High Performance test (Internet Connectivity Evaluation Tool), 94

television
audio receiver connectors, 203-204
component connectors, 202
composite connectors, 202
digital media hub connections, 205
DVI connectors, 203

HDMI connectors, 203
HDTV
CableCards, 200
digital media hub requirements, 201
interlaced scanning, 202
NTSC, digital media hub requirements, 201-202
OTA broadcast signals, 199
progressive scanning, 202
recording to network shares, 225-227
S-Video connectors, 202
tv tuners, digital media hub requirements, 199

Telstra BigPond broadband connections, router configuration, 72

testing
routers, Internet Connectivity Evaluation Tool, 93-95
security, web resources, 295

Traffic Congestion test (Internet Connectivity Evaluation Tool), 94

transport layer (OSI model), 10

troubleshooting
cable, 421-422
Help and Support Center, 415
modems, power cycling, 414
networks
connections, 412, 419-420
general fixes, 413-414
wireless networks, 426-427
NIC, 422-423
offline file synchronization scheduling, 252
online resources, 418-419
Problem Reports and Solutions, 415-417
routers
firmware upgrades, 414
power cycling, 414
resetting, 415
working configurations, reverting to, 414, 427-429

trusted contacts
adding people as, 261
attachments, disabling conversions to vCards, 259
sending data to other people, 260

Turn Off Notification of New Networks command (Network icon), 122

Turn On Activity Animation command (Network icon), 122

turning on/off
computers, as troubleshooting technique, 414
network discovery, 128-129
Network icon, 124
phishing protection (Windows Mail), 310
Preview pane (Windows Mail), 305

tv tuners, digital media hub requirements, 199

twisted-pair cable
RJ-11 jacks, 19
RJ-45 jacks, 19
STP, 18-19, 34
UTP, 19, 34

U

UAC (User Account Control)
least-privileged users, 283
verifying activation, 301

Uninstall options (spyware), 296

updates
automatic updates, configuring, 298-300
Check for Updates but Let Me Choose Whether to Download and Install Them option (Change Settings window), 300
Download Updates, but Let Me Choose Whether to Install Them option (Change Settings window), 300
email viruses, web resources, 305
firmware, routers, 66-70

Install Updates Automatically option (Change Settings window), 299
Never Check for Updates option (Change Settings window), 300
NIC, Device Drivers, 425-426
shared calendars, 221
viewing, 299
Windows Update website, 418

upgrades
computers, digital media hubs, 196
routers, firmware, 414
upgradeable devices, defining, 43

uplink ports, switches, 23

UPnP (Universal Plug and Play). *See also* **PnP (Plug and Play)**
digital media hubs, 205
routers, enabling in, 77-78, 81
UPnP Support test (Internet Connectivity Evaluation Tool), 94

UPnP Support test (Internet Connectivity Evaluation Tool), 94

URL (Uniform Resource Locators), phishing, 307

USB (Universal Serial Buses), registering broadband modems, 107

USB NIC (Network Interface Cards), 16, 45

User Account Control dialog (Network Connections window)
Allow This Device to Wake the Computer check box, 153
Change Settings of This Connection command, 142
Windows Security dialog, 284

user accounts
Administrator accounts, 283
Administrator groups, 283-284
kids, security, 287-288

logon hours
  *automatically logging off users when
  hours expire, 327-328*
  setting, 326-327
password sharing, creating for, 189
Remote Desktop hosts, configuring for,
  367
Standard User groups, 283-285
User Account Control, Windows Security
  dialog, 284
usernames, hiding in logon screen,
  328-330

User security groups, 282

**user-specific wireless network connec-
tions, 168**

**usernames, hiding in logon screen,
328-330**

**UTP (Unshielded Twisted-Pair) cable, 19,
34**

V

vCards, contact attachment, 259

video
  digital media hub connections, 205-206
  HDCP, 199
  HDTV, CableCards, 200
  network cards, digital media hub
    requirements, 200
  OTA broadcast signals, 199
  television
    audio receiver connectors, 203-204
    component connectors, 202
    composite connectors, 202
    digital media hub requirements, 201-202
    DVI connectors, 203
    HDMI connectors, 203
    interlaced scanning, 202
    progressive scanning, 202
    recording to network shares, 225-227
    S-Video connectors, 202

tv tuners, digital media hub requirements, 199
video cards, digital media hub requirements, 199

**View Installed Updates link (Change
Settings window), 299**

**View Network Computers and Devices
option (Network and Sharing Center),
172**

**View Status link (Network and Sharing
Center), 133**

**View Status of This Connection command
(Network Connections window), 144-146**

viewing shared resources, 192

Virtual Directory, adding folders to
  default FTP sites, 471-472
  IIS default websites, 445

**Virus Protection group (Windows Mail),
305-306**

viruses, 304-305

Vista (Windows)
  Automatic Sleep mode, disabling,
    367-368
  Calculator, converting binary values to
    decimal, 26
  Connect to a Network dialog
    Disconnect option, 118
    Save This Network option, 116
    *Start This Connection Automatically
    option, 116*
    wireless network connections, 114-117
  IIS, versions of, 432
  logging off as troubleshooting technique,
    414
  Network and Sharing Center, 125
    Change Network Icon dialog, 136
    Customize Network Settings dialog, 136
    launching, 126-127
    Map area, 127
    Network area, 127
    network discovery, turning on/off, 129

Network map, 132
Sharing and Discovery area, 128
Tasks pane, 128
View Status link, 133
Network Connection Details dialog, 134
network discovery, turning on/off, 128-129
Network icon
    Connect to a Network command, 122
    Diagnose and Repair command, 123
    Disconnect From command, 122
    Network and Sharing Center command, 123
    right-clicking, 122
    status indicators, 123
    Turn Off Notification of New Networks command, 122
    Turn On Activity Animation command, 122
    turning on/off, 124
Network window
    accessing router setup pages, 62
    Details view, 130
    opening, 130
Remote Desktop
    advanced connections, 374-379
    basic connections, 373-374
    host configuration, 367-371
    support for, 366-367
shared folder connections, viewing, 407

W

wake-on-LAN feature (NIC), 153
WAP (Wireless Access Points), 47-49
    firewalls, 50
    router configuration, 85-89
    SSID broadcasting, 86
    switches, 49
warchalking, 335
wardriving, 335, 341

Warn Me When Other Applications Try to Send Mail as Me option (Virus Protection group), 306
web pages, phishing attacks, 307, 494
Web Restrictions page (Parental Controls)
    Allow and Block Specific Websites option, 290
    Block File Downloads option, 291
    Block Web Content Automatically option, 291
web servers. *See* IIS (Internet Information Services)
weblinks, phishing attacks, 307
website limits (IIS), 433
websites
    blocking, 290
    IIS default website
        accessing, 434-436
        adding files to, 441-442
        adding folders to, 443-445
        basic authentication, 454-455
        changing default home pages in, 443
        changing folder location, 448
        configuring Windows Firewall exceptions, 434-435
        default website folder, 437, 440-445
        disabling anonymous access, 454-455
        disabling default documents, 451-453
        renaming, 448
        restarting, 448
        setting default documents, 449-450
        stopping, 447
        viewing server logs, 456-458
        viewing via IIS Manager, 438
        wwwroot folder, 437, 440-445
    Suspicious Website messages (Security Report area), 310
    troubleshooting resources, 418-419
WEP (Wired Equivalent Privacy), 341

Wi-Fi (Wireless Fidelity)
802.11a standard, 41
802.11b standard, 41
802.11g standard, 42
802.11n standard, 42
802.11n standard, 43
detectors. *See* wireless networks, finders
hot spots, 43

Windows Defender, 297, 303

Windows Firewall
activation, verifying, 295
FTP default sites, configuring FTP server exceptions for, 464
IIS default websites, configuring web server exceptions for, 434-435
Remote Desktop
configuring in, 382
exceptions, 368-369

Windows Mail
contacts
adding people as, 261
disabling attachment conversion to vCards, 259
sending data to other people, 260
file types, disabling, 306
Junk E-mail folder, turning on/off Preview pane, 305
phishing protection, turning on/off, 310
Virus Protection group, 305-306

Windows Media Player 11, 207-209

Windows Meeting Space, 256
configuring, 264
handouts, sharing in meetings, 275
invitation files, creating, 271-272
joining meetings, 266
launching, 264-265
People Near Me dialog, 257
Invitation Details dialog, 272-273
Invite People dialog, 269-271
receiving invitations to meetings, 272-273

sending invitations to meetings, 269
setting options, 262-263
signing out of, 264
trusted contacts, 259-261
receiving invitations
from People Near Me, 272-273
opening invitation files, 274
sending invitations to meetings
People Near Me, 269
via Email, 270
shared sessions
controlling, 277-278
ending, 278
starting, 276
starting meetings, 267

Windows Security dialog (User Account Control), 284

Windows Update website, 418

Windows XP
IIS, restrictions in, 433
Remote Desktop
advanced connections, 374-379
basic connections, 373-374
client installation, 372-373
host configuration, 371
support for, 366-367

Wired icons (Network Connections window), 140

wireless DMR (Digital Media Receivers), 53

Wireless icons (Network Connections window), 141

wireless networks, 157
ad hoc connections, 40, 161
administrative passwords, specifying in wireless networks, 336-337, 340
configuring, 113-117, 163
disconnecting from, 117-118
DMR, 53
finders, 51

hardware buyer's guide, 53-57

hidden network connections, 159-160

infrastructure wireless networks, 40

interference, 426

Manage Wireless Networks window, 163-165

NIC

finding MAC addresses of, 356-357

internal NIC, 44

motherboard NIC, 47

PC NIC, 45

purchasing, 54-55

USB NIC, 45

packet sniffers, 341

piggybackers, 335

print servers, 52

radio tansceivers, 40

range extenders, 50

removing, 170

renaming, 166-167

reordering, 167

RF signals, 40

routers, resetting, 427

security

AP, 336

changing default SSID, 352-355

changing properties of, 346

disabling SSID broadcasting, 347-348, 351

filtering MAC addresses, 356-362

minimizing signal leakage, 340

specifying administrative passwords, 336-337, 340

WEP, 341

WPA, 341-346

WPA2, 341-344

signal leakage, 340

signal ranges, 340

SSID, 159, 347-348, 351-355

troubleshooting, 426-427

user-specific connections, 168

WAP, 47-48

firewalls, 50

purchasing, 56

routers, 49

switches, 49

warchalking, 335

wardriving, 335

Wi-Fi, 41-43

wireless NIC (Network Interface Cards)

internal NIC, 44

MAC addresses, finding, 356-357

motherboard NIC, 47

PC NIC, 45

purchasing, 54-55

USB NIC, 45

wireless print servers, 52

wireless range extenders, 50

WLAN (Wireless Local Area Networks). See wireless networks

workgroup names, changing (network configuration), 112-113

working configurations, reverting to (troubleshooting techniques), 414, 427-429

WPA (Wi-Fi Protected Access), 341-346

WPA2 (Wi-Fi Protected Access version 2), 341-344

Write permissions, 319

wwwroot folder (IIS default websites), 437

default home pages, changing, 443

files, adding to, 441-442

folders, adding to, 443-445

permissions, setting, 440

X - Y - Z

Xbox 360, digital media hub connections, 205-206

Register this book!

**Register this book at
www.quepublishing.com
and
unlock benefits**
exclusive to the owners
of this book.

What you'll receive with this book:
- Hidden content
- Additional content
- Book errata
- New templates, spreadsheets, or files to download
- Increased membership discounts
- Discount coupons
- A chance to sign up to receive content updates, information on new editions, and more

Book registration is free and only takes a few easy steps.

1. Go to www.quepublishing.com/bookstore/register.asp.
2. Enter the book's ISBN (found above the barcode on the back of your book).
3. You will be prompted to either register for or log-in to Quepublishing.com.
4. Once you have completed your registration or log-in, you will be taken to your "My Registered Books" page.
5. This page will list any benefits associated with each title you register, including links to content and coupon codes.

The benefits of book registration vary with each book, so be sure to register every Que Publishing book you own to see what else you might unlock at Quepublishing.com!

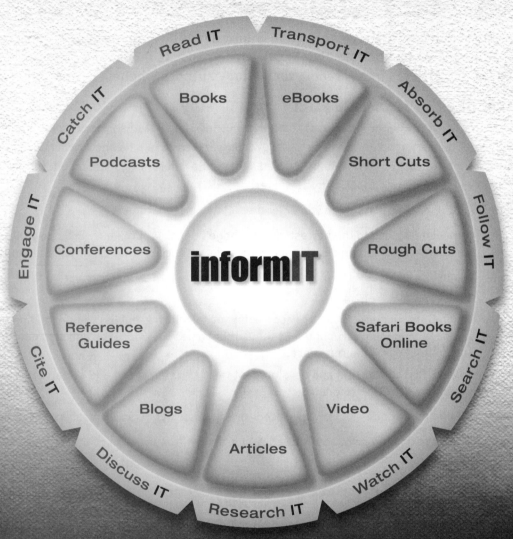